MW00646939

Shreveport Sounds
in Black & White

Shreveport Sounds in Black & White

Edited by

Kip Lornell and Tracey E. W. Laird

UNIVERSITY PRESS OF MISSISSIPPI / JACKSON

American Made Music Series

Advisory Board

David Evans, General Editor
Barry Jean Ancelet
Edward A. Berlin
Joyce J. Bolden
Rob Bowman
Susan C. Cook
Curtis Ellison
William Ferris
Michael Harris

John Edward Hasse
Kip Lornell
Frank McArthur
Bill Malone
Eddie S. Meadows
Manuel H. Peña
David Sanjek
Wayne D. Shirley
Robert Walser

www.upress.state.ms.us

The University Press of Mississippi is a member
of the Association of American University Presses.

Copyright © 2008 by University Press of Mississippi
All rights reserved
Manufactured in the United States of America

First printing 2008
∞
Library of Congress Cataloging-in-Publication Data

Shreveport sounds in black and white / edited by
Kip Lornell and Tracey E. W. Laird.
p. cm. — (American made music series)
Includes index.
ISBN-13: 978-1-934110-41-6 (cloth : alk. paper)
ISBN-10: 1-934110-41-8 (cloth : alk. paper)
ISBN-13: 978-1-934110-42-3 (pbk. : alk. paper)
ISBN-10: 1-934110-42-6 (pbk. : alk. paper) 1. Folk
music—Louisiana—Shreveport—History and criticism.
2. Folk musicians—Louisiana. I. Lornell: Kip, 1953–
II. Laird, Tracey E. W.
ML3551.8.S57S57 2008
781.6409763'99—dc22   2007021404

British Library Cataloging-in-Publication Data available

Contents

IX   Acknowledgments

XI   Introduction

---

3   **Country**

---

7   Introduction from *Louisiana Hayride*
       Radio and Roots Music Along the Red River
       —Tracey E. W. Laird

18   The Grigg Family and the Taylor-Griggs Melody Makers
       The History of a North Louisiana String Band
       —Monty Brown

30   The Cox Family
       —Susan Roach

43   Remembering Hiter Colvin, the Fiddle King of Oilfield
       and Gum Stump
       —J. Michael Luster

46   Sing It Good, Sing It Strong, Sing It Loud
       The Music of Governor Jimmie Davis
       —Kevin Fontenot

58   Louisiana's Honky-Tonk Man: Buddy Jones, 1935–41
       —Donald Lee Nelson

63   Interview with Horace Logan, October 13, 1976
       —Earl Porter

74   Getting the Sound Right
       Bob "Sully" Sullivan, KWKH, and the *Louisiana Hayride*
       —Steven Morewood

105   Beyond Country Music
        —Tracey E. W. Laird

137   **Blues**

140   Fannin Street
        —Charles Wolfe and Kip Lornell
153   Some Negro Songs Heard on the Hills of North Louisiana
        —Vallie Tinsley
178   Jerry's Saloon Blues
            1940 Field Recordings from Louisiana
        —Paul Oliver
192   Jesse "Babyface" Thomas
        —Eleanor Ellis
204   The Flying Crow Blues
        —Paul Swinton
210   The Legend of Old Blue Goose
        —Dan Garner
215   Down-Home Postwar Blues in Shreveport
        —John M. Shaw

223   **Radio, Records, and Rhythm**

226   A Historical Study of Programming Techniques and Practices
            of Radio Station KWKH, Shreveport, LA, 1922–1950
        —Lillian Jones Hall
237   A Friend in Las Vegas
        —H. Allen Smith
248   Stan Lewis
        —Randy McNutt
256   "Reconsider Me"
            Margaret Lewis Warwick and the *Louisiana Hayride*
        —Tracey E. W. Laird
268   The Making of Dale Hawkins
        —David Anderson and Lesley-Anne Reed
302   The Life and Times of Dandy Don Logan
        —Don Logan

316 Shreveport Southern Soul
The Murco Story
—John Ridley
323 Eddie Giles and Reuben Bell
Synonymous with Shreveport
—John M. Shaw
338 Shreveport's Pop/Rock Music Scene
The 1970s and 1980s
—John Andrew Prime

349 Contributors
354 Credits
357 Index

We salute the people of Louisiana
for their spirit and resilience.

Acknowledgments

We owe a debt of gratitude to many people for helping with this project. Foremost are our families for their patience and understanding. Our thanks also go to the University Press of Mississippi for believing in the need for this anthology. We think it is an important addition to the literature related to music in the American South and are pleased to see it published as part of the American Made Music series.

Special kudos to the following people for their help above the call of duty as well as their prompt attention to our requests for photographs, information, and just-plain-assistance: Domenica Carriere, Laura Lyons McLemore, and Mike Rosebery (Archives and Special Collections, Noel Memorial Library, Louisiana State University–Shreveport), and Susan Roach (Folklorist, Louisiana Regional Folklife Program, Louisiana Tech University).

Our thanks also go to Vallie Tinsley White's son-in-law, Jim Karl of Longview, Texas, for her photograph and biographical information; Pam Packer of the Rebel State Historic Society and Louisiana Country Music Museum; John Prime for his generous sharing of photographs; Dan Garner for his good cheer and hard work on blues and gospel music in Shreveport, Maggie and Alton Warwick for supplying photographs and encouragement. Thanks also to C. Joseph Pusateri, Nutchuk (a.k.a. Simeon Oliver), Joey Kent, James W. Joyner, Nancy Fly Bredenberg, Chris Smith, Ray Templeton, Gayle Wardlow, Robert Vaughan, Jan Rosenberg, Donald R. Ross, and Ray Topping, all of whom have contributed to our understanding of music in the Ark-La-Tex. We also thank our contributors who wrote articles especially for this edition and for the periodicals, magazines, and presses who gave permission to reprint other materials. Tracey Laird would like to thank Agnes Scott College for the laptop loaner and for the remarkable level of support among friends, colleagues, administration, and staff.

Introduction

Southern Music

Since minstrelsy swept the country in the decades before the Civil War, the South has dramatically shaped musical sounds of the United States. Genres as diverse as jazz, blues, and country emerged from the southern heartland in the early twentieth century, influencing music not only in the U.S. but eventually across Europe and then other parts of the world. Despite its origins on opposite coasts, even hip-hop, which today reigns as the most influential form of popular music on the planet, increasingly looks to southern cities like Atlanta, Houston, and Memphis for up-and-coming artists.

Southern music has been written about in thousands of books, articles, and record liner notes by authors across the globe. Although most of these writers initially rose from the non-academic ranks, scholarly interest in blues, country, jazz, and other southern genres has blossomed since the late 1960s.[1] At times, those interests intersect, for example, in the magazine *Oxford American*, which devotes one issue each year to southern music. Its contributors include the most respected writers working in the field—people like Peter Guralnick, Tom Piazza, and Charles K. Wolfe—writing on topics as diverse as Uncle Dave Macon and the legendary mid-70s Memphis rock band, Big Star. New digital formats like the online "Digital Southern Music Magazine" *Gritz* (gritz.net) celebrate "Southern Music, Americana, Country, Southern Rock, Bluegrass, Pickin', Blues, Gospel & Southern Life." Published since 1998, *Gritz* features reviews, articles, gossip, and interviews encompassing artists like southern rocker Marshall Tucker, bluegrass legend Ralph Stanley, blues diva KoKo Taylor, and the inimitable Kinky Friedman. Not surprisingly, the internet also hosts sites like www.thesoutherngospel.com and www.bluegrassworld.

com that serve as portals to information such as touring schedules, artist pro-files, and industry awards for these specific musical styles.

Likewise, individual genres of southern music have seen a proliferation of writing, both broad and regional in focus. For example, several dozen books appear every year that address aspects of country music ranging from the trivial to the esoteric, from coffee table photograph collections to important scholarly reference books.[2] Meanwhile a smaller number of books, usually written by scholars, focus on the country music traditions of individual states, regions, and even cities. These began with a 1977 survey of country music in the "Volunteer State" by the late Charles Wolfe, covering topics from Uncle Dave Macon to the development of bluegrass and from the Grand Ole Opry to the contemporary Nashville scene. Similar treatments of Kentucky, West Virginia, West Texas, and Atlanta flesh out the picture of country music in discrete regions or past eras.[3]

Blues has experienced a surge in popular and scholarly interest since the early 1960s when the English magazine *Blues Unlimited* began publication. By the decade's end Paul Oliver, also English, published the music's first compre-hensive history, *The Story of the Blues*.[4] Books continue to examine the blues from the broadest to the most narrowly focused viewpoints, ranging from overviews to regional studies. Some cover times and places when blues culture flourished within black American communities, like Chicago in the late 1940s, while others offer intimate accounts of the lives and music of lesser-known players like Sam Myers and Hubert Sumlin.[5]

In a similar fashion, jazz enjoys an immense body of literature, both aca-demic and popular.[6] Books on styles from swing to fusion, and on jazz cit-ies (New Orleans, Chicago, New York) continue to appear in print every year. Moreover, magazines like *DownBeat!*, first published in 1935, have profiled thousands of musicians.[7]

The "Ark-La-Tex" and Music Research

Within the whole field of writing on southern music, very little addresses the distinct region that radiates from the civic center of Shreveport, dominated geographically by the Red River and a landscape of thick piney woods, and characterized by a cultural mix that is equal parts black and white. The easi-est, if not scientific, way to locate the Ark-La-Tex on a map, is to place one end of a protractor on Shreveport, stretch the other end to the distance that would equal between ninety and a hundred miles on the map and draw a circle. To the west, the Ark-La-Tex extends just past Tyler, Texas, located almost halfway between Shreveport and Dallas. The small city of Natchitoches, Louisiana, delineates the southernmost boundary of the Ark-La-Tex, while Monroe, Louisiana, marks the east. Hope, Arkansas, birthplace of President Bill Clinton, is the northernmost small city usually associated with the Ark-La-Tex. Texarkana is another city with a noteworthy musical legacy.

It has been historically a "land between," most broadly speaking between the southern and the western United States. In the first half of the nineteenth century, many migrants used the Texas Trail, a westward trek that originated in the southeastern Piedmont region of Georgia and North Carolina; a number of them ended their journey in Shreveport. In 1867, what became known as the Chisholm Trail began at the northwestern tip of the Ark-La-Tex, along the Red River. Shreveport is now the principal transportation, economic, communication, cultural, and educational center between Dallas and Little Rock. Culturally and geographically, the city is closer to Little Rock and Dallas than it is to New Orleans.

Shreveport, Louisiana, sits at the commercial center of an area that crosses the borders of three other states: Texas, Arkansas, and (the southeastern tip of) Oklahoma. Locally, as attested by area business names and promo spots for the local news broadcasts, the region is known by the shorthand "Ark-La-Tex." Despite a strong regional identity, music in and around the Ark-La-Tex gets relegated to conventional state borders in books and magazine articles on southern music. As a result, the region's distinctiveness too often is ignored or subsumed into a broader state identity. For example, *Our Own Sweet Sounds: A Celebration of Popular Music in Arkansas* by Robert Cochran looks almost exclusively at African American music in the Delta region or country music in the state's upland north to the exclusion of the state's southwestern corner, the part that resembles Shreveport more than Memphis.[8]

Documentation of Texas music is much more extensive, and its literature covers thriving musical cities like Austin, Dallas, and Houston, as well as deep-rooted traditions of blues, country (especially western swing), and norteño music. Broader surveys in the past few years vary wildly in coverage and depth, yet each recognizes the importance of music in a state that produced ragtime progenitor Scott Joplin (who was born in the Ark-La-Tex), recent Tejano diva Selena, the pioneering blues guitar of T-Bone Walker, as well as pop/rockabilly legend Buddy Holly, and Willie Nelson. Nevertheless, with very few exceptions, the piney woods of northeastern Texas remain absent from these pages.[9]

Popular perceptions about music in Louisiana are clearly skewed towards the southern part of the state, and writing about its music has followed suit. The result is a colorful yet incomplete musical picture of a state with a long-held cultural mystique. The mention of an upcoming trip to visit friends and relatives in Shreveport inspires inevitable questions about walking the French Quarter, eating lunch at K-Paul's, or heading over to Eunice to catch some Cajun music. Now it includes questions about surviving the terrible hurricanes of August 2005. Likewise, for most music fans, New Orleans jazz and R&B, along with Cajun and zydeco music from the southwestern parishes, constitute Louisiana music.[10] In academic and popular discussions of Louisiana's unusually diverse musical culture, Shreveport has been overshadowed by New Orleans jazz, R&B, and carnival music as well as the Cajun and creole music found due west of the Big Easy. In an effort to correct this regional imbalance, we focus this book on vernacular music in Shreveport and its surrounding metropolitan area.

New Orleans's jazz heritage has inspired hundreds of articles and books over the past decades and helped make the city a prime draw for tourists. The large statue of Louis Armstrong, the downtown park, and the international airport bearing his name underscore the associations of early jazz with New Orleans, as do the French Quarter clubs catering to tourists. Local academic institutions celebrate the importance of jazz, including the world-class research facility at Tulane University, the William Hogan Jazz Archive, and programs in jazz performance and jazz studies at the state-supported University of New Orleans and at Loyola University. In short, New Orleans has successfully marketed its jazz tradition to the world, indelibly linking the music with the city and, by extension, with the state. R&B also remains a strong tradition in New Orleans. With roots in jazz and blues, this tradition emerged during the 1940s. Musicians like Fats Domino, Irma Thomas, Professor Longhair, and Smiley Lewis gained national attention beginning in the 1950s. The Neville Brothers are among more recent artists associated with black popular music in New Orleans over the past forty years. The body of popular and scholarly writing supports the strong association of New Orleans with R&B.[11]

Music and culture of the Acadians of southwestern Louisiana have gained attention in print sources as well, most recently in *Accordions, Fiddles, Two Step & Swing: A Cajun and Creole Music Reader*, edited by Ryan Brasseaux and Kevin Fontenot, which brings a variety of voices together.[12] These writings are welcome support for the Cajun and Creole recordings periodically released on Smithsonian Folkways, Rounder, and a handful of other labels. Once largely unknown or overlooked, over the past twenty-five years Cajun music, foodways, and speech have emerged as widely regarded national treasures. Across the United States it is now possible, even fashionable, to do things Cajun like eat crawfish etoufée and then dance a two-step to the sound of a button accordion. The related regional phenomenon of swamp pop also emanates from the southwestern section of the state. A laconic musical genre influenced by African American R&B and other popular trends (most notably doo-wop), swamp pop flourished during the late 1950s into the 1960s.[13]

Defining Shreveport

The United States Government defines the Shreveport metropolitan area, (or "Shreveport-Bossier" in local acknowledgment of the smaller "twin city" across the Red River) as encompassing Bossier, Caddo, and Desoto parishes (Louisiana's equivalent of counties). Both Webster Parish as well as Harrison County, Texas, are within an hour's drive of downtown Shreveport, and look to this city for employment, broadcast media, and shopping. Including Webster Parish and Harrison County, the area is home to approximately 490,000 residents, mainly black and white. In 2005 the Shreveport-Bossier metropolitan statistical area (MSA) had a population base comprised of 56.2 percent White, 38.9 percent African American, 2.5 percent Hispanic, and 1 percent Asian. According to the 2000 census Shreveport's 200,145 residents broke down along racial lines as follows: 50.80 percent African American, 46.66 percent White, 1.55 percent Hispanic or Latino, 0.79 percent Asian, 0.31 percent Native American, 0.03 percent Pacific Islander, 0.95 percent from two or more races, and 0.45 percent from "other races." Shreveport's median income was well below the national median of $42,148 for a household. Shreveport's household median was $30,526, 72 percent of the national median; the local median income for a family was $37,126.

Cultural geographers define distinct areas like the Ark-La-Tex by the people, who share one or more cultural traits such as foodways, linguistic patterns, transportation patterns, or religious affiliation. Cultural geographers have used sports such as lacrosse, folk house types, or the pervasiveness of a musical style like southern gospel to identify distinct regions across the United States. The Cajun culture that straddles state borders between southern Louisiana and Texas provides a distinctive example of this phenomenon.

In ways less dramatic than the French-speaking country to the south, Shreveport forms the heart of the Ark-La-Tex region with a feel and sense of identity all its own. Its tangible clues are found in a certain sweetness and texture to the beef barbecue or a way of seasoning the locally caught fried cat-fish. Maybe it's the proclivity to root for the Dallas Cowboys football team over the New Orleans Saints. Or it's the rhythm of life shaped by local trans-portation: once the Red River, now Interstate-20 and the newer I-49. A quick glance at the telephone book confirms that many local businesses and other organizations embrace the regional shorthand, although its spelling is not consistent. The Ark-La-Tex Speedway, Arklatex Modular Train Club, Ark-La-Tex Crisis Pregnancy Center, Ark-La-Tex Caged Bird Club, and the Ark-La-Tex Blueberry Growers Association are only a handful of names associated with the region. Local media report Ark-La-Tex weather conditions in a manner that, like the weather itself, utterly ignores state boundaries. Even the airport describes itself as the primary hub for "the Ark-La-Tex Region that encom-passes north Louisiana, east Texas and southwest Arkansas."[14]

Once the prime motivator for founding the city of Shreveport, the Red River recently has reemerged as a boon to the local economy. Since the early 1990s Shreveport-Bossier has become a major gambling hub with no less than five full-service casinos permanently moored along the riverbanks, close to the I-20 corridor that runs through the heart of the two adjacent cities. Gambling annually pumps millions of dollars into the local economy and has created several thousand jobs. The casinos have also provided a destination for tens of thousands of gamblers who do not wish to drive hundreds of miles to similar emporiums in southern Louisiana, Mississippi, or Oklahoma. Local casinos offer not only jobs, but a wide range of musical events. However, nearly all the headlining acts are from out-of-town. Most casinos employ local musicians to play in their smaller lounges, performing a wide range of popular music from contemporary rock to country. In some respects, the casinos have replaced the clubs that, during the 1950s and 1960s, once dotted the infamous "Bossier strip," not far from Barksdale Air Force Base. The clubs entertained service men and local residents eager to hear a range of R&B, rock, popular, and country music.

As we write this in the winter of 2007, several civic groups are working to preserve and sustain Shreveport's musical life. Notable among these is the non-profit organization FAME (Foundation for Arts, Music & Entertainment of Shreveport-Bossier, Inc.), founded by long-time participants in Shreveport's civic, cultural, and musical life Alton Warwick and Maggie Warwick. Begun during the mid-1990s, FAME's focus on local music and music history includes plans to further revitalize the Municipal Auditorium, a project already under-way, to build new hotels and residential units in downtown Shreveport, to develop artists' workspace, and to establish several cultural museums. FAME's centerpiece proposal is the *Historic Music Village* (awarded plan of the year by the Louisiana American Planning Association in 2003), which aims to include a Digital Media Center and the Southern American Music Museum to showcase, in its words, the "music that changed the world." The Southern American Music Museum will house exhibits that use innovative technology, not only focusing on performers but on business people within the industry, including broadcasting and music distribution. We agree that attention to music in Shreveport, in particular, as well as the surrounding Ark-La-Tex is long overdue.

Shreveport Sounds

Shreveport Sounds in Black and White includes a variety of writings about vernacular music found in and around metropolitan Shreveport. Vernacular refers to the everyday lives of people and their cultural expressions, including architecture, language, and music. While many of the articles examine a particular musician (Lead Belly) or group (the Cox Family), we also include pieces about local record companies (Jewel) and local radio stations (KWKH, in particular) that have helped to document and disseminate the region's vernacular musical landscape. These articles about record stores, radio stations, and record companies are placed in various sections of the book. Thus, *Shreveport Sounds in Black & White* emphasizes the inescapable fact that local musical traditions are intertwined with the local community and its mass media. Most of the radio announcers, record company owners, recording artists, *Louisiana Hayride* participants, and so on have been men and women who grew up in the Ark-La-Tex, some of them in Shreveport. Most of them were not full-time music professionals; their music or music industry-related work was part-time.

Individual articles about Shreveport area blues, country, and pop musicians have appeared in dozens of magazines, liner notes, and book chapters. We have brought together some twenty-five of these writings in one place, to create a starting point for future book-length analyses of music among blacks and whites in this unique and dynamic city. Pieces on country music cover groups like the Taylor-Griggs Melody Makers as well as individuals like Hiter Colvin. We include writing related to blues, such as a piece about Lead Belly's early years living near Shreveport and an oral history with Jesse Thomas. The pop music section encompasses individuals as disparate as Gene Austin and

Dale Hawkins. Nearly one-half of the authors come from outside academia, including musicians (Eleanor Ellis and Dan Garner), journalists (John Andrew Prime and Randy McNutt), and a disc jockey (Don Logan).

Outside the Ark-La-Tex, the musical contributions of Shreveport-Bossier too often go unnoticed or, at least, underappreciated. Many have heard of the cultural icons we include, like Lead Belly, who grew up near Shreveport and briefly lived there in the early twentieth century, and the *Louisiana Hayride*, which played a significant role in the early careers of Hank Williams and Elvis Presley.[15] Others know something of the importance of Shreveport guitarist James Burton in shaping the sound of rockabilly and early rock-and-roll. Yet, it is only the American vernacular music specialist or local music enthusiast who is aware of the role that soul singer Eddie Giles played on the local and national music scene in the 1960s. We hope this volume inspires others to uncover the wealth and diversity of grassroots music from Shreveport and perhaps even the rest of the Ark-La-Tex.

We intend this book not to be comprehensive. For instance, our vernacular focus precludes treatment of formally sanctioned western art music activity like the Shreveport Symphony Orchestra, which has been operating continuously since 1948, or the Centenary College Choir, formed in 1941. We include neither pieces on black and white gospel nor on jazz, not because those traditions held no sway in Shreveport but because so little has been written on them. Likewise, our space constraints forced choices among the writings on certain rich topics, for example, the blues guitarist Jesse Thomas who has been profiled in several magazines or journals. There are many noteworthy institutions of Shreveport music, like the Tri-State Singing Convention or the Calanthean Temple, and many musical figures who deserve a fuller accounting, among them the Ever Ready Gospel Singers, Kenny Wayne Shepherd, Dorsey Summerfield, Fred Carter Jr., Buddy Flett, Dorothy Prime, Dori Grayson, Rev. Utah Smith, Raymond Blakes, Merle Kilgore, Claude King, Brian Blade, and Brady Blade.

In the end, we hope to have set a precedent for expanded attention to vernacular musics in specific cities in the South such as Atlanta, Nashville, or Charlotte, all of which also cross racial boundaries much like Shreveport. Closer to home, we sincerely hope that *Shreveport Sounds in Black & White* stimulates a greater interest in the region's homegrown musical culture that is waiting to be discovered, appreciated, documented, and shared with the rest of the world.

—Kip Lornell and Tracey Laird
February 2007

Notes

1. Bill Malone and David Stricklin's *Southern Music, American Music*, 2nd ed. (Lexington: University Press of Kentucky, 2003) remains the topic's broadest overview. A wide ranging collection is *Sounds of the South: A Report and Selected Papers from a Conference on the Collecting and Collections of Southern Traditional Music*, ed. Daniel W. Patterson (University of North Carolina Press, 1991) which includes topics like researching blues from a European perspective, the interactions of traditional and revival folk musicians, and the study of Acadian music at Louisiana State University–Lafayette since the 1970s.

2. Of the latter, recent monumental contributions to country music scholarship include *Country Music Sources: A Biblio-Discography of Commercially Recorded Traditional Music* by Guthrie T. Meade Jr., Richard K. Spottswood, and Douglas S. Meade (Chapel Hill: University of North Carolina Press, 2002); and *Country Music Records: A Discography, 1921–1942* by Tony Russell (with editorial research by Bob Pinson) (New York: Oxford University Press, 2004).

3. Charles Wolfe, *Tennessee Strings* (Knoxville: University of Tennessee Press, 1977); and *Kentucky Country* (Lexington: University of Kentucky Press, 1982). Also, Ivan Tribe, *Mountaineer Jamboree* (University of Kentucky Press, 1984); Alan Munde and Joe Carr, *Prairie Nights and Neon Lights* (Lubbock: Texas Tech University Press, 1995); Wayne Daniel, *Pickin' on Peachtree* (Urbana: University of Illinois Press, 1990).

4. Paul Oliver, *The Story of the Blues* (Philadelphia: Chilton, 1969; reprint Boston: Northeastern University Press, 1998).

5. See, for example, the survey by Francis Davis, *The History of the Blues: The Roots, The Music, The People* (NY: Hyperion, 1995; reprint Cambridge, MA: Da Capo, 2003). David Evans's *Big Road Blues: Tradition and Creativity in the Folk Blues* (Berkeley: University of California Press, 1984; reprint, Da Capo, 1987) concentrates on country blues in west-central Mississippi from the 1920s through the 1970s. Barry Lee Pearson's *Virginia Piedmont Blues: The Music and Art of Two Virginia Bluesmen* (Philadelphia: University of Pennsylvania Press, 1990) discusses the blues tradition in one section of that state, while Mike Rowe's *Chicago Blues: The City and the Music* (Da Capo, 1981) chronicles the late 1940s electric blues scene. For the southeastern blues tradition see Bruce Bastin, *Red River Blues: The Blues Tradition in the Southeast* (Urbana: University of Illinois Press, 1986).

6. A milestone among this work is *Jazzmen*, edited by Frederick Ramsey and Charles Edward Smith (NY: Harcourt Brace, 1939), one of the first important books on the topic published in the U.S.

7. See William Kennedy, *Chicago Jazz: A Cultural History 1904–1930* (NY: Oxford University Press, 1993) or Charles Suhor, *Jazz in New Orleans: The Postwar Years Through 1970* (Lanham, MD: Scarecrow, 2001).

8. Robert Cochran, *Our Own Sweet Sounds* (Fayetteville: University of Arkansas Press, 1996; reprint, 2005). Aside from Bill McNeil's extensive work on folk life in northern Arkansas, Louis Guida's *Blues Music in Arkansas* (Philadelphia: Portfolio, 1982) concentrating on the eastern portion, and Vance Randolph's work on folksongs and folklore of the Ozarks, little has been written about vernacular music in the "Natural State."

9. Notable examples published in Denton by the University of North Texas Press include the following, both focused on the Dallas metroplex: Alan Govenar and Jay Brakefield, *Deep Ellum and Central Track: Where the Black and White Worlds of Dallas Converged* (1998); and John Mark Dempsey, *The Light Crust Doughboys Are on the Air: Celebrating Seventy Years of Texas Music* (2002). Govenar also honed in on the state's blues tradition in *Meeting the Blues: the Rise of the Texas Sound* (Dallas: Taylor, 1988; reprint, Da Capo, 1995). Two books by Roger Wood and

photographer James Fraher cover distinct aspects of Texas music: *Down in Houston: Bayou City Blues* (Austin: University of Texas Press, 2003) and *Texas Zydeco* (Austin: University of Texas Press, 2006). Recent statewide surveys include Michael Corcoran, *All Over the Map: True Heroes of Texas Music* (Austin: University of Texas Press, 2005); Rick Koster, *Texas Music* (NY: St. Martin's, 1998); and Roy R. Barkley, ed., *The Handbook of Texas Music* (Austin: Texas State Historical Association, 2003).

10. *Louisiana Music: A Journey from R&B to Zydeco, Jazz to Country, Blues to Gospel, Cajun Music to Swamp Pop to Carnival Music and Beyond,* by Rick Koster (Da Capo 2002), doesn't even include the "Ark-La-Tex" or "Shreveport" in its index and mentions Lead Belly only in passing. The Interstate-10 corridor across Baton Rouge, Lafayette, and Lake Charles seem to be his northern boundary for Louisiana as a cultural concept.

11. See for example, Jeff Hannusch, *I Hear You Knockin: The Sound of New Orleans Rhythm and Blues* (Ville Platte, LA: Swallow Books, 1985); and Jason Berry, Jonathan Foose, and Tad Jones, *Up from the Cradle of Jazz: New Orleans Music Since World War II* (Athens: University of Georgia Press, 1986; reprint, Da Capo, 1992).

12. This was published by the Center for Louisiana Studies, University of Louisiana at Lafayette, 2006. Other books in this area include Michael Tisserand's *The Kingdom of Zydeco* (NY: Spike Press, 1999); Ann A. Savoy, *Cajun Music: A Reflection of the People* (Eunice, LA: Bluebird Press, 1984); and Charles Stivale, *Disenchanting Les Bons Temps: Identity and Authenticity in Cajun Music and Dance* (Durham: Duke University Press, 2003).

13. Shane Bernard, whose father Rod was a swamp pop star, published an in-depth book on the topic *Swamp Pop: Cajun and Creole Rhythm and Blues* (Jackson: University Press of Mississippi, 1996); Cookie and the Cup Cakes and Johnny Preston are among its best-known practitioners.

14. http://www.mytravelguide.com/attractions/profile-81088006-United_States_Louisiana_Shreveport_Shreveport_Regional_Airport.html

15. The *Hayride* was the subject of a book by this collection's co-editor Tracey Laird, whose *Louisiana Hayride: Radio and Roots Music Along the Red River* (NY: Oxford University Press, 2005) is excerpted in this volume. Other interesting sources on the topic include a 1984 Louisiana Public Broadcasting television documentary *Up from the Cradle of Stars* that received funding from (among other sources) the Louisiana Endowment for the Humanities. Memoirs by *Hayride* participants include Horace Logan and Bill Sloan, *The Louisiana Hayride Years* (St. Martin's Press, 1999; originally published as *Elvis, Hank, and Me* the previous year); and Tillman Franks, *I Was There When It Happened* (Many, LA: Sweet Dreams, 2000).

Shreveport Sounds in Black & White

Country

The term "country music" suggests a range of styles, most closely associated with Southern white working-class culture and evolving over the first two decades of the twentieth century. The pioneering "hillbilly" recordings that began in 1923 emphasized stringed instruments like the guitar, fiddle, and banjo, along with the harmonica. Within thirty years love, relationships, home, and nightlife had become staples in country music lyrics. Although contemporary commercial country features a slick pop and rock-influenced hybrid emanating from Nashville, country as a genre covers a wide variety of musical sounds: old-time, bluegrass, honky-tonk, western swing, new country, Bakersfield sound, progressive country, alt(ernative) country, and so on. These subgenres grew whenever country music planted itself in the fertile grounds of particular times and places. Thus, country music sounds different in the mountains of West Virginia than in the valleys and flat lands of central California or in the humid, piney woods that characterize the Ark-La-Tex.

The *Louisiana Hayride* dominates any notion of Shreveport's importance in country music history, and with good reason. Radio station KWKH's 50,000-watt signal beamed the program into homes hundreds of miles away, and these weekly broadcasts allowed listeners to hear such highly regarded musicians as Hank Williams, Kitty Wells, Jim Reeves, and Elvis Presley. The *Hayride* also brought acts of more circumscribed renown like Merle Kilgore and Claude King, as well as local performers like Ray Hendrix or Jimmy and Johnny, into living rooms throughout the country's heartland.

Likewise, the *Hayride* dominates this country music section of *Shreveport Sounds*, framed with excerpts from the book on the topic by one of this collection's co-editors.[1] We also include excerpts from a 1976 interview with longtime

Hayride director, Horace Logan, and one of a handful of new pieces written for this collection, Steven Morewood's essay about long-time radio and recording engineer Bob Sullivan. Sullivan worked the board at Shreveport's Municipal Auditorium on most Saturday night *Hayride* broadcasts; and he often recorded after hours in the KWKH studios, creating beloved cuts by Slim Whitman, Jim Reeves, Dale Hawkins, and other 1950s legends.

Before the *Hayride*, its host radio station KWKH already drew country musicians to its studios eager to take advantage of its powerful signal. Most famous among these, Jimmie Davis aired a weekly live broadcast during the late 1920s and recorded on the station owner's "Hello World" label. (Station owner W. K. Henderson also surfaces in the section of *Shreveport Sounds* titled "Radio, Records, and Rhythm"). A string of regional performers made their way to the city for a chance to broadcast over KWKH's mighty radio signal in these early years. Monty Brown's piece on the Taylor-Griggs Melody Makers offers an oral history of one family band's experiences broadcasting at KWKH, as well as cutting commercial records in the industry's early era. As a companion to that piece, Susan Roach writes an account of the Cox Family, a contemporary family band who gained fame via their inclusion on the film and soundtrack, *O Brother Where Art Thou?*, but remain bound to their northwestern Louisiana roots.

Both groups draw on a tradition of string music that blended Anglo and African influences beginning in the era of slavery. The Shreveport region is fertile ground for this tradition, which started in the early nineteenth century when white farmers and merchants, some bringing slaves, arrived along a westward track from the Piedmont region of the southeastern United States. Those who settled in northwestern Louisiana found a life fueled by the cash crop agriculture of cotton and the commercial navigation of the Red River to New Orleans, then a world-class port. Music-making in this context occurred at house parties, among both blacks and whites, and in formal dances of the elite white plantation culture. It also happened in established churches and at tent revival meetings, aboard the steamboats that plied the Red River, or with the traveling minstrel shows that entered town by wagon or, later, by train. All these experiences shaped the region's musical culture, including its country music.

White rural bands with guitar, bass, fiddle, and mandolin are by no means unique to the area. Shreveport's location, however, is such that influences of black music, Cajun and Creole, and Texas music gave these bands a distinct regional flavor. In addition to the Taylor-Griggs, other regional artists include the East Texas Serenaders and the Pelican Wildcats. The East Texas Serenaders were from just north of Tyler; their twenty-four recorded sides for Columbia, Brunswick, and Decca offer a rich picture of the region's distinct string band style.[2] Closer to Shreveport, from the small Webster Parish town of Pelican, the Wildcats formed as an "old-time" band during the late 1920s and played for venues ranging from the Mansfield Female College to the Logansport Fair. They broadcast over KWKH's competition in Shreveport, including stations KWEA and KRMD. With members Willie Ross Mayes (fiddle), Dolphus Hill (mandolin), and Kenneth Mayes (guitar), the Pelican Wildcats recorded for Columbia Records in Atlanta on October 27, 1931. Their one released selection, "Walkin' Georgia Rose," initially appeared as Columbia 15755-D, with Charles B. Smith performing "My Little A-1 Brownie" on the other side. "Walkin' Georgia Rose" was reissued on *Roots 'n Blues: The Retrospective* (Columbia/Legacy C4K-47911, 1992); their other selection recorded at that time, "Love Flower Waltz," has never been issued.[3]

A brief sketch of the elusive loner and fiddle master, Hiter Colvin, written by Michael Luster, appears in this volume as a counterpart to the pieces on the Taylor-Griggs and the Coxes. The latter both point to an extensive tradition of traditional string band music shared by the East Texas Serenaders, the Pelican Wildcats, and other groups; while the former suggests the kind of solo virtuosity that inspires rumors of pacts between fiddlers and the devil.

Meanwhile, other area musicians explored a variety of styles in a number of different circumstances. Onetime member of the Pelican Wildcats Buddy Jones later recorded a large body of western swing–tinged music during the late 1930s and early 1940s. Around this same period, Jimmie Davis also recorded with a western swing band, including the 1940 cut of "You Are My Sunshine," kicked off by Shreveport country music trumpeter Sleepy Brown. Both these musicians incorporated blues and jazz idioms into music that maintained its country identity. In addition to Kevin Fontenot's overview of Jimmie Davis's long career, we include in this section a reprint of Donald Lee Nelson's portrait of western swing/honky-tonk guitarist Buddy Jones. This writing further broadens the perspective on country music in and around Shreveport.

The Horace Logan interview and the essay on Bob Sullivan bring this section inevitably back to the *Hayride*. The final entry looks beyond country music to the legacy of sidemen, studio musicians, and producers that began during the *Hayride* era and extended to the decades that followed.

Notes

1. Tracey Laird, *Louisiana Hayride: Radio and Roots Music Along the Red River* (NY: Oxford University Press, 2005).

2. See Nancy Fly Bredenberg, liner notes to *East Texas Serenaders*, County Records LP 410, 1977.

3. A very brief sketch of this group appears in a local history publication: James W. Joyner, "The Pelican Wildcats and Their Role in the Early Broadcasting Industry in Shreveport, Louisiana," *DeSoto Plume* III, 297.

Introduction from *Louisiana Hayride*

Radio and Roots Music Along the Red River

—Tracey E. W. Laird

Most discussions of the *Louisiana Hayride* focus on Hank Williams, Elvis Presley, and its list of other nationally recognized acts. In her book *Louisiana Hayride*, however, Tracey Laird argues that the show's significance extends beyond the run of famous personnel taking its stage between 1948 and 1960. Its significance reaches back into the history of Shreveport, long before the *Hayride* began, and it extends long after, as local musicians like Merle Kilgore, Jerry Kennedy, Joe Osborn, and Nat Stuckey made their way into studios as producers, songwriters, and artists well into the 1980s.

We reprint here an excerpt from the book's introduction that places the *Hayride* within its unique local context. This piece outlines how the *Hayride* story became a critical lens for examining key themes in U.S. southern history during the latter twentieth century: the relationships between black and white culture, the impact of modern media, and the cultural fusion that revolutionized popular music in the post–World War II era. In so doing, it makes clear that, even in the present volume, categories for music (in this case, country) never seem to stay neat and tidy.

By Horace's watch, it's time.

The white of Saturday night stars illumines the bas-relief eagle watching over the building's dedication to "those who served in the world war." The lamp moons of Leadbelly's Fannin Street wax across the hood of a '53 Louisiana Ford as it slips into the last parking space between two Texas Chevys. The Municipal Auditorium lights up tonight—as it does nearly every Saturday—a monolith, warm and alive beside Shreveport's cold grey Confederate sepulchers and tombs of gentry long

ago buried in Oakland Cemetery. From open second-floor windows, the build-
ing breathes out the hum of amplifier tubes, the whine of microphone feedback.
Behind the drawn velveteen curtain inside, a snare drum snaps its sound test beats
through the electric gab of a crowd just now easing into their wooden slat seats.

In the wings, Horace Logan adjusts his gun holster and fingers the slipknot of
his planter's tie. He jabs his arm out straight, clearing the sleeve from his wrist-
watch face. Sure enough, it's 7:59—show time. The Hayride *producer, program*
director, and emcee sidles onto the stage, up to the mike—a crowd conductor ready
to kick off the weekly broadcast of the radio barn dance. He coughs into his fist to
clear his throat. Mister Logan, as Elvis politely addresses him, winces into the spot-
light and beams at the audience.

"How many folks are here tonight from our fine neighbor to the north,
Arkansas?" His question draws a slim salvo of hand claps and hollers. Horace
pauses, runs a forefinger casually across the felt brim of his cowboy hat. "How
many of you all out there are from right here in Louisiana?" Louder applause and
a few swill-bellied whoops rise from the settling throng. Horace inconspicuously
pulls back the sleeve from his wrist and calmly glances down to see the second
hand tick to 50. He looks up and out, grins wide, and, in a stentorian voice that
intuitively cues an audience to cheer, bellows:

"And how many people are here from the great state of Texas?" The tiers and
coliseum floor explode in revelry. Riding the raucous pitch, fiddles saw and steel
guitars slide into the top-of-the-show theme. So it begins, just as it does every
Saturday night for thousands of listeners from Amarillo to Yazoo: three hours of live
music blow through the wireless like a rush of new wind through an open window.[1]

This and many scenes like it played out across the nation during the
golden era of the radio barn dance. KWKH's *Louisiana Hayride* staked its ter-
ritory in the ethereal radio universe, one among many shows funneling live
dobros and fiddles into parlors from the Gulf to the Great Lakes. The history
of this radio genre reached back into the earliest days of mass broadcasting.
WBAP in Fort Worth, Texas, created the prototype on 4 January 1923, when it
broadcast a variety program led by fiddler and Confederate veteran Captain
M. J. Bonner.[2] The next year, Chicago's WLS christened its *National Barn
Dance* and Nashville's WSM soon followed with the debut of the *Grand Ole
Opry* in 1925. Soon after, a long line of radio barn dances poured into Saturday-
night living rooms from Virginia to California, manifestations of a pop culture
phenomenon lasting the next two-and-a-half decades.[3]

But of all the barn dance radio shows, the *Louisiana Hayride* rises to the
fore in country music after World War II, assuming a uniquely powerful role

second only to the *Grand Ole Opry*. For all its sway, however, the Shreveport broadcast earns only scattered mention in books that address the dramatic shifts in music during the era. Synoptic histories of country music generally allot the *Hayride* a paragraph or two, or at least briefly conjure a metaphor that situates the show in terms of comparative influence: for example, the "high minor leagues" of country music, as one of Hank Williams's earliest biographers dubbed it.[4] Bill C. Malone, country music's preeminent historian, writes that "few could equal Shreveport's Louisiana Hayride as a forum for musical exposure, nor as a launching ground for future stardom."[5] Yet, despite the quotidian nods, the *Hayride*'s significance (and the regional importance of other barn dance shows in the roster, for that matter) remains largely overshadowed by the music scene in Nashville.

The paragon in the early story of the *Louisiana Hayride* is Hank Williams, country music's legendary songwriter and singer, and one of the most influential musicians in all of U.S. popular music. Williams's *Hayride* association is certainly one of the show's greatest claims to fame; while there, he exploded into the national spotlight with "Lovesick Blues" and launched a whirlwind career of hit recordings cut short by his untimely death in 1952. Williams's son, Hank Jr., also a successful performer in his own right, writes about the *Louisiana Hayride* and its impact on his father's career:

> Between the late forties and the late fifties, [the *Louisiana Hayride*] became an innovative force that changed the style and sound of country music and its impact on the American listening public. . . .
> 　The Hayride also did a lot to refine and redefine what was then called "hillbilly" music and make it a respected part of America's musical culture. It helped make it possible for country artists like my daddy to break out of the narrow "hillbilly" category and cross over into the mainstream of popular music.[6]

Hank Williams's fame via the *Louisiana Hayride* sealed the radio show's status as a forum from which hopeful country musicians of the postwar era could gain exposure and success; and Williams's fortune alone might have garnered a mantle of historical significance for the *Hayride* and KWKH. But Williams's association with the show was just one of the most conspicuous factors among many that multiplied the influence of the *Louisiana Hayride* on country music and rockabilly. There were idiosyncratic and local matters like the personal pluck of *Hayride* management, and the chance circumstance and human connections that drew specific personalities to the station at key moments.

And there were broader aspects: the nature of the radio medium, the location and milieu of Shreveport, and the convergence of media opportunity that contributed to the *Hayride*'s success and, in turn, secured it a lasting legacy.

The *Louisiana Hayride* matters much more than its occasional acknowledgements allow. The radio show played key roles in the rise to prominence of both country and rock-and-roll. The *Hayride*, in fact, presents a microcosm of the post–World War II dynamic in the southern United States. A generation of white musicians began to play sounds that merged all the musical impulses—black and white—that surrounded them growing up. No form of popular music remained untouched by this phenomenon. But while the decade following World War II clearly builds to a cultural watershed (what Greil Marcus called "the rockabilly moment"), the roots of this momentum extend far back into the troubled yet intimate history of contact between southern blacks and whites. For this reason, I will not detail the week-to-week minutiae of operations or recount every individual performer on the *Louisiana Hayride*. Instead, I hope to examine the context of the radio show within a complex web of historic, geographic, and commercial realities that began shaping the region's culture during the 1830s.

The story begins as early as Shreveport's founding as a commercial port of the Red River, binding land to water, South to West, black to white, with thick, sticky, and often dirty fibers of cotton. It traces Shreveport's changing identity as railroads killed river trade, and oil and gas became the region's lifeblood. The rise of media—both phonograph and radio—and of country music enters this story with a fresh relevance wrought from a simple shift in point of view, away from commercial centers of power in New York or even Nashville, and toward the peripheral position of Shreveport and its radio barn dance.

Many familiar popular culture tropes about the rise of media, about country music, about Elvis Presley, and about the emergence of rock-and-roll look different from this shift in perspective southward and westward. And the questions raised in this book point to other useful inquiries: How do social and cultural forces within a particular time and place shape the ways people make and appreciate music? In this case, what can be learned about a region's identity—and, therefore, about a collective national identity—through a show like the *Louisiana Hayride*? Perhaps less philosophical, but no less important: Why should we concern ourselves with the *Hayride* if it was, in the words of one writer, just "another, more Southern-fried, version of the Opry"?[27]

First and foremost, the *Hayride* operated with a style and attitude completely different from the *Opry*. *Hayride* producers, in contrast to those at the more established *Opry*, took risks more willingly. They kept an entrepreneurial eye out for new talent and an ear to the ground for changes in what people might like to hear and when they would like to hear it. For instance, about a month before the *Hayride* aired, on 1 March 1948, KWKH began an early morning country music variety program, the *Ark-La-Tex Jubilee*, broadcast Monday through Friday from 5:00 to 6:00 in the morning. Featured performers on the show were Johnnie and Jack and the Tennessee Mountain Boys, Al Robinson and his Red River Ramblers, and announcer Horace Logan with his puppet sidekick, Cosmo. The *Jubilee*, as well as *Hayride* precursors such as *The Saturday Night Roundup* and *Hillbilly Amateur Show*, prefigures the station's willingness to play with the schedule and tenor of its programs to showcase untried artists and new music.

While the show benefited from its start by fortuitous associations with some established country music names, *Hayride* producers were also more ready than most to take chances. Artists whose styles did not easily fit into increasingly discrete musical categories, artists who would have been rebuffed by the self-consciously traditional *Opry*, found a welcome at KWKH. Hank Williams, in fact, failed to secure a position on the *Opry* before he came to Shreveport; and it was only after he proved successful on the *Hayride* that WSM became interested. In fact, because of its conservatism, even established artists were sometimes constrained on the *Opry*. Western swing trumpeter Sleepy Brown recalls that, while touring with the country paragon and cowboy politico Jimmie Davis and his ten-piece band, he enjoyed a respite at gigs in the Ryman Auditorium in Nashville: "[E]very time we would go on tour or go through the Grand Ole Opry, I was a trumpet player. And no horn or drums were ever used on the Opry, so the drummer and I would have to sit backstage. They just didn't allow it." [8] A more famous anecdote recounts Bob Wills's standoff with *Opry* management over drums during his orchestra's sole guest appearance there.[9] (Wills refused to play without his entire band, rejecting a compromise offer to place the drums behind a curtain; his band became the first to use drums on the *Opry* stage.)

The inherent quality of radio broadcasting—that of a theater of the mind, which captures imagination with far less venture capital than other media (e.g., movies, television, phonograph records)—aided the *Hayride* producers in creating a show vital to country music a full day's drive from Nashville. Recollections of Williams's early performances of "Lovesick Blues" underscore the unique opportunity for creating reality when experienced through the ears only. Tillman Franks, a local musician and *Hayride* notable who played bass with Williams the first time he performed "Lovesick Blues," explains what the live audience saw, and what their radio counterparts could never have imagined, during Williams's performance: "Ray Bartlett was an announcer here on KWKH. Ray Bartlett would get right in the orchestra pit and he would turn a flip when Hank would start doing that yodel. And he would get everybody clapping. So Ray Bartlett deserves lots of the credit for getting the people kicked off on that 'Lovesick Blues.'"[10] At other times Bartlett might have incited the crowd by dancing a tango with the curtain.[11] Only the enthusiasm of the live audience came through the speakers to radio listeners, whose stirred imaginations then filled in the visual spaces.

The radio station enjoyed the dual benefit of a strong signal and a strategic location. KWKH's 50-kilowatt transmitter allowed the AM signal to cover a huge geographic area. It reached listeners in twenty-eight states, but much of its audience was in the lower South and Southwest, the direction toward which its potent transmitter pointed after sundown. This partially explains the program's ascendancy throughout communities across the rural expanses of Texas and why a *Hayride* tour could sell out as far from home as Phoenix. Arizona.[12] Not only did the live *Hayride* broadcast win a large radio audience, but it drew weekly crowds to the Municipal Auditorium as well. Shreveport was advantageously located in this respect, an easy trip from town in southwest Arkansas, east Texas, and north Louisiana. A 1951 article in *Shreveport Magazine* estimated that 65 percent of the live *Hayride* audiences were from out of town, and most of these were from Texas.[13]

Even before the *Hayride*, Shreveport's central location gave KWKH a growing reputation as a place where country performers could make a successful living. During the 1930s, the station had drawn a handful of country performers with impressive credentials and national notoriety, starting with Jimmie Davis and the Sheltons (known as The Lone Star Cowboys when the duet played with guitarist Leon Chappelear).[14] The later move by industry notables Dean Upson and the Bailes Brothers to KWKH countenanced the regional popularity of the show and the influence of the station.

Other well-established performers came to Shreveport in their wake, including fiddler Tex Grimsley and guitarist Cliff Grimsley with their band, the Texas Showboys; harmonica wizard Wayne Raney; the Mercer Brothers; Curley Williams and the Georgia Peach Pickers. Several performers who came to Shreveport because of their connection to Upson and the Bailes had been part of the *Grand Ole Opry* before, including Curley Kinsey and the Tennessee Ridge Runners, the Four Deacons, the Delmore Brothers, and Johnnie Wright and Jack Anglin and the Tennessee Mountain Boys, featuring the singing of Johnnie's wife, the future "queen of country music," Kitty Wells.[15] If this list were not enough to affirm KWKH as a viable and influential radio signal for live country music performance, then Roy Acuff's personal appearance on KWKH in March 1948 shortly before the *Hayride* started was nothing short of approbation from the era's most notable country music icon.

Once the *Louisiana Hayride* began, its immediate popularity with audiences and advertisers furthered the reputation of KWKH as a significant center for country music and the area as a place where country musicians could earn a living. After Hank Williams became a star, hopefuls gravitated to Shreveport expecting to follow Williams's trajectory of joining the *Grand Ole Opry* and finding stardom. Many of them did, including Red Sovine, Slim Whitman, Leon Payne, Webb Pierce, Jimmie C. Newman, Johnny Cash, George Jones, Johnny Horton, Jim Reeves, Floyd Cramer, the Browns, and Faron Young. For this reason, *Hayride* producers later dubbed the show "The Cradle of the Stars."[16]

Four additional factors synergistically transformed the hokum of a hayfield wagon into a launching pad for country music fame: FCC regulations, the CBS radio network, the station KTHS, and the Armed Forces Radio Services. Perhaps the most critical factor in the drawing power of the early *Louisiana Hayride* was the absence of television. The FCC freeze on television licensing from 1948 to 1952 gave the Shreveport program a tremendous boost. Even a major city like Houston, Texas, had only one television station at the time; no television station operated in Shreveport until January 1953. In effect, the freeze created an entertainment void, filled in part by the *Hayride*'s live weekly broadcasts.[17] Around the same time Shreveport experienced its first glance at television, the extensive CBS radio network picked the *Louisiana Hayride* as part of its program called "Saturday Night, Country Style."[18] CBS broadcast six barn dance programs in rotation, airing two shows each Saturday night. Thus, a twenty-five-minute segment of the *Hayride* broadcast live nationwide every third Saturday. The CBS interest and investment made it clear that country music was ensconced in U.S. popular culture, and the tradition of the Saturday night barn dance was indeed an institution. The late Johnny Cash, another of country music's most enduring performers, wrote about how this network promotion affected his career:

> The nationwide exposure I got on the *Hayride*, via the CBS Radio Network, was the key factor in making my early records successful. Within a year, my name and voice were familiar to country music fans from coast to coast. The *Hayride* gave me the boost every successful recording artist has to have, just as it had with Hank

Williams, Kitty Wells, Webb Pierce, Faron Young, Slim Whitman, Jim Reeves, and Elvis Presley before me.[19]

The third factor that maximized the influence of the *Hayride* was KTHS, the Little Rock, Arkansas, station acquired by the Ewing family (who already owned KWKH and the Shreveport *Times* newspaper) in a trade following FCC restrictions on multiple ownership. By this time, KTHS was also a 50,000-watt powerhouse. It began broadcasting the *Louisiana Hayride* in its entirety every week, giving *Hayride* performers even greater exposure to the north and east. A final boon came on 26 June 1954, when the Far East Network of the Armed Forces Radio Services picked up the *Hayride* for a weekly thirty-minute segment.[20] All these broadcasts further boosted the prestige of the *Hayride* and the influence of KWKH.

By the early to mid-1950s, the country music mèlange on the *Louisiana Hayride* had reached a large national audience. The list of country musicians who either began their careers on the *Hayride* or were significantly associated with the show was already extensive. They traveled from as far away as Canada (in the case of singer-songwriter Hank Snow), California, and West Virginia, all drawn to Shreveport by the *Hayride's* promise of a shot at fame; but a number of *Hayride* house band musicians, particularly those who played around the mid-1950s, came from the immediate northwest Louisiana area. Whereas *Hayride* headliners presented a wide range of regional sounds and idiosyncratic styles, the local musicians' attitudes and repertoire reflected an ongoing interaction of white and black music characteristic of the flatland region around Shreveport since the nineteenth century.

The *Hayride*, a white country music show with a mostly white audience, employed these young musicians who performed country on the stage every Saturday night, but went home and listened to rhythm-and-blues stars Wynonnie Harris and Al "Stomp" Russell. During the same period KWKH broadcast the *Louisiana Hayride*, the station also featured late afternoon rhythm-and-blues shows, announced by the disc jockey Ray "Groovie Boy" Barlett, who impersonated an African-American disc jockey during his show, *In the Groove*.[21] In hindsight, Bartlett's shows could very well be seen as an adaptation of blackface minstrelsy that began a century earlier.

KWKH program listings in the Shreveport *Times* include an early morning show called *Jive Parade* on New Year's Day in 1948. By at least August of that year, Bartlett was broadcasting his thirty-minute disc jockey program from 4:30 to 5:00 every weekday afternoon. By 1950 the show had expanded to 45 minutes, and by the following year was a full hour.[22] The late 1940s, in general, saw the beginning of radio shows featuring what would (after 1949) be called rhythm-and-blues in stations throughout the country, many of them featuring African-American disc jockeys, rather than whites imitating black dialect.[23] These shows influenced white youth of the period, whose searching for cultural expression has been the subject of reflection from commentators as divergent as Bill Malone and Norman Mailer. Cultural analyst W. T. Lhamon found a continuous thread of "deliberately speeding" mid-1950s culture connecting the method acting of James Dean and Marlon Brando to the writings of Jack Kerouac to the paintings of Jackson Pollock to the rise of rock-and-roll.[24] Adding Shreveport to this discussion of post–World War II cultural shifts offers the chance to add two elements often missed in analyses of the 1950s: real names and faces of the generation of white southern players whose coming-of-age after the war indelibly marked their careers and musical sensibilities; and a direct, specific example—the *Louisiana Hayride*—of rock-and-roll's deep roots in both rhythm-and-blues and country.

Ray Bartlett's *In the Groove* takes on particular significance for the Shreveport country music scene because many young, white *Hayride* musicians during the 1950s had been exposed to his predominantly black playlist. These musicians include Jerry Kennedy, Joe Osborn, James Burton, D. J. Fontana—all of whom went on to find extensive success outside of Shreveport. Not incidentally, it was this type of young musician—with one ear to country music and the other to rhythm-and-blues—who created the white southern sound that would become rockabilly. Elvis Presley, the "Memphis Cat" who began headlining *Hayride* shows in late 1954, was only the most renowned of their ilk. The image of Presley's earliest performances of "That's All Right, Mama" and "Blue Moon of Kentucky" parallels Hank Sr.'s first renditions of "Lovesick Blues" on the *Hayride*; and Presley's signing of a KWKH contract on 6 November 1954 is the other half of the twain that meets to secure the enduring legacy of both country and rock-and-roll on Shreveport's Red River.

Notes

1. This is a creative retelling of Horace Logan's account included in his memoir (with Bill Sloan) *Elvis, Hank, and Me: Making Musical History on the Louisiana Hayride* (New York: St. Martin's, 1998), 7.

2. By 1927 this show aired two or three times per month. See Bill C. Malone, *Country Music, U.S.A.: A Fifty-Year History*. 2d rev. ed. (Austin: University of Texas Press, 1985), 33–34;

and David Ewen, *All the Years of American Popular Music* (Englewood Cliffs, N.J.: Prentice-Hall, 1977), 306.

3. WSB in Atlanta first began broadcasting hillbilly music prominently as early as 1922, though it did not use the barn dance format. Examples of shows that emulated the early prototypes include: the *Wheeling Jamboree* on WWVA in Wheeling, West Virginia, beginning in 1933; the *Boone County Jamboree* in 1938 on Cincinnati's WLW (who renamed in the *Midwestern Hayride* in 1945); the *Renfro Valley Barn Dance* in 1939 on WHAS in Louisville, Kentucky; the *Tennessee Barn Dance* in Knoxville on WNOX in 1942; the *Old Dominion Barn Dance* in Richmond, Virginia, on station WRVA in 1946; the *Ozark Jubilee* over KWTO in Springfield, Missouri, in 1947; the *Big D Jamboree* on Dallas station KRLD, also in 1947; the *Town and Country Jamboree* on KMAL in Washington, D.C., 1947; and the *Town Hall Party*, a television broadcast over station KTTV begun in 1950, Compton, California. This list is taken from Steven R. Tucker, "Louisiana Saturday Night: A History of Louisiana Country Music" (Ph.D. diss., Tulane University, 1995) 393–94. A list of radio barn dances also appears in Linnell Gentry, *A History and Encyclopedia of Country, Western, and Gospel Music* (Nashville: McQuiddy Press, 1961), 168–75.

4. Roger M. Williams, "Hank Williams," in *Stars of Country Music: Uncle Dave Macon to Johnny Rodriguez*, Bill C. Malone and Judith McCulloh, eds. (Urbana: University of Illinois Press, 1975), 238. Writing from the centrality of Nashville, Williams refers to the show as the "Farm club," the "minors," or (abandoning the parallel to baseball) one of the "way stations on the country music line" in his biography *Sing a Sad Song: The Life of Hank Williams*, 2d ed. (Urbana: University of Illinois Press. 1980), 73, 198, 1.

5. Malone, *Country Music, U.S.A.*, 207.

6. Hank Williams Jr., foreword to *Elvis, Hank, and Me*, by Horace Logan, vii–viii.

7. Gerald Natchman, *Raised on Radio* (New York: Pantheon Books, 1998), 158.

8. Thomas E. "Sleepy" Brown, interview by Rachel Stone, 19 February 1995, *Sunday Stage* radio program, KWKH, Shreveport, tape recording in author's files.

9. Monte Mountjoy (Texas playboys drummer), liner notes to Bob Wills, *The Tiffany Transcriptions*, vol 6, *Sally Goodin*, Bob Wills and His Texas Playboys, Kaleidoscope Records, C-27, 1987; also see Joe Carr and Alan Munde, *Prairie Nights to Neon Lights: The Story of Country Music in West Texas* (Lubbock: Texas Tech University Press, 1995), 62; and Charles R. Townsend, *San Antonio Rose: The Life and Music of Bob Wills* (Urbana: University of Illinois Press, 1976), 103, 289.

10. Tillman Franks and Murrell Stansell, interview by Rachel Stone, 17 September 1995, *Hank Williams Special* radio show, KWKH studio, Shreveport. Tape recording in author's files. Escott identifies the upstaging gymnast as Ray Atkins, who performed with Johnnie and Jack; Franks asserts that it was Barlett.

11. Ray Bartlett interview, 27 June 2003, Shreveport, tape recording in author's files. All interviews are by the author, unless otherwise indicated.

12. Frank Page interview, 23 February 1996, Shreveport, tape recording in author's files. According to announcer Page, the *Hayride* toured four or five times per year, selling out most shows.

13. "Louisiana Hayride," *Shreveport Magazine* (May 1951), 32–33; in Tucker, "Louisiana Saturday Night," 425.

14. Davis recorded with the Sheltons and Chappelear during his last recording session for Victor Records in Chicago, 4–5 August 1933, before he moved to Decca. Tony Russell describes session details in notes to *Governor Jimmie Davis: Nobody's Darlin' But Mine*, BCD 15943 E1, Bear Family, 1998. This is the first box of a two-box set of Davis's entire opus.

15. For more discussion of these performers recruited by Upson and the Baileses, see Tucker, "Louisiana Saturday Night," 408–11. A picture of Curley Kinsey and the Tennessee Ridge Runners shortly after their arrival at KWKH appears in the Shreveport *Times*, 11 January 1948.

Announcement for the beginning of daily broadcasts by Johnnie and Jack and the Tennessee Mountain Boys, at 5:45 A.M., 1:30 P.M., and 10:30 p.m. Monday through Friday appears in the Shreveport *Times*, 8 February 1948; both articles in the scrapbook compiled by Robert Gentry, *The Louisiana Hayride*, vol. 1, *1948–55*, 3, 5. In the early 1960s, Johnnie Wright changed the spelling of his first name to "Johnny." I will use the original spelling, as he was still using it during the period discussed.

16. Malone, *Country Music, U.S.A.,* 207. A brief entry listing some other stars appears in Paul Kingsbury, ed., *The Encyclopedia of Country Music* (New York: Oxford University Press, 1998), 304–5. Also of interest is an essay from the late 1950s written by Horace Logan and printed as part of a *Louisiana Hayride* publicity layout in Robert Gentry, *The Louisiana Hayride, "The Glory Years–1948–60: A Compilation of Newspaper articles, Pictures, and Advertisements,* vol. 2, *1956–60* (Many, La., 1998), 362–63.

17. Tucker, "Louisiana Saturday Night," 396–97.

18. Lillian Jones Hall, "A Historical Study of Programming Techniques and Practices of Radio Station KWKH, Shreveport, LA, 1922–1950" (Ph.D. diss., Louisiana State University, 1959), 183. See also Harrison B. Summers, ed., *A Thirty-Year History of Programs Carried on National Radio Networks in the United States, 1925–1956* (report compiled by the Department of Speech, University of Ohio, 1958; reprint, New York: Arno Press, 1971), 208.

19. Johnny Cash, introduction to *Elvis, Hank, and Me,* by Logan, xii.

20. Hall, "A Historical Study," 183.

21. Barlett's program also went by the name *Groovie's Boogie.* Bartlett was the same *Hayride* announcer who turned back flips during "Lovesick Blues." In discussing the instrumental "Juke," released by Chess Records in 1952, Muddy Waters reflected on a tour his band made in that year to Monroe and Shreveport, Louisiana, set up by a "disc jockey, called him the Groovy Boy [*sic*]". See Robert Palmer, *Deep Blues: A Musical and Cultural History from the Mississippi Delta to Chicago's South Side to the World* (New York: Penguin Books, 1981), 211.

22. See KWKH program logs in Shreveport *Times,* 4 August 1948, 4 April 1950, and 23 June 1951; in Gentry, *The Louisiana Hayride,* vol. 1, 23, 78, 101. A photo caption of KWKH announcers in the Shreveport *Times*, 15 January 1950, describes Bartlett's program as "the most popular locally produced program heard in Shreveport"; in Gentry, *The Louisiana Hayride,* vol. 1, 75. Disc jockey programs of all types expanded and a glance at KWKH radio logs underscores the eclecticism of the era. For example, Bartlett's show during one period immediately followed a live hillbilly show by Harmie Smith. Performer Johnnie Bailes also hosted a hillbilly program, and Frank Page hosted both a pop program and a rhythm-and-blues show in addition to his *Hayride* announcing.

23. Rufus Thomas on station WDIA in Memphis is among the most famous of African-American disc jockeys of the era; he began in 1951 doing an hour-long Saturday program and, by 1954, he was doing four hours late night every day. See Rob Bowman, liner notes to Rufus Thomas, *Can't Get Away from This Dog,* CD sxd 038, Stax Records, 1991. A number of stations started between 1948 and 1952 that were solely aimed at an African American audience; many of these were white-owned, but there were exceptions, like WERD in Atlanta. See Erik Barnouw, *The Golden Web: A History of Broadcasting in the United States,* vol. 2, *1933–1953* (New York: Oxford University Press, 1968), 289–90.

24. W. T. Lhamon, *Deliberate Speed: The Origins of a Cultural Style in the American 1950s* (Washington, D.C.: Smithsonian Institution Press, 1990). Bill C. Malone writes of the dynamic in *Southern Music/American Music* (Lexington: University Press of Kentucky, 1979), among other places.

The Grigg Family and the Taylor-Griggs Melody Makers

The History of a North Louisiana String Band

—Monty Brown

This article originally appeared in the 1988 volume of *Louisiana Folklife*. Here, Monty Brown recounts the history of an Ark-La-Tex musical family extending back into the 1870s. The family's oral history is fascinating in its own right, even more so as it includes encounters with prominent figures in radio and recording. Moreover, the Grigg story relates how one family in northwestern Louisiana experienced transformations of life resulting from the early twentieth-century revolutions in media and transportation. Whereas the Griggs drove a horse-drawn wagon to their first gig as a family band, they traveled by automobile for their first recording session in Memphis, held under the auspices of the famed hillbilly, blues, and gospel record producer Ralph Peer. They learned much of their repertoire via the phonograph recordings they purchased at the local furniture store and performed this music over KWKH during the 1920s, from the studios of station owner W. K. Henderson's country estate. This part of the story offers a window of insight into KWKH's importance long before the era of the *Hayride*.

The Taylor-Griggs' recorded legacy provides a brief but colorful look at one string band in northwest Louisiana at the beginnings of the "hillbilly" music industry. We see the Griggs navigate the different demands of local performances in schools and churches, and the changes in those performance practices exacted by radio and records. As Brown explains, Peer's concerns over copyright make this small body of recording not likely their best work; even so, the story of how they came to be recorded makes listening to those sounds all the richer.

On July 16, 1988, during the performance of *Louisiana Saturday Night* at the Natchitoches-Northwestern Folk Festival, Ausie Grigg, Sr., was presented an award in recognition of his place in Louisiana musical history. The KWKH Country Music Pioneer Award was presented by singer Dolly Parton on behalf of the Shreveport radio station, which carried the show "live," and the Louisiana Folklife Center.

KWKH holds a unique position in the history of country music in northwest Louisiana. During the late '20s and early '30s, pioneering days of radio, owner W. K. Henderson started to program local and regional musicians, most of whom played some form of "hillbilly" music. In those days KWKH's signal could easily be heard over most of the United States, and very often, beyond. The signal was not stronger then, but there were far fewer competing signals. Anything broadcast reached a very wide audience, and mail poured in from all over the continent. Henderson himself used the airwaves as his own private pulpit, holding forth freely and helping define the Federal Communications Commission's standards of decency. Though Henderson is largely forgotten, his efforts as a country music pioneer live on through KWKH.

During the 1930s, KWKH began broadcasting live shows along the lines of the *Grand Ole Opry; Saturday Night Roundup* was cancelled by the disappearance of talent during World War II, and after the war, in 1948, the *Louisiana Hayride* was established. The *Hayride* ran for about fifteen years at the Municipal Auditorium in Shreveport, and has continued sporadically ever since. As of October 1988, there were still plans afoot to re-establish the *Hayride*, which is undoubtedly one of the most influential institutions in the history of country music. The Pioneer Award presented to Ausie Grigg, Sr., was in recognition of the contribution he, his family, and his fellow players were making two decades and more before the inception of the *Louisiana Hayride*. With the Griggs, it has always been a family affair.

The Griggs trace their American ancestry back to Charles City County, Virginia, near Jamestown, in the seventeenth century. In a classic migratory pattern, they moved gradually southwest. By the mid-eighteenth century, they had moved about fifty or sixty miles; then came the first long jump to Polk County, North Carolina, where Ausie's great-grandfather, Wesley Jackson Grigg, was born in 1818.

Ausie's father, Robert Crowder Grigg, was born in North Carolina in 1870. The family moved to Louisiana in the fall of 1873; by train from Shelby, North Carolina, to Vicksburg, Mississippi; by ferry across the Mississippi, and by stage coach to Trenton (West Monroe). From there they traveled by covered wagon drawn by four mules to their new home in the Brush Valley-Liberty Hill communities of Bienville Parish.

Most early settlers in the area lived by subsistence farming. Cotton was the cash crop; corn, peas, sugar cane, potatoes, and pumpkins were grown for the family to eat. Pioneer families such as the Griggs also fished, and hunted for wild turkey, deer, and squirrel. They had large families, easing the work load and constituting a self-sufficient social group in the sparsely settled backwoods.

There were nine children in the Grigg family, and the four boys, when they became young men, formed a vocal quartet. Three of the girls also sang, and they were all much in demand at church socials and other social gatherings. Most Grigg children became singers and played musical instruments. Robert, Ausie's Father, was given a violin by a black man who lived close by. However, when Robert's father saw that he wanted to play it, he made Robert get rid of it. Robert's father associated the violin (or "fiddle") with the rougher social elements, people who drank, partied, and fought.

In January, 1896, Robert married Annie Jones, and their first child was born in December of that same year. This was a son, Shelly. Soon after the marriage, Robert, in a spirit of independence, bought himself a violin and began to satisfy his old yearning to play. When Shelly was old enough, Robert fixed two straws, each about a foot long, and taught his son how to "beat" or "rap" on the strings to provide a rhythmic accompaniment. Robert showed Shelly how to keep the correct time for different tunes. The Griggs played well enough so that neighbors would often drop by to listen, and the family would be asked to play for social functions. In 1910, however, tragedy struck the family. Late in the year, Shelly became ill with typhoid fever, and, after several weeks of suffering, he died on his fourteenth birthday, December 2. Robert put his violin away; he was grief stricken and had lost the desire to play.

Robert and Annie's second child, a daughter, had died as an infant of three months. Ausie was born on September 16, 1900. During the next few years, until 1908 when the family moved to the Bear Creek area ten miles north of the old home place, three more children were born. There were two girls, Berkie and Ione and a boy, Crockett. A third girl, Lorean, was born at Bear Creek, and the last child, a girl named Johnie Maude, was born two and a half years after Shelly's death.

Among the other farm families in the region were the Greers and the Caskeys. Virgil Greer was, by all reports, an excellent fiddle player, and Till Caskey could pick the guitar. Greer belonged to a dance band with Benny, Paul, and Raymond Roper; the band played a selection of old time waltzes and ragtime music. The instrumentation of this band was violin, bass violin, guitar, and mandolin. They lived in the neighborhood, and one night they came to the Grigg house and serenaded the family.

"They were on the porch, playing, before we knew it," says Ausie. "We all got up, dressed, and invited them into the living room where they played several selections for us. In the meantime, of course, mother had served cakes and coffee. I got my desire right there to play a bass violin. It was five years after that before I really did."

The serenade was in 1915. It was on a Sunday, after Sunday school, in 1920 that Ausie was standing around talking with Till Caskey and Virgil Greer about their music when Mr. Euwell Bott, principal of the Bear Creek public school, suggested that the four of them organize a band. Mr. Bott avowed that he had never played an instrument but that he would buy a mandolin and try. Ausie announced that he would dearly love to play the bass violin, and Caskey said that he knew where there was a used bass for sale.

Within the next few days, Ausie hitched up his horse and buggy, and he and Caskey drove the fifteen miles to where the bass was for sale. There were a few cracks in it, only one string remained, and there was no hair on the bow. He paid $25.00 for the instrument, and they headed back to Bear Creek where Virgil Greer fixed it up. He applied glue to the cracks, coated it with varnish, ordered hair for the bow and strings for the bass. By the time it was in playing condition, the mandolin that Mr. Bott had ordered had arrived, and the quartet was ready to rehearse.

These rehearsals were held at the Grigg home where there was an organ which could also be used; Berkie, the eldest sister, was an accomplished organist. According to Ausie, the life of this band was "far too short": Mr. Bott found himself too pushed for time and had to give up, and Till Caskey moved away from the area. However, it was during this time that Robert took his old fiddle out of storage and went back to playing with a renewed enthusiasm that never again left him. Also, the other children began to take up a stringed instrument, or at least to add their voices, and with Virgil Greer as teacher, the sound of stringed instruments became a regular part of the Grigg household.

Ausie puts it this way: "After we got to playing, my daddy would be sitting there listening, and he just began playing with us. Greer would tell us where to make the notes on the guitar and the bass violin; we knew no music. But when Greer moved, there was the Grigg Family Band."

Virgil Greer moved away from the area in the mid-1920s, but his work had been done. Robert was back to playing the fiddle, Ausie was a bassist, and the four daughters and Crockett could sing and play some of the instruments with varying degrees of expertise. One of the pastimes they would indulge in was sort of musical chairs with the instruments: they would pass on the guitar, or mandolin, fiddle, or bass to the next family member for the next tune, and so on, until everyone had played each instrument. If Robert was unable to get to a performance, Ausie would play the fiddle and Crockett would take over on the bass.

During this time there were very few radios. The radio station which became KWKH when W. K. Henderson bought it in 1925, had been on the air since 1923. That was about it for radio broadcasting in their region, and so it stands to reason that everyone hadn't automatically gone out and bought radios. There were probably a lot more record players around; the recording industry had been steadily growing since the last decades of the nineteenth century, but there wasn't much country music on record. In fact, it was the late-1920s that saw the first great burst in the recording of hillbilly music which the Griggs were to be a part of. All this meant that "live" music was very popular.

The Grigg Family Band was in demand in Bienville Parish for gatherings and social occasions of different kinds. They didn't play for dances, but rather for school and church socials, house parties, theaters, and openings of businesses.

"We'd go serenading, too," says Ausie, recalling the time that Greer and his band had arrived on the Grigg front porch some years earlier. "We'd ease up to a place and they wouldn't know we were there. It was a customary thing to do. We'd begin to play all at once and kind of shake everybody up. We went to a place one night, and this man had a vicious dog. He was a big ol' dog and he met us at the gate, bristles raised and growling. Well, who's going in under conditions like that? So, Johnie Maude said, 'You go ahead with that bass violin; he can't get to you.' Everybody laughed, but I went ahead with the bass violin, the ol' dog ran up and I came down on the ol' E string of that bass and got the growl out of that dog; he whirled around, went under the house, he bumped his head and we heard him come out the back, bumping his head again, and he went down across the pasture just a-hollerin' for dear life. These were our neighbors, you see. We went on in and played, and in a few days someone said, 'We haven't seen our old Tuck in a long time.' And old Tuck stayed gone about a week."

Ausie carefully explained the family didn't play for dances, but it had nothing to do with religious attitudes which found dancing sinful. It was for much more practical reasons.

"Back in those days, things got pretty rough at some of those dances. It was during Prohibition and there was a lot of that 'white lightning' being made. Now somebody who had indulged in that white lightning to excess, even in a mass group of people, could cause a little disturbance. I knew it was a possibility, so we didn't take that chance because we didn't know what was going to be involved. Not that we had anything against playing for a good, clean dance."

The Griggs used mules and a wagon, or a horse and buggy, for transportation long after the advent of the automobile. Ausie doesn't remember when they got their first car, but he recalls that it was "some time" before they bought one.

"The first time we made a trip to play for a school, my daddy's brother lived down in the lower part of Bienville Parish, close to the Bryan community. They asked us to come down and play for the closing of the school. It was in the spring of the year and pretty warm. We had a wagon, and we had a neighbor that had a covered deal to go on the wagon. So we borrowed that, put it on our wagon, and drove down there in a covered wagon. We drove through what we call the 'Piney Woods.' All those trees were huge—virgin timber—it was a beautiful sight to see. We went down there to that schoolhouse and played until midnight. That was our first experience and we were pretty rough; we enjoyed it, though."

When the band members were more proficient and more mobile, they would even get paid for playing on some occasions. One time there was a Grand Opening of a furniture store in Ruston, and the Griggs were hired to attract a crowd. But for special causes in the local towns, for school or church events, the Griggs contributed their services. Sometimes it even cost money.

"In those days, all the roads were gravel," says Ausie. "We played Ruston one afternoon and we started home, and I had the bass violin strapped on the running board of the Model T Ford. Well, a man attempted to pass us and he ran into the side of us and knocked us over into the ditch. It didn't turn the car over, but we went over sideways into the ditch, and that bass fiddle was hanging there, getting full of water. We got it out and got the water out of it. At that time there was a violin maker in Gibsland. He was a German gentleman. We carried it to him and he took it completely apart. He had the parts scattered all over the room. But he put it back together, and he told me, 'You're going to have a better sounding bass than you had at first,' and I said, 'Why?' and he said, 'One side of the front of that bass was thicker than the other, and I planed it down.' He glued it back together and I said, 'Will it stay?' He said, 'Unless you dip it up and down in the creek it'll stay.'"

Later on the bass violin went through two more near disasters, making it one of the most storied instruments in the region. Ausie rescued it from a burning house one time and again in 1982 from his house in Herbert which was destroyed by a tornado. Strangely, the bass was the only thing in the house that didn't get wet.

"It was the only thing that couldn't have stood any water. There was an outside closet that had quilts and things stacked up inside, and I had my bass violin sitting in the corner, and there was a chest-of-drawers sitting beside it. After the tornado had got the top of the house, and the house was all bent up, I walked in there and the water must have been two or three inches deep on the floor. The roof was gone, you see. I looked over there and there stood my bass. I walked over and got it and it was just as dry as it could be. Which was almost a miracle," he laughed.

Two things happened in 1928 which led the Griggs onto radio and into the recording studio. First, they met Foster Taylor; and second, there was a sudden commercial burst in the recording of hillbilly music. Foster Taylor was a lawyer from Arcadia. He had a telephone and was accustomed to business dealings; and, most importantly, he was an avid and talented fiddle player. Aware that the Griggs comprised a close-knit family band, Taylor proposed he come in with them and, effectively, work as their agent. All agreed, and Taylor was soon in contact with W. K. Henderson, who invited the group to come and perform on KWKH.

Henderson ran his radio station, studios and all, from his estate, Kennonwood, a few miles north of Shreveport. It was his policy to go into the studio and personally broadcast whenever he got the urge. He held strong opinions on many matters; he ran a national campaign against chain stores, and in favor of local businesses. He also kept up a running battle with the newly evolving board that eventually became the Federal Communications Commission. He was an enthusiastic proponent of free speech, though his blind spot may have been in not seeing his own situation as more free than most. After all, not many people own radio stations.

The first time that the Griggs [who by now called themselves the Taylor-Griggs Louisiana Melody Makers] went to perform on KWKH was also the first time they had been in front of a microphone. Mr. Paul Carriger, director of programs, organized the session. They drove to Henderson's country home, which was some sixty miles from Arcadia. The room they were shown into had curtains all around it and one microphone which they were to gather around.

"We played, and it was the nearest to nothing that I had ever gotten into, playing to a bare room; nobody hearing you . . . we played an hour and we went back home, and we got a letter from Mr. Henderson. He asked us to come back to the studios and play again! He had gotten telegrams from that first program, a stack of them three inches high, and he read some of them to us. Well, we could really get into it then! Somebody was hearing us!"

On one occasion the band returned to Henderson's station to play during the election campaign of 1928. Henderson, of course, had strong political opinions. He was campaigning on behalf of Al Smith, the governor of New York, who was running against Republican Herbert Hoover. Mrs. Henderson, it seems, was a Hoover supporter and so W. K. would grudgingly give some time to the opposing point of view. The show with the Melody Makers was arranged so that Henderson would make his pro-Smith speeches, and the musicians would entertain between times. Their first number was "The Sidewalks of New York" which was popular at the time. The Griggs knew the song; they had learned it from a record, which was the way they learned much of their music.

There were no record stores, as such, in those days. The record outlets were often the furniture stores that stocked the equipment which played the records. The huge machines—Victrolas, for instance—were regarded as pieces of furniture. The Victrolas were manufactured by the RCA Victor Talking Machine Company. To promote the sale of the machines, Victor had to make sure there was a steady flow of material to play on them, so the company also made recordings.

Country music, referred to as "folk" or "hillbilly" at the time, received a shot in the arm from radio shows such as the *Grand Ole Opry* which began in 1925. Soon, country folk were buying Talking Machines and it was discovered that there was a market for their kind of music. Ralph Peer was sent out from Victor headquarters to discover and record some hillbilly entertainment, and in 1927 he discovered both the Carter Family and Jimmie Rodgers at the same session. With these two acts, sales of hillbilly music broke new ground, and a demand for new acts was created.

The owner of the local furniture store in Arcadia, the one that dealt with Victrolas, was Ed Conger, a friend of Foster Taylor's who often listened to the group during their practice sessions. At one of the rehearsals, Conger announced that he knew Ralph Peer through his business dealings, and Conger thought the Victor record scout would listen to the group and perhaps want to record them.

The next time Peer was in Dallas, Conger telephoned him and asked him to stop by in Arcadia during his eastward journey, and listen to the Taylor-Griggs Louisiana Melody Makers. It was arranged. The musicians set up their instruments in the furniture store and were ready and waiting when Peer's train arrived at the station. Peer came to the store and the musicians played. He would alternately walk around the store and sit and listen. Finally, he said, "Can you folks come and meet me in Memphis, Tennessee, in September?" This, as Ausie has said, was music to their ears, and they readily agreed to the dates suggested.

Long before daylight on September 12, 1928, two vehicles bearing the Taylor-Griggs Louisiana Melody Makers set out from Arcadia on the day-long trek to Memphis. Even today this is a seven-hour drive, but in 1928 there were no Interstates, and the roads were primarily gravel. There were six Griggs in the group: Robert, his two sons, Ausie and Crockett, and three of his daughters, Ione, Lorean, and Johnie Maude, who was just sixteen at the time. Foster Taylor took his Model T Ford; he also brought his nephew, Clavie Taylor, who supplied the other vehicle, a Chevrolet. They drove through southeast Arkansas and took the Mississippi River ferry at Greenville. There was no bridge south of Memphis at that time. Apart from a slight delay when one of the cars overheated, they made good time, getting to Memphis by nightfall.

The next morning they arrived at a makeshift studio on the second floor of the City Hall. The recording companies would carry their equipment with them to a central location in a region, and arrange appointments for various musical groups. Musicians in Louisiana generally had to go to New Orleans, Dallas, San Antonio, or Memphis. There was one recording session in Shreveport, in 1930. The Melody Makers quickly found out the realities of the commercial recording world: tune after tune that they offered to Ralph Peer was rejected. "We already have that one," was the standard reason. The Melody Makers' best known material had been learned from other recordings, or was otherwise too well known. Peer was looking for the unusual or the original.

Only three tunes, all hastily put together, were accepted on that first day. Foster Taylor had a couple of melodies to which he put some lyrics: the romantic "Sweet Rose of Heaven" (blushing in the noonday sun), and "Ione," to which they all contributed, and Mr. Taylor dedicated to Ione Grigg. Taylor played the fiddle on both these tunes, and Clavie got in on the act by doing the vocals. The third tune was a breakdown titled "Big Ball Uptown." Robert Grigg came up with the words and the arrangement to this tune which "must have been in his memory somewhere." Being a breakdown fiddler, Robert played on this cut, and shared the boisterous vocals with Crockett:

> Big ball uptown, boys, big ball uptown
> Big ball uptown, my darlin', don't turn me down
> Drink your whiskey and I drink my wine,
> You tend your business, I tend to mine.

The same tune was adapted by Bob Wills some years later. It became a West Texas dance hall standard under the name, "Big Ball in Cowtown." One of the obvious disadvantages to this recording system, from an artistic standpoint, was that the ensemble playing which the Griggs had developed over the years was wasted. None of the girls' voices was recorded, and none of the songs could be thought of as their best material. During the practice takes, which were made to set levels, the bass could not be played. Therefore, Ausie never did hear what his part was like until the actual record was made.

"Let me tell you a little bit about it. In this room they had big, thick curtains hung all around about two feet from the wall. There were no cooling systems. They had electric fans, but they couldn't use those fans when we were recording. So they'd pull those curtains over the windows. It was as hot as it could be. There was a red light over in the corner, and this engineer came in, and he talked to us and said, 'When that red light comes on, just be quiet. When that green light comes on, start playing. Let it be over in two minutes, but not more than three.' And we played.

"He came back in and said, 'I want you to see how it sounds,' but he told me before he went out, 'Don't put the bass in there.' I thought, my goodness, am I not going to get to play? He saw that I was confused about it and he said, 'This test is cut on wax, and the vibrations from that bass violin will shatter that wax. So we can't take it on the test. So, he played it back and the rest of it sounded pretty good. I didn't know what I was doing, though. He saw that I was still wondering about that, so he said, I'm going to show you.' He went back and set up again and said, 'Play your bass violin,' and I did, and he came back and turned it back on. Oh! The screeching and scratching and going on you had never heard. It sounded like cats and dogs!"

It is worth noting that by the time Ausie returned to Memphis one year later, studio equipment had been improved so that the bass could be recorded on the tests. Ausie said that it helped them all because they could tell where to "lighten up a little" and where to increase their volume. As a result, they had a much easier time and were able to make three complete records.

After this first, frustrating day, the Melody Makers retired to their rooms at the Peabody Hotel to come up with some fresh material for the next day. They met some of the members of an Arkansas string band, Dr. Smith's Champion Hoss Hair Pullers, who had run into the same problem. Dr. Smith's group had written three new tunes for their second day in the studio, but only one of them was ever released. The Melody Makers came up with four more songs that evening, but only one of them was released.

"My daddy had an old tune that he knew, and he added some words, 'When the Moon Drips Away into Blood'. I got to searching in later years and I found where those words are in the Bible, there in Revelations [sic]. And then we recorded a song, 'When I Was Single'; my daddy came up with that, but it was never released."

There are two other waltzes listed (in *The Victor Book*) in the recording session of Friday, September 14: "Dreamy Eyes Waltz" and "Doris Waltz." Both are listed as unissued, as is "When I Was Single," which may have been the only tune on which both Robert Grigg and Foster Taylor fiddled. Clavie Taylor had left Memphis the day before, presumably by bus or train, so Ausie, Crockett, and Lorean drove back in the Chevrolet. The others drove back with Mr. Taylor, and Johnie Maude recalls that they got into an accident in El Dorado, Arkansas. Nobody was hurt and the car was able to continue the journey back home.

"Big Ball Uptown" and "Sweet Rose of Heaven" were released on a 78 rpm disc just in time for the Christmas season. Conger's Furniture Store would play the songs on its outside loudspeakers, and the local newspaper was generous in its coverage of the local celebrities. Conger's sold out of the record more than once, and found that stores in Shreveport, Ruston, and Gibsland were having similar trouble keeping it in stock. There are also reports of its being popular as far away as Hawaii, and, of course, as was noted earlier, the Taylor-Griggs Louisiana Melody Makers had gained widespread reknown through KWKH broadcasts.

Ausie Grigg continued to play and record for several years, but the Grigg Family Band started to fall apart after the 1928 session in Memphis. When they were invited back, in September, 1929, Ausie was the only Grigg to go along. The new band consisted of Foster Taylor on fiddle, Byron "Bun" Hiser on mandolin, Henry Galloway on the guitar, and Oscar Logan, vocalist. Two of the records that came out of the session were released under the name, "Taylor's Louisiana Melody Makers." The Grigg girls began to take an interest in raising their own families, and Robert felt that Ralph Peer was not that interested in "breakdown" fiddlers.

A month after the 1929 session, the stock market crashed, and the Great Depression set in. All the record companies cut back on their activities, recording only those artists who could assure profitable sales. Both the country and the blues (or "race") record markets suffered from the bad economic times. It was the end of a great surge in activity, and the Melody Makers never recorded again. Ausie worked on a series of morning radio programs with Foster Taylor, and others on KWKH. This was *The Alarm Clock Program* in the early 1930s, sponsored by the Monticello Nursery Company and broadcast from the new studios in downtown Shreveport.

Ausie also did some recording with Jimmie Davis in Dallas, in 1932, and worked on a show for a vaudeville company (with Davis) that never materialized. In 1935 he moved to Hebert, Louisiana, to be closer to Rilla Hebert, whom he married in 1936. They have a son, Ausie, Jr., who plays the piano and has performed with his father at many local functions. Ausie Grigg, Sr., is a retired farmer. His wife, who taught school for many years, died in 1976. Crockett and Johnie Maude still reside in Bienville Parish. Lorean lives in Bossier City.

The Cox Family

—Susan Roach

The Cox Family lives in Cotton Valley, Louisiana, some thirty-five miles from Shreveport. Their roots remain deep in old-time, bluegrass, and gospel music that they picked up from local musicians, heard on phonograph records and radio stations, and learned at church. They are modern exponents of the same "old-time music" tradition carried on decades before by the Taylor-Griggs Melody Makers, and full participants in a vital subculture that sustains itself via informal gatherings of family and friends, rural (particularly Pentecostal and Baptist) church settings, and fiddling contests.

A tradition grounded in nostalgia, this country music subculture continues to thrive quite apart from the mainstream commercial country industry. One notable exception is the mainstream attention brought by the sensational success of *O Brother, Where Art Thou?* in 2000. The Cox Family remains close to the roots music of northeastern Louisiana and Shreveport despite the blossoming of their fame through this film and their interactions with bluegrass star Alison Krauss. Roach sketches their history as a family of musicians and their challenges in pursuing a professional life while staying close to home.

Carrying on a long family musical tradition, the Cox Family, from Cotton Valley, Louisiana, exemplifies the best of both the preservation and promotion of folk music. Echoing the old-time country sounds typical of the north Louisiana hill country, they draw on, as Nashville writer Michael McCall says, "the bedrock of American music, combining traditional country, Southern gospel, rural blues, and old-styled pop into a sweetly casual, homespun sound that is as refreshing as a soft summer breeze across a back porch."[1] The family band includes father Willard Cox on fiddle and vocals; son Sidney on banjo, Dobro, and vocals; and daughters Evelyn on vocals and guitar and Suzanne on vocals and mandolin. Another daughter Lynn, who initially played bass with the band and then stopped for a period, again plays bass and sings. While their traditional musical background and beautiful family harmony have much in common with many of this region's musicians, their accomplishments and awards, including Grammy award–winning recordings, songwriting, and film, go far beyond the norm.

Family Background

Continuing to live in their hometown of Cotton Valley, the Cox Family has a background in music characteristic of many of the traditional old-time country families of north Louisiana, in that they learned their music "by ear." The family patriarch and spokesman, Willard, who started the family band, describes his style as "country, bluegrass, and gospel; we mixed it up."[2] Born June 9, 1937, Willard Cox grew up in rural Webster Parish, where traditional music was a part of family life. His grandfather on the Etheridge side and his uncle played country fiddle, which he says made him want to play. In addition, his mother sang, and as Willard recalls: "I first learned to sing in church when I was a small boy. It just came naturally to me to learn. We sang the old One Hundred songs at the First Baptist Church."[3] His country music was inspired by other musicians in the community as well as the radio broadcasts from both the *Grand Old Opry* and the *Louisiana Hayride*; by the time he was eleven in 1948, the *Hayride* had begun, providing him with many inspirations:

> I listened to KWKH every afternoon, especially to Harmie Smith's program, where he played the guitar and sang, and on Saturday nights, the *Louisiana Hayride* and the *Grand Ole Opry*. I was especially inspired by Johnny and Jack, the Tennessee Mountain Boys, Red Sovine, Wilburn Brothers, Mac Wiseman, Johnny Horton, and Jimmie Davis. It was all country. Every once in a while Jimmy Martin, Flatt and Scruggs would come down and do bluegrass.[4]

The *Hayride* first aired about the same time as Bill Monroe, the father of bluegrass, and his band, with Flatt and Scruggs, hit its stride. While the Cox

Family often is categorized as bluegrass by the music world, they actually think of themselves more as old-time country. The family's emphasis on harmony singing, with female voices dominating the sound, and the subject matter of their work does set them apart from the hard-driving, fast-paced instrumentation and aggressive singing style of typical bluegrass. Also their instrumentation, particularly Willard's fiddling, points more toward country, which is not surprising, given how he learned the fiddle.

Willard describes how he obtained his first instrument and learned country fiddling in the folk tradition from other fiddlers: "I got my first fiddle from a guy at school. Darrell Stevens taught me how to tune and put strings on it. I learned to play from listening to other people play." One of those teachers was Pat Patterson, the husband of the First Baptist Church organist.[5] A true fan of the *Louisiana Hayride*, whether listening to its broadcasts or in the audience, Willard absorbed much of his fiddling style and learned "fill in fiddle" style from the *Hayride* house band, as well as visiting fiddlers: "Two fiddlers—Buddy Attaway and Dobber Johnson—really inspired me. I would watch them play the fiddle."[6] Thus, with a foundation in gospel, family old-time music, commercial country from the *Hayride*, and a touch of bluegrass, Willard had the basis he would use to build his family band's composite sound.

Like many other traditional musicians, Cox learned to play more than one instrument and played different styles with various bands; he tells how he got his first guitar as a teenager and formed his first country band: "My daddy sold a hog to buy me a guitar, and Johnny Sonoff taught me to play it, and we started us a band called Cotton Valley Ramblers. We played in front of Rittles store and at different peoples' houses and even at Rocky Mt. School. The band played on to 1956, when some of the guys joined the Navy and broke the band up." After he finished high school, the men came back from the Navy, and the band got back together. It is interesting to note that he did not play the guitar in church then because it was seen then as a "bar hall thing."[7] Today when the Coxes perform in churches, they often use their instruments, including guitar, since that stigma from the earlier era has faded.

In 1958, he married Marie, also from a musically talented family in Webster Parish, and they formed a band with her family, playing schools, churches, and rest homes around Cotton Valley: "My brother-in-law and I played music together while Marie and her sister sang."[8] In addition, Willard played guitar in another band, Dewey Keene and the Country Squires, from 1964–68.[9] Music was a part-time job at best, so Willard's chief occupation then was working in oilfield-related jobs. Beginning as a roustabout, he then worked six years for Louisiana Nevada company doing jobs such as pipeline contracting. Beginning in the mid-sixties, he worked fourteen years as a gauger in the laboratory at Kerr-McGee Corporation, an oil refinery, loading tank cars. He did the gauging in the specifications for jet fuel going to nearby Barksdale Air Force Base.[10]

As Willard and Marie's children were born—Evelyn, Sidney, Suzanne, and Lynn—they were raised in the country music tradition; they "just heard it from the time they were crawling."[11] It is not surprising that the children soon were eager to play as well. Willard tells how quick Evelyn, their first child born in 1959, was to learn: "After the kids got big enough to play, when Evelyn was about seven, she wanted to learn to play the guitar. I wrote down some chords, and in about an hour, she came back, and said, 'Dad, I know them, and I want some more.'"[12] Willard tells how he would create a makeshift microphone by taping a hairbrush to a broom handle for the children and prop it against a chair in the living room. The family had fun singing and playing their instruments. "That's how we got started," Willard said. "Anytime we were going somewhere, in a car or whatever, we were singing."[13]

As the children began to sing and play, Willard decided that they needed a bass since he played the fiddle, and Evelyn played the guitar. He purchased a bass in Shongaloo for Lynn to play, and the family band began with Willard and the two girls. An anecdote from one of their earliest performances notes that the daughters, suffering from stage fright, became even more frightened when a clown grabbed Willard's hairpiece, and the audience began laughing.[14] The other younger children grew up hearing the music. Willard explains to a local newspaper reporter how Suzanne learned to sing:

> We didn't even know Suzanne could sing harmony, she would just sit down and play with a Barbie doll and listen to us sing. One day, they needed a third part, and my wife said, "Well, why don't you teach Suzanne the part?"
>
> They asked Suzanne, "Can you sing that part?"
>
> She said, "Yeah."
>
> "Can you sing the words?"
>
> "Yeah." She sang the tenor part. She's been the tenor ever since.
>
> They asked her, "Well, why haven't you been singing with us all along?"
>
> She said, "Because you hadn't asked me." She was just a little thing at the time, no more than eight. She was afraid to go out on the stage with us. She finally grew out of it, though.[15]

Suzanne's voice would develop into a haunting high tenor described as dazzling, smooth as glass, and one of the finest voices in country music.

As the children grew older, the Cox family band took form with Sidney
on banjo, Evelyn on guitar, Suzanne on mandolin, Lynn on bass, Willard
on fiddle, and everyone on vocals. Just as they still do in their performances
today, they all learned to sing the lead (the soprano line), as well as different
parts, observing Willard's important rule of not singing another's part. For
example, if not singing lead, Willard might sing baritone, Suzanne tenor or
high baritone, Evelyn tenor or high baritone, and Sidney baritone. While most
liner notes list the vocal performers, notes for the Cox Family's four commercial albums specify who is singing what part, even noting whether it is high
or low tenor or baritone if the part is sung an octave higher or lower than is
customary. This kind of detail reveals the importance of the parts in creating
the family harmony sound.

With this vocal versatility in pitch, their genetic talent, and the frequent
family practice, they learned to blend their voices the way only family members can. Performing almost every weekend, they developed tight, harmonious
vocals and instrumentation. Willard remembers the early travels and how they
led to a full-time music career:

> We sang all around, and we got in the bluegrass at the Old South Jamboree in
> Baton Rouge. We began to get bookings in the surrounding states. After I got off
> work on Friday, we left and played music all weekend and came back in time for
> school and work. We did this for about five years. I was working in at Kerr McGee,
> and in 1975 we made our first gospel album on Wilcox label in Chattanooga,
> Tennessee. I quit my job to play music full time. We started playing festivals and
> spreading on out, and it then became a way of life for us.[16]

It is significant that their first album-length recording on their own Wilcox
label, *I Shall Not Be Moved*, is all gospel, but it was followed by other albums,
Heartaches on the Horizon, and *Favorites*. Willard remembers being ridiculed
for leaving his job with Kerr McGee in 1979 to pursue the music business, but
remains proud of his decision to "do it my way."[17] Sidney and Suzanne both
attended Louisiana Tech University on music scholarships, but the family
touring took them away from their studies, so they did not pursue their classical music training. This period of touring from their home base in Cotton
Valley continued as they built up fans in the bluegrass circuit, mainly in
Mississippi, Texas, Arkansas, Louisiana, and other states as well.

The Alison Krauss Connection

Around 1988, when Suzanne and Sidney were in Nashville, they first saw Alison Krauss performing in a bluegrass band contest, sponsored by SPBGMA.[18] Prior to this, they had been listening to each other's tapes. A friend had given Krauss's first album, *Too Late to Cry*, to the Coxes, and Krauss had first heard the Coxes on a live tape of one of their shows. As Krauss recalled, the tape belonged to one of her band members: "Mike Harman would play the tape in the van. We'd listen to it all the time."[19] In 1989 at a Perrin, Texas, festival, the family finally met Krauss when they were booked on the same festival bill. At that festival, the band spent time with Krauss, who asked Sidney for a tape of all his songs. She loved them so much that she chose four of them, including the title song for her next Grammy-winning record, *I've Got that Old Feeling* (1990). Suzanne also sang harmony on that album on another song of Sidney's, "Tonight I'll Be Lonely Too."[20]

According to Willard Cox, Krauss "was very instrumental in getting us a record deal with Rounder Recorders, where we made two albums"—*Everybody's Reaching out for Someone* (1993) and *I Know Who Holds Tomorrow* (1994), which won a 1994 Grammy for Best Southern Gospel, Country Gospel, or Bluegrass Gospel Recording, and a DOVE award.[21] Krauss, who produced and arranged both albums, comments on their live performances on the liner notes to *Everybody's Reaching out for Someone*: "They can't be compared to anyone—they've created something in Cotton Valley, Louisiana, that is so incredibly special. When you reach the Pearly Gates, they'll be playing the Cox Family."[22] The gospel album, reflecting Krauss's Nashville connections, has slick Nashville arrangements with drums, piano, Dobro, as well as the usual instruments. While the Coxes play their own instruments for their live performances, on all the recordings produced by Krauss, the family does not provide the instrumentation. Instead they use professional musicians, usually including Dan Tyminski on guitar (the lead musician and vocalist in *O Brother's* performance of "Man of Constant Sorrow"), and other members of Krauss's band. This makes for a smoother, Nashville-type sound on the recordings, which do not have the authenticity of the live performances.

The Krauss collaboration continued with Sidney becoming a staff writer for her, having a big influence on her repertoire. Willard agrees with the many Cox Family fans who believe that Suzanne's high tenor voice also influenced Krauss's vocals; the similarity between their voices is uncanny.

They have continued to work together, and Krauss is still a frequent visitor at their Cotton Valley home, where she is regarded as family; as Willard says, "I didn't have but three girls; now I have four."[23]

On the National Scene

A big dream of Willard's—to play at the *Grand Ole Opry*—also materialized during the early 1990s. His memory of the specific date and time reveals how the importance of this event is etched in his mind: "I always had a desire to play the *Grand Ole Opry*. Well, it came to pass on August 15, 1992 at 9:48."[24] They have played it a total of six times to date. After recording for Rounder, the family's national prominence grew, and they were recruited to sing harmony background vocals with singers such as Randy Travis, Emmylou Harris, and Charlie Daniels. Both Krauss and Suzanne Cox were featured on Dolly Parton's live album *Heartsongs*. In 1995 they shared a Grammy for Best Southern Gospel, Country Gospel, or Bluegrass Gospel Album with their contribution to the album, *Amazing Grace: A Country Salute to Gospel*.

The Cox Family sound was introduced to younger rock fans, when T Bone Burnett invited the family to tour with Counting Crows as the opening act. After hearing the rock band's recording, at first Willard refused because he did not think their music would fit, but with encouragement he agreed, and in 1994 they began a fifteen-show tour, including Louisville, Toronto, New York, and the east coast playing to sold-out crowds.[25] Lead singer Adam Durwitz subsequently contributed to liner notes for their 1995 *Beyond the City* album, which also received a Grammy nomination. Durwitz's note describes the first time he heard the family on a tape while on a New Orleans trip: "the next song was about as beautiful a piece of country music as I'd heard in years. We arrived at the bar we were looking for just as the song ended. My friends went inside to see the band, but I stayed in the car to listen to the rest of the tape. It turned out to be the Cox Family. . . . I stole the tape."[26] *Beyond the City* ranges from the traditional "Little Birdie," to A. P. Carter's "I'll Be All Smiles Tonight," to Roy Orbison's "Blue Bayou." It also includes two songs written by Sidney Cox, "Cowboy's Dream" and the title song, with Sidney singing lead on both, as he often does on his own songs. Also on this album are two versions of the Louvin Brothers adaptation and arrangement of "Broken Engagement"; Evelyn sings lead on both, but the second version, produced in 1974 by Willard and released as a 45 with Lynn on alto and bass, has a much more old-time country sound than the first. Since their early recordings are not readily available, fans will be interested to hear this earlier sound, before the days of Krauss's production.

After this tour, in 1996 they released a major-label album on Asylum Records, *Just When We're Thinking It's Over*, also produced and arranged by Alison Krauss. Like the other albums, this one ranges from country to pop, including four original songs (two written by Sidney and two by Sidney and Suzanne), two Del McCoury songs, Larry Gatlin's "Love of a Lifetime," Hank Williams's "I Just Don't Like This Kind of Living," and even the popular "Runaway" by Del Shannon and "That's the Way Love Is." On this album, as well as the prior three, Willard sings the lead on the older country songs, including the Hank Williams. Suzanne and Evelyn switch off on the others, their voices sometimes being hard to distinguish, which is typical of sisters' voices.

In their albums and on stage, the Cox Family's subject matter and style stand out as distinctive. Whether singing one of their original songs or covering popular numbers such as "Blue Bayou" or "Runaway," the Coxes make the song their own, with their own pacing, instrumentation, and harmony. Their selections for albums and concerts evoke moods from sweetness and light to longing and melancholy. For example, Sidney's "Backroads" and the popular "Blue Bayou" exhibit deep wishes for a special rural place, which is often romanticized. Like typical old country, many of the songs deal with fears of losing love, lost love, heartbreak, grief, and death. Their close harmonies with the ethereal female high tenor add a haunting sadness to many of their sad songs and a bittersweet nostalgia to their more sentimental numbers, in the tradition of the classic Victorian parlor songs.

O Brother, Where Art Thou?

After their touring and recording successes, T Bone Burnett selected them specifically again for the *O Brother, Where Art Thou?* soundtrack and film. According to Willard, the family went to Nashville thinking they had to audition; the Coen brothers were in the room, and Willard asked, "When are you going to audition us?" They were told there was no need to audition; they were already in it.[27] Given that the film was set in 1937, the year of Willard's birth, and that it uses a composite of early country sounds as well as some original songs written in period style, it is not surprising that the producers would find their music perfect for the film. Along with musicians Chris Thomas King, the Fairfield Four, and the Whites, the Cox Family not only performs music for the film, but also appears in it. In the film, the Cox Family performs "I Am Weary" in the scene where the main character, played by George Clooney, talks with his daughters at a political speech. In their 1930s period dress, the Coxes fit into their roles, and their sweet harmony in the melancholy song is a counterpoint for Clooney's Ulysses character. They "spent four days on location in Mississippi" to film their short scene, Willard said.[28] The film's closing credits feature the Coxes' version of "Keep on the Sunny Side," although it is not on the soundtrack album. Their involvement with the film brought them a Grammy for Album of the Year at the 2001 Awards, held February 27, 2002, and awards from the Academy of Country Music and Country Music Association.

As a follow-up to the film, T Bone Burnett produced the *Down from the Mountain* concert, which was released as an album and broadcast from the Ryman Auditorium on public television on May 24, 2000. The Coxes performed in two numbers, "I Am Weary" and "Will There Be Any Stars in My Crown?" Between the two songs, Willard introduces his children individually, and jokingly adds, "And I've got the papers on all them." In that television broadcast, Willard also shows off his country humor backstage telling jokes and stories.

The aftermath of this tremendously successful film brought many opportunities to the family to tour, including the Great High Mountain Tour (done in conjunction with the film *Cold Mountain*). However, a near-fatal accident interfered with the possibilities. In July 19, 2000, Willard and Marie were in a serious car wreck near Cotton Valley: an "empty log truck slammed into the back of their car as they were attempting to make a turn." Marie broke her "arm, collarbone, back, and neck" and "Willard broke a vertebrae in his back" and was paralyzed below the waist, leaving him unable to walk and in chronic pain.[29] His recuperation was slow, and the children had to do much of their national touring without him. In spite of the severe pain, Willard did manage to perform with them for their June 13, 2002, Carnegie Hall concert featuring most of the artists on the *O Brother, Where Art Thou?* soundtrack. The Carnegie Hall trip put Cox's strength and resolve to the test, Sidney says. "We've never had to go to a place and wonder if they've got a ramp, or if we can roll up this way or that. We ended up having a great time, and that show was wonderful. Carnegie was everything people ever said about it. He was himself, as far as I'm concerned and everybody else. He just sat down in a chair that had wheels on it. He was in good humor, and he was as feisty as ever. He was himself for a few hours. It was like this whole thing hadn't happened."[30] Because of his injury, Willard has not been able to take advantage of all the opportunities; for example, when the Coen brothers offered him a part in another film as a wheelchair-bound sheriff, he decided to turn it down because of his ongoing back pain and difficulty maneuvering. However, in spite of these problems, he perseveres: "I can still play the fiddle, and I'm learning to build and repair fiddles since I cannot tour as much."[31]

Back Home in Cotton Valley

Currently, the family is planning more touring and has been setting up their own state-of-the-art recording studio so that they can all continue to live and work in their Cotton Valley homes and produce their own records on their old family Wilcox label. There they can also be available to help care for their aging parents. The family has always been close-knit and still is. Daughter Lynn and her two children now live with Willard and Marie to help care for them. Suzanne, her husband, and two sons live next door to Willard. Sidney, his wife Christie (formerly the band's road manager and now a licensed publishing administrator and Sidney's agent), and three daughters, live up the hill within sight. Evelyn and her husband live nearby as well.

This proximity makes it easy to collaborate on songwriting and recording projects. Sidney, along with Suzanne, continues to write songs for and with major country music stars such as Garth Brooks and Reba McEntire and other songwriters such as John Randall and Robert Lee Castleman (of "Lucky One" fame). One of his latest songs for Alan Jackson, "Had It Not Been You" was released in fall 2006, and focuses on three little girls—inspired by Sidney's three daughters; Jackson also has three daughters. Sidney has had his own publishing company, Sidney Lawrence Music, for fourteen years and is starting a new company; he's in Nashville about one week out of every six. In fact, musicians such as Brad Paisley have encouraged him to move to Nashville, but he believes that the ideas and inspiration for his writing come from his home, so he remains in Cotton Valley where his father's stories about their family inspire poignant songs such as one of his latest—"Gone like the Cotton," which brought tears to Willard's eyes when he heard it. In addition to Sidney's songwriting, both Willard and Lynn have done some writing and are planning to do more.

According to Willard, their next big project is a gospel album featuring original songs written by the Coxes, as well as another Rounder album

produced by Krauss. All but three songs are ready for the project.[32] Gospel
music is a staple in their repertoire; they always have a couple of gospel numbers in their live performances, although their three commercial recordings
focus on country/bluegrass. As Sidney puts it, "That's where we came from,
our roots, in the Southern Baptist tradition; we all sang in church."[33] Their
commercial gospel album with Alison Krauss, *I Know Who Holds Tomorrow*,
again shows their eclectic taste with its assortment of works, including
Thomas Dorsey's "Walk over God's Heaven," "Will There Be Any Stars?,"
Stamphill's "I Know Who Holds Tomorrow," and Paul Simon's "Loves Me Like
a Rock." Given the variety of periods and styles on this album, it will be interesting to see what influences their original gospel songs will have.

Even with their national acclaim and busy touring and recording schedules, the Cox family has remained humble, modest, and committed to the
Cotton Valley community and north Louisiana. Their recent area performance venues range from the 2002 Louisiana Folklife Festival in Monroe to
the Centenary College's Annual President's Convocation in Shreveport to the
Louisiana Hayride fundraiser and the Jimmie Davis Memorial Homecoming in
2004. At their live performances, the love, respect, and care the family members
hold for each other and for their audience illuminate the stage, and they always
stay late to sign autographs and chat with fans. They still play benefits for
injured or ill community members and, today as always, their heartfelt family harmonies bring comfort at community funerals. In return, when Willard
Cox was injured, groups such as the North Louisiana Bluegrass Club raised
money for him, and to show their admiration for them, the club worked with
folklorists to nominate them for the 2004 Louisiana Governor's Arts Award for
Lifetime Achievement, which they received. The state arts community and folklorists equally respect their work. As folklorist and music critic Ben Sandmel
writes in his letter of support for their nomination: "They mine the old-time
and bluegrass repertoire, and tastefully apply the aesthetics of these genres to
contemporary pop material. Their re-invention of such comparatively recent
sounds with traditional interpretation is a fascinating and effective example of
the folkloric process in full circle."[34] In receiving the award, Willard, speaking
for the family, modestly gave credit and thanks to God and their fans, and then
reciprocated by performing a few songs for the crowd:

> The first thing we want to do is to thank the Lord Jesus Christ for giving us the
> talent to do it. . . . I want you to know that every place we've gone in the United
> States, everybody recognizes us being from Louisiana in the first place, and we

always had them put it on the bill that we was from Louisiana, and we're proud of the state; we're proud it's given us a chance to be recognized. And you folks have done a great service to us here today. And I will say this, if it had not been for you folks, well, we could play at the house, but you folks bought our records, and you come to our shows, and you write letters.[35]

Whether their music is for a national commercial audience or a local cause, the Cox Family provides beautifully crafted, professional and personal music that entertains, comforts, and displays the complex country, bluegrass, and gospel heritage of Louisiana. With their unaffected performance style, north Louisiana hill country accents, and a varied repertoire focused on rural settings, everyday life, and lost loves, they bring an authenticity and emotional timbre to this regional music that cannot be duplicated. Music is central to their family and a major way of communicating, as Willard puts it: "Music is a way of life for us. Playing music is an emotional outlet. I think if you do not feel the music, you cannot play it. You have to feel it, or it doesn't mean anything to anyone. We generally are always singing all the time. We relate to each other with music."[36]

Notes

Acknowledgments: My deepest thanks go to Willard, Sidney, and Christie Cox for their help with the information on the family. I first heard the Cox family perform as one of the featured groups in a small area bluegrass festival in the 1980s and admired their old-time country style and their close family harmonies. I also taught Sidney Cox freshman English in 1985 at Louisiana Tech, where he had a music scholarship. I presented and interviewed the Cox Family in the 1991 Louisiana Folklife Festival, where I first heard Willard Cox talk about his love for the old country fiddle music and the importance of this music in his family. I recommended them for the 1994 Louisiana Folklife Festival concert in Monroe, and again as headliners at the 2002 Louisiana Folklife Festival. I am also grateful to Kerry Davis, research associate for the Louisiana Regional Folklife Program, for her assistance with electronic research, photograph processing, and proofreading and to Peter Jones for his insightful comments.

1. Michael McCall, "Family Trip: The Cox Clan Takes Off," *Nashville Scene*, 5 August 1995, 23–24.

2. Christie Cox, "Re: Answers," email to Susan Roach, 24 February 2005.

3. C. Cox, "Re: Answers."

4. C. Cox, "Re: Answers." For a history of the development of country music, see Bill Malone, *Country Music U.S.A.* (Austin: University of Texas Press, 1968). For an overview of bluegrass, see Thomas Goldsmith, *The Bluegrass Reader* (Chicago: University of Illinois Press, 2004).

5. "The Cox Family, Biography," *Century of Country*, 13 February 2006, http://www.countryworks.com/artist_full.asp?KEY=COXF.

6. C. Cox, "Re: Answers."

7. Christie Cox, "Re: Willard Cox," email to Susan Roach, 23 February 2005.

8. C. Cox, "Re: Answers."

9. "The Cox Family, Biography."

10. Willard Cox, personal interview with the author, 24 July 2006. A gauger oversees mixing the fuels and monitors the levels in the tanks.

11. C. Cox, "Re: Answers."

12. C. Cox, "Re: Willard Cox."

13. Josh Beavers, "Fame Hasn't Changed Cox Family, *Minden Press-Herald*, 3 March 2002: 13 February 2004, http://www.press-herald.com/news/Mar02/0225news.html.

14. "The Cox Family, Biography."

15. Allen J. M. Smith, "Webster's Cox Family Wows Crowd," *Minden Press Herald*, 8 August 2002: 13 Feb, 2004, http://www.press-herald.com/news/Aug02/0813.html.

16. C. Cox, "Re: Willard Cox."

17. W. Cox, interview, 24 July 2006. Willard believes that his leaving this job for the music business was divinely guided and saved his life since this area of the plant exploded on 22 May 1986.

18. Sidney Cox, personal interview with the author, 31 July 2006. SPBGMA is the Society for the Preservation of Bluegrass Music of America.

19. Jack Hurst, liner notes, *Everybody's Reaching out for Someone*, CD Rounder Records, 1993.

20. Hurst.

21. C. Cox, "Re: Willard Cox." Sidney Cox, interview.

22. Hurst.

23. W. Cox, interview, 26 July 2006.

24. C. Cox, "Re: Willard Cox."

25. W. Cox, interview, 26 July 2006.

26. Adam Duritz, liner notes, *Beyond the City*, CD Rounder Records, 1994.

27. W. Cox, interview, 26 July 2006.

28. Beavers.

29. "The Cox Family Update, Aug. 10, 2000," CMT.com: The Cox Family, 13 February 2004, http://www.cmt.com/artists/news/1478109/09112003/cox_family_the.jhtml.

30. Edward Morris, "Recovering Willard Cox Mulls Returning to the Road," *CMT News*, 10 July 2001: 27 July 2006, http://www.cmt.com/artists/news/1445024/07092001/cox_family_the.jhtml.

31. W. Cox, interview, 24 July 2006.

32. C. Cox, "Re: Willard Cox."

33. Sidney Cox, personal interview, 31 July 2006.

34. Ben Sandmel, letter of support to Governor's Arts Awards Committee, 17 February 2004.

35. Willard Cox response at Presentation of Governor's Arts Awards Ceremony, Bienville Depot, Arcadia, Louisiana, 10 July 2004.

36. C. Cox, "Re: Answers."

Remembering Hiter Colvin, the Fiddle King of Oilfield and Gum Stump

—J. Michael Luster

Hiter Colvin is a little-known master fiddler from northwestern Louisiana, who made his local reputation dazzling crowds at dances, fiddling contests, and Pentecostal worship services. As Michael Luster explains in this short sketch that draws from the memories of family and friends, Colvin's recorded legacy is quite small: only a handful of sides recorded for Victor at a 1929 session in Dallas, Texas. Nonetheless, these selections testify to the musical prowess and the flair for showmanship described in this brief piece.

The great Hiter Colvin was born in 1900, one of nine children, on Boardtree Creek near the community of Fellowship, northeast of Dubach, Louisiana. His father, Thomas Mayberry Colvin, bought a fiddle at a pawnshop in Monroe and told the children that whichever one of them could play it best would get to keep it. Hiter earned the fiddle, and the fiddle would eventually earn him the only livelihood he would ever know. Hiter used the fiddle to follow the oilfield money, moving first to the country around El Dorado, Arkansas, where in 1926 he married Eloise Torrence, an eighteen-year-old girl from nearby Sandy Bend. The young couple followed the various oil booms and would have three children, including their first, Hyter Colvin, Jr., (so he spells it) born at Smackover in 1927, before the huge oilfield discovered at Kilgore, Texas, drew them there about 1935.

Hiter Colvin had already been to Texas once and come as close to striking it rich as he would. In October of 1929 he and his guitarist friend Herbert
Sherrill traveled to Dallas and recorded six sides for Victor records. These tunes,
"Indian War Whoop," "Monroe Stomp," "Dixie Waltz," "Old Lady Blues," "Hiter's
Favorite Waltz," and "Rabbit Up a Gum Stump," his evocative showpiece said to
be a portrayal of the dogs pursuing rabbits down along Boardtree Creek, reveal
him to be a fiddler of extraordinary skill. The records sold well for Victor and
the company even ran a two-page display ad in one of its catalogs with Jimmie
Rodgers pictured on one page and Hiter Colvin on the other, but Colvin saw
little money from them and refused to record again. Beyond his playing, Colvin
was also a consummate showman who played the fiddle behind his back, behind
his head, on the floor, and he always drew a crowd and sometimes played on the
radio out of El Dorado. Jimmie Rodgers himself came to town, trying to convince Colvin to join him on the road, but the fiddler refused, opting instead to
keep company with his buddy Sherrill or with a peg-legged guitarist and follow
the oilfield money. Before long, Sherrill too headed for Kilgore.

In Texas, Colvin continued to play for boomtown dollars and cleaned up at
local fiddle contests. His honky-tonk dances were legendary. On one occasion,
he played at a highway nightspot while the celebrated Light Crust Doughboys
played to a largely empty house at another across the road. At the end of the
evening, the Doughboy bus pulled into the yard at the Colvin house trying to
get the man they couldn't lick to join them, but again Colvin chose to stay put
to play in the clubs and sometimes even in the Pentecostal church. He remained
in Kilgore for seven or eight years during which time his marriage broke up and
his family moved back to Sandy Bend. He followed them to Arkansas and there
was a reconciliation that lasted a couple of years, but they split for good in 1938.

In the years following his divorce, Hiter Colvin returned home to
Louisiana, to the area which had earned the nickname "the Pint Country"
because of the availability of vernacular whisky, where he continued to play
to packed dance floors backed up by his nephew Bill Bagwell or others. Back
home, folks called him "Pee Wee," for his small size, but remember that the
fiddle he carried in a flour sack had a sound that would carry an unusual distance. Hunters in the woods would pause to listen to Colvin playing at some
far-off dance. E. N. "Nig" Robertson, who used to squirrel hunt with the
diminutive fiddler himself, remembers walking the five miles to Bernice to
attend a Colvin dance. Times were hard and when Colvin passed the hat he
got only nineteen cents. "Alright, I'm going to play you nineteen cents worth
of music and then we're going to pass it again," and Hiter cut loose with all

his fiddler's tricks. Owen Perry tells that on riding home horseback from such a dance, Colvin would frequently stop and serenade a sleeping farmer named Campbell who loved a particular waltz and would be good for a generous tip. Perry also remembers well fiddling against Colvin in those years at many a regional fiddle contest, frequently coming in second to the perennial winner. "Owen's going to beat me one of these times," Colvin would say but Perry says he knew he couldn't even hold the master's bow.

Without question, all regarded Hiter Colvin as the greatest fiddler in north Louisiana and probably far beyond. His genius was singular and beyond his skill with the fiddle, the squirrel gun, and the garden hoe, he seemed to have little aptitude. His own son says he was woefully inadequate at even driving a nail. But he could play and he continued to, on into the television age, appearing on the *Happiness Exchange* on Monroe's pioneering television station KNOE, a product of the oilfield success of Governor-for-a-Day James Noe. Colvin began spending time with his brother Brown Colvin down near Colfax, Louisiana, where he played for friends and in the local Pentecostal church near which he would eventually be buried.

In a sad and confusing set of circumstances, he set his own death in motion. According to his son, Hiter Colvin had been suffering from a toothache when he decided to try and get some relief. He used a shotgun, perhaps in a less-than-expert attempt to remove the tooth. Others contend he was out to end all suffering. Whatever his intentions, he failed and instead inflicted horrible damage to his face and head which required lengthy but ultimately unsuccessful reconstructive surgery. He lived another two or three years before he was laid to rest in 1975 in a country cemetery between Colfax and Bentley.

Besides the six sides he recorded for Victor and the countless stories still told by the numberless Colvins and Colvin kith and kin of Lincoln Parish, there is one other monument to the great talent of Hiter Colvin. I heard it fleetingly in the tape deck of my truck, a recording made in his brother's yard in the summer of 1966. Moving easily from breakdowns to swing standards to hymns, Hiter Colvin still conjures, with consummate skill from an assemblage of horsehair and wood, the rabbits and dogs and gum-stump hollers of Boardtree Creek.

Note

Hiter Colvin's "Rabbit Up a Gum Stump" and "Indian War Whoop" can be heard on *Echoes of the Ozarks, Volume Two*, County CD-3507.

Sing It Good, Sing It Strong, Sing It Loud

The Music of Governor Jimmie Davis

—Kevin Fontenot

Nineteen twenty-eight marks the recording debut of Jimmie Davis, perhaps best known as Louisiana's "Singing Governor" or the man who collected royalties for "You Are My Sunshine" (though, most likely, he did not actually compose it). Davis made his name on the national political scene as the state's two-term governor and as a recording artist who made hundreds of commercial records mostly between the late 1920s and the early 1950s. His professional musical career began in Shreveport, after he gravitated to the city from his birthplace (September 11, 1899) near Beech Springs, Louisiana, on the southeastern edge of the Ark-La-Tex region. His first recordings were custom made at KWKH and issued on a W. K. Henderson-sponsored label, Doggone Records. Two years later, however, the recordings he made for RCA Victor launched a music career that lasted more than six decades.

Much of Davis's recorded output reflects the mutual influence of black and white musical life in Shreveport, even during a time of harsh race-based legal segregation. Likewise, the attention paid to Davis by RCA Victor underscores the unequal access to professional opportunities afforded white musicians over black musicians. Although Davis's custom recordings on the Doggone label ("Ramona," "You'd Rather Forget Than Forgive," "Think of Me Thinking of You" and "Way Out on the Mountain") give no hint at his understanding of black music, Davis's 1930–31 Victor recordings clearly demonstrate his affinity for the African American blues tradition. Songs such as "She's a Hum Dum Dinger from Dingersville," "Midnight Blues," and "Pea Pickin' Papa" place Davis in the same yodeling blues-influenced basket as country music icons Jimmie Rodgers and Gene Autry. Like Rodgers, who recorded with both Louis Armstrong and members of a Louisville-based Jug Band, Davis brought in two

local black musicians—guitarists Oscar "Buddy" Woods and Ed Schaffer—on a handful
of these bluesy and salacious recordings. Both Woods and Schaffer made commercial
records as well, and Woods was documented by the Library of Congress several years
later. (For more about these black musicians, please see Paul Oliver's piece in the "Blues"
section of this book.)

As this article makes clear, Davis loved both music and politics. Fontenot breaks
down his musical career into three sections and also explores the delicate question of
the authorship of "You Are My Sunshine." Although this is an article about music, the
author also briefly describes Davis's political career and his status as a much admired
and recorded southern gospel artist in the three decades before his death in 2000.

James Houston Davis is one of Louisiana's most important contributors to the
field of country music and, along with artists like Louis Armstrong, to American
popular music in general. Throughout the 1930s and the 1940s, Davis registered
hit after hit on the "hillbilly" charts and saw several of his compositions cross
onto the popular charts as well. His songs, including "Nobody's Darling But
Mine" and "You Are My Sunshine," became hits for artists as diverse as Gene
Autry, Bing Crosby, Ray Charles, and Satchmo himself. Davis has been honored
with induction into the Country Music Hall of Fame, the Nashville Songwriters
Hall of Fame, the Louisiana Music Hall of Fame, and the Gospel Music Hall
of Fame. Judging by some of the inductees, including Jimmie Rodgers, Hank
Williams, and Leadbelly, he also deserves induction into the "pioneers" wing of
the Rock and Roll Hall of Fame. Despite his importance, Davis has yet to garner
great attention from the scholarly community. Perhaps this lack of concern is
due to Davis's political career, which some find objectionable, or to the fact that
folk music scholars find little appealing in an artist who actually made money
rather than suffered abuse by the industry. Davis, for his part, only reluctantly
granted interviews to researchers whose interest extended beyond the usual
journalistic foray. More to the point, Davis's career was so lengthy, his catalog so
large, and his music so diverse that the task seems daunting.

The existing scholarship on Davis easily breaks down into three categories. First, several scholars have written broad general discussions of Davis's
life and music. Usually these studies make little effort to connect his career
to the larger trends in country music history, and are often rife with factual
errors. A tendency also exists to downplay the Governor's rich gospel career.
The novelty of a "singing politician" dominates these accounts. Music scholars
find themselves unable to navigate the complicated Louisiana political bayous

and political historians often fail to take the music industry seriously.[1] To the problems within this group of general studies may be added the mistaken attempt to interpret all of Davis's music as "Celtic" in origin.[2] Though greatly appealing and wildly romantic, this theory quickly evaporates upon listening to Davis's songs—they exhibit a deep debt to African American styles and to popular culture, as well as to the Anglo traditions of Davis's youth.

Second, scholars have spilled a great deal of ink concerning Davis's early risqué recordings.[3] These articles usually focus on the debt Davis owes to his black sidemen and the often "unbridled carnality" of some of the songs. Seldom do these scholars admit that Davis was working in a tradition well known among Southern folk artists and that the "dirty" element owes as much to white tradition as to black. Only Nick Tosches approaches the songs with the tongue-in-cheek humor that Davis so obviously saw in the songs.

The third group of research focuses on the origins of Davis's most famous composition, "You Are My Sunshine." The song has one of the most complex genealogies in the history of recorded music, and most scholars tend to agree that Davis did not write the song, but merely was the first to copyright it.[4] A close examination of the evidence, however, reveals that Davis and Charles Mitchell, while not being the primary authors, may be responsible for the song as we know it today.

These three areas of investigation fail to reveal the diversity and importance of Davis's legacy. Scholars have tended to concentrate on the mundane or the controversial, with the latter seeming intent on damaging Davis's contributions. The facts remains that had he never recorded a risqué line in his life or had he never given us "You Are My Sunshine," Jimmie Davis would still deserve the honors given him. His is the only country music life rooted in the nineteenth century who remained active across the twentieth century, providing the art form with one of its strongest links to the past.

James Houston Davis was born into a musical family. His father, Sam Davis, played a passable fiddle and was in demand for local dances. His repertoire included such southern classics as "Turkey in the Straw" and "Arkansas Traveler." Davis's mother, Sara, sang the traditional southern ballads of loneliness, death, and social bandits—songs like "The Letter Edged in Black" and "Jesse James."[5] She also played the harmonica and taught her children religious songs.

Perhaps the most important person in young Jimmie's formative musical years was his paternal grandfather, Henry Cicero Davis. A native of Georgia, the elder Davis lived an adventurous life, walking to Arkansas when he was not yet a teenager, winning the hand of his employer's daughter, and donning the Southern uniform during the Civil War. But what most people remembered about Henry Davis was his remarkable singing voice, a voice that was clear and deeply emotional. He summoned up "old Georgia tunes"[6] with ease, and his devil-may-care attitude may indicate that he was more than familiar with risqué folk songs such as "Keyhole in the Door"—a paean to voyeurism that his grandson later recorded. Henry Davis's exact repertoire is difficult to determine, but it is highly possible that many of his Georgia-based lyrics found their way into Jimmie's future compositions. At least two songs that the Governor claims credit for are strongly linked to Georgia—"Columbus Stockade Blues" and "You Are My Sunshine." It is entirely possible that Davis learned at least part of these songs from his grandfather.[7]

Jimmie Davis drew influence from the music that surrounded him as a child. Besides the music he heard at home, young Jimmie heard music at the local dances and play parties, at traveling circuses and medicine shows, and from the neighboring African Americans. Determining the extent of black influence on Davis from direct exposure is difficult; he often denied that any such influence was strong. However, he has admitted that he heard black church music, listened to blacks in the field, and he may have encountered a traveling black minstrel (like Henry Thomas, the famed east Texas songster, who often worked in north Louisiana[8]). In his film autobiography, *Louisiana*, Davis even has a fanciful scene where he learns the basics of rhythm from an African American blacksmith.[9] Davis also heard a black jazz band on a steamboat during his abortive trip to New Orleans in 1919.[10]

But the place young Jimmie learned the most about music and the power his singing potentially could command was in the local church. Singing instructors from east Texas periodically came to Quitman and the surrounding area to teach "shaped note" singing and the basics of harmony. These singing schools provided Jimmie with his first formal musical education and introduced him to the use of choruses to drive home the central idea of a song.[11] They also established a deep and abiding affection for religious music, an affection that would later lead him in pioneering commercial gospel music. Davis's decision to pursue music as a career came at one of the camp meetings near Quitman. There Davis heard a local farmer named Del Grissom do a solo number and the young boy was deeply moved. Grissom "had a beautiful tenor voice" and encouraged Davis to sing. He told Jimmie that the boy's singing "wasn't all that bad and maybe (he) ought to sing some more."[12]

A major change in Davis's music came when he attended Louisiana College in the early 1920s. At the college located in Pineville, Jimmie received formal voice

training as a member of the Boys Vocal Quartet and the choir.[13] He also belonged
to a quartet called the "Wildcat Four," which specialized in popular tunes. Davis
continued to sing in glee clubs and quartets when he pursued his master's
degree at Louisiana State University. (Davis earned his undergraduate degree in
1924 and completed the M.A. in 1926.) These experiences taught Davis to control his voice and utilize it for its maximum effect. The college years also taught
him that people gladly paid to hear his singing. He soon abandoned his job
washing dishes and mopping floors to sing on the street corners of Alexandria
and Baton Rouge, and found performing both more entertaining and profitable
than manual labor. Despite his high degree of education, Jimmie seems never to
have learned to read or write music. He did develop his own system of writing
music and then sought the help of others to transform his crude notation into
formal style. (His longtime protégé Charlie Mitchell was his primary assistant
in this regard.) Surprisingly Davis also seems to have never learned more than a
few chords on the guitar. But his true genius lay in associating himself with fine
musicians who could complement his style and his rich warm vocals.

College also exposed Jimmie to the final and perhaps most important
influence on his music—recorded popular and hillbilly music. The record
industry was only just beginning to boom when Davis entered college in
1921, but companies like Victor already had plans to target specific markets.
While Davis was at Louisiana College, touring groups from Victor sang in
the school's auditorium and then plugged their records. Jimmie quickly took
to the medium and absorbed the recordings of popular artists such as Gene
Austin, famous for his versions of "My Blue Heaven" and "Ramona." When
Davis made his first recordings in 1928, one of the songs was "Ramona."

But while Jimmie admired Austin's control and sweet vocals, it was another
voice that captivated him and the southern people. The other song Jimmie
recorded in his first session was "Away Out on the Mountain," a close cover of
Jimmie Rodgers's second release on the Victor label. Rodgers's influence cannot
be overemphasized when discussing Davis. Rodgers was the top performer of
hillbilly music during his lifetime, and his success proved to recording companies that the music was profitable. He also spawned a generation of performers
who began their careers covering Rodgers tunes. Davis became the best of the
Rodgers imitators, and that ability led him to the attention of Victor's agent
Ralph Peer, who signed the young court clerk to a recording contract. Peer also
taught Davis the importance of copyrighting material.

Davis's recording career can be roughly divided into three, perhaps four,
distinct periods. The first lasts from 1928 to 1940 and represents a period in

which Davis experiments with many styles in an attempt to find his own niche in the industry. The second period begins in 1940 and is highlighted by many hits in a distinctive Davis style. The third period (1952–1990) marks Davis's move into gospel music and a growing fascination with the Nashville Sound. A final period in which Davis is reflecting on his career may have begun in 1990 and lasted until his death. The dates used in this outline are rough and overlap occurs, yet this framework helps to understand the growth and development of Davis's career and its relationship to the overarching world of country music.

The first period may be titled the "Formative Years" and represents some of Davis's most interesting work. During this period Davis recorded in a wide range of styles from Jimmie Rodgers blue yodels, the "blackest" and "bluest" of any blues recorded by a white artist, and was backed by jazz bands, Hawaiian musicians, western swing ensembles, and black street musicians. The years that Davis recorded for Victor (1930–1934) are highlighted by his risqué blues, such as "Red Nightgown Blues" (complete with a supercharged nymphomaniac who rapes her fiancée on the way to the wedding), "Sewing Machine Blues" (Davis asks St. Peter for a "high stepping brown" if an angel is not available), and "Organ Grinder Blues" (in which an impotent man extols the virtues of a monkey gland implant). These songs reveal a deep debt to black culture, but not necessarily the black folk tradition. Instead these songs indicate that Davis listened to black recordings, particularly those of the Famous Hokum Boys, a Chicago studio band centering on Bill Broonzy and Georgia Tom Dorsey. The Hokum Boys specialized in risqué numbers that were often covered by country musicians—for example, the western swing innovator Milton Brown, a close Davis friend. The "blackness" of these recordings was further emphasized by Davis's use of the Shreveport-based black musicians Oscar Woods and Eddie Schaffer.[14]

While the risqué recordings are wonderful pieces of playing and singing, the heavy scholarly interest in them has obscured the fact that they represent only about one quarter of Davis's output for Victor. And his risqué recordings were not limited to the black "hokum" or blues style. "Keyhole in the Door" is a well-documented ribald tune from the white tradition, one that was common in the southern region of Arkansas where Henry Davis lived for a short time. Thus Davis's risqué songs represent a wider tradition of "dirty" music, which also existed in the white community.[15] The bulk of Davis's Victor recordings were imitations of Jimmie Rodgers and romantic love ballads. The songs sold moderately for the Depression era, but Victor seems to have developed an interest in turning Davis into another Rodgers. As much as Davis admired his friend and mentor, he wanted to create his own style and sell more records. Thus, when Jack Kapp formed Decca Records in 1934, Davis quickly signed on as a hillbilly act.

Decca was founded on the premise of making money by selling quality records at a low price, hoping that higher sales would offset the lower profit margin on each individual record. Kapp seems to have permitted Davis free rein in his recording style and Jimmie continued to explore new styles, but increasingly settled into his own sound. The blues and yodels decreased significantly and the arrangements began to reflect the western swing style emanating out of the Dallas-Tulsa axis. For his Decca recordings Davis drew on the bands of his friends Cliff Bruner and Milton Brown, leaders of two of the finest western swing groups then performing. Bruner and Brown did not follow the lead of Bob Wills into the sound of the big bands; instead they kept to small string ensembles that were in fact proto-honky-tonk bands. Yet their style was smooth and perfectly complemented Davis's pop leanings. Thus Davis consciously chose musicians who could perform hillbilly songs with a pop flair. The recordings made for Decca during this period reveal a degree of technical strength found in few contemporary country bands.[16] The sound was tight, but never forced. Since he almost never used his own band for recordings, but instead created a "perfect" band from those of his friends, Davis presaged the studio bands of the Nashville Sound during the 1950s and 1960s.[17]

By 1940 Davis entered what might best be called the "Sunshine" period, after his most famous song. The Davis style had gelled around a string band with lead and rhythm guitars, a fiddle played in the longbow Texas style, string bass, and a piano or accordion. A muted cornet often makes an appearance. Basically this was an early form of the honky-tonk band that became the basis of country music to this day. Davis did not originate this style alone, but his recordings did much to popularize this musical lineup. Davis's warm rich vocals dominated his recordings during this period. He also began the practice of recording monologues and recitations, inserting them into his songs. Davis's spoken voice was just as expressive as his singing voice, and his recitations added strength to his recordings. Perhaps the best examples are "I Just Dropped In to Say Goodbye," in which a jilted lover speaks to his love on her wedding day, and his 1953 rendition of the gospel classic "Suppertime." Recitations and the "spoken song" became strong parts of the country music tradition as a result of Davis's pioneering work.[18]

Davis's songwriting truly blossomed during this period. His lyrics usually dealt with love lost or found and occasional uptempo songs found their way into his repertoire. Davis maintained a close working relationship with some of the finest songwriters of the period—Floyd Tillman, Ted Daffan, and Shelly Lee Alley. These relationships have led to some vexing questions of authorship. In many cases, Davis purchased songs from fellow songwriters and signed on as a co-writer. This was a commonly accepted practice and many aspiring songwriters readily agreed to this arrangement in hopes of furthering their careers.[19] To Davis's credit, he generally only signed on as a co-author and not as sole author, although the common practice was to do so. He also expressed a willingness to relinquish his rights when time came for renewal, as he did in the case of "It Makes No Difference Now," which had been written by Floyd Tillman. Further, no one who entered such an agreement with Davis has expressed great distress. Most have only kind words to say about Davis and view his aid as a major advance to their careers.

This brings up the question of the authorship of "You Are My Sunshine." Toru Mitsui has discussed the complicated history of the song in his article "You Are My Sunshine: A Question of Authorship." Briefly, the song appears to have been a folk song that emerged from northern Georgia or western South Carolina in the mid-to-late 1930s. The song was brought to Shreveport by the Rice Brothers who took it to Davis and his bandleader Charles Mitchell. They purchased it for thirty dollars. (Mitchell later sold his interest to Davis.) Davis then copyrighted the song and the rest is history or controversy. There is no doubt that a song that became "You Are My Sunshine" came out of Georgia or South Carolina and was brought to Louisiana by the Rice Brothers. But the question that has never been answered is what condition was the song in at the time? Was it complete? Or was it in need of a professional makeover? The Rice Brothers sold something to Davis, but he says that he and Mitchell "had some verses, got to playing around with them, and came up with 'You Are My Sunshine.'"[20] Perhaps Davis and Mitchell did just what Davis said they did—took some ill-formed verses and created or at least polished into being "You Are My Sunshine." As a result Davis would be responsible for the song as we know it today. In the end, the last person left who knew the true story was Jimmie Davis and he spoke in couched terms. Nevertheless, Jimmie Davis is responsible for the great popularity of the song. He kept it alive and on all our lips. Because of this, "You Are My Sunshine" is truly his song.

The Sunshine period lasted until the late 1940s. By this time Davis's smooth pop-country sound was displaced by the harsher, more earthy honky-tonk sound of Hank Williams and Ernest Tubb. Davis was older and four years in the Louisiana governor's chair had kept him from the cutting edge of the music. Around 1950 he returned to radio and began broadcasting the "Fill Up with Billups" show, underwritten by Davis's political ally and gas station magnate Buddy Billup. Davis made a regular policy of answering requests, and he soon noticed a heavy demand for religious numbers. These requests, coupled with his own love of religious music, led him to attempt to revive his sagging career (pummeled by both the harder honky-tonk sound and the rise of rock and roll) by venturing into gospel. Thus the early 1950s marks the beginning of the gospel phase of Davis's music.

White gospel had largely been dominated by quartets and singing families. It was viewed largely as a subset of country music and quite often ignored by promoters. Davis, Red Foley, and Martha Carson began to change that situation in the 1950s by bringing a kind of star system to gospel. They were individual performers singing the music and began to introduce new songs, not just old hymns. Davis shifted his publishing interests firmly into gospel and churned out songs with an otherworldly bent. Humility before God (for example "On Your Knees") and the future life in Heaven (the classic "Suppertime" and "I Wouldn't Take Nothing for My Journey Now," a song from black gospel tradition) became the common themes in Davis's gospel songs.

In addition to his songwriting abilities and personal drawing power, Davis infused gospel with the slick "Nashville Sound." Recording at Decca was managed by Owen Bradley, one of this sound's architects (along with Chet Atkins and Steve Sholes). He was also the regular piano player on Davis's radio program. The Nashville Sound derives its name from the use of studio musicians handpicked by the producer to make a tight consistent sound, usually with pop influences. The Nashville Sound is best represented by Eddy Arnold and the later recordings of Patsy Cline. This meant that performers' road bands seldom made records and a small group of house musicians essentially determined the arrangements. Davis took this new sound whole and used it to great benefit on his classic gospel album "Suppertime."[21] In 1959 he recorded a greatest hits package for release on LP and remade his hits using a Nashville Sound backup (including the Anita Kerr Singers). Most of his albums during this period were produced by Bradley, who was busy molding Patsy Cline into the Queen of the Nashville Sound.

Davis remained at the top of the southern gospel scene throughout the 1960s and early 1970s. Yet by the 1980s religious music began to move away from its southern roots and closer to popular music and, eventually, rock-and-roll. Davis pressed on, doing the circuit of bluegrass festivals that willingly made room for the older gospel performers. In 1968 he married Anna Carter Gordon of the famous Chuck Wagon Gang, and the two began to perform together. Davis moved to a small combo of guitar and piano and emphasized harmony with his wife. As a result Davis was probably closer to his country roots in the early 1980s than he had been since the 1940s. The 1980s witnessed a return to traditional styles in country music. Ricky Skaggs, George Strait, Randy Travis, and Dwight Yoakam began to produce a roots-based music thoroughly aware of the history of country music. Skaggs invigorated bluegrass, Strait western swing and honky-tonk, Yoakam hardcore honky-tonk. Amid all the new stars, Davis named his favorite—Randy Travis, because he had a rich warm voice and sang decent songs.[22] Travis also comes the closest to being what Davis was in the 1930s and 1940s, a hillbilly singer firmly rooted in country music, yet having smoothness and warmth of a pop singer.

During this later period, more and more of the old country songs he sang in the thirties and forties crept into his concerts, edging out gospel numbers. By 1994 his New Orleans Jazz Festival appearance featured a full recreation of the Davis sound of the 1940s, with gospel to a minimum and a newly recorded risqué tune to boot ("The Ding Dong Song"). Later that year he celebrated his ninety-fifth birthday with a hundred-dollar-a-plate dinner and the Davis sound back in full swing, bringing him into what may well be a fourth phase of his career, a return to hard country. As Jimmie Davis returned to his roots, country music itself was bracing for the rise in popularity that would come in the 1990s.

Thus, far from just being the singer of dirty songs and the copywriter of songs of questionable origins, Jimmie Davis remains a major figure in the history of country music. He was the only protégé of Jimmie Rodgers who not only had his work issued on compact disc, but whose digital reissues included new material. He helped to initiate trends and he also followed, always guided by the uncanny ability to know where he should move next. Davis was the last living link to Rodgers and a world of music that seems distant now. As a result his is the longest and quite possibly most successful career in the industry, one that lasted nearly seventy years until his death in 2000.

Notes

This piece is based on nearly four years of research into the career of Governor Jimmie H. Davis. The primary sources are a series of interviews that the author conducted with Governor Davis beginning in August 1991. Copies (both taped and note) of these interviews are in the author's private collection. The author would like to thank Bill C. Malone, Bruce Raeburn, Ronnie Pugh, and Bill Meneray for their help and insight over the years. My friend Courtney Page encouraged me throughout this project and has probably heard more about Davis than she ever cared to know.

1. The best of these studies are Peter Mikelbank, "Places in the Sun: The Many Splendored Careers of Jimmie Davis," *Journal of Country Music* 10, no. 3 (1985): 28–32 and 49–56; and Ronnie Pugh's liner notes to Jimmie Davis, *Country Music Hall of Fame*, MCAD-10087, 1991. The only book-length biography of Davis is Gus Weill, *You Are My Sunshine* (Waco, TX: Word Publishing, 1977), an uncritical book as much about the American Dream as it is about Davis. However the book is a significant insight into how Davis saw himself. Political discussions of Davis's life are even weaker. The best general political assessment is Floyd M. Clay, "Jimmie Davis," in *The Louisiana Governors: From Iberville to Edwards* (Baton Rouge: Louisiana State University Press, 1992).

2. Grady McWhiney and Gary B. Mills, "Jimmie Davis and His Music: An Interpretation," *Journal of American Culture* 6, no. 2 (Summer 1983): 54–57.

3. The very best discussion of the early risqué recordings is Nick Tosches, "Stained Panties and Coarse Metaphors," in *Country: Living Legends and Dying Metaphors in America's Biggest Music*, rev. ed. (New York: Scribner's Sons, 1985), 120–56. Tony Russell concentrates on Davis's debt to the black musical tradition in *Blacks, Whites and Blues* (New York: Stein and Day, 1970), 80–85. See also John Morthland, *The Best of Country Music* (Garden City, NJ: Doubleday, 1984), 68–69, who speculates more on Davis's race relations than on his excellent recordings. I have commented on these recordings in "Sunshine Jimmie and Georgia Tom: Two Gospel Pioneers Reflect on Their Blues Past," a paper presented at the Louisiana Historical Association meeting in New Iberia, Louisiana, in 1994.

4. The best summary of the origins of "You Are My Sunshine" is Toru Mitsui, "You Are My Sunshine: A Question of Authorship," *Old Time Country* VI (Winter 1990): 15–19. Also helpful on the origins is Wayne W. Daniel, *Pickin' on Peachtree: A History of Country Music in Atlanta, Georgia* (Urbana: University of Illinois Press, 1990), 149–51. Ron Nethercutt has written an excellent appreciation of the song in "You Are My Sunshine: Theme and Variations," *Regional Dimensions* 5 (1987); this is a publication of the Center for Southeast Louisiana Studies at Southeastern Louisiana University in Hammond. Also see Ryan Banagale, "You Are My Sunshine: The Recorded Lineage of an American Folk Song," *Musicological Explorations* 6 (Spring 2005): 7–24. Claimants to the authorship of the song are numerous; I personally know two people who have told me that they wrote the song.

5. Alan Lomax advanced the theory that mothers, because of their mundane existence and hard lives, expressed their emotions by preserving the traditional songs. Sara Davis certainly lived the hard life of a plain folk mother and wife, but she also was estranged from her parents, perhaps explaining her penchant for morbid songs.

6. Davis used this phrase in describing his grandfather's repertoire to the author and in Weill's biography, 7.

7. My understanding of Henry Davis is based on Weill, 6–10, and Arey Love Daniel, "Henry Davis," in *Jackson Parish, Louisiana* (Jonesboro, LA: Jackson Parish Chamber of Commerce, 1982), 168–69. The governor often waxed nostalgic for his Grandmother Davis, but seldom mentioned his grandfather. Jemimah Davis seemed to fascinate her grandson as some sort of paragon of virtue, perhaps for living with the very worldly Henry. See, for example, Jimmie Davis, "Country Music Is Part of the People" *Louisiana Heritage* I (Summer 1969): 16–17. Jemimah's photograph was prominently displayed in his Baton Rouge office.

8. Thomas's recordings are diverse and provide an excellent example of what Davis may have heard from a wandering black minstrel.

9. Such scenes are common in both country music biographies and movies. Note the manner in which Hank Williams's relationship with "Uncle Tee-Tot" is portrayed in *Your Cheating Heart*, a horribly inaccurate movie that plays on nearly every stereotype available.

10. No one knows exactly which band Davis heard since the name of the boat he was on is not known. At one time Davis said the incident occurred on the *President*, but that steamboat did not

ply the Mississippi until 1933, according to Davis Chevan's "Riverboat Music from St. Louis and the Streckfus Steamboat Line," *Black Music Research Journal* IX (1989): 153–80. Perhaps Davis was on the *Capitol*, which may mean that the band was Fate Marable's and that Louis Armstrong was one of the players.

11. The classic discussion of the singing schools is to be found in George Pullen Jackson, *White Spirituals in the Southern Uplands* (Chapel Hill: University of North Carolina Press, 1933). Chapter 6 focuses on the tradition in Texas, including the area of Tyler, home to some of the teachers who went to north Louisiana.

12. Davis quote from Weill, 17.

13. His instructor was Marion Dunwoody.

14. Compare Davis's risqué blues on Oscar Woods and Black Ace, *Texas Slide Guitars*, Document DOCD-5143, 1992, with the early recordings of the Famous Hokum Boys on *Famous Hokum Boys Volume One*, Wolf WBCD-011, 1993. This leads me to believe that Davis was less influenced by Woods and more by the recordings of black musicians like Dorsey and Blind Willie McTell. Peer recorded McTell in the early 1930s and several Davis songs share lyrics with McTell tunes. These may have been floating lyrics that both were aware of or perhaps Peer provided them to Davis. Davis said that Peer often provided him with lyrics to "make songs." Jimmie H. Davis, interview by Kevin S. Fontenot, 22 August 1991, Baton Rouge, LA, tape recording in author's collection.

15. For an examination of this white risqué tradition see Guy Longsdon, *The Whorehouse Bells Were Ringing* (Urbana: University of Illinois Press, 1989); and Vance Randolph, *Roll Me in Your Arms* (Fayetteville: University of Arkansas Press, 1992). Both contain a discussion of "Keyhole in the Door," and Randolph is interesting because many of his sources were people who may have been descendants of Henry Davis's neighbors.

16. Waylon Jennings called Davis's 1930s and 1940s Decca recordings the equal of anything to come out of Nashville in the modern (post-1960) era.

17. Little true criticism of Davis's recordings exists. My ideas here rest on my listening and interpretation of Davis's recordings, my interviews with him (particularly the previously cited 1991 interview), and a telephone interview with Cliff Bruner on November 30, 1991 (notes in author's collection). I have utilized as many of Davis's recordings as possible, but the most succinct introduction to his music is Jimmie Davis, *Country Music Hall of Fame*, which covers his Decca material. *From the Vaults: Decca Country Classics* (MCAD3-11069) and *The Smithsonian Collection of Classic Country* provide excellent overviews in which to examine Davis's work. My understanding (and nearly everyone else's) of country music history comes from Bill C. Malone, *Country Music USA*, rev. ed., (Austin: University of Texas Press, 1985).

18. Davis's disciples in this style include Jimmy Dean and Cal Smith.

19. I have documented Davis's purchase of several songs. Most helpful in this regard were the Shelly Lee Alley papers, Country Music Foundation Library and Archive, Nashville, TN, and Mrs. Wilma Kennison, who kindly provided me with photocopies of correspondence between Davis and Charles Davis regarding the purchase of a song.

20. Davis made this comment several times, including to the author in August 1991 in direct response to a question concerning the origin of the song. Thus Davis carefully avoided answering whether he actually wrote the song.

21. *Suppertime*, Decca DL 78953, 1959; re-released as MCA-150 during the 1980s.

22. Davis to the author, August 15, 1991. Davis first named George Jones as his favorite "young" or "new" star. This comment emphasizes the fact that Davis is a member of Jimmie Rodgers's generation of performers, since Jones is now regarded as an elder statesman of country music.

Louisiana's Honky-Tonk Man

Buddy Jones, 1935–41

—Donald Lee Nelson

Although he was born in Asheville, North Carolina, guitarist Buddy Jones (born Oscar Bergan Riley) spent most of his adult life to the west, first in Port Arthur, Texas, but later in Shreveport. Jones began his musical career as one of the many emulators of Jimmie Rodgers. By the time he recorded nearly seventy selections for Decca in the 1930s his music sounded more like western swing, the up-tempo dance music that combines jazz-based swing rhythms with a hot string band, often augmented with drums, saxophones, pianos, and, notably, the steel guitar. Originating with Milton Brown and Bob Wills in the early 1930s around Dallas-Fort Worth, the style became the most popular form of country music from the mid-1930s to the late 1940s. Jones's Decca recordings often included such western swing stalwarts as pianist Moon Mullican and bassist Bill Mounce.

Jones had met officials at the Decca Record Company late in 1936 through another legendary musician with Shreveport connections, Jimmie Davis. Like Jones, Davis played in and around Shreveport during the late 1920s. Buddy Jones lived in or near Shreveport for about twenty-five years. After his full-time musical life diminished, the Shreveport police department provided him steady employment. Jones continued playing regularly in the area until he died of a heart attack in 1956.

As the first third of the twentieth century was drawing to a close, mountain music fans listened with relish as Jimmie Rodgers sang of rounders, fast women, gambling, and the generally rowdy side of life. Few who heard his mildly rakish style, however, felt that his songs were anything but stories and observations of others, gleaned from his railroading experiences. Some two years after Rodgers's untimely passing, a young Shreveport resident began to record in a similar mode, but with more pronounced subject matter. He told of being staggering drunk, living off street women, nights in jail, and other wanton ways which convinced listeners his songs were autobiographical. In truth, by the time Buddy Jones was making records, he was a soft-spoken, model husband and parent—and a career policeman.

Buddy began life as Oscar Bergan Riley at Asheville, North Carolina, in 1906. (The exact date was supposedly December 25, but this is apocryphal, in that his three brothers' birthdates were July 4, February 22, and Thanksgiving.) His dad was lost at sea when Oscar was young, and he spent most of his remaining childhood in foster homes, and finally, a school for wayward boys in Georgia. In his late teens, he joined his mother, now Mrs. Joe Jones in Port Arthur, Texas; ever after he referred to that as his native city, and adopted his stepfather's surname. Thus Buddy Jones came into being.

It was Joe Jones who probably introduced Buddy to the guitar. Joe played a variety of instruments, and taught Buddy's younger brother Allen Walter (now called Buster) a certain proficiency on all of them. Buddy, however, played only flatbox; he was a straight "chord knocker," and he picked good rhythm.

Joe, Buddy, and Buster began to play for house parties and dances in the Port Arthur area. Handsome and charismatic, Buddy quickly realized he could increase his earning power by working in that oil city's brothels. When his mother learned of this, a violent disagreement ensued and Buddy left home with Buster in tow.

When the two youngsters couldn't earn their fare with music, they worked as short order cooks, bellhops, plant guards, and anything else that came their way. They began travelling with a variety of tent shows and circuses, learning the "carnie lingo" they would ever after use between them. It was during this period that the fundamentals of timing and showmanship were grasped.

In the late twenties, Buddy landed in Shreveport and settled temporarily. It was Shreveport's first live hillbilly music show and was broadcast each Saturday night. The trio acquired a good following, as their fan mail indicated. Buddy had very limber vocal chords and often imitated Jimmie Rodgers and Roy Faulkner, a local cowboy singer over rival station KWKH.

Within two years, the wanderlust had Buddy (and Buster) again on the road. A half decade of itinerant rambling, countless two-man shows in hundreds of towns all over the midwest and south, and an unsuccessful marriage for Buddy, culminated in his final return to Shreveport. KRMD was glad to have him back, and he formed the "Ward's Cowhands" under the sponsorship of the Montgomery Ward stores. The group broadcast every day at noon and were paid two dollars per show.

Using magic, comedy routines, and blackface, as well as singing and playing, Buddy and Buster spent most nights working saloons and dances. At one of the latter, in 1934, Buddy met Mrs. Lucille Donaldson. She was educated refined, reserved, and had three young sons from a previous marriage. Within a year, the two were wed.

Entering into a ready-made family had an instantaneous effect on Buddy. He stopped playing bars and dance halls, stopped staying out all night, and generally made a one-hundred-eighty degree change in his lifestyle.

For some years, he had been friendly with a young college professor who was now Clerk of the Court. This was Jimmie Davis, and he had carried Buddy with him to Chicago in 1931 to play backup guitar at a Victor recording session. Later, when Jimmie signed with the fledgling Decca Company, he persuaded their A&R people to audition Buddy, whose flexible voice would complement his own. The duet had two sessions together.

A gift for imitating other hillbilly artists, as well as his own pleasing style, convinced Decca officials to grant him his first solo recording date at Dallas in February 1937. Brother Buster backed him on steel guitar, using raucous barroom licks which added impetus to the often risqué lyrics.

Buster Jones's duties were twofold. He was in charge of the music for the sessions and was also composing and "borrowing" much of the material to be recorded. Even the songs which Buddy wrote were generally polished up by his younger brother.

Not long after his marriage to Lucille, Buddy joined the Shreveport Police Department. He settled in the traffic division, and there remained for the rest of his life. Jimmie Davis had been elected Public Service Commissioner, and by an odd coincidence, many policemen were in his band, or at the very least, musicians. Cliff Bruner, whom Buster nicknamed "Prints" for his lawman specialty, Tex Swaim, Leon Chappelear, Tillman Franks, Moon Mullican, Herschel Woodal, and Charlie Mitchell were all gendarmes under Davis.

Buddy, however, was a full-time officer. He would play a few local gigs during his off-duty hours, or accrue leave to attend recording sessions in Dallas, San Antonio, or Houston. Buddy was a policeman, first; even the Shreveport city directory so read.

The Jones musical portfolio had a number of suggestive pieces, delivered tongue-in-cheek, a few reworks of Davis's Victor material (like "She's a Hum-Dum Dinger"), several Rodgers standards, an occasional tear-jerker, some "beer joint heartache," and a couple of talking blues. Ironically the one song which should have been most accurate, "Shreveport County Jail Blues," had a twin flaw in the title. Louisiana calls such divisions "parishes," not counties, and the parish name is "Caddo." In Caddo Parish, the phrase "High Five" does not refer to overpaid athletes who cannot master the common handshake; it is the archaic designation for the jail. This, in spite of the fact that the cell blocks are on two levels above the fifth floor.

Although Buster was present at all of Buddy's sessions he occasionally yielded steel guitar duties to Bob Dunn, now a fellow member of Brown's Musical Brownies, and Charlie Mitchell. Mitchell, known to history as co-author, of "You Are My Sunshine," had a plaintive style which accentuated sad songs. At most of the later Jones recording dates. It was the Davis-Bruner musicians who were backup.

As record buyers noticed Buddy, so did his superiors on the police force. He made desk sergeant, then patrol sergeant, then commander of the evening division. He is often remembered for singing "Ragged But Right," an old Riley Puckett tune, in the traffic office.

Years of handling show audiences had given Buddy an insight into people, making authoritarian posture virtually unnecessary. Although he could be firm when the situation so demanded, those who knew him during his police career speculate he probably never had to fire his pistol on duty, and seldom unholstered it.

Buddy's public musical career began to draw to a close by his own choice; he preferred to be at home with his family. Buster had moved to Port Arthur, and when they got together they played only for their personal amusement.

Charles Justice, another musician and career officer recalls one of Buddy's last personal appearances, "It was in January 1955 at a March of Dimes benefit. Buddy and I were there in uniform and there was Floyd Cramer, Elvis Presley, and Johnny Horton. They came in a car with the Sun Records' inscription on the side. Buddy sang 'Little Red Wagon"; he did it so beautifully, and the audience went wild. It was so cold that day that Floyd Cramer wore rabbit fur gloves to play piano."

In the late forties, Buddy had been promoted to lieutenant and in the early fifties made captain. He and Charlie Justice would frequently jam together, but shows were a thing of the past.

Buddy, who was heavyset, was fond of Louisiana-Texas cooking. For his noon meal on October 20, 1956, he consumed two bowls of chili and some catfish at a local restaurant. An hour or so later, he received a call to assist another officer, and was driving to that location when he had a heart attack. His car crashed into a tree, and he died instantly.

A floodtide of affectionate tributes rushed forward at news of his passing. All segments of the community were saddened by the loss of the man many had called "Mr. Buddy." Jimmie Davis summed up a quarter century of friendship by sadly declaring. "I could depend on him."

Interview with Horace Logan, October 13, 1976

—Earl Porter

Horace Logan's name will always be uttered in the same breath as the *Louisiana Hayride*. His decisions as program director for ten years and his talents as an announcer imbued the *Hayride* with its special character. Logan published his own remembrances several years before his death, in a 1998 memoir *Elvis, Hank, and Me*, written with Bill Sloan (and reprinted the following year under the title *Louisiana Hayride Years*). As the title suggests, along with the book jacket images of Elvis Presley, Hank Williams, and Johnny Cash, this memoir self-consciously positions its author as a key figure in the stories of these three popular culture icons.

By contrast, the interview excerpted here, occurring on October 13, 1976, more than two decades before the memoir, finds Logan in a different place in life. He was working at the time as station manager at KREB in West Monroe, Louisiana. Talking with Earl Porter, a student in an upper-level oral history seminar at Louisiana State University-Shreveport, Logan seems relatively unguarded and unrehearsed. There is a refreshing, human quality to the conversation between Porter and Logan, lacking that weight of posterity and posturing that pervades the later published memoir.

As Logan shared with his interviewer, his entry into radio during the early 1930s was accidental. As a high school student, he accompanied a friend to the KWKH studios, then housed within the Washington-Youree Hotel in downtown Shreveport. His friend planned to participate in an announcer's contest, sponsored by Half Past Seven Coffee. When one of the other participants failed to show up, Logan was recruited to take his place in order to maintain the radio segment's timing. With the description, "The delicate, volatile oils of Half Past Seven Coffee," Logan won the contest and a job as KWKH announcer for fifteen dollars per week. From that moment, radio shaped the course of Logan's life.

The bulk of the interview concentrates on Logan's memories of the *Hayride*. Throughout his conversation with Porter, Logan stakes his claim as the *Hayride*'s originator. As other sources have argued, this is a title he shares in varying degrees with other early *Hayride* figures like the Bailes Brothers, Dean Upson, and even Henry Clay, KWKH's general manager at the time. Despite the static between different points of view, it cannot be denied that Logan, as program director, dictated the show. In the interview, he reflects on his own guiding vision for encouraging performers to do their best, and for pacing and rotation among the emcees. He also touches on the show's relationship to the musicians' union, to commercial sponsors, and to Shreveport's civic leaders. In the end, we gain a greater sense for the unpredictable and freewheeling spirit that so distinguished the *Louisiana Hayride* from other barn dances.

Tucked for three decades in an archive folder at the Noel Memorial Library Archives and Special Collections at Louisiana State University-Shreveport and known to only a handful of scholars, this interview finds Logan in a more reflective and thoughtful mindframe. We have edited the interview from the typed transcript housed in the Oral History Collection. Ellipses points replace portions of the transcript omitted from this reprint. In addition to portions that become redundant or off topic, we excluded Porter's questions, leaving only the voice of Logan.

We initially began the *Hayride* by everybody in it sharing in what was left over after all the expenses were paid. After it was obvious, the first several weeks, and it was obvious that the *Hayride* was going to be a monetary success, KWKH then assumed the financial responsibility for the program and started paying the talent. Union scale at that time was $12.00 for a side man, $18.00 for a soloist, and $24.00 for the leader of a band. . . .

Steve Grunhart was the head of the local union there in Shreveport when we started the *Hayride* and he was still head of it when I left, and the relations were very amiable. He asked that since the majority of the artists on the show were recording—most of them on little labels or unknown labels—he requested that we stick strictly to union musicians which was a reasonable request because, in those days, you basically had to be in the union in order to get on a record or even to play on a record. But he was very generous in that he would let new people, who we were trying out temporarily, perform for thirty or even sixty days and sometimes longer without having to join the union. Then, when it was obvious they were going to begin to do something and make it, he would let them join the union with a moderate amount down and pay them so much a month. He was very good about that, and it was never any problem for the union. Therefore, everybody that was on the *Hayride* as a regular was a union member. Now, that had its advantage to me.

The *Hayride*, although it did not require that an artist be internationally known before he joined it—because none of them were when they joined it—we did require that they have background and experience to be able to advance at the speed with which we could promote them because of the publicity and the area wide publicity and the national publicity we could give them. If they were rank amateurs and unable to handle the situation, they might set their careers back by years by coming on and failing dismally. So, I would usually require that a man had been on record or be on record. Now I didn't require a RCA or Columbia. It could be the Po dunk label—a little small label—but we had to have something we could play on the air and promote. In fact, some of the artists that first came to me, I told them they would have to be on record and they left and came back a year later on record and I put [them] on the show. Johnny Horton, one of my dearest personal friends of the whole bunch—when Johnny first came to me, he was not on record. I said, "Johnny, you've got to be on record. You have to be ready to move, man, so we can promote you. Go get yourself a recording contract." And he came back with a contract with Fabor Robison who, initially, started a great many people—Jim Reeves and the Browns and others—and joined the show.

So, at this point, the station began paying the artists and it became completely a station promotion and we began selling the broadcast time to local advertisers and to regional and national advertisers and it was then that the Jax Beer network was set up. And we actually broadcast over several states. I don't know how many states were involved, but as I understand it, at its peak, it had about eighty stations. So, that would have been quite a few states more than likely.

Incidentally, one of the very first sponsors—in fact, the first sponsor—of the *Hayride* and a man who sponsored a portion of the *Hayride* every single night that I was there for ten years, was Southern Maid Donuts. . . .

But, as I said, it was the custom of your major stations to have all sorts of live acts on each day, and we had the group of them and that's the way we started the *Hayride*. Well, I was immediately besieged by people from all over the country wanting to get on the show and we did try a lot of people. We had a constant attrition going on the show. Every week, almost without exception, I would add one or two new acts and drop one or so. If an act showed any promise—real promise, I would keep them on the show for three months, or six months, or nine months, or twelve months, or longer if they showed any promise. If it was obvious that they weren't going to do very much at this stage, I would drop them and take another group. Now, this was solely, completely, and absolutely my responsibility. No one else had any say-so whatsoever as to who would be on the show. Not only that, I even picked the material that the artists would sing. Each artist would submit to me each week what they wanted to sing on the next week's show and I would pick out what they would sing and the order in which they would sing it. Now, my reason for that was this. Not that I thought I was so superior, I wasn't, but I put it together for the purposes of programming. I didn't want two artists to follow each other—two men singing songs very similar in nature or about the same tempo. I would invariably put between them . . . at this stage of the time in 1948 and '49 there were very few girl singers in the country field—mostly men, the Eddy Arnolds and the others and the Hank Williamses and the others to develop, but very few girls. But I would put girls on the show in between the male soloists or quartet groups or some variety group to break up and try to make each fifteen minutes and thirty minutes a separate, complete package show. And another thing was I forced them to be extremely competitive with each other. . . .

The *Hayride*, initially, when we started, it was three hours long, but shortly after that expanded to four hours. And we presented what amounted to two shows. An artist would go on stage—a man—scheduled to sing two numbers. If he didn't encore, that's all he did, was two numbers. Now two hours later he would come back and he was scheduled again to do two numbers. If he didn't encore, that was it. When the girls went on, they were scheduled to do one number and, if they didn't encore, that's all they did. In other words, when Kitty Wells went on the *Hayride* for a four-hour show, she was scheduled to do two numbers in the entire evening. And if she didn't encore—they fought like fiends to get encores. It made them do the best they possibly could. And little Ray Bartlett who was the announcer with me that went on as co-emcee right from the beginning . . . Ray Bartlett said, "Hoss, you're not going to make many friends this way." And I said, "No, but I'm going to make stars. I'm going to make them. I'm going to force them to do their best." And that was it. I made them so competitive they had to do their best or they didn't get a chance to do anything.

When Hank Williams encored seven times, it was because the people wanted to hear him, not because he was scheduled to encore because he wasn't. And that was the way the *Hayride* ran the entire time—a very competitive thing that forced the artist to do his dead level best. Everybody on the show was good and they had to be good to compete with the other guys on the show or they'd be nothing compared to them. And we had this slow attrition process of taking acts off and adding new acts constantly, keeping in mind the necessity for variety, etc., etc. And, it was a funny show.

Ray Bartlett, who I just mentioned, was an announcer on the station—a young man, I think, from Little Rock, Arkansas, originally—very enthusiastic— and he was hilariously funny. He was my co-emcee for the first year or so on the show and later on we added Frank Page and Hi Roberts and Norm Bale and some others at different times, and Bill Cudabac, but Ray Bartlett was the first. He and I were the only two on the show, initially, and Ray would . . . some big tassels would hang from the curtains there and so forth. Ray would dance with those tassels and kept the audience in absolute hysterics most of the time, and it was a funny, relaxed show.

There was one night that a quartet—the Deep South Boys—were singing "Cool Water." Well, Ray and I came out with a cup of water in each hand and gave each of the men a cup of water. Then, we brought another cup of water for each one of them so they had both hands full of water. Then, we brought the entire water barrel out and gave it to them. Well, the audience, as you can imagine, was having hysterics but we never explained on the air what was happening. You could hear the audience laughing and roaring and so forth. We never told anybody on the air what was making them laugh, and it intrigued the people and they wanted to come to the show to see what the heck was going on. That was the whole idea of it, see. And, people came to it by the thousands from all over the area. The average attendance for the *Hayride* for the ten years that I ran it was 3,300 people each Saturday night. That's over a ten-year period. Now the building seated 3,800 and there would be nights when it was cold winter weather and so forth that we wouldn't have 1,200–1,500. So, you can see, obviously most of the time the building was pretty well packed full. . . .

I doubt if 10 or 15 percent of them were from Shreveport. They came from all over the area. There was one night that we had over sixty high school classes—graduating classes—there as part of their senior trips. They came mostly out of Texas, but they came out of Mississippi and Arkansas and Georgia and Alabama and Oklahoma and Arizona, New Mexico, to see the *Hayride* because KWKH covered a large area and because we were on the network—on the CBS network for so long, we were known throughout the country and in particular in the south, southwest. If we had had to depend on the attendance from the city of Shreveport, it would have died after the first three or four weeks, and that's true of any show. If the Opry had to depend on the attendance from Nashville, Tennessee, it would go out of business next week. It's people coming in by the thousands and that's the way we began the show. When we hit the air at eight o'clock, I'd go on stage in front of the curtain, just before—five minutes, usually—before air time and I'd greet everybody. And "Hello, welcome to the *Hayride*, etc., etc. and you're such a very important part of the show. There'll be points in the show, particularly on the network, where we must ask you for applause because it punctuates and makes the show sound live and better and we'll give you this kind of applause. Now let's try it." And we'd give them that business, waving the hands and Bartlett would jump up and down and they'd scream their heads off. And then I would tell them about the network and how we couldn't encore during the network because it had to be carefully timed and all that sort of thing, but after the network was over then we could encore whatever they wanted to hear and so on down the line. . . .

[The name *Louisiana Hayride*] had been a Broadway production which is, obviously, about as alien to a country music show as it's possible to get. And it had been a political book, *The Louisiana Hayride*, about the life of Huey Long. Yes, so, it had an entirely different connotation.

The night of the show, we still had no theme and Red Sovine, I believe it was [one] of the Bailes Brothers, or Red in combination with the Bailes Brothers said, "We need a theme." And they wrote one in just a few minutes. "Come along, come along. The sun is shining bright, the moon is shining bright. Gonna' have a Louisiana hayride tonight," which is a variation of an old song that had been around for many years.

Later on, a few months later, when Johnny Fair Syrup became one of the sponsors on the show—quite a bit later, in fact—I asked Red Sovine and Tillman Franks to write a theme song for Johnny Fair Syrup, and they said they would. And I thought it would be, perhaps, weeks before I heard from them, and they were back in about ten minutes. They had written a thing called "When I die, just bury me deep with a bucket of Johnny Fair at my head and my feet, and put a cold biscuit in each of my hands and I'll sop my way to the promised land." (laughter) The guys were pretty tough, really. . . .

Well, that was the way with the show. It was my sole responsibility to determine who would be on the show, when they would appear, what they would sing, the order in which they would sing it, and who would accompany them. Now, if I put a guy on in the first half hour of the show, of the first show, and the first half hour of the second show one week, the next time he was on he'd go on maybe in the last half hour. Nobody was ever set in the same position. You couldn't tune in at any specified time and say, "I'm going to hear so and so." In fact, you never knew who was going to be on the *Hayride* until you got there because I would have some artists gone—because I did let artists off every Saturday night so they could make more money—so we didn't advertise that Hank Williams was or was not going to be there that night, or later Elvis Presley was or was not going to be there. We just simply didn't say who was going to be on it. You came to the show and saw whoever was there, but you certainly got your sixty cents worth because that's what we charged to get in—sixty cents at that time, thirty cents for kids—and at one time for sixty cents you could have seen, oh, Webb Pierce and Faron Young, and Johnny Horton and Elvis Presley and Johnny Cash—all on the same show for sixty cents. That's a pretty good buy all things considered. . . .

In that ten years the *Hayride*, because of its very competitive nature, elevated more artists to national prominence from obscurity than all the other shows in history combined to this date. Because remember now, the *Opry* doesn't make artists. It takes them after they are made, but the *Hayride* developed more artists . . . in fact, the late Jim Denny, who at the time was in charge of the *Opry*, referred to the *Hayride* as the *Grand Ole Opry* farm club. By then, so many artists had left the *Hayride* and gone to the *Opry* that I referred to the *Opry* as the Tennessee branch of the *Louisiana Hayride*. And Jim Denny and I were close friends for many years. That's what happened.

Hank Williams was the first to get famous. Hank called me before we ever got on the air about joining the *Hayride*. Well, he was working with a radio station in Montgomery, Alabama. He already had a reputation as a drunk and being rather undependable, which he was, and I told him that if he could stay sober for a few months and prove it, then I would put him on the *Hayride*. Well, he called every couple of weeks or so and had the radio station call every week or so and, apparently, he did stay sober entirely because the radio station said, "Yep, he's here every morning"—he, too, was doing a morning show there—"he's here every morning in good shape, no drinking, no nothing, and doing fine." So after about six months I hired him to come to Shreveport to join the *Hayride*, and he rode into Shreveport with everything in the world he had on the top of an old Chrysler. He had springs and a mattress and everything, and he had his wife, Audrey, and her daughter by a former marriage in the car with him and that was it. They just moved to Shreveport. And I put him on the air in the morning, by himself, doing a fifteen-minute program. And

that's when Johnny Fair Syrup first came on. Red later wrote the *Hayride* . . .
the theme for it. I'll tell you about that in a moment. But, Hank Williams went
on the air and we could pay him a moderate sum for doing this daily show for
Johnny Fair Syrup and it was enough for him to live on. After he joined the
Hayride, then he organized a band of local guys. Felton Pruett played the steel
guitar and various others who were on the *Hayride* joined in his group and he
started making personal appearances throughout the area. . . .

We expanded to four hours. I added another emcee and that was Frank.
Frank was added as a Master of Ceremonies for this reason. By then we had
sold thirty-minute segments of the *Hayride* to various sponsors, and when I
came on with, say, Sal Hepatica or Lucky Strike cigarettes, I wanted a different
voice emceeing it and a different voice doing the commercials than had done
the preceding half-hour. So I needed more guys on the show, and I finally
wound up with four emcees so we could alternate doing the commercials and
doing the emceeing so we wouldn't have the same voice reading commercial
after commercial for different sponsors, because we had people like, well, Sal
Hepatica, Liggett Meyers tobacco—that's Lucky Strike Cigarettes—and many,
many others. The Southern Maid Donuts and so forth, that we would do live.
All the commercials were done live on stage, etc. . . .

Dean Upson was working with the commercial department of the station at the time we began the *Louisiana Hayride* in 1948. Dean was a salesman.
He was selling in national sales, and Dean knew some artists out of Nashville
because he had been associated with a radio station in the Nashville area. And
when we started the *Hayride*, he contacted a number of artists and they, in
turn, were considered by the station as joining the *Hayride*. So he was used,
initially, or was very valuable initially, in contacting artists and contact with
artists. But as far as actually working directly on the *Hayride*, no, he didn't. His
biggest value was giving us some initial contacts—from the artists to us, initial
contacts—when we were just beginning to form the *Hayride*. . . .

Henry Clay and Mr. Upson had really nothing to do with it. B. G.
Robertson and I put the show together because he and I had run the old former
show before World War II called, as I've mentioned several times, the KWKH
Saturday Night Roundup. Now, Mr. Clay's experience in this field was nil. He'd
had no experience. At this point, now remember, Henry Clay was still quite
young. He was our manager of the station but it was because of marriage to the
boss's daughter, the owner's daughter, not because of his background in that
field. He later developed into a heck of a good guy in the field, but at this stage

he wasn't really too familiar with it. Upson was reasonably familiar with the country music field, having worked in Nashville, and he did make a great many contacts. But he did not determine who would or would not be on the show, nor did he determine who would go on and what time they would go on and what they would sing. All of that was thrust on me, for which I was very grateful because I liked it, and I had had several years experience in that from the old previous show, you see. I mean working with the live acts. You see, I had worked at the station and on the station for years in the mornings, specifically, and had emceed and presented the vast majority of those live acts from the studio day after day, week after week, year after year, so I was thoroughly familiar with the live acts—what they could do and what they couldn't do. So it was logical that this burden would fall on me, which was fine because I loved it. I really did. I mean I could do it and it was something that I was experienced in.

Now, these other men were more at the executive level at that time. While they could say, "Yes, you can do it." They'd just say, "Do it." They didn't tell you how. "We're interested in results. We don't care about the methods, get results."

Upson was in that position because he was head of the national sales for the thing, but I don't know that he ever even walked on the stage on the *Hayride*. I don't believe he did. Neither did Henry Clay. In fact, Henry Clay came over one night to come in the front door of the *Hayride* and he was so unknown to them they wouldn't let him in. He had to come around the back and call for me to get in the back door (laughter). . . .

The City Council or the City Government agreed to let us have the auditorium for a modest sum. I believe, initially, it was seventy-five dollars a week, and we paid the union stagehands and we paid ticket sellers and ticket takers. In fact, we used a teller from the bank as our head ticket seller, and he was in charge of that. He was very good with money; he was excellent. And we paid the policemen. We had a few policemen there, normally—one of them in plain clothes and a couple in uniform just in the event there was trouble. And there never was any trouble. They were just there because it was expected in a public building. And the city agreed that we could have the Municipal Auditorium every Saturday night except five a year. And on those five, they would have to use it for various other things. Bear in mind, in those days they didn't have the Hirsch Coliseum and other places. This was the only large assembly place in the city of Shreveport and on those five times a year, we would take the show out in its entirety to . . . well, to San Antonio, to Corpus Christi, to Houston, to Oklahoma City, and to Little Rock a number of times and to other cities—even to Monroe one time, put it on in the Neville High School auditorium. And we would originate our broadcasts from there, but we carried the entire show and run just the same show but in a different city. We would immediately get protests from the motel and hotel owners and the restaurants that they didn't get any business this weekend because the *Hayride* was out of town. It was estimated that the *Hayride* attracted approximately three thousand people into the city of Shreveport every weekend that it was held there and the majority of them spent the night. So financially it was an excellent thing for the city and the city was aware of that. That's the reason they gave us so many concessions price-wise on the use of the building and so on down the line. . . .

Frank Page joined the *Hayride* as one of the emcees after it had been on for a while. I think it had been on a year or so before Frank actually joined it or maybe even longer, but I made Frank the chief announcer. Well, theoretically, the boss did but I went in and said, "Hey, we need a chief announcer and I think it ought to be Frank because he's been here longer than anybody else, seniority and so on down the line." And the *Hayride* was taking more and more of my time. We had an average of a hundred artists on it, including musicians, every Saturday night. That was the general average—seventy-five to a hundred—and the mere contact with them during the week and keeping up with all of them was getting to be quite a job. See, I was program director of the station so we made Frank chief announcer so he could basically take a whole lot of the burden of program directing off of me, which isn't really that big a burden because after a while things are following a set pattern anyhow. And Frank later joined the *Hayride* and then when I left the *Hayride* after ten years, Frank was given the sole charge of the *Hayride* and he ran it for the remaining eight months that it existed and then it folded up as a regular show.

So the *Hayride* did fold in the fall of 1958. From its beginning in 1948 until the fall of 1958, it had been presented every single Saturday night without missing a Saturday night and other than the first few weeks it had never used an outside artist. Well, after I left the *Hayride* and moved out to California, they began using some outside artists, bringing them in. Then, in the fall— I think it was October of 1958—it closed as a regular show, and for several years they ran the *Hayride* regularly only during the summer months. And during the winter and fall and spring months, they ran it only when they could book in some large outside acts as an attraction. So after 1958, the fall of 1958, the *Hayride* lost its character as the show of artists that are exclusively with us, etc. without outside artists coming in on it. . . .

The original *Hayride* was carefully designed to be as alien to the type of show that the *Opry* was presenting and the others [as possible]. The *Opry*, for example, would have Red Foley on, and Red Foley was an emcee for a half-hour and in that half-hour he would open, sing a song or so, bring on a guest artist, and then he'd sing a song, and then the guest artist, and so on down the line, and then Foley would emcee it and sign it off. That isn't competitive. How can you compete with Red Foley when you're on a Red Foley show? The thing to make them competitive would be put Red Foley on for two numbers and then put George Jones on for two numbers and let them fight head to head and see who came out the best. That's what I did. So I deliberately listened to the other shows, discarded their formats as being not the one I wanted because I wanted to develop stars, and set up a very aggressive, a very competitive format that forced them to become famous whether they wanted to or not. They had to become famous or fall off the show, one or the other. They either had to make it or quit, and a great many of them made it. Now, some of them got mad at me. Some of them really did because I made them be competitive. I wouldn't let them . . . oh, some of them drank but I couldn't stop some of them. But I roved all the time looking for it and stopping it—sat on them. If one of them was late, I'd jump all over him. And like Bartlett said, "You're not making friends." I said, "No, but I'm making stars." . . .

Yes, Jim [Reeves] joined the show, incidentally, as one of the announcers, not as a singer, initially. He joined the *Hayride*. Well, Jim came to see me first about a job as an announcer. He was working at the little station over in Henderson, Texas. He later bought it. And I didn't have an opening, listened to him, he was pretty good, but I didn't have an opening. You don't fire somebody just to put somebody on. I told him I didn't have an opening, to come back. He came back in a few months and auditioned again, and again I didn't have an opening. And the next time he came back, his wife was with him and he made the comment, "I know you're not going to like this, but I want to audition again." And it made me mad. I said, "Man, if I'm not going to like it, why're you wasting my time and yours. You come back when you think I'll like it." He said, "I think you'll like it." I actually had an opening but I didn't tell him. And I listened to him again and hired him and he joined the station as an announcer and went on the *Hayride* as one of the emcees, so we could have the voices that I talked to you about. We needed the different voices on the different commercials, and when there was time, which was rarely, he would sing a song. And he developed from that. Then, this young songwriter came up from Nacogdoches, fellow who wrote "Mexican Joe" [Mitchell Torok] and taught it to Jim and we recorded it there in the studios one night after sign-off again and Fabor Robison picked it up and it went on to become a big, international hit and Jim went on from there.

Getting the Sound Right

Bob "Sully" Sullivan, KWKH, and the *Louisiana Hayride*

—Steven Morewood

Although he did not make a living as a musician, Bob Sullivan is one of the key figures in Shreveport's musical history. As a sound engineer, his contributions to radio and recording resonate from the Ark-La-Tex to the broader popular music scene of the 1950s and after. Sullivan for years worked a daily shift at KWKH in Shreveport and operated the broadcasting board during the Saturday night *Louisiana Hayride*. In addition, he produced records for a long list of nationally famous and local musicians after hours in the KWKH studio, which remained Shreveport's only viable recording facility for most of the *Hayride* years. Along the way "Sully," as he was known, interacted with Hank Williams, Elvis Presley, Jim Reeves, Rose Maddox, and a host of other *Hayride* artists. As a deeply engaging person with a sharp wit and talent for weaving a good yarn, it is surprising that his biography remains so little known.

The memories and anecdotes from these encounters by themselves make a colorful and revealing narrative. Yet, even beyond these, Sully's story opens insight into a vanished era of recording and radio history. It was a comparatively raw and spontaneous time for both media, a character bespoken by Sully's entry into the profession by way of accidental experience acquired in U.S. Army service and personal connections. Sullivan's vivid memory for detail and Morewood's prose make these stories anything but remote.

Steven Morewood first met Bob Sullivan in 1995 and has since spent many hours with him, reflecting on and recording his experiences as a KWKH engineer, as well as corresponding from across the Atlantic. This piece is part of a longer biographical project, printed here for the first time.

Of all the thousands of words written about the *Louisiana Hayride*, famous "Cradle of the Stars," too few have been devoted to one of its unsung heroes: Bob "Sully" Sullivan, a key KWKH recording engineer. Tillman Franks called him "the best radio engineer I have ever known" and "one of the best kept secrets in country music."[1] He has still to be inducted into the *Hayride* Hall of Fame and does not even warrant a mention in the memoirs of two *Hayride* luminaries despite being closely associated with them.[2] And yet it was Sully who oversaw the weekly live radio broadcasts from the *Hayride* stage (at their peak second in popularity only to the *Grand Ole Opry*) and recorded acts after broadcasting hours, capturing career-launching releases for the likes of Slim Whitman, Jim Reeves, Mitchell Torok, The Browns, and Dale Hawkins. He also captured the final recording of Hank Williams and cut a demo for Elvis Presley. His is a fascinating story worth telling for the insights it brings to a seminal period of country music's history which took place not in Nashville, Tennessee, but in Shreveport, Louisiana. Moreover, since he has no axes to grind or an ego to feed, Bob Sullivan's memories are as close, at this far remove, to what really happened during several critical moments in *Hayride* history.

Finding a Vocation

Robert Carl Sullivan was born in Bossier City, Louisiana, on 3 December 1926. His early life was unremarkable except for a growing love of blues and country music.[3] His family came through the Depression, not least because his father, Wimberley Parker Sullivan (known as "Wim") managed to hold down a job in the oil industry. Around the age of twelve the Sullivans moved to a farm in Bienville Parish, Louisiana, owned by Wim. It was here that Robert began attending Rosenwald Baptist Church, a black church just half a mile from his home. At the same time he acquired his first guitar from a Montgomery Ward catalog, a three-quarter size Gene Autry model. An accompanying book showed him the basic chords. Once he mastered the intricacies of "Wildwood Flower" he teamed up with three friends and an older fiddle player and began playing local country dances. Here he honed his skills as a musician and eventually added steel guitar and dobro to the instruments he could play.

The expansion of the Second World War to the Pacific saw "Sully," as he became known, conscripted, and in 1944, once past the age of eighteen, he was sent to serve as an infantryman in the Philippines. Fortunately the serious fighting was over by then and his typing skills soon led to his recruitment as

a cryptographist. There was a military radio station in Manila, which broadcast transcriptions of programs by Bob Hope, Glenn Miller, and other acts
to entertain the troops. Fascinated by what went on, Sully hung around the
station when off duty. He came to the attention of a lieutenant who was disgruntled at the lackluster attitude of a sergeant responsible for the continuity
of programs. The sergeant would get drunk, fall asleep, and instead of another
program listeners would hear the scratching of the record needle as it reached
the end of the disc. Sully readily volunteered to step in and acquired his first
taste of the life of a recording engineer.

After leaving the army at the end of 1945, turning down a commission,
Sully went first to Louisville, Kentucky, finding employment at a Roi Tan cigar
plant. Disenchanted, he soon returned to the town of Caster, Louisiana, in
Bienville Parish where he had lived on the farm around two miles outside. Here
he began making a few dollars as a musician playing country dances, hooking
up with some of his old buddies and new acquaintances. Sully became, in his
own words, a "half decent musician." Later on at KWKH, he would occasionally be called upon to fill in for a missing band member, provided a *Hayride*
act was not playing too far outside Shreveport to enable him to get back for his
early morning shift. More importantly, his musical experiences gave him an
unerring instinct for how to capture the raw energy of live music whether in
the studio or at the *Hayride*.

During this period he first saw Hank Williams, playing at Ashland,
Louisiana, as the guest act with Johnny and Jack and Miss Kitty Wells.
Coincidentally, the janitor of the school was another Sullivan who let his relative in free through the back entrance. Walking through the backstage area Sully
encountered ol' Hank sitting on a metal chair playing "Sally Gooden" on the
fiddle. "I didn't know you played the fiddle," remarked Sully. "I don't play it
much, Ace." "How about playing another one?" Williams duly obliged. It was his
way of relaxing before a show, even though he only ever played guitar on stage.

What life in the army did for Sully was to imbue in him a sense of adven-
ture, a desire to see the world and take chances rather than return to Bienville
Parish, listen to the radio, and sink back into anonymity. So he ventured to
Louisville, Kentucky, where he found work at a tobacco plant turning out
cigars and cigarettes. From there he managed a series of gas stations in the
vicinity called Aero Gas before moving on to Birmingham, Alabama. The dete-
rioration in the situation in South East Asia in the late 1940s, which would
lead to the Korean War, produced speculation in the national and local press
that the draft might be reintroduced. Fearing he might be enlisted again, Sully

returned to Louisiana to stay close to his home army base. It was at this point that his personal life changed dramatically.

> That's when I met Judy. I was sitting in a café with my old friends shooting pool when these schoolgirls came in from the school just down the street. Somebody introduced me to her. We just sort of hit it off. I asked her if she wanted to go out and she accepted. I went out to her folks at the Texas Eastern Transmission Company which was a gas pipeline pumping natural gas from the coast up to the Northeast and had a pumping station about every 150 miles to keep the gas flowing over 3,000 miles. When I came back from Louisville, Kentucky, I got a job building one of those pumping stations about two miles from my house. Judy's parents lived out at the plant because her father worked for Texas Eastern as an operator running this huge pumping station. I worked there when they were building the thing. We saw each other quite often. We kept dating and dating and I kept fighting off the rest of the boys and I guess I won out because we got married in 1949 and had children. Little Judie was born in November 1950, Ronald, born in 1951, and Tim in 1956. All three of my kids were born in Shreveport.

In Shreveport Sully got a job with the local steel mill; the money was good, but he detested the work, especially perching precariously on the steel girders that were the framework for new high rise buildings. Fortunately, salvation was at hand. Tillman Franks was a leading figure at the *Louisiana Hayride*, a Saturday night radio show aired by Shreveport's KWKH, a 50,000-watt clear-channel radio station beaming right across the eastern half of the United States and beyond. The show had started on 3 April 1948 and became renowned for introducing new talent, whereas the much more conservative *Grand Ole Opry* in Nashville generally played it safe by only allowing acts with at least one hit to their name. The industrious Tillman delved into a multitude of areas to earn a living, which included running a music shop in Shreveport. It was a natural port of call for Sully and he quickly struck up a friendship with Tillman, an affable and kindly person who got a big kick out of helping others. Tillman learned of his new friend's disenchantment with his job, love of music, and his brief experience in radio during his Army days.

It was Tillman who told Sully of an opening at KWKH. One of the existing engineers was a frustrated radio announcer, but there was no opening at KWKH. Ironically he stuttered off air but had a beautiful speaking voice behind the microphone with a delivery as smooth as silk. He had secured a job with a small radio station in Arkansas but could not leave until a replacement engineer was found. Tillman phoned Sully to alert him to the situation. Sully jumped at the opportunity and went up to see the chief engineer, Jack Jones, who was impressed by his musical prowess and rudimentary radio experience, sufficiently so to offer Sully the job on the spot. What swung the situation for Jones was Sully's ability to play guitar and steel guitar, figuring that he could empathize with musicians. "There's not a soul on the staff who's a musician."[4] But he also now had a wife to consider. At thirty-five dollars a week the starting salary was less than half what he was getting, but job satisfaction was a big drawing card. Judy was nothing less than fully supportive. So he took the job and never regretted the decision. In his first week Jones showed Sully the ropes and then left him to it.

Sully was the first engineer to clock on at KWKH, which meant arriving at 4 A.M. to get ready for the day's first broadcast at 5 A.M. At the start Sully had no transport, so Jones went to see Henry Clay, the station manager notorious for his frugality, for authorization to pay for a taxi. A negative might have ended Sully's radio career there and then. But while Clay would not go the whole hog (a taxi to and from home) he did sanction expenses for the journey in to the Commercial National Bank Building, where KWKH was located, leaving Sully to find his own way home after his shift concluded at 1 P.M. When he arrived, the sleep-in janitor had not risen to work the lift, which meant climbing two stories to arrive at KWKH's floor. For a brief period in the afternoons Sully attended radio school to acquire more technical knowledge of the equipment he was working with. However, Henry Clay said that as soon as Sully earned a first class licence from the FCC he was going to be transferred to the transmitter around twenty miles north of Shreveport. This was a prospect that filled him with dread: "All you do is sit there for eight hours watching gauges and take readings every hour or so to make sure the transmitter is working properly. It had to be the worst job in the world as far as I was concerned." So he quit school to avoid this fate.

On Saturdays, when the *Louisiana Hayride* went out, Sully signed the station on as usual. Then later, at 5 P.M., he would go back to KWKH and pick up the broadcasting equipment (microphones and a broadcast amplifier) to load into the company van to take it down to the Municipal Auditorium to set up and work there until the *Hayride* finished. Then he took the equipment back to the station before returning home around 1 A.M. Sully could not have a Sunday morning lie-in, however, because he needed to sign KWKH on at 6 A.M. for a seven-hour shift. Later, when he did recording sessions immediately after the

Hayride, he never returned home at all. His was not a job for the fainthearted. The other broadcasting engineer who assisted was Elmo Davis, and for much of the time when Sully first went to KWKH, they were running the shifts at the studio seven days a week. A brief respite came when Hershel Pace, who had left to do army service, returned for a time before he went to Channel 12 TV station where he felt his technical skills could be put to better use.

Life as a Recording Engineer at KWKH

During KWKH's heyday the opening few hours from 5:00 to 9:00 A.M. were taken up with live performances by *Hayride* acts who would play Monday through Friday, generally for a few weeks or months at a time, before being rotated to give them a break and allow another act to come in. Most performers received no fee, despite the ungodly hour, but were content to rise to the challenge because they could increase their fan base and attract bookings in the vicinity and beyond. Sometimes acts would play too far out of town the previous night, or succession of nights, to be able to get back to Shreveport in time. In this instance, Sully would record them on aluminum discs to play in their absence. The Maddox Brothers and Rose, for instance, were in the habit of recording a week's worth of programs on Sundays.[5] As Rose recalled:

> We'd go back to Shreveport and stay there for four months. On Saturday night we'd do the *Hayride* broadcast over KWKH. On Sundays, we'd tape all day long for the early morning radio programs. Those were sponsored by a company that sold mail-order baby chicks out of Chicago. We also had a fifteen-minute program that aired at midnight, which reached all over the South and Midwest. During the week we'd work every night, travel around that part of the country, but we were always back in Shreveport for the Saturday night broadcast.[6]

On one occasion, Judy Sullivan, Sully's wife, provided the Maddoxes with chicken sandwiches and sundries for refreshment, which were much appreciated by the hungry musicians. Whether acts went out live or not, Sully's job involved setting up the five KWKH microphones (the collective total available), making adjustments during changeovers, and putting on ads, which were the lifeblood of the station. Each act played for fourteen minutes, leaving just a one-minute turnaround time before the next came on air. It was like juggling cats, but somehow everyone managed and normally transitions went smoothly. What helped was that bands tended to feature the same instruments (drums being conspicuous by their absence) and the lead singers were adept at working their microphone.

KWKH carried a program between 8:30 and 9:00 A.M. called *Contact*, which featured an interview with a celebrity in town. It was a way to promote their activities and to fill air time.[7] One particular day a big Hollywood actor, John Payne, was in Shreveport to appear in a musical. He arrived around 8:10 A.M. with his secretary and a personal attaché, looking dishevelled from the night before. His hangdog expression advertised that this was the last place he wanted to be. Five minutes later Webb Pierce and his accomplished band[8] began their regular fifteen-minute early morning show. Webb kicked off with his first hit, "Wondering," but went flat on a high note. At this moment Sully observed Payne flinch. After Webb finished, he noticed Payne and asked Sully who he was. "By God," said Pierce, "I am going to stick around and meet him." When Payne finished his interview, Webb approached him like a besotted fan. "Mr. Payne, I am sure glad to meet you. You are one of my favorite actors." "I'm pleased to meet you too, Mr. Pierce," Payne replied, "but I have a question for you. How in hell do you sing in one key while that band plays in another one?" It was a barbed comment, but Webb took it as a compliment. "Well," he responded, "that's just my style."

The highlight of the week at KWKH was the Saturday night *Hayride* staged at the Municipal Auditorium in Shreveport. Sully was the principal broadcast engineer on duty throughout the three-hour show from eight to eleven except for two brief interludes when either Elmo Davis or his boss, Jack Jones, stepped in to the broadcast booth to give him a break. The broadcast system was rudimentary by today's standards but proved more than equal to the task, including a fortnightly live feed to CBS of a portion of the show. The sound system was fed off a broadcast amplifier at the stage. Sully had only three big speakers to play with so their positions were absolutely crucial. He situated one down on the floor in the center of the huge stage; the other two were placed on each side of it around ten feet off the floor. The noise level was sufficient to carry to all parts of the auditorium but not so overwhelming that conversation could not take place. As each act came on, the majority would wave or say hello to the amiable Sully in his broadcast booth to the left of the stage facing the audience, situated just out of view. At no time during his tenure at KWKH were there ever any complaints over the sound.

Curiously, the city authorities did not care much for the Saturday night *Hayride*, notwithstanding the fact that it drew most of its audience from Texas, thereby bringing in extra revenue over a weekend. On several Saturday evenings throughout the year they would commandeer the Municipal Auditorium for their own purposes, such as a carnival or a big band concert. On such occasions the *Hayride* was compelled to go on the road, which required Sully to oversee an outside broadcast. This was no easy task given the unfamiliarity of the venues and the fact that the parsimonious management of KWKH would only sanction the cheaper "B" line feed back to KWKH rather than the more expensive "A" line. Examples of these outside broadcasts include the High School Gymnasium, Gladewater (twice in 1955), the Heart of Texas Coliseum in Waco, Texas,[9] and the High School Football Field at Conroe, Texas.[10]

Taking the *Hayride* out of town led to several amusing incidents that are still etched in Sully's memory. Jim Bulleit, the owner of Bullet Records, was hired briefly by Henry Clay to run artists' services for the *Hayride*. The first gig he booked was in Gladewater, Texas, at the High School Gym on 30 April 1955.[11] Bulleit was in ecstasy after selling three hundred reserved tickets for $1.50 each, a reflection of the burgeoning popularity of Elvis Presley. The problem was that the *Hayride* had never sold reserved seats. Tickets were seventy-five cents each on a first come first served basis. By the time those with reserved seats began to arrive, all their seats had been taken up. Arguments developed and when the show went on the air at 8:00 P.M. three fights were still going on. The first few minutes were like a wrestling match with extraneous noises breaking into the feed to CBS but because it was live and national radio, the show continued until eventually the melee subsided.

On another occasion the *Hayride* road show was due to play at the Louisiana Tech University in Ruston, Louisiana, on its football field. Sully arrived around 5:45 P.M. and commenced setting up. As he did so, he noticed a big dark cloud looming threateningly overhead. It was late August, there had been a six-day drought, and the heat was sweltering. "Man, I sure hope it don't rain," Sully muttered under his breath. Just before show time the skies began ominously to open, at first with a sprinkling of raindrops. At the opposite end of the football field was a field house which had been closed since Friday afternoon. Horace Logan, the KWKH program director, managed to get someone to open it up. Inside the temperature was even more intense than outside but it was the only possibility of avoiding the storm and staging the show. Everyone grabbed some equipment and made a dash for safety as the skies became even more threatening: Sully clutched the broadcast amplifier while Ray Baker, then a local disc jockey, scooped up the microphones and the stands. Just as they reached the field house torrential rain fell. Inside it was like a sauna and everyone was soon perspiring heavily. Sully searched desperately for a phone line and located one. Ideally he needed two lines so that he could hear the transcribed spots from KWKH in Shreveport, and know when to go on and off the air. With just one line available, this was impossible and posed a dilemma: he could send but not receive. Baker saved the day by locating a battery-powered radio which enabled him to listen to KWKH. He stood at the door and used hand signals to let Sully know when to go on and off because some of the radio spots resonated from Shreveport.

Resolving how to feed KWKH efficiently did not end the troubles of this particular occasion. Between 9:00 and 9:30 P.M. the program was sponsored by Jax Beer. At 9:01 P.M. there was an announcement to this effect. Ten minutes into the slot the back door burst open as the university chancellor appeared with three heavies dressed in uniform. His face livid with rage, he demanded that Horace end the broadcast: "You are advertising beer. This is a Christian school and I won't have it! Shut it down now or I will have everything you have hooked up yanked out." It says much for Logan that he remained calm and collected. "Wait a minute, wait a minute. Let's go talk about this." The chancellor agreed and the two went off to one side. As this went on, Sully was mixing the music and watching Baker for cues, fully expecting one of the guys in uniform to cut the phone wire at anytime. Horace impressed upon the chancellor that the show was going out nationally over CBS, but the latter remained insistent that the show must be shut down. Logan managed to keep the chancellor talking until the next sponsored segment of the show went on air at 9:31 P.M., which was for Purina Feeds. Horace then seized the moment: "It is a moot point anyway. We are now advertising animal feed." "Well, I guess that's okay, but no more advertising for beer!" At this the chancellor and his entourage left in a huff and the crisis was over.

Hank Williams

In his still vivid reminiscences of his time with KWKH, Sully's association with Hank Williams figures prominently. They met again after their brief encounter backstage at Ashland, Louisiana, early one morning on a program sponsored by Johnny Fair Syrup.[12] Hank started to appear on 10 January 1949 but it was some time after this that they renewed acquaintances. Hank had become an overnight star thanks to "Lovesick Blues," an old vaudeville song he launched on the *Hayride* that had a tremendous impact, so much so that he then recorded it over the objections of his producer, Fred Rose, and went to number one.[13] "Hank did it," recalls Sully, "and the crowd went absolutely berserk. From the first night he was on the show, people just loved him."[14] The singer looked at the new KWKH broadcast engineer with a puzzled expression and then vented his thoughts: "Don't I know you, Hoss?" "Well, probably so," came the reply. "I saw you down at Ashland playing fiddle." "Ah yes," shot back Hank. "I remember you." From then on Hank always recognized Sully who (like so many others) he referred to affectionately as "Hoss" or "Ace."

Sully observed many a Hank Williams performance at close quarters. His early morning radio shows as "the ol' Syrup Sopper" between January and May 1949, with just him singing to his guitar, were magical to behold at first hand. "I think," judges Sully, "he was most effective with just him and his acoustic guitar."[15] Often Hank would try out a new composition in its raw form and frequently perform songs he never cut in the studio. Better still were his stage performances with a backing band where, if he was on form and sober, he would blow an audience away. Sully considers Hank the best live performer he ever witnessed, ranking him above the likes of Elvis Presley, Johnny Cash, George Jones, and Slim Whitman. Getting to know Hank gave Sully an insight into the reasons for his mood swings. Williams would crouch over the microphone and many subsequent singers imitated his posture. It was not a gimmick, though, but derived from the curve in Hank's back. As a child he suffered from spina bifida and a severe back problem still afflicted him into adulthood. The excruciating pain that resulted was alleviated through taking pills, but this gave Hank a very low tolerance for alcohol. Just a few drinks would make him as high as a kite, marring his set and occasionally rendering him incapable of taking the stage.

Hank's Achilles' heel was his alcoholism. When he was sober, being in Hank's company was a delight as the witticisms flowed from his tongue like a cascading waterfall. When he was drunk, however, Hank's personality transformed, making him mean-spirited and obnoxious. Sully was not alone in preferring not to be around him at these times. Keeping the bottle away from Hank became a fixation with those close to him and the KWKH management, especially Horace Logan. For instance, if Hank came on sober at 8:30 P.M. for his first spot he could easily become inebriated once in his dressing room and his second spot an hour later would be an embarrassment to one and all. At a show in Lake Charles, Louisiana, Red Sovine opened with his theme song, "On My Farm in Louisiana Where the Old Red River Flows." Just as he finished the first verse the curtains came down, inadvertently yanked away by Hank who was behind them getting drunk. Red looked at Hank in shock. "By God," burst out the latter, "It's time for ol' Hank!"

Since he was the main draw, a drunken Hank Williams was Horace's nightmare scenario and he went to great lengths to try to stop him from drinking. Sometimes he succeeded, sometimes not. On one outside date for the *Hayride*, Horace bribed fellow artist Tommy Trent to keep Hank from imbibing hard liquor. The tour bus headed for Little Rock with Tommy sitting attentively next to Hank, watching him like a hawk. Hank was wearing tight clothing—jeans and a western shirt—with no room to hide whiskey. Each time the bus stopped Horace would pat Hank down as if he was a cop searching a criminal for a hidden gun. Nothing was found and Horace was convinced his plan had succeeded and that a sober Hank would tear the house down in Arkansas. Instead Hank's drunken half showed up and it was a disaster. When the troupe boarded the bus to return to Shreveport, Hank looked mischievously at Horace. "I know what you did, Hoss," he said in a drunken stupor. "You gave Tommy twenty bucks to keep a bottle from me. The problem is I gave him fifty bucks to carry it for me!"[16]

On one occasion in the fall of 1952 the *Hayride* was booked to play a large auditorium in Brownwood, Texas, with Hank set to top the bill. Sully arrived with the broadcast equipment at 5:30 P.M. and within half an hour had set up. Then, with Tommy Trent he started to mosey around town, killing time before the show. They soon spotted a familiar figure across the street in front of a hotel. The gaunt male beckoned them over and invited them up to his hotel room to escape the sultry heat whereupon he removed his shirt and sprawled his lanky figure across the bed, his boots hanging over the foot of the bed. There was a knock at the door and in walked a bellhop with a sack containing a fifth of whiskey. It now became apparent why Hank Williams had been standing outside the hotel in the oppressive heat. Brownwood was dry and he was seeking a bootlegger. Hank paid for the whiskey, added a generous tip and opened the bottle, offering a swig to his companions, which they refused. The singer then returned to the bed and began working the bottle. All this time Hank's vivacious new bride, his second wife Billie Jean, had been taking a shower, from which she now emerged. When she spotted Hank with the whiskey she immediately assumed that Sully and Tommy were the perpetrators and cussed them with a vengeance. Hank tried to explain but his new bride wasn't listening and the pair made a quick exit. That evening at the show Hank laughed at their tongue lashing. "I'm sorry you got the blame, Ace. She just wouldn't listen."

Hank Williams had left Shreveport for Nashville in mid-1949, on the back of the huge success of "Lovesick Blues" and "Wedding Bells." His sudden and unexpected return to the *Hayride* on 13 September 1952, after being fired by the *Grand Ole Opry*, has spawned almost as many different stories as when Elvis Presley made his *Hayride* debut. One story has it that if he returned to Shreveport for three months and stayed sober, the Ryman Auditorium was willing to take him back. Another version insists that Horace Logan called Hank and asked him to come back. It's also claimed that Hank cajoled Henry Clay not to pay him scale but two hundred dollars a show.[17] The Bob Sullivan version of events supports an impulsive return by Hank to his natural home. Sully recalls that one Saturday night he was working the *Hayride* broadcast booth as usual when he heard a commotion outside that included a familiar voice of old. When he opened the door and looked out to determine who was talking he was surprised to see a gaunt Hank talking to Horace. "He looked like a skeleton," recalls Sully. Hank was not dressed in his usual western attire but instead sported a black serge business suit, shoes, and a Fedora hat. Hank had seemingly just showed up out of the blue. He had walked in off the street and hung out at the back of the auditorium before being spotted. No one knew he was coming and Horace almost threw a fit! Recovering his composure Horace asked Hank whether he wanted to sing. When the answer was in the affirmative Hank was introduced to an exuberant crowd, who acted like they had witnessed the Second Coming, and he proceeded to do two numbers. The first was his current chart topper "Jambalaya (On the Bayou)," which Hank co-wrote with Moon Mullican to the melody of the old Cajun tune, "Gran Texas." Its uplifting quality fitted the occasion perfectly and the crowd was further enticed with the promise that Hank would be back the following Saturday when he made his official return to the Municipal Auditorium. It was, ironically, "Slim Whitman Appreciation Day."[18]

The following Monday Hank and Horace Logan came into the KWKH control room. Horace was clutching an acetate that Hank was really excited about. Logan asked Sully to "put this on" whereupon Hank interjected, "Yea, this is the next hit." The song was "Kaw-liga." As it played, Hank kept nudging Horace and insisted, "That's a hit record right there. What do you think, what do you think?" Horace agreed and then asked Sully for his opinion. "Well it sounds good to me." At this Hank remarked mischievously: "He likes fiddles so much he'd like it 'cos it's got a fiddle on it! That don't mean it's gonna sell." "Yea, I really like it Hank." The singer recorded "Kaw-liga" at what turned out to be his last recording session in Nashville on 23 September 1952. Despite the quality of the other songs recorded (including "Your Cheating Heart" and "Take These Chains from My Heart") Sully remembers that "Kaw-liga" was the one song he enthused about.[19]

All was not well, however. Hank struggled to reconstitute a band. He was in very poor health, which was exacerbated by his constant imbibing of whiskey, a problem that was now on a much worse scale than when he left Shreveport for Nashville. A date that sticks in Sully's mind is 3 December 1952: it was his birthday but more than that he was visited in the KWKH studio by Hank, who wanted to commit a song to disc. He said he intended to record it on his next session, but in fact wanted to do it as a present for his father. Hank went back into the studio he'd last sung from in 1949 to find the same microphone. The song, which turned out to be the last he ever recorded, was called "The Old Log Train."[20] After Sully committed it to disc and handed it to Hank, the latter asked what was the cost. "You don't owe me nothin'. Glad to do it."

A few days later Hank returned to the studio to get his mail. He sat in the control room, opened his letters and chatted a little. Sully told him that he looked good compared to what he looked like in September because he had put on weight. "Hoss, I'm feeling better than I have in years. I'm eating three squares a day. That's helping a lot." Williams was upbeat about feeling better and doing well. In what turned out to be their final conversation, Hank mentioned to Sully his plans to spend Christmas in Montgomery and then play some New Year show dates he was committed to. They did not fill him with relish—"I've got two more dates to play for those sons of bitches and then I'm through with them."

Crucially, Hank alluded to his intention to return to regular *Hayride* performing.[21] His first stint in Shreveport had been the happiest time of his singing career, and he yearned to rekindle those days and perhaps indulge in some hunting and fishing, favorite pastimes for which he seldom found time. Hank got up and walked to the door, turning round to wish goodbye: "See you later, Hoss." It was not to be. Sully was working the board at KWKH on New Year's Day 1953 when the teletype bell rang. The man who took the message immediately came into the control room with the devastating news: "Sully, Hank Williams just died. His driver found him dead in the back seat of his car." The immediate dilemma of the announcer was whether to inform listeners there and then, or to refer the matter to Horace Logan, who was not on duty. As it happened, CBS broke the news. Sully felt he had lost a dear friend, but his meager salary prevented him from traveling down to Montgomery, Alabama, for the weekend funeral. Horace led a small party from Shreveport, which was overawed by the large party that came in from Nashville, many of whom reportedly got drunk after the Sunday service.

Suddenly the aluminum acetates that Sully had made of Hank's early morning radio program became invaluable. Most had long since been taken away to aluminum centers by the scrap merchant who recycled them, but a precious few with Sully as the broadcast engineer miraculously survived, stashed in the corner of a room. They mysteriously disappeared but later materialized in a record release that took advantage of the surge in Hank's popularity following his tragic passing.[22] So too did a tribute record by Jack Cardwell, "The Death of Hank Williams," which Sully engineered at KWKH. Released on King Records, it reached number three in February 1953.

Recording Sessions at KWKH

It was a natural progression for *Hayride* acts to want to record in Shreveport. Before he moved to Nashville in the summer of 1949, aside from some demos, Hank Williams either recorded at a radio station there or in Cincinnati. But traveling so far away was not an option for the lesser lights. Apart from one very inadequate local facility, there was no other recording studio in town. While Jim Beck's studio in Dallas sometimes drew *Hayride* acts to record there, it was sufficiently far removed to repel more than attract customers. This opened up an opportunity for KWKH. Its studio was built as a room within a room. About two feet away from the outside walls of the building another wall was constructed stuffed with fiberglass. The only windows faced the announcer's booth and an area in front of the studio where the coffee machine and several chairs and tables were situated. The latter was a viewing area for people who came up to the studio in the morning when acts were broadcasting. This guest room was often filled with people who could listen through a speaker to the program as it went out live. It also served as a lounge for KWKH employees where they could take a break and drink coffee.

The dimensions of the studio were approximately twenty-five by thirty feet with a twelve-foot ceiling, which was similar to the Beck facility. Not that KWKH's studio was state-of-the-art. Recording facilities there were primitive in the extreme: a one-track broadcast board with no echo or equalizer and just five knobs to turn to achieve a good mix. Again, only five microphones were available, which meant their positions had to be carefully chosen to achieve a good balance between singer and musicians. Everything needed to be recorded live and there was no possibility of an overdub. Nevertheless, Sully excelled in being able to make the most out of what was available. For instance, he discovered that an echo effect was possible through feeding the output back into the board, which is what he did with "Indian Love Call." On another Slim Whitman release, "By the Waters of the Minnetonka," the singer wanted the sound of running water to start and end the song. Sully went into the KWKH library and, after some searching, found the sound of a babbling brook the closest match to what was needed. The splashing noise was prominent at the beginning and close of the song, being pushed into the background when the musicians came in. When the single was first aired on KWKH the assistant manager called Sully to raise Cain, dismissing the water effect as "surface noise" that distorted the record and asking never to hear it again. Despite the general age of the equipment, the announcer microphones in the KWKH studio were the RCA 44BX ribbon type, which was top of the range. These microphones so captivated Jim Reeves because they could capture his precise diction and warm baritone that he insisted on their employment when he moved to RCA Victor in 1955.[23] KWKH also had 77DX microphones, which was the latest model available and they were used predominantly by singers. The absence of drums from country acts of the day further helped to simplify the mixing process.

Mac Wiseman, just signed with Dot Records in California, was the first act to cut a record at KWKH. Mac had previously recorded with Molly O'Day, Bill Monroe, and Lester Flatt and Earl Scruggs before signing with Dot. Unable to travel to his label's studio, Mac asked to cut two sides in Shreveport and Sully was happy to oblige. The recording date for Mac's first solo session was 23 May 1951, which also happened to be his twenty-sixth birthday. The songs laid down were "'Tis Sweet To Be Remembered" and "I Wonder How the Old Folks Are at Home." Mac didn't have a hit with the single, but the record did establish him as a viable artist. It got played on KWKH and earned him a spot on the *Hayride*, blazing a trail for others to follow. In fact it attracted some attention by being covered by Cowboy Copas and Lester Flatt and Earl Scruggs, who took it to number eight and number one respectively on the *Billboard* country chart early in 1952.[24]

The first big hit to be recorded at KWKH was by a yodeling tenor balladeer, Slim Whitman, who joined the *Hayride* in May 1950. Recently signed to Imperial Records, his day job as a postman prevented him from traveling to California for a recording session. Slim turned to Bob Sullivan in seeking a solution to his dilemma. "Sully, can you cut me a record?" The answer was in the affirmative with the proviso that the session could only take place when KWKH was off air. In November 1951 "Love Song of the Waterfall," "My Love Is Growing Stale," "Bandera Waltz," and "End of the World" were recorded one morning. Slim had recorded before (1950) at RCA without success. But from this session the opening song, a Bob Nolan composition, gave him his first Top Ten record in the *Billboard* country chart (May 1952). Two months later another KWKH recording, "Indian Love Call," went to number two and became a million-seller, heralding Whitman's arrival as a major recording artist.

Suddenly Sully found himself in great demand. The extra work deprived him of sleep and seriously eroded his home life, but his willingness to record beyond the call of duty led to KWKH spawning several hits that have become legendary. There was no set pattern to recording other than a preference for recording after the *Hayride*. Acts were warmed up and on a high after their appearance at the Municipal Auditorium. More important still, KWKH opened up at 6 A.M. on Sundays; this gave an extra hour of studio time, which often proved invaluable. What it meant personally for Sully, however, was that after he finished broadcasting the *Hayride*, he had to stay up through the night for the recording session and then sign on the station for his Sunday morning shift. When someone wanted to record they sometimes contacted Sully by telephone to determine when the studio was available. Generally, though, he would be approached during the *Hayride* and if the facilities were available afterwards then the recording would happen that night. The one rule which Sully applied was to accommodate only one act at a time. Other than that, he was free and easy with his time. Even so, three was the most recording sessions he ever held in a week and sometimes a week or two would pass without any being booked.

As his reputation spread, the range of acts that passed through the KWKH studio broadened considerably. While much focus has naturally been accorded to the big names and their resonant hits, it should be emphasized that more routine recording took place that garnered little attention. Second tier *Hayride* artists who never achieved a chart breakthrough were recorded for a local label. They included Tommy Trent and Johnny Johnson, both with their own bands, who would cut records not for single release or to attract big label attention but more to sell on their personal appearances. The KWKH studio also generated business from Stan Lewis, who owned Stan's Record Shop in Shreveport, and furnished a procession of black artists to record blues records. Lewis's *modus operandi* was to turn up with a singer, book an hour's studio time to record them singing and strumming a guitar, pay for the session and then take off.

Some notion of the pressures attending sessions in the small hours of the morning can be gleaned from Maxine Brown's memory of The Browns' first recording session at KWKH:

> We couldn't begin recording until ... KWKH went off the air. It took about an hour to set up and make sure everything was balanced on one mike. We had only about three hours recording time because the station went back on the air at 6 A.M. We had to be completely cleared out of the studio by then so the disc jockey could start his newscast. The studio was so full of musicians and technicians we were almost lost in the shuffle.[25]

These time pressures notwithstanding, Sully managed to take a remarkably relaxed approach to recording as well as capturing the raw energy and exuberance of the performances. Somehow the occasion brought out the best in him and the acts he recorded.

East Texan Jim Reeves, a quietly spoken junior announcer and disc jockey for the Saturday night *Red River Round Up*, an hour-long broadcast which followed the *Hayride*, joined KWKH in December 1952.[26] Sully often worked with Jim,[27] finding him very pleasant but difficult to get to know, so much so that Sully had no idea that his new colleague was an aspiring singer. That was until the California-based owner of Abbott Records, the flamboyant Fabor Robison, asked Sully one day if he could record Reeves. Robison had seen Jim perform at the Reo Palm Isle club in Longview, Texas, and been sufficiently impressed to sign him up. Originally, Fabor wanted Herchel Pace for the Reeves session until somebody told him of Sully's success with Slim Whitman.

The resulting session (18 January 1953) produced "Mexican Joe," a fast-paced light-hearted novelty song with an infectious beat written by Mitchell Torok, who soon became a *Hayride* act in his own right. Sully would also record the same song using the very same musicians and arrangement for Billy Walker, who had joined the *Hayride* in July 1952 and was still seeking his first hit. His label, Columbia, sensed a killing and felt confident it could easily outsell a minor competitor. But while the cover, which infuriated Jim, did take away some sales from the original,[28] it failed to deny Reeves from enjoying his first hit. His own version became no less than a chart topper, voted *Cash Box* magazine's Top Country and Western Record of 1953, that would allow him to leave announcing and seek his fortune as a singer. After the KWKH session, Robison sent a

Western Union telegram to Torok informing him that Jim had cut his song: "He did fine job singing."[29] Ironically, Reeves had been extremely reluctant to record "Mexican Joe" because it only had two chords and he considered it overlong at seven verses. To overcome the singer's disinclination, Fabor needed to persuade Jim's wife, Mary, to intercede. Crucially "Mexican Joe" started Jim Reeves's career and he went on to greater fame as a crossover ballad singer nicknamed "Mr.Velvet" and "Gentleman Jim" until his untimely death in a plane crash.[30] "Mexican Joe" remained part of his live act throughout his career.

In a 1961 interview, Jim articulated to Texan disk jockey Bill Mack about his greatest thrill.

> Well I think actually the greatest thrill was one Sunday morning I went to work as an announcer at KWKH in Shreveport. And at that time we had announce booths like you and I are in now, and all the controls were handled in another room, in what we called the control room. You didn't twist your own knobs in those days, you know, you had an engineer to do that. And I sat down to look through the book to see what I was going to have to read, and the engineer punched the button on the intercom and says, "Your tune 'Mexican Joe' is on the hit parade in *Billboard* magazine." And I said: "Go away. I don't feel good this morning." He said: "No kidding, it's in there. It's tied with 'Kaw-liga' for tenth place." And I thought, well, gee whiz, let me see that thing. And I went in the control room and there it was and I saw my name and I thought, well now this surely has got to be a misprint, you know, not me surely? And I don't think I read a commercial right, or got on the network right, or anything all that day.[31]

"Mexican Joe" climbed to the top and Hank Williams's posthumous classic fell from thirteen weeks as number one.

On 24 January 1953, a week after cutting "Mexican Joe,"[32] Jim got his first chance to perform on the *Hayride* when Sleepy LaBeef failed to show because of a flat tire.[33] As it happened, because of the cold weather the 3,800 capacity Municipal Auditorium was only half full. Moreover, since Jim had yet to incorporate "Mexican Joe" into his live act, he sang the two sides of his first single release of late 1952, "What Were You Doing Last Night" and "Wagon Load of Love."[34] The single had flopped miserably,[35] but Jim managed to generate enough applause to return later in the program when he performed "How Many."[36] Ironically, it would be the up-and-coming Billy Walker who first performed "Mexican Joe" on the *Hayride*, when an incredulous Jim stared daggers at him.

The first Reeves session went smoothly with Jim obediently following Fabor's instructions as producer. Subsequent Reeves sessions at KWKH, however, quickly degenerated into shouting matches between the pair over material and singing style. Jim, as his friend Tom Perryman continually impressed on Fabor, was essentially a baritone balladeer who excelled in the lower registers. Jim wanted to sing slower and croon sincerely to evoke heartfelt meaning from lyrics. Robison, though, was determined that his protégé record predominantly novelty songs sung at a fast pace and in the high pitch that the prolifically successful Webb Pierce had made fashionable. At times Jim was almost shouting as he strained to hit the notes outside his natural range. On one occasion, musicians Jimmy Day and Floyd Cramer walked out. "When you two finish fighting," they told Jim and Fabor, "we'll be back. Otherwise we are leaving."

Although another hit followed, the jolly "Bimbo," there was nothing jovial about these sessions, which Sully came to dread. At one session, on 16 August 1954, following Reeves's appearance on the *Hayride*, a novelty number, "Penny Candy," was cut about a young girl who loved gorging herself on candy. After the playback someone pointed out that Jim had mispronounced Penelope in the lyrics.[37] Indeed he had, but Reeves adamantly refused to do another take and consequently the single went out with the glaring mistake. It still made number five in the hit parade. The other side recorded was "I'll Follow You," which became the flip side. This session was the first to feature Leo Jackson, then a teenager, who became Jim's lead guitarist. Jackson recalled:

> I don't remember all the musicians who were there but I do know Jimmy Latham was on steel guitar, probably Evelyn Rowley on piano, perhaps Jerry Rowley on fiddle and I played lead guitar. We had to hurry up and get out of the studio because Slim Whitman, who was a bigger star than Jim back then, came to record, so we had to hurry up and get out of there.[38]

To Sully's relief, this Reeves session turned out to be his last at KWKH: two further Abbott sessions followed in California before the singer joined a major label, RCA Victor, and the *Grand Ole Opry*, drawing him away from Shreveport to Nashville.[39]

Sully had been initially reluctant to record acts because of the rudimentary recording equipment and the unsocial hours. Once Whitman and Reeves enjoyed considerable chart success, though, he created a rod for his own back and naturally other acts wanted to jump on the bandwagon. Jimmy and

Johnny[40] managed one major hit, "If You Don't Someone Else Will," which was recorded at KWKH and made number nine on *Billboard* in the fall of 1954. It had originally been recorded in early summer 1952 for the Feature label, a Louisiana record company owned by J. D. Miller, whose greater claim to fame lies in his composition, "Release Me."[41] When they were signed to Chess, their manager, Tillman Franks, arranged for the song to be re-recorded at KWKH on 14 July 1954. "Though not particularly different," Tillman wrote in his memoirs, "the Chess version stands out for its superior sound quality."[42]

More of Fabor's acts were recorded at KWKH, including Floyd Cramer ("Fancy Pants"), Ginny Wright, Caroline Bradshaw, and The Browns. Mitchell Torok, the composer of "Mexican Joe," came up with another Tex-Mex flavored up-tempo tune, "Caribbean," which Fabor Robison earmarked as Jim Reeves's follow up single. Mitchell wanted it for himself and in the ensuing argument Fabor told him: "Jim's hot and you're not!" Torok's obstinacy won him a recording contract from Fabor and in April 1953 he recorded two self-penned sides at KWKH for single release: "Little Hoo-Wee" and "Judalina." It was the next KWKH recording, however, which broke Mitchell. At this session, in May 1953, "Caribbean" was captured along with another of his compositions, "Weep Away." He recalls: "I remember we couldn't come up with a proper kick-off to go with the fast tempo and I finally said, 'Fabor, how about if I throw my little Martin [guitar] up the mike and we just go?' . . . We tried it and it still sounds like a truck coming through when it starts!"[43] Surprisingly, for such an infectious number from a minor label, there was only one cover version, which left the field open for the Abbott single to reach number one in August 1953. A few years later it was re-released in Europe and became a hit all over again.[44]

The Browns, then comprising Jim Ed and Maxine, held their first recording session on 15 March 1954 with Jim Reeves on rhythm guitar and Floyd Cramer on piano. The resulting single, "Looking Back to See," made the Top Ten that summer and kick-started their career.[45] Ginny Wright paired up with Jim Reeves on stage for a rendition of "A Dear John Letter," a big hit for Jean Shepard and Ferlin Husky. Fabor Robison liked what he heard and instantly decided to pair them on record with "I Love You," written by Billy Barton, which set Jim's narration against Ginny's insistent "I love you." The session took place in the fall of 1953.[46] As Ginny remembered in a 1977 interview:

> We left straight for Shreveport, Louisiana, and we cut the session the next night, after the radio station went off the air at 1 A.M. in the morning. We cut "I Love You" as the A side. "I Want You Yes (You Want Me No)," written by Mitchell

Torok, was on the backside. Then I also cut "Please Leave My Darling Alone," which was written by Jim Reeves, a song I love dearly.[47]

The same session also saw Reeves record "Bimbo," written and also recorded by Rod Morris. This provided Jim with his second number one record. Amid strong competition, his upbeat rendition of the story of the little boy with the grown-up mind managed to hold onto the top spot for three weeks.

The hits that poured forth out of KWKH intrigued outside producers. British-born Don Law, Columbia's A&R man, came along with Billy Walker to see for himself how it was being done. Swigging liberally from a whiskey bottle, Law was astonished when he observed Sully in action. "Hell, you know as much about this as I do." Lew Chudd, the owner of Imperial Records, also visited the Shreveport radio station's studio to find out "what the secret was." The primitive equipment amazed him. "My God, man," he remarked to Sully, "I have more equipment than this in my office! I can't believe that you are cutting hit records." What helped was the stellar cast of musicians, many of whom would later join the Nashville "A" Team: Jimmy Day (steel), Floyd Cramer (piano), Tommy Bishop (lead guitar), "Big Red" Hayes and "Little" Hayes (fiddles), and Don Davis (bass). The musicians would contribute to the arrangements. They were also capable of improvisation. On a Jimmy and Johnny session for Chess, a snare drum was called for that wasn't available. It says much for the comradery at KWKH that singers with hit records often played on sessions to help their fellow artists. One such was Bill Carlisle, famous for his hit records, "Too Old to Cut the Mustard" and "No Help Wanted," who was playing rhythm guitar on this session. It was Bill who came up with a solution by taking a newspaper, cutting it into strips and winding it through the strings on the neck of his guitar to imitate the instrument.

Soon after this, on a Johnny Mathis session (this was "Country" Johnny Mathis, not the African American balladeer of the same name), a man showed up just after it had concluded. This was most unusual but Sully established that the man owned half the song that had been cut. Shortly, two other gentlemen came in with the same story and all three sat together. It transpired that Johnny had sold half the song for fifty dollars to the first man three weeks previously and then did the same twice over. When Johnny returned to the studio and saw all three together, his face turned white and he made a quick exit. Despite the considerable additional hours engendered by the impromptu recordings, Sully only received five dollars from the twenty-five per hour that KWKH charged acts to record. In fact, Maxine Brown was under the mistaken impression that when Sully recorded Fabor and Abbott artists, he was being paid by Fabor Robison, who became notorious for not remunerating his label mates for their chart successes or tour appearances. Fabor told Sully on one occasion that his expenses were such that he was not making any money. Another time he dreamed up an outlandish scheme to set up a recording studio in Brazil to cut costs and approached Sully to become the recording engineer. Wisely he declined to become involved and the venture came to nought.

Elvis Presley

Today a statue of a young and strutting Elvis Presley with a guitar slung across his back stands outside the Municipal Auditorium, a singer with attitude if ever there was one. Far and away the *Hayride*'s most successful act, his coming to the show on 16 October 1954, after a failed audition at the *Grand Ole Opry*, is shrouded in controversy.[48] Since that famous occasion so many have claimed the credit that it has become virtually impossible to disentangle fact from fiction. Bob Sullivan is not an ego tripper. Possessed of a remarkable memory that can recall distant events as if they happened yesterday and with no axe to grind, his perspective is an objective one. He can throw light on how the famous Sun single, "That's All Right Mama," coupled with "Blue Moon of Kentucky," came to the attention of Horace Logan. Tillman Franks always claimed that he brought it to Logan and Sully confirms this. He was with Logan when an excited Franks came in with the single, urged Logan to book Presley for the *Hayride*, and both sides were played. Sully wasn't too impressed by the A side, which he'd heard done better by black singers, but the Bill Monroe cover blew him away. It was refreshingly different. Tillman revealed that rival station KCIJ was playing the single a lot on T. Tommy Cutrer's show. Logan then asked whether Presley was white, which Tillman did not know. Thereupon he was ordered to call Sam Phillips, owner of Sun Records, to find out. Phillips was known to have several black blues acts signed to his label, but none of them sold well, particularly among whites at a time when racial segregation and prejudice pervaded the United States, especially its southern states. Once it was established that the boy wonder might sound black but was actually white, arrangements were put in hand to bring Elvis and his tiny band (lead guitarist Scotty Moore and bassist Bill Black) to Shreveport.

The outcome was that Elvis, the "Hillbilly Cat," made his *Hayride* debut after an all-night drive. A good quality recording survives of Frank Page introducing him before he went nervously into his two songs.[49] "The first night he appeared on the *Hayride*, nobody knew who he was," recollects Sully. "He was nervous."[50] The audience was mostly comprised of middle-aged to elderly people and the nineteen-year-old teenager was received politely—enough to merit an encore—but failed to bring the house down. As Sully recalls, his attire didn't help Elvis's cause: "They were used to seeing cowboys walking around in their cowboy clothes, and he shows up in a pink sports coat and white buck shoes!"[51] Elvis was more reassured on his second appearance that evening, and unlike the more conservative *Opry* management, Logan could see the kid had something and invited him back the following Saturday. In the days between, KWKH played the Sun single to death and made recurrent announcements that Elvis Presley was to appear on the next *Hayride*. When it came around, the audience was full of teenagers. Elvis came on in black pants and a pink sports coat. The older spectators still did not know how to react, but the teenagers did and went berserk. Elvis now became a regular. "By the fourth or fifth night," remembers Sully, "the crowd began to wake up to who he was and young girls would smother the first ten or fifteen rows."[52]

One Saturday night soon afterwards Elvis sought Sully out. He had recently bought a new Volkswagen, which was parked at the back of the auditorium. "What is that ugly thing?" "Pres, that's my new car." After finishing his opening set, Presley made for Sully's booth seeking to borrow his car. As a truck driver, he was used to the stick shift, which reassured Sully that he could handle the German model. Elvis went for a spin and then returned the keys. The trouble was that he would take some girl with him, which left a strong scent of cologne. Despite Sully winding the windows down on the way home, the smell still lingered when his wife Judy went to church the next morning. The situation was embarrassing. "Pres," Sully told Elvis, "I don't mind you using my car, but see if you can't find a girl who doesn't take a bath in that darned cologne!" Fortunately, after three or four weeks, Elvis grew tired of his new toy, and his requests to borrow the Volkswagen ceased.

The Elvis Presley that Bob Sullivan became acquainted with was naïve, shy, and as polite as could be. Elvis got into the habit of picking up his fan mail from KWKH on a Sunday afternoon. On one occasion he came in, got his usual Coke, and confessed to Sully: "Man, I am just beat. I worked five nights last week and have to head to Oklahoma from here." "Pres, why don't you slow down? Tell them to stop booking you so heavy." At this well-intentioned advice Elvis shook his head. "Man, I can't. A year from now they ain't going to know who Elvis Presley is. I've got to make it while I can." Another time during the day Elvis went with Sully to a local café where the engineer saw firsthand how, without even trying, the rising star attracted ardent female attention. Although Elvis never formally recorded at KWKH, one night following a *Hayride* he wanted to lay down a demo, and Sully was happy to oblige. The song in question was "I'm Left, You're Right, She's Gone." When it came out on Sun as the B side of "Baby Let's Play House," the arrangement was exactly the same and it became a little hit in its own right as disc jockeys flipped the single over.[53]

Once Colonel Tom Parker got wind of Elvis he instinctively sensed that there was big money to be made. The problem was that his new protégé was contracted to perform regularly on the *Hayride*. The Colonel first tried to persuade Henry Clay to let him run the show for the remainder of the contract but the stubborn station manager would not hear of it. Parker then proposed buying out the rest of the Hillbilly Cat's contract, to which Clay readily agreed, thinking he had hoodwinked the Colonel when in fact the latter was willing to pay much more. It was not the first or the last of Clay's misjudgments. At least he ensured that Elvis would appear one more time, for charity. During 1956 Presley had become a phenomenon and his final *Hayride* appearance, at the end of the year,[54] had to be moved to the Hirsch Coliseum, which held 11,000 against the Municipal Auditorium's 3,600. Sully took care of the sound, as usual, and observed at first hand the hysterical teenage adulation that the once shy Memphis teenager generated.[55] He wondered how Elvis felt but never got the chance to ask as he was now cocooned away from everyone—even his band, except on stage. But underneath the superstardom Elvis remained, at heart, the decent human being his doting mother brought him up to be and he did not forget his friends. Although Sully would never see him again, there was one occasion during the 1960s when he managed to convey his best wishes to the King in Los Angeles, where he'd become trapped making movies with the same plot and singing mostly woeful songs to beautiful women and animals. The message came back that Elvis did indeed remember Sully, said hello, and invited him to visit if ever he was in LA. Their paths, however, were destined never to cross again.

A Missed Opportunity and a New Career

In the mid-1950s KWKH had a unique chance to rival Nashville and stop the emigration of its homegrown stars to what would be dubbed "Music City, USA." To do so Shreveport needed services to match: a recording facility that could be utilized around the clock, an artists' bureau to book dates across the country, and television for greater exposure.[56] None came to pass, not least because of the head-in-the-sand attitude of Henry Clay.[57] Sully found him the most tightfisted man he'd ever known. He could only see the immediate expenses involved and adopted a lukewarm approach which infuriated those like Sully who had a vision for Shreveport. Clay did not even believe in upgrading station equipment because there was a cost attached. Thus the microphones used for the *Hayride* and the RCA broadcast amplifier remained through Sully's tenure despite requests to upgrade them.

In response to the migration of talent to Tennessee, Clay had reluctantly hired Jim Bulleit out of Nashville, a promoter who owned Bullet Record Company, to handle artists' bookings, but he proved to be a disastrous appointment. Sully initially elicited some interest from Clay regarding a new recording studio, but then the station manager visited Nashville, where he spoke with Owen Bradley who opened a recording studio in 1955 on 16th Avenue South. Bradley impressed on Clay that recording studios were risky ventures, and he advised against indulging in them. "There's no money in it. I'm thinking of shutting mine down." Clay was gullible enough to take Bradley's counsel at face value, returning to convey the immensely disappointing news to Sully that he'd decided not to finance a new studio.[58] All was not lost, however, because Texas disc jockey Tom Perryman, who had become a good friend of Sully, got the backing of a Texan oil millionaire to finance a new studio, with Sully penciled in as the engineer. "Man," beamed Tom, "we have all the backing we need! Locate us a building, and then start looking for the equipment you need to go first class!" Sully set about the task and found an old theatre that could handle any size group. He also drew up a list of recording equipment for his dream studio featuring state-of-the-art four-track recording. Just as the $50,000 deal was about to be sealed, Sully received a devastating phone call from Tom: their erstwhile backer had just died from a heart attack and the venture was off.

By 1959 Bob Sullivan could sense that the *Hayride* was in its final throes, having degenerated largely into a glorified local talent show. The majority of the stars that the *Hayride* created had migrated to Nashville where regular *Opry* appearances, recording studios, music publishing companies, and booking agencies provided what Shreveport did not and could optimize their potential earnings. Of the big names the *Hayride* had nourished, only Johnny Horton, managed by Tillman Franks, remained loyal. Horace Logan had left the year before. The *Hayride* now even featured the occasional guest from the *Opry*. Through Dale Hawkins, Sully learned of an opening for a recording

engineer at the new studio in Fort Worth owned by Clifford Herring who traveled to Shreveport to discuss a contract with Sully which was negotiated after a
Hayride show. Ironically, except for a brief visit to Jim Beck's studio in Dallas,
Sully had never seen a proper recording studio before.[59] He arrived to find a full
band waiting and recording equipment, which gave him everything he needed,
including an echo chamber. The spacious studio also included all the microphones he desired.

The session started at 2 P.M. and ended at midnight, at which point
Herring told Sully his new job had just started. Leaving KWKH was a gam-
ble that meant exchanging regular hours and the $125 a week wage that now
came with them for studio sessions which could occur any time of day or
night according to when the client wanted to record. And where KWKH sessions were strictly limited in duration because they only happened when the
station was off air, studio sessions might be extended by several hours. It was
the one occasion which caused serious differences in the Sullivan marriage.
But Sully knew instinctively that this was the right time to leave, to look for
new challenges before the *Hayride* folded completely. In his eighteen months
at Herring he would record three number one records, two of which, "Hey
Baby" and "Hey Paula," are still played frequently today. After this, Sully went
to Sumet Sound in Dallas, a big three studio complex managed by Ed Burnett.
Among the many acts Sully worked with there were Sonny and Cher, Bob
Wills and the Texas Playboys, Patti Page, and the Rolling Stones.[60]

An Overview

What recording at KWKH instilled in Sully was a preference for recording live
without overdubbing, which has never left him. Despite all the computer wiz-
ardry that has emerged since, Sully believes that the standard fare produced
by recording studios today "is not real music" because of its artificial nature.
Autotune machines can now put even the most horrendous singer in tune
while tracks are generally assembled factory style, imitating the ingredients in
songs that have succeeded. Drum machines that never tire have replaced session drummers; synthesizers substitute for orchestration. Today's Nashville is
bereft of distinctive voices to the extent that the late Billy Walker dismissed its
released output as "the best of the bad."[61]

When Sully made a nostalgic return to Shreveport's Municipal Auditorium
in 1999 for a concert to mark the fiftieth anniversary of the *Hayride*, a sound

company came in from Nashville. The board looked like a computer; twenty-six microphones were on stage; gigantic speakers hung from the ceiling; acts needed earphones to hear themselves. It was a million miles removed from the heyday of the *Hayride* where musicians played on the spacious stage as if it were their living room and volume was achieved simply by amplifying it. Standing at the back of the auditorium for the sound check, Sully was horrified by the blast of sound which was so loud he could not hold a conversation. His mind went back to the fifties when the audience was able to appreciate every nuance of the largely acoustic music they heard. There were no complaints—no one wanting the sound higher or lower. It was just right.

Over recent years Bob Sullivan's contribution to Shreveport's musical heritage has at last begun to be recognized in some quarters, none more so than Bear Family Records of Germany. One of its employees, Yurgen Koop, visited Bob at his Oklahoma home in search of new material. His eyes lit up when he was shown a disk with an unreleased recording by Johnny Horton. It featured the late singer playing piano. Koop took away the item, phoning back a few weeks later seeking final confirmation of its authenticity because like Hank Williams playing the fiddle for amusement backstage, the piano was not an instrument associated with Johnny Horton. The story behind this unique recording is an interesting one. On a Sunday afternoon Johnny called into KWKH to collect his mail. Soon, however, he returned because his car was parked a few blocks away and a fierce rainstorm had set in. Waiting for it to pass he went into the studio and began playing piano. At this Sully asked Horton whether he played any boogie-woogie, to which he replied in the affirmative. Sully then set a tape rolling as Horton played a tune on the piano. This was converted to a disc, which Sully brought home as a present for Judy who loved boogie-woogie. After some plays it sat undiscovered until the Koop visit. Appropriately it appeared on a Horton box set as "Stomping at the KWKH."[62]

Anyone who has the opportunity to meet Bob Sullivan comes away with the feeling that they have a friend for life. As Tillman Franks put it, "He would always go out of his way to help any way he could."[63] It is this affability, combined with musical prowess gleaned from his own experiences as a musician and a technical ability to derive the most from comparatively primitive recording equipment, that has set him apart as a recording engineer. Sully's preference for recording live with real instruments kept him in demand, especially by blues acts and traditional country artists, well past normal retirement age. Apart from the occasional job, he now devotes most of his time to his loving family in Oklahoma, often taking calls from old buddies to reminisce about the past and occasionally to visit with them. His days at KWKH and the *Hayride* occupy a special place in his heart, as well they should. For, as his good friend Tillman Franks put it: "Bob played a big part in the success of the *Louisiana Hayride* and the many recording sessions done at the KWKH studio. Bob is responsible for getting the great sound of those big hits."[64] Sully himself harbors no regrets and is thankful he resisted his father's invitations to leave the recording industry and work for him. "My daddy, bless his heart, thought if you weren't sweating in the sun and freezing in the winter you weren't making a living. But I'm glad I did what I did. I wouldn't take anything for my memories of Hank, Elvis, Lefty, and Horton."[65]

Notes

Where stories are not referenced they derive from the extensive interviews the author has conducted with the subject.

1. Tillman Franks, foreword to Bob Sullivan's forthcoming autobiography.

2. Horace Logan, *Elvis, Hank and Me: Making Musical History on the Louisiana Hayride* (New York: St. Martin's Press, 1998); Tillman Franks, *I Was There When It Happened* (Many, Louisiana: Sweet Dreams Publishing, 2000). Colin Escott's near definitive life of Hank Williams (*Hank Williams: The Biography* [Boston: Little Brown, 1994]) also fails to mention Bob Sullivan. Making amends is Tracey Laird, *Louisiana Hayride: Radio and Roots Music Along the Red River* (New York: Oxford University Press, 2005).

3. Like so many others, Sully's first initiation into country music was through listening to the *Grand Ole Opry* radio broadcasts.

4. Quoted in J. Beaty, "Musical Memories: Tannehill Man Recalls His Days Working with Some of the Greats," *McAlester News*, 15 October 2006, p. 2.

5. Subsequently many of the surviving recordings surfaced on a Bear Family release. Jonny Whiteside, *Ramblin' Rose: The Life and Career of Rose Maddox* (Nashville: Vanderbilt University Press, 1995), refers to "Shreveport, Louisiana, where they cut dozens of acetates during their later stint at the *Louisiana Hayride*" (p. 90).

6. Quoted in Whiteside, *Ramblin' Rose*, p. 139.

7. *Contact* went out once or twice a week, depending on who was in town.

8. Webb Pierce's band featured Floyd Cramer (piano), Jimmy Day (steel), Tommy Bishop (guitar), and Don Davis (bass).

9. 30 April 1955. Among those appearing that night were Elvis Presley, Slim Whitman, Jim Reeves, and Jimmy Newman.

10. 24 August 1955. At this gig a young George Jones first appeared.

11. Stanley Oberst, *Elvis Presley: Rockin' across Texas: An Audiovisual Journey 1954–1977* (Sony BMG Denmark: Follow that Dream Records, 2005), p. 70.

12. Colin Escott, "The Stories," liner notes to *The Complete Hank Williams* (Mercury Records), p. 77.

13. Laird, *Louisiana Hayride*, pp. 94–5.

14. Quoted in Beaty, "Musical Memories," p. 2.

15. Ibid., p. 2.

16. This story was told to Bob Sullivan by Tommy Trent.

17. Escott, *Hank Williams*, pp. 213–17.

18. Hank Williams loathed Slim Whitman whom he considered a pop singer.

19. *The Complete Hank Williams* contains a demo of "Kaw-liga" from August 1952, which has two false starts.

20. Later Sully heard that Hank took the recording to his father's house, intending to give it to him for Christmas, but found he wasn't home. The song is available on *The Complete Hank Williams* box set but is incorrectly listed as a Nashville demo.

21. Horace Logan had given Hank a leave of absence to allow his health to recover.

22. Red Sovine filled Hank Williams's radio spot sponsored by Johnny Fair Syrup.

23. Colin Escott, liner notes to Jim Reeves, *Welcome to My World* (Bear Family Records, 1994), p. 7.

24. I am grateful to Eddie Stubbs for providing illuminating detail on the Mac Wiseman KWKH session.

25. Maxine Brown, *Looking Back to See: A Country Music Memoir* (Fayetteville: University of Arkansas Press, 2005), p. 49.

26. Jim also worked on other radio shows for KWKH.

27. As well as the *Red River Round Up*, Reeves also had a weekday show on KWKH.

28. Walker later claimed sales of 220,000. See Colin Escott, liner notes to Billy Walker, *Cross the Bravo at Waco* (Bear Family Records, 1993), p. 4.

29. Quoted in Colin Escott, "Mitchell Torok," liner notes to Mitchell Torok, *Mexican Joe in the Caribbean* (Bear Family Records, 1996), p. 8.

30. 31 July 1964.

31. Quoted from "Bill Mack Interview with Jim Reeves Part 2," *The Jim Reeves Fan Club Magazine*, no. 106, June 2006, p. 10. This interview is available on Jim Reeves, *Heartbreakin' Baby*, Voice Masters, VM 1104 OD, www.voicemasters.biz.

32. 18 January 1953.

33. Jim would claim in interviews that he had replaced Hank Williams. This does not chime with the evidence: Hank was not scheduled to appear on the *Hayride* in December 1952, when Jim first arrived, and by the time "Mexican Joe" was released Williams had died. A recently discovered acetate in Jim Reeves's possession suggests that Jim's first *Hayride* appearance was in fact on 14 July 1951, when he performed "I Can't Help It (If I'm Still in Love with You)," a Hank Williams hit from earlier that year, "Unfaithful One," an Ernest Tubb number, and Hank Thompson's "Today." Correspondence between Monroe Smith, an early fan who recorded Jim's live performances on radio at KRGI, and Jim seemingly provides confirmation. (Arie den Dulk, "Jim Reeves' start at the *Louisiana Hayride*," *The Jim Reeves Fan Club Magazine*, no. 108, December 2006, pp. 3–5.) If this was the case, then it begs the question as to why Jim did not return immediately.

34. Reeves had cut these sides at Jim Beck's studio in Dallas.

35. "Wagon Load of Love" received some plays on KWKH.

36. See the informative sleeve notes by Joey Kent and Frank Page for the CD release *The Louisiana Hayride Archives Volume Four—Jim Reeves* (Music Mill Entertainment).

37. The subject's name was Penelope Pendance, otherwise known as "Penny Candy."

38. Leo Jackson, "My First Recording Session for Jim Reeves," *The Jim Reeves Fan Club Magazine*, no. 108, December 2006, p. 6. Slim Whitman actually only recorded one song in the following session, "You Have My Heart".

39. Jim Reeves's KWKH session details have been extracted from Arie Den Dulk, Kurt Rokitta, and Richard Weize, "Jim Reeves: The Discography," within the Bear Family box set, Jim Reeves, *Welcome to My World*. Jim made his last regular *Hayride* appearance in September 1955.

He returned a final time, in December 1958, as a guest star, by which time his ambition to be recognized as a ballad singer had been achieved through "Four Walls," a song he performed that night.

40. Duo of Jimmy Lee Fautherlee and "Country" Johnny Mathis.

41. "Release Me" was a country hit for several acts in 1954 but the more famous version came years later when English balladeer Englebert Humperdinck (the name was stolen from an Austrian composer after his real name, Gerry Dorsey, failed to make any impact) had a worldwide career-making hit with it.

42. Franks, *I Was There When It Happened*, p. 76. The musicians on the KWKH session were Dobber Johnson (fiddle), Sonny Harville (piano), Sonny Trammel (steel guitar), and A. J. Lewis (drums).

43. Mitchell Torok email to the author, 16 June 2006.

44. Escott, "Mitchell Torok," pp. 10, 17.

45. "Looking Back to See" made number eight on Billboard in June 1954.

46. A precise recording date is missing but it fell between October and November 1953.

47. Arie Den Dulk, interview with Ginny Wright, 17 July 1977, *The Jim Reeves Fan Club Magazine*, no. 104, November 2005, pp. 8–14. Ginny also recalled that whenever one of his singers protested at the high key he wanted songs recorded in, Fabor would respond by demanding an even higher register.

48. For full details of the controversy see Frank Page and Joey Kent, *Elvis: The Hayride Years, 1954–1956* (Chicago: JAT Publishing, 2004).

49. Horace Logan took the view that he rather than Frank Page had introduced Elvis to the world as he had emceed the CBS portion of the show.

50. Quoted in Beaty, "Musical Memories," p. 2.

51. Ibid, p. 2.

52. Ibid, p. 2.

53. Occasionally, as with Elvis, Sully was asked to cut demos. When the studio versions came out, they frequently sounded like the KWKH-generated demo, and sometimes not as good. This baffled Sully until one day he spoke with a major label producer who said that invariably the songs would be cut again for job security.

54. 15 December 1956.

55. The screaming was such that Elvis could not be heard in the coliseum—although he came across clearly over the air.

56. The explosion in the popularity of television also had a detrimental impact on the size of *Hayride* audiences.

57. Television was an area KWKH wanted to get into but FCC officials ruled against a license because the owners of KWKH also owned the local newspaper, the Shreveport *Times*, and they feared a monopoly would be created. Instead a television license was accorded to rival radio station KTBS.

58. Only two years later, RCA built a recording studio just a block away from Bradley's Barn (as it was known). The latter was sold to Columbia in 1962 and remained in operation until 1982. See entry on Owen Bradley in Barry McCloud, *Definitive Country: The Ultimate Encyclopedia of Country Music and Its Performers* (New York: Perigree, 1995).

59. Sully had dropped by Beck's studio while on vacation. Sonny James was recording, who was a friend of Sully's, and he introduced him to Jim. At this the latter went ballistic, berating Sully for "taking" money from him.

60. The Stones were in the habit of undertaking unofficial recording sessions when they were on the road. On this occasion, Sully did not complete the session because he wanted to go to the car races.

61. Overheard by the author at the Country Music Foundation where Walker was giving an interview. One of Walker's final appearances was at a *Hayride* reunion at the Municipal Auditorium where he gave the most outstanding vocal performance, notwithstanding the fact he was then in his seventies.

62. Johnny Horton, *The Early Years* (Bear Family Records, 1998).

63. Franks, foreword.

64. Franks, foreword.

65. Beaty, "Musical Memories," p. 2.

Beyond Country Music

—Tracey E. W. Laird

We reprint this sixth and final chapter of *Louisiana Hayride: Radio and Roots Music Along the Red River* as an end cap to the introduction—one looking forward from the *Hayride* where the other looked back. This piece highlights four musicians whose experiences in Shreveport during the post–World War II era—most of them closely associated with the *Hayride*—shaped their future professional lives as studio musicians, band members, and producers. The collective stories of D. J. Fontana, Jerry Kennedy, Joe Osborn, and James Burton stand as testimony that the importance of the *Hayride* did not end with the cessation of its regular broadcasts around 1960. Each of these men drew on instincts formed in Shreveport during an era when jive and R&B co-existed with country music on KWKH radio, when Shreveport's "Bossier strip" offered a steady and varied diet of live performance opportunities across genres, and when the *Hayride* left an enduring legacy for music in Shreveport, in the Ark-La-Tex, and in the nation at large.

> Shreveport was a great place to cut your teeth on music because there was so much going on.
>
> —Jerry Kennedy, musician and producer

On 16 October 1954 the *Louisiana Hayride* scheduled a guest appearance of nineteen-year-old Elvis Presley, calling himself "The Hillbilly Cat." From that moment, in the fertile ground of a KWKH radio show, a new sapling was successfully planted, one that conspicuously exposed its country roots. On this autumn night during the dawn of nuclear anxiety, no one could foresee the megaton explosion of popular music aimed at teenagers. The mostly white audience at Shreveport's Municipal Auditorium saw an unsung "cat" with herky-jerky legs sing a few quirky covers, including a high-octane version of Bill Monroe's bluegrass standard "Blue Moon of Kentucky" and a driving rendition of Arthur Crudup's rhythm-and-blues tune "That's All Right, Mama." He introduced his trio as the Blue Moon Boys, referring to the Monroe song or to the Rodgers and Hart tune "Blue Moon" they had played around with some, or to both.[1] To anyone there that night, it was just another Saturday evening at the *Hayride*.

The *Hayride* had a six-year history of taking chances on unproven artists with unique styles. It was a young show with a young staff, and its entrepreneurial producers always sought artists they thought might captivate and expand the audience, increasing both revenue and the program's stature as a prominent forum for country music entertainers. Thus, KWKH hoped to find in Presley another example of that which it consistently sought— a new artist with the distinct sound and the charisma to boost profit. What they got was a pivotal performer destined for a life and musical career that mixed triumph and tragedy in proportions extraordinary enough to inspire countless writers to reflect on his place and meaning in U.S. popular culture. They got a performer whose image and recordings between the years 1954 and 1958 represent a transformation of musical aesthetics on the *Hayride*, in country music at large, and within the whole society.

Presley's story on the *Hayride* reflects the snowballing of changes following World War II on both a national level and a local level in Shreveport. For U.S. culture as a whole, these changes culminated in the most dramatic social markers of the mid-to-late 1950s: the emergence of youth culture, the breakdown of legal race-based segregation, the transformation of media industries, and the rise of rock-and-roll. In ways both tangible and emblematic, Presley connects these same social forces to a generation of Shreveport musicians who, like him, grew up steeped in black and white music that came to them on phonograph records, radio, and through live performance. The stories of four famous sidemen who musically matured in Shreveport during the *Hayride* era form a critical counterpart to those of the *Hayride's* headliners from Hank Williams to Elvis Presley. These sidemen make it apparent that the dynamic musical atmosphere in post-war Shreveport fed on a rich local culture with at least a century-long history. Two of these players, D. J. Fontana and James Burton, share a direct connection to Presley, since they spent long portions of their careers in Presley's band. The other two, Joe Osborn and Jerry Kennedy, eventually brought the instincts they developed in postwar northwest

Louisiana to the newly dominant arena of recording studios. Through these musicians, the unique energy of their native region reached places even beyond the powerful reach of the KWKH radio signal.

Yet a mid-1950s Shreveport—like anywhere in the United States, especially the South—must be understood against the social back story of the postwar era. If it is true that Shreveport and other southern cities were hotbeds of mutual sharing between black and white musicians, it must be understood that these exchanges often crossed tempestuous rivers. These rivers broke their banks in the postwar United States. For African Americans, the 1950s was a decade when the gross social inequality and economic disparity that had defined their citizenship in the legacy of slavery looked to be a waking steppenwolf at the doors of the Supreme Court. Obversely, for many institutions of Euro-American power, the civil rights movement that emerged during the 1950s and threatened radical shifts of power constituted little more than a barbarian at the gate.

Throughout the postwar decade, the entire nation experienced the most radical social upheaval since the Civil War and the subsequent passing of the Thirteenth Amendment. Working-class blacks and whites migrated from the South to the North, and from the rural South to its urban centers. Suburbia began its crawl across the nation, slowly becoming the landscape of a new middle class. Pre-planned Levittown-styled communities appeared around cities, populated almost exclusively by young whites with a government-subsidized college degree, a newly expanded pocketbook, and a newly utopian image of an American social order.[2] Beneath the image, discontent rumbled softly as the bankruptcy of older frameworks for how gender and race dictated relationships between people became increasingly apparent. Women, many of whom had sensed new possibilities in pursuing college or gainful employment in industrial jobs vacated by drafted soldiers, experienced deep conflicts when, after the war, they were expected to resume domesticity. African Americans who had served in the military returned to their homes with a heightened sense of dissatisfaction and unwillingness to tolerate continuing racial inequalities.

Earlier in the same year Presley first performed on the *Hayride*, the Supreme Court challenged the established social order, particularly in the South, in its decision in the case of *Brown v. Board of Education*. The process began more than a decade before, through a series of cases that gradually overturned the 1896 *Plessy v. Ferguson* decision that legitimized racial segregation. In this case, which addressed Jim Crow seating on south Louisiana railroad cars, the Court legalized segregation by establishing the theoretical criterion of "separate but equal" facilities for blacks in the South. In reality, however, separate facilities were rarely close to equal. In the case of Shreveport in 1910, for example, 62 percent of the total 58,200 residents of its Caddo Parish were African American, but only 6.5 percent of the total value of Caddo Parish school property was dedicated to facilities for black students.[3]

In 1938, *Gaines v. Canada,* the Court ruled against Missouri, which maintained a law school for whites but not for blacks; rather, Missouri paid tuition for blacks to attend law school in a different state. The Court ordered Missouri to either build a separate facility for black law students or admit black students to the white school. In June 1950 two cases involving African Americans, George W. McLaurin in Oklahoma and Heman Sweatt in Texas, called into question the idea that separate could also be equal, based on intangible benefits such as intellectual exchange with other students, tradition, and prestige offered by the graduate programs at the University of Oklahoma and the University of Texas. The watershed, however, was May 1954 *Brown v. Board of Education,* which unequivocally affirmed that the racial segregation of educational facilities rendered them necessarily unequal.[4] In May 1955 the Court issued a dictum that school desegregation should proceed "with all deliberate speed."

It was not incidental that the phenomenon of rock-and-roll emerged during a period when the legal strictures of segregation in the South were breaking down. Presley's early recordings and performances, particularly those during his subsequent year-and-a-half stint with the *Hayride,* assume paramount significance within the context of *Brown* v. *Board of Education.* The watershed court decision became a gestalt for the erosion of a racially determined social order. Likewise, popular music has a foreshadowing moment in Presley's *Hayride* debut, when the tensions underlying the long and tangled history of musical exchange between southern blacks and whites began coming to a head. As a southern white musician, Presley did more than appropriate or mimic African American music. He fused the southern musical aesthetics in which he had been immersed since childhood— country, rhythm-and-blues, pop, gospel—into a hybrid musical identity that was equally indebted to them all. On the *Hayride,* Elvis Presley performed country songs like "Just Because" by the Shelton Brothers (recorded by them as the Lone Star Cowboys in 1933) and "I'll Never Let You Go (Little Darlin')," a 1941 song by Jimmy Wakely. He also performed rhythm-and-blues songs like "Mystery Train" by Junior Parker, and "Good Rockin' Tonight" by Wynonnie Harris. Presley performed "I Don't Care If the Sun Don't Shine," originally written for the Disney animated feature *Cinderella* by Mack David, and the Rodgers and Hart "Blue Moon."[5]

The Pelican Wildcats played string band music in and around Shreveport in the late 1920s, including a show on KWKH competitor KRMD. Photo courtesy of Rebel State Historic Site, Marthaville, Louisiana.

Conference program for the Southern American Music and Shreveport Conference, sponsored by the FAME Foundation and funded in part by the Louisiana Endowment for the Humanities, 2002. Permission given by Maggie and Alton Warwick.

The Municipal Auditorium in December
2006. Photo courtesy of Tracey E. W. Laird.

The Stage of Stars Museum opened in the
summer of 2004 to commemorate the musical
history of Shreveport's Municipal Auditorium.
Photo courtesy of Tracey E. W. Laird.

R. C. Grigg Family Band, most likely around the time of the first Memphis recordings. Photo courtesy of Monty Brown.

Louisiana Hayride cast shot in 1952. Photo courtesy of LSU Shreveport Archives—Noel Memorial Library, Joey Kent Collection.

The Cox Family performing at the 2004 Jimmie Davis Memorial Homecoming. Photo courtesy of Susan Roach.

Record label for Hiter Colvin's release on Montgomery Ward. Photo courtesy of Kip Lornell.

Jimmie Davis with his late 1930s band that broadcast over KWKH. Photo courtesy of Kevin Fontenot.

Jimmie Davis in a promotional shot for Decca Records, ca. 1940. Photo courtesy of Kevin Fontenot.

KWKH Program Director and Hayride emcee Horace
Logan in July 1957. Photo courtesy of LSU Shreveport
Archives—Noel Memorial Library.

Bob Sullivan returned to the mixing board as sound
engineer for the Louisiana Hayride Reunion show,
"One More Ride" at the Municipal Auditorium in late
June 2003. Photo courtesy of Tracey E. W. Laird.

A young Jerry Kennedy onstage at the Louisiana Hayride in the late 1950s.
Photo courtesy of LSU Shreveport Archives—Noel Memorial Library.

Statues of Elvis Presley and James Burton flank the entrance to the Municipal
Auditorium (December 2006). Photo courtesy of Tracey E. W. Laird.

Moreover, Elvis Presley's music and his presentation stood as an overt expression of the social and cultural implications that *Brown v. Board of Education* portended. In sound, in repertoire, and in posture, Elvis Presley of the mid-to-late 1950s represented nothing short of a desegregation of musical aesthetics. This signaled a degree of desegregation of the music business itself, as companies marketed him and rock-and-roll artists like Little Richard, Fats Domino, Carl Perkins, and Jerry Lee Lewis to teenagers across racial lines. But the implications extended far deeper than a new market category somewhere between white country and black rhythm-and-blues. Presley's presentation inadvertently set off an earthquake. Although he was not the first musician to manifest the rock-and-roll impulse, he touched a cultural nerve as no one had before him.

Two years before Presley appeared on the *Hayride*, a moderately successful Western swing bandleader and country music disc jockey from New Jersey named Bill Haley recorded the song now considered the first white rock-and-roll record. In 1952, still known as Bill Haley and the Saddlemen, his band recorded a 1949 rhythm-and-blues hit by Jimmy Preston and his Prestonians, "Rock the Joint." The flip side of this record was "Icy Heart," based on the Hank Williams song of the year before, "Cold, Cold Heart." The following year, 1953, Haley changed the name of his band to Bill Haley and Haley's Comets, and became famous for both his recording of "Shake, Rattle and Roll," written by Charles Calhoun and originally recorded by rhythm-and-blues singer Big Joe Turner, and of "(We're Gonna) Rock around the Clock." The latter song won prominence in the 1955 movie *Blackboard Jungle* and sold more than twenty-five million copies.[6] "Rock around the Clock" became famous for setting the tempo and mood for rock-and-roll music to come, despite its origins (like Williams's "Lovesick Blues") in Tin Pan Alley.[7]

To a level that alarmed some onlookers, Haley excited audiences just as pop crooners like Frank Sinatra before him. However, his music ignited neither the hysteria of fans nor the obloquy of critics that Presley sparked, both of which were unprecedented in degree. By the time Presley left the *Hayride,* headlines read "Beware Elvis Presley" in newspapers across the country and warnings appeared in *America* magazine in June 1956; his effigy was burned in Nashville; the East Berlin newspaper *Neues Deutsch-land* called him a "Cold War Weapon" against communism and a NATO conspiracy to infiltrate East German society.[8] Presley's sexuality and the frenzied reaction it evoked among teenage girls only exacerbated the disquiet he inspired in many adults. In the context of postwar America, that disquiet seems to have less to do with sexuality, per se, and more to do with the tempestuous social changes occurring at the same time. More specifically, in the context of white southern resistance to African American demands for full civil rights, Presley's stage persona and his music conveyed a rebellion of manners through an intuitive blend of black and white styles. This was the quintessence of rockabilly—its definitive musical integration—and, for this, it caused a stir.

As a potent manifestation of the broader rock-and-roll phenomenon, rockabilly was the music of the emerging youth culture, which strove to create new means of expression—in dress, attitude, patois, and soundtrack—that would distinguish teenagers from the world of adults. For white teenagers, this involved the open embrace of aesthetics identified with African American culture, which entered wider cultural circulation after the war. Beginning in the late 1940s, radio and recordings offered broader access to the music of African American performers. At the same time, white teenagers of the post–World War II era had money to spend on entertainment as had no generation before them. Much of this money went to purchasing records. A whole new market of young record-buyers snatched up releases by white rockabillies and by black rhythm-and-blues artists. Among whites, young musicians first tapped into the rich resources of rhythm-and-blues records in the late 1940s, but that interest spread during the early 1950s to white teenagers in general.[9]

This process fit into the same postwar cultural phenomenon that Norman Mailer pondered in his essay on the late 1950s stereotyped figure, "the hipster." In "The White Negro: Superficial Reflections on the Hipster," originally published in 1957, Mailer characterizes the hipster as a racially hybridized individual, born when "the bohemian and the juvenile delinquent came face-to-face with the Negro."[10] In Mailer's view, the hipster faced the new challenges of the postwar world head-on, when the larger society suffered from "a collective failure of nerve."[11] Elvis Presley's *Louisiana Hayride* debut occurred three years before Mailer published his portrayal of a phenomenon he observed largely in New York's Greenwich Village. Taken out of its East Coast context, Mailer's prose could easily have described the early performances of Presley—suggesting hedonism, youth culture, and African American culture—in the context of a white country music radio barn dance in Shreveport.

The manifestation of this hybrid aesthetic that took place among southern white youth took on the name "rockabilly," coined around the mid-1950s for the obvious mixing of elements from country or hillbilly music with, as country music historian Bill Malone puts it, "rocking" black music.[12] In June 1956 the term appeared in the lyrics to Gene Vincent's first release, "Be-Bop-A-Lula," and, later that month, in print as a description of a new release by Ruckus Tyler in a *Billboard* review column, "Reviews of New C&W Records."[13] Rockabilly music existed before then, however, the product of musically fecund environments like Shreveport, where white country musicians could incorporate the energy from African American rhythm-and-blues into country music. It was then a musical impulse without a name. During Presley's *Hayride,* tenure, contemporary Shreveport newspaper writers wrestled to find adequate descriptors of Presley's "unusual singing style" or "wriggling style of song delivery" or the "unique musical arrangements" of his band. Shreveport *Times* writer Pericles Alexander described him in March 1956 as the "twenty-one-year-old guitarist-singer who straddles the fence as a purveyor of both country and western songs and the type of ballads you expect to emanate from the larnyx [*sic*] of Perry Como, Sinatra, or Der Bingle."[14]

Even as Shreveport journalists groped for words to describe it, rockabilly's most striking characteristics—including backbeat rhythm, slap bass, prominent electric guitar, instrumental solo breaks, and spontaneous whoops and hollers—had direct precedents within country music tradition. For one, attention to and influence from contemporary black music extended to the genre's commercial beginnings in the 1920s and long before. But the musical energy and onstage intensity that distinguished rockabilly had forerunners as well, even on the *Hayride.* One of the best examples is the family act known as the Maddox Brothers and Rose, whose long career included *Hayride* cast membership for parts of 1953 and 1954. During these periods the group worked out of Shreveport, with a daily KWKH radio show sponsored by a Chicago company selling baby chicks.[15] Before coming to Shreveport, the Maddox family, originally from Alabama, had hitchhiked and jumped boxcars to California, where they spent several years working as migrant fruit pickers. They began performing music and won such local acclaim that they soon pursued entertainment full time, creating a high-energy, colorful stage act. In elaborate sequined costumes, they delighted crowds with spontaneous antics, comedy bits, and brassy singing by sister Rose.

Their sound foreshadowed rockabilly in the melodic guitar work by Roy Nichols and the slapped-bass technique of Fred Maddox.[16] Music writer Nick Tosches, citing in particular their late 1940s version of Jimmie Rodgers's "Blue Yodel No. 8" titled "New Muleskinner Blues," comments that the group "recorded stuff that not only rocked, but also contained many of the vocal fireworks—yelps, screams, howls—that became watermarks of rockabilly."[17] Elvis Presley admired their showmanship and their flashy costumes.

As Rose Maddox recalled in an interview with country music historian John
Rumble:

> We was backstage there [at the *Hayride*], and the boys had their jackets to these
> pink costumes hanging in a room . . . and we went back there and Elvis . . . had
> one of the boy's jackets on, looking in the mirror, just so proud. You know, he
> said, "One of these days, I'm going to have me a suit like this." And Mama came
> back there and seen him with that on and she made him pull it off. She didn't
> want nobody else wearing their clothes.[18]

In both their sound and their flamboyance, the Maddox Brothers and Rose
presaged many of the future qualities that distinguished rockabilly.

The Maddox Brothers and Rose continued a distinctly rowdy tradition
long part of country music at the same time they anticipated the mid-1950s
musical transformation. The tradition that engendered Jimmie Davis's ribald, sometimes downright dirty songs of the early 1930s found its mid-1940s
and early 1950s manifestation in the style known as honky-tonk. Rockabilly,
as a hallmark of the postwar atmosphere of accelerated cultural interchange,
exploded and exploited this raucous tradition in country music, just as it drew
from the characteristic bawdiness of rhythm-and-blues. Rockabilly epitomized
in music the same breakdown of aesthetic borders across racial boundaries
that Mailer portrayed in his late-1950s hipster.

In a dramatic way, Presley's debut on Shreveport's *Hayride* stands as a pivot
point where the natural extension of a long tradition made a sudden abrupt shift
toward a new musical paradigm. Like several other southern cities—Memphis,
New Orleans, Atlanta, Dallas, Houston, St. Louis, Kansas City—Shreveport had
a tradition of white and black musicians listening to and borrowing from one
another. During the late 1940s and early 1950s, this dialogue became national.
Cultural exchange across racial lines accelerated and intensified, spurred on by
records and radio, in a way that permanently altered conceptions of popular
music in the United States. Shreveport presents this process in microcosm at the
same time the live music and records broadcast over station KWKH helped to
push it forward.

Records sales to a growing, enthusiastic, and youthful audience during the postwar era led to the success of a number of independent labels that
had up until then barely kept afloat. The result was upheaval in the record
industry as a whole, which only a few years before had been dominated by a
handful of big companies.[19] A glut of small postwar independent labels, like

Chess, Modern, Specialty, Imperial, and Sittin' In With Records, captured an unprecedented wealth of blues and rhythm-and-blues by African American musicians. Besides being a boon to black audiences, young white musicians now more than ever took these records home and studied them, unconstrained by the ubiquitous borders—social, political, and especially in the South, legal.

Many of these small labels depended on a less formalized, less centralized model of product distribution than the bigger companies. Radio stations like KWKH played an important role in getting these records into the hands of young consumers. For instance, during the early 1950s Shreveport's KWKH began broadcasting *Stan's Record Review,* sponsored by local music store entrepreneur Stan Lewis and hosted by Frank "Gatemouth" Page.[20] Lewis had opened his record shop in 1948 on Shreveport's downtown Texas Street and, from the beginning, built a symbiotic relationship between his business and KWKH. Lewis purchased time for a radio show that sold records on KWKH and eventually expanded to KTHS in Little Rock, Arkansas. As he recalled:

> Frank Page did the show on KWKH. We had a program on which we sold records by mail. So I would program and tell him what to play— I'd make a list every night. And we would have, like, six records for $3.49—the same way that they do today on TV with the big artists you see on TV . . . I started with fifteen minutes, and then I went to thirty and then to an hour.[21]

Lewis's mail-order records and radio shows became an important avenue for young white musicians across the region to absorb African American music, as well as experiment with new styles and new sounds.

The same could be said of the rhythm-and-blues disc jockey shows that began airing after the war all over the South. Beginning in the late 1940s, *Hayride* announcer Ray Bartlett, calling himself "Groovie Boy," spun the newly introduced single-song 45-rpm records in nightly KWKH disc jockey shows called *In the Groove* or *Groovie's Boogie.*[22] *Like* many southern stations of the postwar decade, KWKH juxtaposed its rhythm-and-blues with a variety of other music, particularly country music on the still-popular Saturday night barn dance shows. A generation of future professional musicians from Shreveport, like guitarist James Burton and musician-producer Jerry Kennedy, developed their musical ears by tuning into both the *Louisiana Hayride* and Bartlett's rhythm-and-blues disc shows. This juxtaposition of the *Louisiana Hayride* and *Groovie's Boogie* on KWKH speaks volumes about the postwar rise of rock-and-roll. And the iconic moment of Presley's debut comes out of this intensified mingling of white and black music on the airwaves.

A few overlapping, sometimes competing stories account for Presley's first appearance on the *Hayride*. Sam Phillips at Sun Records in Memphis had recorded the covers of Monroe and Crudup during the week after Independence Day in 1954.[23] Both cuts showed promise, generating a positive response from Memphis radio audiences right away. Phillips looked around for ways to promote his label's young artist. On 18 July Phillips called Bob Neal, a prominent local disc jockey who hosted an early morning country radio show called the *High Noon Round-up* on Memphis station WMPS. Neal also did booking and promotions in the area.[24] Neal had put together a show that featured *Louisiana Hayride* headliners Slim Whitman, who was riding the success of "Indian Love Call," "Rose Marie," and "Secret Love," and Billy Walker, whose recording of "Thank You for Calling" had just entered the top ten on country charts. As Walker recalled it, Neal approached them before their scheduled show at the Overton Band Shell in Memphis on 30 July:

> Bob Neal came to me and Slim and said, "I've got this kid here. Would you mind if I put him on for a couple of songs?" And I said, . . . "Well if he's good enough for you, I guess he's good enough for us." And so I watched this kid. . . He knocked the crowd out. We got back the next week and I was in Horace Logan's office talking about Elvis Presley. I got the kid's phone number. And I was talking to Horace about him and Slim walked in about that time and Slim said, "Yeah, but he's got some kind of funny name." And I said, "Yeah, his name is Elvis Presley." So I gave Horace his phone number and Horace called him up and gave him an audition shot to be down on the *Hayride*.[25]

Logan's own recollection likewise includes the connection with Whitman and Walker.

According to Tillman Franks, Thomas Clinton "T. Tommy" Cutrer, singer and country music disc jockey on Shreveport's station KCIJ at the time, played a Presley record on his show. The sound caught Franks's attention and, as he recalled, "I called him up and I said, 'T., boy, that record by that black boy that you're playing is unreal.' He said, 'Tillman, he's not black, he's a white boy and Sam Phillips has got him. He got [*sic*] a funny name.'"[26] At that time, Franks both managed and played bass for a *Hayride* duet known as Jimmy and Johnny (Jimmy Lee Fautheree and "Country" Johnny Mathis). Jimmy and Johnny wanted to play a lucrative gig in Carlsbad, New Mexico, on an upcoming

Saturday night, but Horace Logan hesitated to free them of their *Hayride* commitment. As Franks continued:

> I said, "Well, I'll get the boy with the funny name." He said, "You can't get him."
> I said, "Well I'll call him up." And I didn't have a phone and I called him from
> [bandleader/booking agent] Pappy Covington's office. Told Sam who I was and
> I said I'm in Pappy Covington's office. He called Pappy. Pappy handed me the
> phone. . . . That's the way he come [*sic*].[27]

In the meantime, Sam Phillips had arranged with *Grand Ole Opry* manager Jim Denny for Presley to appear as a guest in early October. Presley and his fellow band members, guitarist Scotty Moore and bassist Bill Black, performed the two songs to a lukewarm reception from the audience and left Nashville feeling defeated. On the bright side, they would play a guest spot on *the Louisiana Hayride* in only a couple of weeks. Regardless of the precise circumstances leading to the *Hayride* invitation, Presley's trio performed with enough success that they entered into a one-year KWKH contract three weeks later. Still a minor, Presley signed along with his parents on 6 November 1954. Before long, the show's producers began placing Presley's group at the end of *Hayride* performances to avoid upstaging other performers. Bob Neal, who had become Presley's manager in early 1955, negotiated the bandleader's second one-year contract with the *Hayride* in September 1955 (to become effective the coming November). By that time, Presley's salary raised from the union scale of $18 per appearance to $200 per appearance, with a side agreement that stipulated a penalty of $400 per show for missed performances beyond the allotted five.[28]

In March 1956 Presley adopted Colonel Tom Parker as his new exclusive manager. Parker bought out the second year of his client's contract for $10,000 the next month, with the stipulation that Presley return to perform a charity concert at Shreveport's Youth Building (later renamed the Hirsch Coliseum) before the year's end. Presley's final Shreveport performance took place on 15 December 1956, and the proceeds of the concert aided the local YMCA.[29] The ride cymbals crashing and tom-toms pounding in time with Presley's farewell burlesque on KWKH made the performance a watermark for Shreveport's *Louisiana Hayride* in the story of rock-and-roll. According to Logan, female fans after the show mangled his Mercury automobile climbing onto it to get into the high windows of the coliseum's backstage area. Inside the coliseum, Logan admonished the teenagers leaving en masse for a glimpse of their hero to keep their seats for upcoming acts, famously assuring them: "Elvis has left the building."[30]

Ironically, Presley's ascendance to fame on the *Louisiana Hayride* also marks the beginning of the show's gradual decline. According to some Hayriders, the Saturday-night crowds at Shreveport's Municipal Auditorium began to look and act differently after Presley. For one thing, more teenagers attended, particularly girls who screamed and rushed the stage, often even before the music began. Jimmy C. Newman cites the resulting audience shrinkage as a reason he sought a position at the *Opry*: "When he [Presley] came there, the older audience, a lot of them didn't come back to the *Hayride* because it was such a change, you know, to a young audience. But once he left, the younger audience left and the older ones didn't come back much."[31] Pianist Sonny Harville, who performed for years in Slim Whitman's band and in the *Hayride* staff band, remembers Presley's impact as less immediate. He felt that the show suffered more from attempts by the *Hayride* management to replace Presley with young singers of similar appeal: "Elvis is a phenomenon and that was all right.... The country people could take him, but when they got ... too many Elvis imitators, the country folks just quit coming."[32]

In this way, Presley represents a cultural phenomenon that shook the country music industry to its core and resonated far outside the region of Shreveport. Even at the *Opry* where Presley never again performed, ticket sales decreased by almost 44 percent during the period 1953–1960.[33] Country music as an industry eventually responded to the threat of rock-and-roll by adding mellow-toned choruses and swelling strings, and de-emphasizing the fiddle and steel guitar in a cross-over country-pop style intended to have broader appeal—the "Nashville Sound." The *Hayride* tried to do as it always had and find the next shining talent. After Presley, other rockabillies appeared on the *Hayride* stage, but never filled his blue suede shoes.

Rockabilly luminary and native Louisianan Jerry Lee Lewis actually auditioned for the show, but was turned down. As Sonny Harville recounted with some bemusement:

> Before Jerry Lee Lewis was known, he came in to the *Hayride* and went to Horace Logan who was boss of the *Hayride* at that time and asked Horace for a job playing the piano.... Horace sent him to me, 'cause I was playing piano at that time on the *Hayride*, to listen to him and I told Horace that he wouldn't work out. He's too show but no music, you know. Couldn't play well enough to be on the staff band.[34]

The Lewis anecdote attests that *the Hayride's* timely instincts about musical flair were not always infallible. At the same time, it points to the dilemma rockabilly brought to the *Hayride*, as well as to white southern roots musicians in general. How would a white country musician, or a white country barn dance for that matter, carry on in a world where older ways of understanding music—black and white, race and hillbilly—were proving less and less adequate? Either during or after Presley's tenure, George Jones, Johnny Cash, and Johnny Horton upheld the popular momentum of the *Hayride* just as the *Hayride* searched for direction. Each of these performers reckoned the impact of rockabilly in different ways around this period. Yet, as noteworthy as they were in sustaining the show's standing, the *Hayride* never again regained the edge it had in late 1940s and early 1950s country music.

Other prominent rockabilly performers appeared during the late 1950s and specifically appealed to the newer teenage audience, including Tommy Sands and, most notably, Bob Luman. While Luman later won notoriety between 1965 and his untimely death in 1978 as a country-pop singer on the *Grand Ole Opry*, his early musical style from recordings between 1955 and 1957 reflected his immersion in the rockabilly sounds of the day and the singular impact of Elvis Presley on white southern teenagers of his generation. After seeing Presley perform at a *Louisiana Hayride* package show in his hometown of Kilgore, Texas, as Luman put it, "That's the last time I tried to sing like Webb Pierce or Lefty Frizzell."[35] Shortly thereafter, Luman won a talent show in Tyler, Texas (judged by Johnny Horton, Johnny Cash, and Carl Perkins), and subsequently joined the *Hayride* in 1956, filling a vacancy left by Cash. He appealed to a teenage audience with his rakish charisma and gutsy energy. On the strength of his *Hayride* success, Luman also appeared, along with singer David Houston and guitarist James Burton, in the teen flick *Carnival Rock*. Following the film, he gained a regular spot on the *Los Angeles Town Hall Party*, the same show that had earlier in the decade featured Johnny Horton.

But the biggest and farthest reaching story in the *Hayride's* shaping of popular music after the mid-1950s lies not in its stars. For at the same time its status as "Cradle of the Stars" vis-à-vis Nashville slowly slipped away, the *Hayride* nurtured a group of influential sidemen, players who typify the postwar generation of young southern white musicians with one foot in country and the other in rhythm-and-blues. Among this generation, Dominic "D.J." Fontana, James Burton, Joe Osborn, and Jerry Kennedy were all born in and around Shreveport during the era when the Lone Star Cowboys traveled between KWKH and other well-positioned southern radio stations. Members of the same generation as Presley (born between 1931 and 1940) they share his immersion in diverse musical influences.[36] These musicians grew up during the age when radio enriched their lives with a daily dose of music from their own cultural milieu as well as distant sounds they might never have heard otherwise. All four musically matured during the time when the *Louisiana Hayride* carved out a permanent place in the annals of pop music. Each one of these players left Shreveport to achieve high levels of success in the music business. Common threads bind together the stories of their developing musicianship, including KWKH and the *Hayride*, Presley, Luman, and Ricky Nelson, and the power of records, radio, and live musical performance from the mid-1940s through the early 1950s.

Radio echoes throughout their early memories. Jerry Glen Kennedy, a guitarist, record executive, and producer born in Shreveport in 1940, soaked up live country music from the family radio as a child. As he recalled:

> My first memories are of country music and a guy named Harmie Smith on KWKH. He had a daily radio show at . . . 4: 15 in the afternoon. And I was four or five years old and I remember that I would have my mom call me because I couldn't miss that. I wanted to be in the house listening to that whenever it came on.[37]

Bassist Joe Osborn, born in 1937, also recalled the singularity of radio during his childhood, since his family did not own many phonograph records. When he began playing guitar around age twelve after his uncle showed him a few chords, live country radio took on new significance. Eminent guitar picker Chet Atkins in particular caught his ear and, as Osborn recalled, he would "listen to the radio and wait until Chet came on and play along."[38] On Saturday nights, he tuned into the radio barn dances, especially the *Opry* and the *Louisiana Hayride* where, in the early 1950s, he especially remembers hearing guest appearances of Texas honky-tonker Lefty Frizzell. The airwaves likewise brought Chet Atkins to another developing Shreveport musical legend, James Burton. Born in 1939, he picked up the guitar at age thirteen, and quickly absorbed not only the licks of Atkins but also the sense of timing and musical phrasing of early 1950s country singers like Williams, Frizzell, and Carl Smith. Explaining the influence of country music on his budding guitar style, Burton once said: "Also, I really admired the way people like Hank Williams and Lefty Frizzell sang, and I got into their style of singing and overall feeling. I thought that this was how a lead instrument should treat a line—like a lyric—and that was always my approach to playing a solo."[39]

During the same period in his early development, Burton tuned in to the afternoon and late-night rhythm-and-blues shows on KWKH and other stations where he heard the likes of Lightnin' Hopkins, Muddy Waters, and Howlin' Wolf. Enthused by all the sounds, black and white, that poured through the radio speaker, Burton bought records and listened intently, learning new licks and incorporating them into his own playing. Kennedy too discovered early on the sounds of rhythm-and-blues artists like Muddy Waters, Fats Domino, and the Platters via radio shows like the one "Daddy-O Hot Rod" broadcast over the Shreveport station KOKA, as well as Groovie Boy's show on KWKH. As Kennedy grew up, his musical palette continued to expand and by the late 1940s and early 1950s, his ear bent to pop artists like Jo Stafford, Patti Page, and Joni James, as well as close-harmony quartets like the Four Aces and the Ink Spots. All of this music shaped his developing sensibilities from early in his childhood in the same way that blues, string bands, parlor songs, and hymn-singing shaped Jimmie Davis's style from a half-century before. They formed the foundation of his later success in the music business.

Drummer D. J. Fontana also recalls phonograph discs of his youth. Born in 1931, the oldest of the four Shreveport sidemen particularly remembers the Stan Kenton, Woody Herman, and other big band jazz records of his cousin A. J. Lewis. Lewis, an avid collector and later Shreveport music store owner, also owned a distinguishing asset in the local community, a complete set of drums that he encouraged the aspiring musician to use. Fontana gained much of his early technical skill from his band director at the local Fair Park High School. But even more critical to his developing proficiency were the opportunities for live performance abundant in Shreveport during the postwar era. By the time he reached his teens, Fontana worked in local nightclubs like the Carousel, usually with trios who specialized in Dixieland and standards like "How High the Moon" and "Stardust."[40]

The live musical contexts that cultivated Fontana's talent included both informal jam sessions and paid gigs, most often in a nightclub area across the Red River from Shreveport known as the "Bossier strip." Like Fannin Street had been earlier in the century, the Bossier strip was a thriving music scene in mid-century. As Fontana remembered, "Shreveport had a lot of clubs. Bossier, that strip there was just one club after another, you know. They must have had fifteen clubs, it was like a small Vegas is what it was."[41] A musician like Fontana could find plenty of work in Shreveport during the late 1940s and early 1950s. The key to success in this environment was flexibility across a wide range of musical genres. Fontana described the blossoming of the music scene and the demands of playing local clubs:

> Back then they had an influx of musicians. . . . They just started showing up from everywhere, mostly out of the South. They were out of Mississippi, Alabama, and south Louisiana. And some great players come out of there, whether it be country, whether it be blues, pop. You know, back then—you worked a club, you had to play a mixture. You just couldn't play country or rock or whatever.[42]

Eventually, this local music club scene beckoned all four future sidemen and played a formative role in the directions their talents would take them. While still in high school, for instance, Burton fine-tuned his instincts in . these area clubs—for which he needed a special underage permit—building a reputation around town as a guitarist of unique ability. Likewise, Joe Osborn played in local clubs, mostly around the Bossier strip, beginning at age fourteen or fifteen. There, he first gained experience with the commingling of country and rhythm-and-blues music that would prove essential to his later success. Like Fontana, Osborn recalled the liveliness of the club scene and the music that resonated together there:

> At that time [the Bossier strip] was really booming. It was like just alive, you know, wall-to-wall clubs and music. You can still see some of those old places boarded up and see what it was, or what it must have been. It all [country and rock-and-roll music] sort of gelled. . . . You could go ahead and do your old country standards but maybe with more drums, you know.[43]

Shreveport's 1950s music scene emerged from the same dynamic postwar southern musical atmosphere that wrought rockabilly. But while the area's clubs mingled music styles in a way akin to the era's radio, the clubs accomplished what radio never could. These nightclubs became sites for face-to-face interaction between black and white musicians themselves. In Shreveport clubs and along the Bossier strip, the racial constraints of the segregated South loosened among musicians much as they had on Fannin Street when Leadbelly played its brothels. As Fontana recalled his experience:

> If we had a jam session, you'd call everybody you knew. And they'd show up . . . black, white, . . . they didn't care. If you played, come on, bring your horn, bring your drums, whatever. We'll all have a good time. Sometimes we'd play all night.

Different songs, you know. Guys would sing, everybody'd just work together, have a good time and go home. We used to do that about once or twice a month.[44]

This open attitude among musicians extended to paid gigs as well. Fontana further reflected upon his experiences during the postwar era:

> Amongst musicians we had no problems. We could play and have a good time. I think it was just the people, the people who wanted to be segregated. But we didn't care. If the guy could play his horn or play saxophone or whatever, well, hey man, come on and play something tonight. We'll be at such-and-such a place. They'd show up and nobody would bother them. We'd go to a black club maybe and play and they wouldn't bother us cause we were with that band.[45]

Fontana's experiences suggest that the status as a musician sometimes eased the turbulent waters that separated whites and blacks during the era.

Jerry Kennedy also absorbed music from African American contemporaries, not only as a fellow musician but as a member of the audience. As a teenager, Kennedy attended shows of rhythm-and-blues artists who traveled to the area, particularly at a local black nightspot on Shreveport's Texas Street known as Club 66. As Kennedy described it, the African American club allowed whites to attend these shows, but circumscribed their participation:

> I remember that they had a little cage, a glassed-in place where white people could go in. Sort of like the opposite of the way it was during segregation down there with theaters and stuff like that. It was a place set aside. . . . I saw Jimmy Reed there. That's where I saw Bobby Blue Bland. If I'm not mistaken, I probably saw Chuck Berry, Bo Diddley, for sure. But anyway, there was only room for like twelve people to get into this little space.[46]

Even more than Presley's *Hayride* association, the live musical experiences of Fontana and Kennedy point to a long-standing, yet constrained, tradition of cross-racial interaction in the South just as they form a live context for the postwar acceleration of musical exchange that transformed U.S. culture.

Along with the Shreveport club scene, station KWKH and its *Louisiana Hayride* form a meaningful thread in the experiences of these four sidemen. Osborn's *Hayride* connection was the most peripheral of the four, extending past his Saturday nights by the radio to occasional attendance at a live *Hayride* show in the Municipal Auditorium. Osborn recalls one particularly memorable night when he attended the *Hayride* with a friend who knew Presley, as well as Fontana, then a member of the staff band. As Osborn described:

> I met Scotty back in the dressing room, and he showed me the lick he played on "That's All Right, Mama." See, these guys were new too, you know what I mean? Elvis had had his first hit, but he wasn't the star yet. They were accessible. You could go in and meet them and sit and talk with them. "How'd you do your lick?" you know.[47]

For Osborn, the backstage interchange counts as a singular moment of inspiration with one of rockabilly's guitar icons. For the others, the *Hayride* formed a regular laboratory for their training. Fontana, Burton, and Kennedy each served apprenticeships as members of the *Hayride* staff band. In different ways, these experiences pointed the way for their eventual professional accomplishments.

Fontana's *Hayride* association determined the direction of his musical career in a decisive way. Following a stint in the Army, Fontana returned to Shreveport where he helped out in his parents' grocery store, acquired his own set of drums, played in clubs around town, and joined the *Hayride* house band. As staff drummer for several years during the early 1950s, Fontana backed many of the artists who were regulars or guests on Saturday nights. True to the *Hayride*'s typical stylistic berth, it made drums available for any group who wished to use them. At first, in Fontana's words, "most of the artists didn't want me to play behind them anyway." Throughout the early 1950s, drums steadily gained acceptance as a standard part of a country band, and this transformation played out on the *Hayride*. As Fontana tells it, "Gradually one or two of them said, 'Yeah you wanna play—just [play] real quiet.' And pretty soon it got to where I had to work behind everybody. They got used to the idea."[48] The audience grew accustomed to the addition just as the players did.

On Saturday nights at the *Hayride*, Fontana learned the secret of playing drums in country music, which was to use quiet, subtle brush strokes. This introduction to country drumming put Fontana behind the likes of Jim Reeves (with whom he toured), Mitchell Torok, Johnny Horton, Webb Pierce, Faron Young, Lefty Frizzell, and Slim Whitman. The experience served him well in years to come, as an in-demand Nashville studio musician with an instinctive understanding of when to keep his instrument in a subdued, supporting role and when to assert his presence. Fontana later recorded with Tommy James, Patti Page, Porter Wagoner, Dolly Parton, Webb Pierce, Floyd Cramer,

Nat Stuckey, Red Sovine, and many others. However, even more than a portent of his future Nashville success, Fontana's role as staff drummer was a harbinger of the transformations to come on the *Hayride*, as well as within country music as a whole. By allowing an instrument fundamental to rock-and-roll, the same instrument decisively absent from the *Opry* stage, the *Hayride* set in place a key variable in unleashing the pent-up energy of rockabilly. In more concrete terms, the *Hayride*'s openness to drums led to a fortuitous meeting between Fontana and Presley.

According to the drummer's recollections, Tillman Franks and Pappy Covington, both of whom had booking offices on the KWKH floor of Shreveport's Commercial National Bank building, called Fontana into their office one morning to listen to Presley's first single, "That's All Right, Mama," which had also been playing on local radio stations. They asked Fontana if he would like to play with the group when they came to town. In Fontana's words, "I said, 'Well, they don't need me.' They had such a unique sound. I said, 'I'll just make them sound bad,' you know."[49] Not long after, Scotty Moore approached Fontana about their trio's interest in adding drums and suggested they try working up a couple of tunes. The four musicians gathered in one of the dressing rooms at the Municipal Auditorium to experiment. Fontana described his approach early on:

> The secret was not to get in the way. Let them do what they do well. I just played a brush, real quiet and easy, . . . later on I played more, but early on the sound they had with that slapped bass was so unique. I didn't want to clutter that up. Maybe that's why I got the job. Simplicity, you know.[50]

Fontana began playing regularly with the band on the *Hayride*, as well as on tours booked through east Texas and southern Arkansas. In spring of 1955, Fontana officially joined Presley's band, an association that lasted until 1969.

Ultimately, the restraint required by most *Hayride* bandleaders was not what the Blue Moon trio was looking for. Perhaps this fact encouraged Fontana to accept Presley's invitation since, as David Sanjek points out, country music has generally neglected its instrumental virtuosos like Fontana, with the notable exception of bluegrass.[51] For his part, Fontana offered the key element that pushed the Blue Moon trio to a new level of energy. Fellow drummer Levon Helm (of the group known as The Band) once described Fontana's contribution to Presley's band, recalling a performance he witnessed in Arkansas during the mid-1950s where Fontana was "building up to the solos, riding the solos in and riding them out again. He had incredible technique and fast hands . . . he played like a big-band drummer—full throttle. Now Elvis had a real foundation, some architecture, and he made the most of it. D.J. set Elvis *free*."[52]

Throughout their long association, on approximately 460 RCA recordings with Elvis, Fontana employs the full range of his drum technique, even those subtle brush strokes from his barn dance days, which he brought to the tender ballads that entered Presley's post-Sun repertoire. Fontana also created definitive rock-and-roll licks to certain tunes, like his emphatic conversation with Moore's guitar in "Heartbreak Hotel" or the machine-gun punctuation that fills empty spaces in "Hound Dog." Still today, Fontana maintains a steady income from Presley-related events all over the world—from Argentina to Tunisia, and throughout Europe. As a drummer, the flexibility Fontana demonstrates, not only with Presley but as a Nashville studio musician and producer, began during his formative years in Shreveport, soaking in the variety of musical styles that converged in the region. His attitude toward his music is not philosophical, but rather the pragmatism of a musician whose acumen seems to flow naturally from the depth of his experiences. "I never did adapt to a change," Fontana commented, "I just played what I learned when I was a kid and it all fit. It all fit, so why change?"[53]

Guitarist James Burton shares with Fontana both a critical *Hayride* apprenticeship and an intimate connection with Presley, though this came much later for him. At age fourteen, Burton became the *Hayride* staff guitarist. There he played behind George Jones, Jimmy and Johnny, Billy Walker, Johnny Horton, and others, continually honing his craft. The first recording Burton ever made came a year later, when he was fifteen. In the KWKH studio, he played behind a young singer named Dale Hawkins whose "Suzie Q," based on a blues tune by Howlin' Wolf, became his first and biggest hit record. The song is now anthologized as one of the seminal rockabilly recordings of the mid-1950s.[54] Stan Lewis, the local record store owner who was just beginning to dabble in record-making, oversaw the session with KWKH engineer Bob Sullivan at the board.[55] Like other recordings made at the KWKH studio, this one used only three or four RCA ribbon microphones and an aging Collins broadcast board, with no equalizer, no echo—in the words of Sullivan, "just bare bones."[56] Burton devised the distinctive lick later imitated on covers of the song, most famously by the California pop-rock trio Creedence Clearwater Revival. The recording marked him as a guitarist whose style inspired imitation and sealed his association with rockabilly so that when he joined Presley's band in 1969, remaining until the singer's death in 1977, he became what music writer Rich Kienzle referred to as the "sole remaining rockabilly touchstone in Elvis' music."[57]

Between his years on the *Hayride* and his association with Presley, Burton gradually innovated a flatpick/fingerpick style (holding a pick between thumb and forefinger and a fingerpick on his middle finger). The resulting sound, an understated voice that included a staccato, percussive effect he dubbed "chicken pickin," made him one of his generation's most influential and emulated guitarists.[58] As a self-taught player, the evolution of Burton's distinct voice was not so much a deliberate, conscious melding of the influences of country and rhythm-and-blues that he absorbed throughout his childhood, but their innate by-product. As he commented, "It's just the way I started doing it. . . . I didn't notice anything peculiar until I went into a music store one day and some guy said, 'Man, you're doing it all wrong.'"[59]

Burton's career took shape after Bob Luman joined the *Hayride* in 1956 and Burton began playing regularly with him both on Saturday nights and in area tours. When Luman left Shreveport for California in 1957, he took Burton with him, along with bassist James Kirkland and drummer Butch White. The 1958 movie *Carnival Rock* includes lively footage of their rockabilly numbers "All Night Long," "This Is the Night," and an instrumental, "The Creep."[60] Several of the group's recordings, including Luman's version of "Red Hot," remain part of the standard rockabilly corpus.

The following year, Burton and Kirkland joined Ricky Nelson of *The Adventures of Ozzie and Harriet* television show and also an aspiring singer. In the earliest sessions with Nelson, Burton plays the rhythm guitar while another musician, country guitarist Joe Maphis, plays lead. Beginning with Nelson's song "Believe What You Say," Burton played lead. He thus gained wide notoriety among fellow musicians and producers for his sound, and a visual boost via the band's regular *Ozzie and Harriet Show* performances when the camera often focused on the unusual work of Burton's hands. Burton left Nelson's band in 1964, bored with the exclusivity of a contract that left him working for only one month or so out of the year. He began applying his signature technique in studios, on both guitar and dobro, and in 1965, played lead guitar with The Shindogs, house band for the shortlived rock-and-roll television show *Shindig*. Burton's studio work continued, running the gamut from country to pop to rock. During the late 1960s, he recorded with Buffalo Springfield and Judy Collins, as well as Merle Haggard and Buck Owens, where his distinctive guitar helped to define the "Bakersfield sound" of the mid-1960s.[61] By the time he replaced Scotty Moore in Presley's band, Burton often sounds more like a second soloist than a supporting instrument, as he weaves a wah-wah-inflected polyphony against the singer's line, adding new energy to tunes like "Hound Dog," which by that point Presley had been singing for more than a decade.

Following Presley's death, Burton played with John Denver for seven years, and continued to pursue studio recording with Gram Parsons, Joni Mitchell, Emmylou Harris, and others during the 1970s. On his versatility in both country and rock-and-roll, dobro and steel guitar player Steve Fishell once wrote of Burton that he "has refined his country and rock and roll chops with equal mastery: He is equally poised curling a tasty signature flourish around a ballad's chorus line or plunging pell-mell into a double-time country cooker."[62] Since 1984 Burton has toured with an aging but still vital Jerry Lee Lewis, adding his distinct sound to Lewis's mixture of gospel, rockabilly, and country, the same mix in which Burton was schooled during his days in 1950s Shreveport. He returned to his home city during the mid-1990s with his wife, also a Shreveport native, to open a downtown club, James Burton's Rock-and-Roll Cafe, drawing locals along with the patrons of the recently developed casino boats on the Red River. [Editor's note: Since originally published, Burton's cafe closed; he hosted an International Guitar Festival in 2007.]

Joe Osborn shares with Burton a well-worn trail between Shreveport and California, where he likewise crossed paths with Luman and Nelson, and a career built on flexibility in the studio. Between the early 1960s and the late 1980s, Osborn's bass was the lynchpin for hundreds of hits, from rockabilly to pop to soul to country. His own story might be said to include an indirect *Hayride* apprenticeship. Osborn's career reflects the way Shreveport's position as a regional crossroads fostered a unique kind of musical fluency that echoed across a breadth of popular music for decades after the *Hayride*'s final broadcast. Osborn was married and selling hardware at the local Sears Roebuck when his close friend Dale Hawkins had his hit with "Suzie Q." At the time, Osborn regularly played around town. Hawkins's brother Jerry managed his band while Dale was touring to promote his song. The group lived above a Bossier strip joint called the Skyway Club, where they played regular gigs when Osborn joined the band in the latter 1950s. Their repertoire mirrored the same eclectic mix that KWKH blasted over its airwaves. As Osborn described it,

> We were doing that old south Louisiana R&B, I mean whatever was a hit, we just copied whatever was a hit. Jerry Lee had some things, whatever those were— "Whole Lotta Shakin'" and "Great Balls of Fire"—and some of those things like Chuck Willis. And Fats Domino had a few hits by then. So just that kind of stuff. We had a couple of horns. That's where I met [guitarist] Roy Buchanan.[63]

Jerry Hawkins acquired his own record deal in Los Angeles, so Osborn and Buchanan traveled with him to California. Unfortunately, the plans derailed and, as Osborn recalls, "Roy and I were left alone starving to death. Couldn't get our clothes out of the cleaners. Had hair down to there before long hair was supposed to be in."[64] In stepped Bob Luman, whose acquaintance they had made during Luman's membership on the *Hayride*. As it turned out, the association decisively altered Osborn's career. Osborn knew that Luman, by then a *Town Hall Party* cast member, was coming through town on his way to Las Vegas to open the Showboat Hotel along with other *Town Hall* stars. When Osborn caught wind that Luman needed a band, he and Buchanan resolved to "go sit on his doorstep and wait on Bob.'"[65] Luman rehearsed with Osborn and Buchanan and agreed to hire them. In Osborn's account, "He got our clothes out of the cleaners, took us to Las Vegas, got us a hair cut, and so that's how we wound up there. Stayed about a year. And during that time he did his hit record in Nashville. And that's when I started playing the bass."[66]

Until the Las Vegas job with Luman, Osborn played guitar. But two guitars were one too many for the Showboat gig. Since, by his own estimation, Buchanan was a better guitar player, Osborn picked up the electric bass. It was a fortunate turn of events for the musician now considered one of the innovators of the instrument. His guitar background led him to use a pick, a practice uncommon for a bass player at the time. As Osborn recalls,

> I plugged in and turned a lot of treble on the amp, just clicking and clacking and it's great, you know. [Other bass players said,] "You can't do that. You're supposed to feel the bass, you're not supposed to hear it." Well I didn't have a choice. I didn't know anything about playing the bass. It's the only way I knew how to do it. It turned out to be a good thing.[67]

In decades of band and studio work that would follow, Osborn fashioned a fresh melodic type of bass line, a flat-pick style that increased the instrument's prominence, and a characteristic "slide" technique. A pioneer in the relatively young profession of the studio musician, Osborn used the new tools of electric bass and multi-track recording technology to alter notions about the role of the bass in a band.

The Las Vegas job with Luman ended with the bandleader's draft notice in 1960. Osborn and Buchanan played for a while in Chicago, toured out of New Jersey with Dale Hawkins, and finally returned to Shreveport to rejoin Jerry Hawkins at the local Stork Club. Upon the recommendation of Burton, who happened into the club one night and first heard Osborn play bass instead of guitar, Osborn soon returned to California to join Rick Nelson's band. There, at the cusp of a period of musical flowering in Los Angeles studios, Osborn caught the attention of local producers and musicians with the near-human roundness of his sound on Nelson's biggest hit, "Traveling Man." The bassist began a decade-long association with two other session musicians—drummer Hal Blaine and pianist Larry Knechtel—that comprised the rhythm section on innumerable recordings of the 1960s and early 1970s. Lou Adler and Bones Howe are among the notable producers who depended upon the trio. Mean-while, Osborn opened the Los Angeles nightclub called Whiskey A-Go-Go with musician Johnny Rivers and pursued continuous studio work—as many as twenty sessions per week—until 1974 when he grew tired of the hectic big city pace. As Osborn told the story:

> I had to get out of town. I thought we were going to move to the Ozarks and quit. A friend of mine said, "You don't want to do that. You need to do what you're doing but in a different place." Nashville was the obvious place. I might have gone to New York but that would have been worse than L.A. So Nashville. And that whole thing mushroomed again, you know.[68]

Osborn remained active in Nashville studios until 1989, when he retired and returned to Keithville, Louisiana, just outside of Shreveport.

Among the many pop and country acts over the years whose bass lines were laid by Osborn, most often anonymously, were the Mamas and the Papas, the Fifth Dimension, the Carpenters, Neil Diamond, Simon and Garfunkel, Helen Reddy, Barbra Streisand, Kenny Rogers, America, Mickey Gilley, and Hank Williams Jr.[69] This partial list testifies to the flexibility and professional-ism of Osborn as a studio bass player. His pioneering sound is epitomized in the Fifth Dimension's cut of "Aquarius/Let the Sun Shine," where drum, horn, and even vocals seem tethered to the direction of Osborn's undulating deep groove. The variety of musical contexts in which Osborn thrived reflect his past.

In a way, his experiences in the studio extend the musical dexterity demanded of him in local nightclubs around Shreveport. Osborn viewed his talent as a cumulative process of learning that began on the Bossier strip: "If you're just in a band doing whatever's a hit, you know, you learn the record. And you learn to play what's on the record. So that's got to influence your style somewhat, you know, because you're playing that lick." As he moved to the stu-dio, he maintained the same ears-wide-open attitude: "You're always learning.

Especially doing recordings with people that have an idea about what they want to hear, and they lead you into playing things you never played. So okay that's another lesson. And you take all that knowledge with you to the next one, you know."[70] Osborn's upbringing in Shreveport established the foundation for a stylistic breadth that would keep him in demand for nearly three decades. As he said, "I think this has always been a magical place for music. And it could happen again."[71]

Jerry Kennedy's relationship to the *Hayride* goes deep, from his earliest memories beside the family radio to the Municipal Auditorium's wooden seats on Saturday nights to its stage. More closely than the other sidemen, his pathway to studio success mirrored the direct Shreveport to Nashville trail patterned after Hank Williams's initial trajectory. In Nashville, he made a name not only as a musician but as a producer as well. His early experiences all seem to point there. From his childhood, going to the *Louisiana Hayride* every Saturday night was a weekly ritual. Kennedy arrived there at 5:00 P.M. in order to get a front-row seat for the 8:00 P.M. show. In the audience, he became acquainted with Roger Sovine, the son of Red Sovine and now a BMI executive, and befriended the children of Johnnie Wright and Kitty Wells.

Kennedy learned to play guitar from Tillman Franks, and he gained some performing experience playing over the weekly station KCIJ Saturday-morning broadcasts of the *Tillman Franks Guitar Club*. By age ten, Kennedy won first place in the local Bob Wills Talent Contest, then went on to compete in Dallas for second place. Subsequently, RCA signed the young guitarist-singer to a recording contract. At his first session in Dallas he recorded the Johnnie Masters song, "16 Chickens and a Tambourine," also covered by Roy Acuff. Kennedy's version made it to the Top Five on the charts. The following year, he traveled to Nashville, where he recorded under the direction of Steve Sholes in a session backed by Chet Atkins.

By his early teens, he and Roy Dey, a friend who, like Kennedy, eventually became a Nashville record executive, continued to attend the *Hayride* on Saturday nights, now intent on getting a close look at the guitar technique of a player whose recording they tried to "pick apart" already. According to Kennedy, "We'd go up to the *Hayride* . . . and try to listen to this guitar player, but we couldn't hear his guitar because the girls were screaming so loud because this weird guy was dancing."[72] Of course, the gyrating lead singer was Presley, but it was Moore's rockabilly blend of country and rhythm-and-blues that lured Kennedy.

Kennedy's childhood prodigy and his regular *Hayride* attendance gradually evolved into performances, as Franks booked him to play behind artists
like Webb Pierce, the Carlisles, Faron Young, and Slim Whitman whenever
they performed close to Shreveport. As a sophomore or junior in high school,
Kennedy traveled south to Alexandria, Louisiana, where he filled in for Johnny
Horton's guitarist, Tommy Tomlinson. He handled the gig well. Kennedy joined
the *Hayride* staff band the next year as electric guitar player, where he remained
for a year and a half. By his senior year of high school, Kennedy started traveling on long road tours with *Louisiana Hayride* package shows as far away
as Arizona and Colorado, booked by Franks. After returning from a tour of
Canada in 1959, Kennedy lost his taste for road life and quit the stage. He took
a job in a warehouse for the Morris Dickson Drugstore Company, in the meantime marrying *Hayride* singer Linda Brannon.

In 1961 Kennedy met Shelby Singleton, artists and repertoire ("A&R")
man for the Southeast for Mercury Records. Singleton hired Kennedy to
assist in record production and the two cut albums together in Dallas and
New Orleans. Kennedy moved to Nashville and worked as a session musician
and, by 1969, a recording executive for Mercury Records. He left his position
as vice-president over Mercury's country music recordings in 1984, opening
his own JK Productions company. He demonstrated his capability early on
as the producer for Roger Miller's Grammy-winning signature song, "King of
the Road," as well as other Miller albums and singles. That Kennedy produced
the spare, intimate country-folk of Miller attests to the acoustic sensibilities
and country roots of the Shreveport native. On the other hand, two decades
of producing the barbershop-tight country vocals of the Statler Brothers often
demonstrated his studio acumen more dramatically. A good example is their
1964 hit "Flowers on the Wall," whose alternating walking banjo and driving
tom-tom accompanies quirky lyrics and a lurching metrical arrangement.
The staying power of the delightful pop oddity earned it inclusion in the
soundtrack to the 1994 counterculture breakthrough film *Pulp Fiction*.

Kennedy earned many other credits over the decades after he left Shreveport. As a studio musician, he carved a distinct musical voice on both guitar and dobro during the 1960s, playing on Roy Orbison's seminal tune "Oh,
Pretty Woman," Jeannie C. Riley's novelty hit "Harper Valley PTA," and Bob
Dylan's album *Nashville Skyline*. Kennedy's later work as producer includes
recordings of Jerry Lee Lewis, Tom T. Hall, Patti Page, and Reba McEntire, to
whom he signed her first recording contract. In all, he has had one of the most
diverse and long-lasting careers in the Nashville music industry.[73] Kennedy's

coming of age in post–World War II Shreveport, amid the influences of live clubs, records, and, most powerfully, radio station KWKH schooled him for his later pursuits, and he carried these formative experiences throughout his professional life in Nashville. As Kennedy mused,

> Shreveport was a great place to cut your teeth on music because there was so much going on. I wonder if I had been from Tyler, [Texas], I'm not sure that it would have worked. Just being there and hanging around KWKH and going to the *Hayride* and living there, all those things probably set up everything like a domino effect—everything that's gone on up until right now.[74]

Against the backdrop of musicians from the Shreveport region like Leadbelly and Jimmie Davis, along with musicians drawn to the region like Hank Williams and Elvis Presley, the four sidemen illustrate a postwar phenomenon in Shreveport with deep national implications. The cultural milieu that shaped them in youth included the eclecticism of KWKH radio, the plethora and availability of small independent record labels, and the dynamic local music scene. These four players emerged during a period when the accidental momentum and momentous accidents of history—the social, cultural, and geographical forces that shaped the region—set off an earthquake that shook any notion of a simple black and white paradigm of popular music to its foundation. As the *Hayride* faded away, these musicians, no longer subject to the galvanized categories of recorded music, entered the music business during an era when the studio supplanted the stage as a litmus test for industry success. Drawing from cross-racial instincts developed in Shreveport, they recorded scores of songs that would influence the direction of rock-and-roll, country, and rhythm-and-blues for decades to come.

Notes

1. Peter Guralnick, *Last Train to Memphis: The Rise of Elvis Presley* (Boston: Little, Brown, 1994), 96; two versions of the Rodgers/Hart song from early Sun recording sessions can be heard on Elvis Presley, *Sunrise Elvis Presley*. "Blue Moon" had been a 1949 hit for Billy Eckstine.

2. See Kenneth Jackson, *Crabgrass Frontier: The Suburbanization of the United States* (New York: Oxford University Press, 1985); Stephanie Coontz, *The Way We Never Were: American Families and the Nostalgia Trap* (New York: Basic Books, 1992), 28–29; and Elaine Tyler May, *Homeward Bound: American Families in the Cold War Era* (New York: Basic Books, 1988), particularly the discussion of "domestic ideology," 10–11.

3. Joe L. Kincheloe and Theresa Scott Kincheloe, "An Interpretative History of Education in Caddo Parish," bound manuscript in Noel Memorial Library Archives and Special Collections, Faculty Collection, Louisiana State University–Shreveport, 77; originally published in the *Shreveport Journal, Sesquicentennial Edition*, 16 September 1985 as "History of Education Marked by Neglect of Black Students." The authors further report that in 1911 almost 2,000 African American children in Shreveport could not go to school due to a shortage of classroom space; those who did often attended classrooms with between sixty and eighty students. It would take the Supreme Court fifty-eight years to unanimously enjoin this injustice.

4. These cases are discussed in Numan V. Bartley, *The New South: 1945–1980*, vol. 11 of *A History of the South*, ed. Wendell Holmes Stephenson and E. Merton Coulter (Baton Rouge: Louisiana State University Press and the Littlefield Fund for Southern History of the University of Texas, 1995), 15, 154–55, 158–60; David R. Goldfield, *Promised Land: The South since 1945* (Arlington Heights, IL: Harlan Davidson, 1987), 45, 64–69; Charles P. Roland, *The Improbable Era: The South since World War II* (Lexington: University Press of Kentucky, 1975), 33, 35–36; R. Douglas Hurt, ed., *The Rural South since World War II* (Baton Rouge: Louisiana State University Press, 1998) 39–40. Another useful source for southern history after World War II is Pete Daniel, *Standing at the Crossroads: Southern Life since 1900* (New York: Hill and Wang, 1986).

5. See Guralnick, *Last Train to Memphis*, 132; and the CD *Sunrise Elvis Presley*, which contains five tracks of acetates recorded from *Hayride* broadcasts. These are mainly of historic significance because their audio quality is so poor.

6. Craig Morrison, *Go Cat Go! Rockabilly Music and Its Makers* (Urbana: University of Illinois Press, 1996), 35.

7. Nick Tosches, *Country: The Biggest Music in America* (New York: Stein and Day, 1977), 31–33. Lyricist Max Freedman and composer Jimmy DeKnight wrote "Rock around the Clock." Tosches expounds: "Freedman, born in 1895, had written 'Sioux City Sue,' 'Song of India,' and 'Blue Danube Waltz.' DeKnight was really James Myers of Myers Music." When hired as the movie's technical advisor, Myers "suggested that 'Rock Around the Clock' be used as the film's theme song."

8. See Linda Martin and Kerry Segrave, *Anti-Rock: The Opposition to Rock 'n' Roll* (Hamden, Conn.: Archon Books, 1988), 59–68; the chapter titled "From the Waist Up," discusses extreme anti-Presley reaction between 1956 and his entry into the military in 1958.

9. See Bill C. Malone, *Country Music, U.S.A.: A Fifty-Year History*. 2d rev. ed. (Austin: University of Texas Press, 1985), 97.

10. Norman Mailer, "The White Negro," chapter in *Advertisements for Myself* (New York: G. P. Putnam's Sons, 1959), 340; the essay was originally published in the newspaper *Dissent*, by the City Lights Press in San Francisco.

11. Ibid., 338.

12. Malone, *Country Music, U.S.A.*, 250.

13. Morrison, *Go Cat Go!* 2–3; refers to the 23 June 1956 *Billboard*.

14. Articles from May and September 1955 on Presley's participation in the Jimmie Rodgers Memorial Celebration in Meridian and his *Hayride* contract renewal, respectively, are in Robert Gentry, *The Louisiana Hayride, "The Glory Years–1948–60: A Compilation of Newspaper articles, Pictures, and Advertisements* (Many, La., 1998), vol. 1, 190, 195; articles from March and December 1956 are in vol. 2, 207, 225.

15. Rose Maddox, interview by John Rumble, 25 January 1985, Nashville, Tenn. Transcript in files of the Country Music Foundation.

16. Malone, *Country Music, U.S.A.*, 217, 248.

17. See Tosches, *Country*, 29–31. Their tune became a 1960 cover hit for the Fendermen.

18. Rose Maddox, interview by John Rumble. Also see Mary A. Bufwack and Robert K. Oermann, *Finding Her Voice: The Saga of Women in Country Music* (New York: Crown, 1993), 128–29, regarding the group's "fabulously gaudy, flower-encrusted cowboy/Mexican outfits" that "defined the country music look for a generation to come."

19. Peter Fornatale and Joshua E. Mills, *Radio in the Television Age* (Woodstock, N.Y.: Overlook Press, 1980), 40.

20. Stan Lewis, "Comments from Stan Lewis," liner notes to *The Jewel/Paula Records Story: The Blues, Rhythm & Blues and Soul Recordings*, CD 9 42014-2, Capricorn, 1993.

21. Stan Lewis interview, 18 January 1998, Shreveport. All interviews are by the author, unless otherwise indicated. Tape recordings in author's files.

22. On the rise of the 45-rpm, see Andre Millard, *America on Record: A History of Recorded Sound* (Cambridge: Cambridge University Press, 1995), 206–8; Erik Barnouw, *The Golden Web: A History of Broadcasting in the United States*, vol. 2, *1933–1953* (New York: Oxford University Press, 1968), 245; and Malone, *Country Music, U.S.A.*, on the early 1950s sales of 45s by African-American artists to white audiences.

23. A full account of the events is found in Guralnick, *Last Train to Memphis*, 93–97, and 102–5.

24. Again, the story is recounted in detail in Guralnick, *Last Train to Memphis*, 106–14.

25. Billy walker interview, 22 July 1999, by telephone to his office, Nashville, Tenn.

26. Tillman Franks interview, 3 August 1998, Shreveport.

27. Ibid. Guralnick, *Last Train to Memphis*, also reports the difficulty in gaining a clear picture of how Presley came to the *Hayride*, and concluded "I think the scenario I have presented is as logical a version as one might come up with, but that doesn't mean it happened that way." Franks recalled the Carlsbad gig offering $800; Guralnick, 505, writes that it was $500, still substantial compared to the small fee from the *Hayride*.

28. See Guralnick, *Last Train to Memphis*, 129 (*Opry*) and 213; and Horace Logan, (with Bill Sloan) *Elvis, Hank, and Me: Making Musical History on the Louisiana Hayride* (New York: St. Martin's, 1998), 6, 155–56, and 173.

29. Logan, *Elvis, Hank, and Me*, 179–84. Also see Guralnick, *Last Train to Memphis*, 371; and Pericles Alexander, "The Presley Phenomenon," and "Everybody and His Dog Turns Out for Elvis," Shreveport *Times*, 13 December 1956 and 16 December 1956; Bob Masters, "Mass Hysteria: Frenzied Elvis Fans Rock Youth Center," Shreveport *Times*, 16 December 1956. All three appear in Gentry, *The Louisiana Hayride*, vol. 2, 223, 226–27.

30. This can be heard on Presley, *Good Rockin' Tonight*.

31. Jimmy C. Newman interview, 27 July 1999, by telephone from his home, Christiana, Tenn.

32. Sonny Harville interview, 24 July 1999, Shreveport.

33. Chet Hagan, *Grand Ole Opry: The Complete Story of a Great American Institution and Its Stars* (New York: Henry Holt, 1989), 182; in Joe Carr and Alan Munde, *Prairie Nights to Neon Lights: The Story of Country Music in West Texas* (Lubbock: Texas Tech University Press, 1995), 128.

34. Sonny Harville interview. Also Horace Logan, interview by unidentified researcher in Monroe, Louisiana, for 1984 documentary *Cradle of the Stars*, video in files of the Country Music Foundation, Nashville, Tenn.

35. See Bill Millar, liner notes to *Bob Luman: The Rocker*, BFX 15037, Bear Family, 1979. Also Steven R. Tucker, "Louisiana Saturday Night: A History of Louisiana Country Music" (Ph.D. diss., Tulane University, 1995), 496; Morrison, *Go Cat Go!* 159–61; Logan, *Elvis, Hank, and Me*, 178; Barry McCloud, *Definitive Country: The Ultimate Encyclopedia of Country Music and Its Performers* (New York: Berkley Publishing Group, 1995), s. v. "Bob Luman," by James I Elliott, 489. According to Morrison, Elvis did a series of nine one-nighters in a row in the Kilgore area and Luman attended every one.

36. Dale Hawkins and Fred Carter, Jr., are among other notable musicians who characterize the dynamic; Floyd Cramer is another, with status both as sideman and star soloist and a breadth of stylistic capability.

37. Jerry Kennedy interview, 7 March 1996, Nashville, Tenn.

38. Joe Osborn interview, 2 August 1999, Shreveport.

39. Quoted in Steve Fishell, "James Burton: First Call for the Royalty of Rockabilly," *Guitar Player* 18 (June 1984): 90.

40. D. J. Fontana interview, 6 March 1996, Nashville, Tenn.

41. Ibid.

42. Ibid.

43. Joe Osborn interview.

44. D. J. Fontana interview.

45. Ibid.

46. Jerry Kennedy interview.

47. Joe Osborn interview.

48. D. J. Fontana interview.

49. Ibid.

50. Ibid.

51. See David Sanjek, "Blue Moon of Kentucky Rising over the Mystery Train," *South Atlantic Quarterly* 94/1 (Winter 1995): 38, reprinted in Cecelia Tichi, ed., *Reading Country Music: Steel Guitars, Opry Stars, and Honky-Tonk Bars* (Durham, N.C.: Duke University Press, 1988), 26.

52. In Morrison, *Go Cat Go!* 67 (italics in source).

53. D. J. Fontana interview.

54. Rich Kienzle, "James Burton," in *Great Guitarists: The Most Influential Players in Blues, Country Music, Jazz and Rock* (New York: Facts on File, 1985), 192, 194. Colin Escott includes chapters on Dale Hawkins and James Burton in *Tattooed on Their Tongues: A Journey through the Backrooms of American Music* (New York: Schirmer Books, 1996). "Suzie Q" appears, among other places, on the anthology *Rockabilly Essentials*.

55. Stan Lewis interview.

56. Bob Sullivan interview, 26 June 2003, Bossier City, La. Both Lewis and Burton recalled the primitive nature of the recording setup, particularly compared to the multitrack technology soon to emerge. See Fishell, "James Burton," 93.

57. Kienzle, "James Burton," 193.

58. Morrison, *Go Cat Go!* 160.

59. Quoted in Fishell, "James Burton," 90.

60. *Carnival Rock* is available on Rhino Video. Luman's group here includes pianist Gene Garr.

61. Fishell, "James Burton," 88, who lists other artists with whom Burton has recorded, among them Nat King Cole, Dean Martin, Frank Sinatra, Johnny Cash, Tom Jones, Henry Mancini, Ray Charles, the Commodores, the Supremes, Johnny Mathis, the Byrds, Waylon Jennings, Kenny Rogers, the Monkees, and so on.

62. Fishell, "James Burton," 90.

63. Joe Osborn interview. Roy Buchanan was another influential session musician who came to Shreveport when Hawkins heard him playing in a club in Oklahoma. Chuck Willis is the Atlanta-born blues singer and songwriter, best known for tunes like "I Feel So Bad" and "It's Too Late."

64. Joe Osborn interview.

65. Ibid.

66. Ibid. Luman's hit was the Felice and Boudleaux Bryant song "Let's Think about Living," which reached No. 7 on pop and No. 9 on country charts in 1960; Luman followed up with the John Loudermilk tune, "The Great Snowman."

67. Ibid. More information on Osborn's career is found in several articles including John Gibson, "The Anonymous Kings of Top 40," *Entertainment World*, 16 January 1970; David Perry, "Joe Osborn," in *Bass Heroes: Styles, Stories and Secrets of 30 Great Bass Players, From the Pages of Guitar Player Magazine*, ed. Tom Mulhern (San Francisco: GPI Books, 1993), 161–63 (reprint of article that originally appeared in April 1974); and Burton, "Legendary Bass Player Has His Day," Shreveport *Times*, 14 June 1991. All are accessible on the website http://www.shreveportcitylights.com/joeosborn/index.htm.

68. Joe Osborn interview.

69. Ibid; also from an advertisement produced by Lakland Basses in Chicago (for the Joe Osborn signature bass).

70. Joe Osborn interview.

71. Ibid.

72. Jerry Kennedy interview.

73. A lively account of Jerry Kennedy's early career is found in John Grissim, *Country Music: White Man's Blues* (New York: Paperback Library, 1970), 27–34; also useful is Mary Ann Van Osdell, ed., "Music Legends Section" supplement, "Famous Hayriders Return for Glitz and Grits: Kennedy Has Hopes for Industry," Shreveport *Times*, 27 October 1991, 6.

74. Jerry Kennedy interview.

Blues

Blues emerged as a distinctive musical style, the product of polygenesis in the deep South (east Texas, Mississippi, Louisiana, and Alabama), around the beginning of the twentieth century. First heard on front porches and juke joints where black Americans gathered on Saturday evening, early blues was a synthesis of the traditions that preceded it: most notably country dance tunes, minstrel songs, secular ditties, spirituals, field "hollers" (aka "arhoolies"), and so on. Because of its dispersed origins, it is impossible to assign a specific date and geographic location for the first blues performance. By the early teens, however, blues appeared in sheet music and, by 1920, on commercial phonograph records, which helped to standardize the now familiar twelve-bar blues form.

Blues surfaced during a period when Jim Crow racism added misery and hard times to the black community. By the late nineteenth and early twentieth century, mail-order guitars became more readily available and very popular among folk musicians. Black folk musicians found the guitar an ideal instrument—it was portable, its primary chords (I, IV, and V) were easy to play, and its strings bent to accommodate the flatted tonality common to the tradition. Built upon a series of rhymed couplets, blues lyrics often focused on mistreatment, money problems, and difficulty between the sexes. They were played at house parties and dances rather than formal concert halls, while audiences shouted encouragement, danced, and joined in the singing. Thus, blues promoted a dialogue between the musicians and the audience, and provided a critical creative outlet for frustration in response to increased repression and a renewal of hard times after the heady, progressive days of Reconstruction.

Like field hollers, the first blues songs were rather free-form, and early blues musicians played cycles of flexible bar-lengths depending on the words (often between ten and fourteen bars). The standardized twelve-bar format appeared in sheet music as early as 1912, but coexisted with other, more fluid forms in the years of early phonograph recording. Blues developed in distinct areas of the South; thus, the early down-home styles can be assigned to three general regions: the Southwest, mid-South, and Southeast. Blues continues to display the symbiotic, interactive relationship between secular and sacred that has characterized the history of black American music. Many blues players routinely incorporate religious songs into their repertoire. Ark-La-Tex native Lead Belly, for example, felt comfortable playing a mixture of sacred music (including gospel songs and spirituals) and secular music (including blues, country dance tunes, ballads, and protest songs) throughout his life.

Likewise, African American religious music often draws on its secular brethren. The most striking instance of this merging is the gospel blues that originated with Rev. Thomas Dorsey in Chicago during the 1930s. But sacred and secular were also blended in the formalized spirituals performed for concert audiences across the world by the Fisk Jubilee Singers and similar "jubilee" groups at (now) Hampton University and Tuskegee Institute. In a distinct musical style that shares the same word, jubilee gospel singing began with groups like the Golden Gate Quartet in Norfolk, Virginia. The Gates, as they were often called, initiated a style of black gospel quartet singing during the mid-1930s, which featured vocal effects, high rhythmic interest, strong lead vocal, and a "pumping" bass.

The Ever Ready Gospel Singers (who formed ca. 1948) provide an example of this black gospel singing tradition based in Shreveport. Scant attention has been paid their story, which includes a series of recordings beginning with Sitting In With Records in 1950 and a long history with Shreveport media institutions like KWKH, where they were the first African American group to broadcast from its studios. Dan Garner, who contributes a sketch of Shreveport's storied Blue Goose neighborhood in this section, sketched their career as the liner notes to a 1997 recording made at Louisiana Light Studios in Shreveport, *Union of the World*.[1] That recording includes guitar work by the Rev. Eddie Giles, the same Giles who recorded as a soul singer in Shreveport during the small label boom that followed World War II.

Other Shreveport musicians made footnotes in the history of African American music, although sacred music rarely draws the same amount of popular or scholarly interest as its secular counterparts. For example, Rev. Utah Smith, who evangelized with his electric guitar, was raised in Shreveport but spent much of his adult life in New Orleans. His late-1940s recording of

"God's Mighty Hand" remains a classic; however, his life has been poorly documented. Likewise, secular blues players like Ed Schaffer, Will Ezell, and Elzadie Robinson remain sketchy figures captured on all-too-rare recordings that suggest the vitality of blues life in and around Shreveport.

Of the early Shreveport blues performers we know more about, Lead Belly and Oscar "Buddy" Woods thread their way throughout several pieces reprinted in this section. Most prominently, the former is the focus of an excerpt from a biography by the late Charles Wolfe and one of this book's co-editors, Kip Lornell. Woods appears in Paul Oliver's account of a 1940 field recording trip by John and Ruby Lomax, along with an essay on the recording of "Flying Crow Blues." Looking toward an earlier era, we included a short 1928 master's thesis that suggests more broadly a range of musical styles in circulation among some rural African Americans in this area. Looking beyond traditional blues, John M. Shaw's piece on "Down-Home Post-War Blues" reflects on an era following the mid-1950s emergence of rock-and-roll, when blues became largely removed from contemporary African American musical culture. The Shreveport legend Jesse Thomas was recorded playing blues guitar in 1929, during the 1940s, and into the 1990s. The Thomas interview reprinted here represents the vitality of the blues across most of the twentieth century. While the Shreveport native and white blues guitarist Kenny Wayne Shepherd represents a continuation of Thomas's musical legacy, it also underscores why we so deliberately placed "Black & White" into the title of this book.

Note

1. Dan Garner, liner notes to *Union of the World, The Archival Recordings of the Ever Ready Gospel Singers*, LFRS 13, Louisiana Folklife Recording Series, 1997; notes found online at http://profile.myspace.com/index.cfm?fuseaction=user.viewprofile&friendID=85664091. Garner refers to their style as "Southland gospel."

Fannin Street

—Charles Wolfe and Kip Lornell

"Lead Belly" was born Huddie William Ledbetter on Jeter Plantation in Mooringsport Louisiana, ca. January 29, 1885. He is one of the most influential and widely recognized black folk artists of the twentieth century. Taught the accordion and rudiments of guitar by his uncle Terrell Ledbetter, he soon employed his talents at local "sukey-jumps," rural African American house parties. Huddie left home around 1903 to become, by turns, an itinerant musician and a farm laborer working between Dallas and Shreveport and, later, an icon of southern black folk music. The first two years found Lead Belly in Shreveport, honing his skills in the rough-and-ready music scene in its red-light district, centered on the infamous Fannin Street. The formative period is recounted in the chapter from Lornell and Wolfe's award-winning biography, reprinted here. This excerpt reconstructs Lead Belly's coming-of-age in the rural Ark-La-Tex close to Shreveport, drawing on the memories of childhood friends and acquaintants. These include Margaret Coleman, who seems to have borne Lead Belly's daughter when both parents were still in their teens.

The chapters of Lead Belly's life that follow this one include a marriage to his first wife, "Lethe" Henderson (July 8, 1908), and about four years later, an eight-months tutelage with the legendary blues singer Blind Lemon Jefferson. During this period, he acquired the first of his signature twelve-string guitars. Ledbetter's initial brush with the law occurred in 1915, when he was jailed for assault in Harrison County, Texas. He spent much of the next nineteen years incarcerated for crimes ranging from simple assault to "assaulting to kill." This period included the curious turn of events leading to a full pardon granted in 1925 by Texas Governor Pat Neff, who heard him perform at the Sugarland Prison near Houston.

Later, while imprisoned in Louisiana's notorious Angola Penitentiary, Huddie Ledbetter's life changed forever when he met John Lomax and his son, Alan, who were collecting African American folk songs for the Library of Congress in the summer of 1933. Lomax recorded Lead Belly, then returned the next summer with improved equipment. This time Lead Belly reworked his pardon song, addressing it to Louisiana Governor O. K. Allen, as well as recording (what would become) his trademark song "Goodnight Irene."

After release from prison in August 1934, Lead Belly joined Lomax in the northeast, hoping to find a new audience and escape the racist South. Lead Belly proved a sensation upon his arrival in New York City on December 31 of the same year. Newspapers printed lurid and sensational descriptions of his convict past. The publicity helped John Lomax quickly negotiate a contract with Macmillan to write *Negro Folk Songs as Sung by Lead Belly* (1936) and persuade the *March of Time* newsreel to film Ledbetter. Soon, Lead Belly sent to Louisiana for Martha Promise, with whom he had taken up after his release, and married her in Wilton, Connecticut, on January 21, 1935.

In addition to recording for the Library of Congress, John Lomax arranged a contract with the American Record Company (now CBS/Sony). Although these records sold poorly, they sparked the fascination of progressive, white urban intellectuals. For the rest of his life, Huddie Ledbetter entertained and recorded for virtually all-white audiences. Always ready to adapt to his environment, Lead Belly added "topical" and "protest" songs about segregation and natural disasters to his repertoire. He kept company with urban folk musicians like Woody Guthrie, Sonny Terry, Brownie McGhee, Pete Seeger, the Golden Gate Quartet, and Burl Ives. In addition to performing, Huddie eventually recorded dozens of selections for Capital, RCA, Musicraft, and Asch/Folkways. Despite this notoriety, finances remained strained, and the Ledbetters survived these years largely on musical jobs and welfare. Late in 1948, while in Paris, Lead Belly's persistent muscle problems led to a diagnosis of amyotrophic lateral sclerosis, or Lou Gehrig's disease. He succumbed within months, on December 6, 1949. One year later, "Goodnight Irene," a song he once learned from his uncle Bob Ledbetter, became a number one hit for the Weavers.

By the time he was fourteen, Huddie had won a reputation for his guitar playing and singing, and was much in demand for the sukey jumps and house parties. Offers to play now arrived on a regular basis. Margaret Coleman remembered, "As the time rolled on, the white people with stores and drugstores asked Huddie to play Saturday evening and nights at their places to draw the crowd. In that way he made nice change."[1] Though he had grown up in an almost exclusively black community, he was getting a chance to perform for a wider audience, a different audience, the kind of audience he would later learn to cultivate in New York. He also began practicing the craft of entertaining, learning how to sell himself and his music to an often rowdy crowd. Much of it came naturally to him.

For a time he worked on a regular basis Saturday nights at a saloon in Leigh, Texas, out a few miles west on the Blanchard-Latex Road. Huddie was trying hard to grow up—he was a big, strapping boy with muscles toned from working in brutal weather on his father's farm. But he soon realized he wasn't as sophisticated as he thought. A story Huddie told years later illustrates this awareness: "Every Saturday I'd go out to Leigh, Texas, and I'd carry my guitar. Some of them would give me money when I'd get to the saloon, then the man would give me beer and money, too. But I had a good friend, her name was Early Bennett, she would call me 'Six-Shooter,' and Early, she would stash the beer for me; every time somebody would give me some beer, I'd give it to Early and she'd keep it for me." Huddie couldn't abide the raw, bitter taste of the beer, though, and he could hardly bring himself to drink it—though he felt he had to. Finally he hit upon a solution. "I'd get some sugar from my momma at home, you know, and put it in a paper, and put it in my pocket. So when I'd get through, me and Early would get behind the saloon. Early, she drank hers straight, but I had to put a little sugar in mine."[2]

In 1902 this part of Texas and Louisiana was still very much a frontier, a land of bootleg whiskey, disputes over women, knife fights, and shootings. With so much violence a part of everyday life, it was hardly surprising that Huddie soon got caught up in it. Irene Campbell recalled, "At 14 he started running around. I can remember later when he came to his mother's all cut up. He had been out all night, and he had his guitar strapped to his back." There was "blood all over the front of his clothes and his jaw was hanging open because someone had barely missed his eye with a cut on his jaw from top to bottom."[3] Such scenes became more and more familiar, and though Wes and Sallie were upset about them, Margaret Coleman—who was by now his steady girlfriend and confidante—was more sympathetic and more willing to listen to Huddie's side of things. Margaret insisted that it wasn't the life Huddie lived, nor his character which caused him problems. Instead, it was nothing "but jealousy in the heart of the people because he could beat them playing and dancing and made more money. Some began picking on him, telling wrong things. Huddie, being big-hearted, would laugh and try to keep down the confusion. He would say to them boys 'I don't care what you say about me, don't hit me.' He would try to defend himself, regain friendship with his enemies."[4] Another friend of Huddie's, Mary Patterson, agreed this was the official line that reached his parents, but thought there was more to it. "That's what his parents said, 'Everybody picks on Son.' He had them believing that. But I think that . . . he was always crazy about women. They were jealous of him, I guess, but he sure would fight about the women."[5] Another childhood friend from this time, Sallie Hooks, added, "He wouldn't take nothing off of nobody. He didn't go 'round just starting things, but if somebody looked like they want to start, he'd be ready."[6] Obviously, Huddie was a quick-tempered boy in a violent society. His ability to talk his way out of trouble with his parents could mask this only so far.

After a few more nights of watching his only son come home bleeding from cuts and bruises, Wes Ledbetter knew that he had to take some kind of action. When Huddie turned sixteen, Wes presented his son with a typical coming-of-age present in the frontier South of 1903—a pistol. The gun was a Protection Special Colt that comfortably fit under Huddie's coat in a holster. Years later, Huddie could recall his father's exact words when he handed him the weapon. "Now son, don't you bother nobody, don't make no trouble, but if somebody try to meddle with you, I want you to protect yourself."[7]

The gift did wonders to lift Huddie's self-image. And it didn't take him long to try it out. At a neighborhood sukey jump a few weeks after his birthday, Huddie asked a girlfriend named Eula Lee to ride home with him on his new horse. She readily agreed. As they were preparing to leave, however, another boyfriend stepped up and insisted that Eula Lee ride home with him in his new buggy. This boy had been talking big all night, Huddie recalled, and had been thinking that this new buggy made him the "boss over the whole world." An argument developed that quickly evolved into a struggle; the boyfriend grabbed the girl by the arm and she grabbed Huddie to hold on. Huddie remained silent, but as the other boy kept getting louder and more abusive, he eased his hand under his coat, feeling for the Protection Special. He felt the chilly steel, its cold weight reassuring. Huddie listened to the tirade and finally, when the braggadocio's talk "got too big," he lashed out with the gun and pistol-whipped the youth on the side of the head. He went down and Huddie leaped on him, straddling him with Colt in hand. Then he pulled the trigger. The gun misfired—a bad cartridge. Before Huddie could recover from his surprise, the badly shaken boy managed to squirm away and take off around the side of the house. Huddie fired two quick shots in his direction, but it was too late.

Huddie took Eula Lee home, then rode over to his own nearby farm, woke up his father, and told him what had happened. Wes quickly got dressed and rode over to the sheriff's office, only to discover that the parents of the other youth had already arrived. They were crying that somebody had been killed, that Huddie had to be arrested right then. Fortunately, the sheriff was acquainted with Wes, knew of his good reputation in the area, and was willing to cut his son some slack. He eventually fined Huddie $25 for carrying a con-cealed weapon and let him go with a warning.

For the rest of his life this incident stayed with Huddie; it wasn't the first time he had met violence at a frontier dance, but it was the first time he had truly asserted himself . . . and the first time he had gotten himself into a poten-tially lethal situation. This was apparently his first brush with the law, and but for the chance misfiring of his Colt, it could have resulted in something far more serious. As it turned out, the episode became a lesson to him—a les-son about how quickly violence could erupt in a frontier settlement and how easily one could get caught up in it. This lesson was reinforced a short while later when Huddie drew his gun once more. He saw his girlfriend and another boy sitting together in a nearby house; without thinking, Huddie fired his Colt through the door. The bullet apparently flew harmlessly, but it meant another visit with the sheriff.[8]

Huddie was now a grown man. His friend Mary Patterson joked, "Huddie was a good-looking nigger. He wasn't a real good-looking person; had dark skin and pearl white teeth. He wasn't ugly, but he wasn't pretty. Nice look-ing young man."[9] Huddie Ledbetter was about five feet eight inches tall. He had a smooth and very dark complexion and a muscular, athletic figure. Even then Huddie had developed a sense of style. Though he often spent ardu-ous days working in the fields, when he went out at night he was cleaned and well dressed, sporting his eventual trademark red bandanna around his neck. Completing this outfit was a guitar strapped across his back.

The country girls found him irresistible: He had developed into a witty, talented, good-looking young man from a respectable family. He was a "musicianer"—a term used by rural blacks to refer to a performer who had instrumental as well as vocal skills. As such, he was special—a cut above the other farm boys and mule drivers at the local dances. His first real girl was Margaret Coleman, the daughter of a neighboring farmer. By 1903, when Huddie was fifteen and a young man with a Colt and horse, Margaret became pregnant by him and gave birth to a girl. The child died in infancy. The community was much upset both by her pregnancy and the infant's death.

Margaret's parents pushed hard for the couple to get married. Huddie apparently had no real objection to this, but Wes and Sallie had big plans for their son, which didn't include Huddie being trapped into becoming a family man and a dirt farmer at the age of sixteen.

The Colemans finally backed off. Margaret certainly harbored no ill will toward her lover. Her later letters held nothing but respect for Huddie, and affection for his "poor, hard-working" parents. She also continued to see Huddie—and in another year she became pregnant again.

The second baby was another girl, who came out big and healthy. Margaret gave her the name Arthur Mae, but this time, perhaps in self-defense, Huddie denied that he was the father of the child. But his protests fell upon deaf ears and the Colemans were up in arms, rousing much of the community against Huddie. Pressure began to mount for Huddie to either marry Margaret or leave the area. The Colemans themselves soon relocated to Dallas, where Margaret raised her daughter. Huddie continued to deny his paternity, but soon found that his bad reputation with the older folks around Mooringsport was something not easily overcome.

Despite his feelings for Margaret, she was now out of the immediate scene—and Huddie was not often without a girlfriend for very long. However, he found out that the older folks had long memories when he fell in love with a girl known as "Sweet Mary," the sister-in-law of Alonzo Betts, who was a half brother to Huddie.[10] Irene Campbell thinks Huddie felt pretty strongly about Mary—certainly more than for Margaret—and even proposed marriage. Mary's family wouldn't agree to the marriage, though, possibly because of Huddie's growing reputation as a womanizer. Later, after he moved to New York, Huddie wrote and recorded a song for Capitol Records, "Sweet Mary Blues," in which he sings about "going all around the world trying to find my sweet Mary." Although there's nothing in the song specifically referring to Marshall or Mooringsport, his older relatives who still live in the area still believe the song is a lament for this early failed love affair.[11]

Huddie turned sixteen in January 1904. He was still living on the farm with his parents, working in the fields during the day, doting on his ten-year-old adopted sister Australia, occasionally even attending church. Yet he was also a father himself; a respected singer, musician, and dancer; a brawler and scrapper; and a ladies' man, but all of this was only in a small farming community near nowhere. This teenager grew more and more anxious to test himself in the outside world, in a world where the girls weren't so shy, the music not so monothematic, and the dances not as tame as the Buzzard Lope.

Down the road, on the far side of Cross Lake's swampy shores, crouched in an arm of the old Red River, lay Shreveport. It was a mere nineteen miles from Mooringsport in distance, yet decades away in development. In 1904 Captain Shreve's town was still two years away from the Caddo Lake oil strike that would by 1910 turn it into a boomtown and an oil center. But before then it remained a center for the cotton trade, as it had been before the Civil War, a place where planters from a hundred miles around brought their cotton. Shreveport was a town that "gave itself over to cotton," in the words of one guidebook: The very streets and sidewalks were piled with bales of cotton and the talk in shops and restaurants and hotels centered on cotton prices and cotton futures. The cotton was once shipped out on the boats moored along the docks of the Red River, but now traveled recently on the new rail connection to places like Dallas.

In 1900 Shreveport's census showed an official population of 16,913 (a figure that would double over the next decade); about a third of these residents were black. It was second in population only to New Orleans; in fact, the Chamber of Commerce during these early days even sought to imitate New Orleans's famous celebration by staging their own Mardi Gras on Fat Tuesday. Like New Orleans, the town was a loose and open gathering place for all kinds of businessmen and traders from the Ark-La-Tex. Down along the waterfront, especially on Strand Street and on the corner where Gross Bayou spilled into the Red River, was the red light district, just a few blocks from the new Holy Trinity Church and even fewer from the businesses along Commerce Street.[12]

This eventually bothered the city fathers, anxious to move Shreveport forward into the twentieth century and to dispel the image of their town as a collection of frontier saloons. In late 1902 the city council formed a committee to choose a section of the town to serve as a "red light district for the habitation of women of immoral character." They settled on an area west of downtown, away from the riverfront, in a triangle bordered by Fannin Street, Common Street, and the Texas and Pacific Railroad tracks. It was called St. Paul's Bottoms, after the old St. Paul Methodist Church on Caddo Street, and it was a low-lying part of town where the humid summer breezes were few and the mosquitoes numerous.[13] This was hardly choice real estate; the streets and alleys were muddy, the saloons were rough, and the houses were shabby rental properties, many of them taken by black families. In February 1903, the council designated the area as the official red-light district—"the red light district of the city of Shreveport to the exclusion of all others." From all over town, madams loaded up their belongings and began to move.[14]

The center of the new nightlife was Fannin Street, which began on the east side of the bottoms and ran eight blocks downtown, ending at the riverbank. At the head of Fannin, where it ran into Cane (now Baker) Street, stood a sumptuous new two-story house owned by the city's most popular madam, Annie McCune. At the opposite end of the block on Fannin was another fancy house, a late Victorian palace dripping with elaborate gingerbread decoration, run by a redheaded madam named Bea Haywood—"as fine a looking whorehouse as there was down there" recalled a former professional gambler.[15] Tricks cost three dollars each, or two for five dollars and the fancy parlors had all kinds of modern conveniences, such as the new player pianos that reeled off the latest turkey trot for a mere quarter. Within a year after the big move, the bottoms had at least forty whorehouses, not counting the little shotgun houses and dens where individual girls plied their trade. There were also dozens of saloons, dance halls, gambling houses, and even an opium den run by a character named "Ol' Bob" and a smoke house in the back of a Chinese restaurant.

White madams operated the big Victorian houses and they featured white girls. Farther down on Fannin Street, though, were houses featuring black or "mulatto" girls. An elderly white customer recalled that "some mulatto girls as you call them—the high yallers—ran places . . . for white men—didn't allow nigger men in their places. If a nigger got in there they came in by the back door."[16] Some of the famous madams were black, such as Baby Jane, who erected a brilliant electric sign in front of her house on Caddo Street, a block over from Fannin, who had a collection of red, green, and purple wigs, and who had a reputation for letting her drunker customers sleep it off on the premises. Fannie Edwards, another black madam, had a huge house filled with girls and over the years used her insider knowledge of local politics to build up impressive real estate holdings. Another building on Fannin Street housed the Octoroon Club, with many of its women imported from New Orleans—a point upon which its owners capitalized. Working-class customers who could not afford the three dollars charged by the big houses could find dozens of independent black entrepreneurs working out of little shotgun houses for as little as a dollar a trick.

Just a block down the street from Annie McCune's Victorian palace were two places run by blacks for blacks, joints which a contemporary newspaper described as "the most notorious dives in the bottoms." These were the establishments of Caesar DeBose and George Neil, described by local historian Goodloe Stuck as "the center of Negro nightlife—and crime." DeBose's place was next to a Chinese restaurant; its ground floor was a long saloon, but upstairs were rooms reserved for girls and for gambling. It was the scene of

frequent shootings and stabbings, and a regular hunting ground for police and
federal agents after wanted men. Though smaller, George Neil's place included
not only the usual bar and gambling rooms, but also a dance hall, a stage, and
an eatery. Neil, at one time the wealthiest black man in northern Louisiana,
sought only black clientele, and on occasion even complained to the police
when whites wandered into his place.

One Saturday night a retired police chief who had jurisdiction over the
bottoms took some visiting newspapermen to Neil's dance hall and described
what he found:

> The musicians, if so they may be called, were thumping out a hot dancing rhythm
> as I led the way around the edge of the floor. We backed up against the wall by the
> side door. The orchestra stopped for a moment and then swung into a rollicking
> cakewalk. The dancers responded instantly and Negroes certainly do shine in
> a cakewalk. There was no master of ceremonies, no calling the next stunt in
> advance; it was a sort of catch-as-catch-can, the kind of dance being controlled by
> the orchestra.

The chief's rare description of the dance he saw suggests that the new "uptown"
Fannin Street dances were in fact not all that far removed from the rural dances
of the backwoods sukey jumps.

> After a general showing off for a while, a sort of pattern appeared. Pairs of
> dancers would dance into position directly in front of us and proceed to do their
> stunt, breakdown, hoedown, double-shuffle, buck-and-wing and many another
> step for which I knew no name. . . . One couple in particular attracted our
> attention. The man was undersized and coal-black. He was shovel-footed, buck-
> kneed and agile as a cat. The woman was chocolate colored, broad, rather squat,
> bulged high in front and low behind, sort of a shed-room-rumped effect, and
> badly pigeon toed. They faced each another and danced, turning 'round slowly,
> his huge foot slapping the floor with loud thwacks and her feet keeping time with
> a sort of forward and drag back movement. It was really comical.[17]

In such places, a young Huddie Ledbetter could see that, while music
was extremely important, the dancers often took center stage, and they
managed to merge courtship, celebration, and tradition into some new and
exciting synthesis. There was, of course, an uglier side to places like Neil's.
The Shreveport *Times* complained that in Neil's "police have been openly
assaulted by Negroes" and that there had been so many fights and scrapes that
"the walls of the dance hall are peppered with bullet holes." In a violent age,

Fannin Street was a crucible of violence. In some ways, the dens and dance halls of the bottoms were as far removed from the courts and the police and due process as were the remote hamlets around Caddo Lake; blacks in the bottoms tended to settle problems by themselves, by skill with a knife and quickness with a gun, and this, too, was an impressive lesson for a young teenager just in from the swamps.

In the story he inevitably told to accompany his famous song "Fannin Street" (or "Mr. Tom Hughes' Town" or "Follow Me Down"), Huddie implied that he had never been able to go to Fannin Street until he was sixteen. "I been wantin' to go down on Fannin Street all my life," he says in his Folkways recording of the story; his mother, however, heard the stories about the newly created red-light district and was afraid for him to go. It was only when his folks finally allowed him to put on his long pants—a frontier rite of passage—that he got up enough courage to defy his mother. "When you put on long pants you ought to act like a man, if you ain't no man." In fact, his song about Fannin Street has very little about the bottoms in it; most of it revolves around the act of defying his mother. It describes both his mother and his "l'il adopted sister," Australia, begging him not to go; it broke his mama's heart, he sung, and she walked away from him with her hands behind her, crying. Unable to stand the sight of her crying, Huddie went to her, fell to his knees, and begged her to forgive him—but then walked away "with tears runnin' over the back of my head."[18]

The scene described in the song doubtless took place and was probably every bit as traumatic as Huddie remembered it; but in a later interview he admitted that this trip to Fannin Street was by no means his first. Huddie had gone there with his father when he was just a small boy, when Wes Ledbetter had taken his cotton to sell in Shreveport. When he was sixteen, he said, he had gone there when his father had given him some money for the fair. But Huddie went to Fannin Street instead, defying his father, not his mother:

My papa would take me to Shreveport on some bales of cotton. He'd lead me all around in Fannin Street, that's what I'd like, you know, see people dance, and play and sing and pianos, and the women dance. (I love to see women dance anyhow.) And so my father carried me down there, I was a little boy, I wasn't much knee high to a duck at that time, but I was staring. Sure, your children don't forget nothing. My father'd lead me around by the hand in the daytime, and then he'd put me in the wrong yard, too. 'Cause I'd be sleeping, and he'd be gone. When I'd wake up and he'd be gone, it'd run around in my mind (I was a little boy, too), he's going right back down there where he carried me that day. So I say, well, when I get to be a man I'm going down there, too.

And when I got to be about sixteen or seventeen years old, see, I was wearing long pants at that time. So my father put me on a bale of cotton and carried me to the train, and give me forty dollars in my pocket. I was a big shot, too, when I had that forty dollars. Sent me to go to the fair, five times, he says, "Son, don't go down on Fannin Street none at night." Just thinking about Fannin Street, and I said "No, sir. Papa," and that was just where I was going. I wasn't going to tell him. He shouldn't have asked me.[19]

Anyhow, when I got to Shreveport, I never did forget how to go down on Fannin Street 'cause there's a little hill you drop off. I knows exactly where the big place sitting up on Texas Street—I guess it was a church, I don't know what it is, I never did pay that much mind— 'cause when I was getting ready to go down that little hill, I was studying about that church. But I knowed how to go down there. So I went on down on Fannin Street, and that's where I'd go every time I'd leave home.

It was a whole different world to a boy from out in the parishes, and as he walked along beside his father, his eyes grew large at the marvels of Fannin Street. In the store windows were dress mannequins, staring at the boy with unmoving eyes. Huddie admired them as he and his father walked past, and when they returned a couple of hours later he noticed they were still there—in the exact position, in fact, their eyes still staring. "Papa, don't these people never go home and get nothing to eat?" he asked, to the great delight of his father. "No, son, that's fashions."

Later on, he would pretend to be more sophisticated:

I was down there, and two girls, you know, high browns, and I was so young, and they asked me, "Where'd you come from?" And I told 'em, "Chicago." Well, I was dead out of the country, and I knowed it, but they didn't have to know where I come from. When they found out, they said, "Daddy, take us up there and buy us some beer." So I took 'em up, you had to get beer in a pigeon-hole, you know, wouldn't let women inside of a bar (a saloon what they call it down there). So I ordered three glasses, these big tumblers, and so when they got up the beer, the women says, "All right, let's drink, Daddy." So I grabbed my glass and got on to it, and I got a big mouthful, but I went to spitting it out on the floor. They said, "Oh Daddy, you from Chicago and can't drink beer." And I said, "No I can't drink it, stuff's too bitter for me. You got to put some sugar in it!" And so the women jived me a whole lot.

They jived him, but Huddie soon became a favorite of the girls at Neil's and DeBose's; his work on his father's farm had made him strong, and his naïveté added to his charm. He learned about women on Fannin Street, but he also began to learn more about his music. This was one of the big reasons he kept thinking of going into town on Fannin Street: the attraction of pianos and guitars in the barrelhouses.[19]

Shreveport did not have the rich kind of early jazz culture that the downstate city New Orleans enjoyed, but a number of the better pianists and singers were on a circuit that took them through Shreveport. As he listened to them, Huddie began to hear some new sounds to add to his own music. One was an early form of the blues; he remembered a singer and piano player named Pine Top Williams, who boomed out off-color versions of "The Dirty Dozens" and sang it "right to a gal in the audience." He also sang versions of "Take Me Back" and one of the early archetypal dirty blues, "Salty Dog." Huddie later could still recall fragments of Pine Top's song:

> Baby, let me be your salty dog,
> I don't want to be your man at all, you salty dog.
> Yes, honey babe, let me be your salty dog, your salty dog.

> Little fish, big fish swimming in the water,
> Old man, can I marry your daughter, you salty dog?
> God made woman, made her mighty funny,
> Kiss her 'round the mouth, sweet as any money.[20]

Another blues he learned very early—one which he said was his very first blues—was "I'm on My Last Go Round," which he recorded for Bluebird in 1940. The blues songs, he found, were more popular on Fannin Street than the older country songs, work songs, and ballads he had been singing. He quickly added the blues to his repertoire.

His guitar playing also took a new turn. Though he was still playing a six-string at this time, he could adapt the barrelhouse piano style to it. He said, "Boogie woogie was called barrelhouse in those days. One of the best players was named Chee-Dee. He would go from one gin mill to the next on Fannin Street. He was coal black and one of the old-line players and he boogied the blues. At that time anyone could walk into a barrelhouse and just sit down and start playing the piano. I learned to play some piano myself by picking it out." At dances and in saloons he would always sit near the piano so he could hear the rolling bass, what he called "walking the bass." This was novel in 1904 or 1905, and quite the rage. Huddie recalled, "It was about 1904, 1903, piano players were walking the bases. [You'd] walk up to a man and tell him, 'Walk the bases for me,' give him a drink or something."[21] Some of the best of this new style can be heard on his Shreveport song "Fannin Street," a dense, complex composition that became a Lead Belly standard.

Whether or not Huddie, as some early biographies have suggested, was "kept" by some of the girls in the Fannin Street houses, or whether he was simply a familiar figure and favored entertainer, he stayed there almost two years. What other musicians he might have met, what other girls he could have loved, what scrapes he fought his way out of there, remain unknown. But he always remembered the street, always spoke and sang about it as if it were one of his most vital formative experiences. By 1909 efforts were being made to clean up the district (prostitution would be legally voted out in 1917), but by then Huddie was miles away and entering another chapter of his life. His mother had been right about one thing: It was a testing time for him, and when he came back to Caddo Lake, after two years, he came home a man.

Notes

1. The Library of Congress, "Leadbelly" files letter.
2. "Last Session" Folkways FP 2942D, Band 1.
3. Campbell manuscript, Leadbelly file, Archive of Folk Culture, Library of Congress.
4. The Library of Congress, "Leadbelly" files letter.
5. Wyatt Moore, 1972 interview with Mary Patterson.
6. J. L. Wilson, "Kinfolk Remember Their 'Leadbelly,'" *Shreveport Times Sunday Magazine*, October 20, 1974, p. 3.
7. John A. Lomax and Alan Lomax, *Negro Folk Songs of Lead Belly* (New York, Macmillan, 1936), p. 6.
8. Ibid., p. 7.
9. Moore interview.
10. Huddie's mother, Sallie, had been formerly married to Joe Betts before she wedded Wes Ledbetter, and Alonzo resulted from that union.
11. In her unpublished typescript (Leadbelly file, Archive of Folk Culture, Library of Congress), Irene Campbell talks about the mysterious "Sweet Mary."
12. The *WPA Guide to Louisiana* provides our background information about the development of early twentieth century Shreveport.
13. Goodloe Stuck, *Annie McCune, Shreveport Madam* (Baton Rouge: Moran, 1981), p. 10.
14. Ibid. p. 70.
15. Ibid. p. 13.
16. Ibid. p. 54.
17. Ibid. pp. 70–72.
18. *Negro Folksongs of Lead Belly*, p. 169.
19. This lengthy description of Fannin Street and Huddie's adventures with his father are found on "Leadbelly's Last Session," Folkways 29400, Side 4.
20. Ross Russell, "Illuminating the Leadbelly Legend," Down Beat 37 (1970), p. 12.
21. "Leadbelly's Last Session," Folkways 29400, Side 4.

Some Negro Songs Heard on the Hills of North Louisiana

—Vallie Tinsley

We include this piece as an item of historical interest, a snapshot of scholarly inquiry into the musical practices of rural African Americans near Shreveport from an era long past. The Louisiana Folklife Program's database of theses and dissertations identifies this work as a "M.A. 1928 Louisiana State University." Because of the absence of notated music, we assumed it to be a thesis in English. As it turns out, Tinsley wrote her paper for the School of Music, fulfilling a requirement for her concentration in music history and literature. In the context of contemporary music study, during a time when Eurocentric work predominated, this late 1920s graduate music thesis is interdisciplinary, focuses on black American music, and looks in its own backyard. Thus, it may be viewed as forward-thinking, even groundbreaking, for almost any music department to sanction such a topic for graduate work at this time. That said, it occasionally lapses into language that reflects the embedded racism of 1928 society. When the substance of the work is not affected, we have edited out demeaning language.

While outside the mainstream for historical musicology, Tinsley's study was in line with folk song scholarship during the late 1920s. Scholars like John Lomax and Robert Winslow Gordon scoured the South collecting the words to American folk songs, mostly from black and white performers. Tinsley, in fact, refers in passing to the work of Dorothy Scarborough, Howard Odum and Guy Johnson, and Thomas Talley. Although scholars increasingly used sound recordings beginning in the mid-1920s, these earliest folk song collectors were most interested in the words rather than the music or performers' lives. These rural words presented challenges to the researcher intent on writing down an essentially oral tradition. Struggling with transcription of the dialects she recorded, Tinsley used *Kenyon's American Pronunciation* as a guide to "give through phonetic transcription the dialect of the negro as used in these songs" (p. 1). [1]

Tinsley focused her study directly out her front door, in the "fields, kitchens, churches, and in the memories of the old and the young" she found within a circumscribed area of northwestern Louisiana. She notes that her findings are "only a few rays from the million sunbeams of songs pouring over those hills and valleys." Her collection includes secular and religious songs classified by Tinsley as "spirituals, blues, lullabies, reels, and rhymes" (p. 1). Tinsley's section divisions are somewhat idiosyncratic to our modern sensibilities and she does not distinguish between oral, recorded, or other sources of the songs she collected. "Searching for Spirituals," for example, contains largely nineteenth-century spirituals, along with discussion of her methods and locations for song collecting. "From My Father's Collection" contains short verses of non-religious songs Tinsley gathered from her father, who learned them through job experiences as "the 'Mister Mun' or 'cap' to the negroes" (p. 12). These include words to fiddle tunes like "Sally Gooden" and minstrel show songs. Similarly, "My Mother's Contribution" contains songs from "the kitchen and at the wash-place," learned by her mother from African American women she encountered in the domestic sphere (p. 21).

An odd section titled "If I Can" contains a hodgepodge of songs Tinsley characterizes as "spontaneous outbursts of real feeling," unified, it seems, by texts that all imply movement—often to a better place. Several sections refer to the people from whom she collected. She named "Azzie's Songs," for example, for the woman who accompanied her to several local churches; these most notably include a version of "The Midnight Special," a song closely associated with Lead Belly. Similarly, "Dorthula's Songs" come from a singer identified only as "Mis Hester's colored girl." "Bob's Song," a brief fragment she posits as from "some old phonograph record," (p. 33), is in fact the opening line of Blind Lemon Jefferson's 1927 race record hit "Black Snake Moan." Likewise, "Fannie and Angeline's Song" is the opening of the gospel hymn "Just Over in the Gloryland." The final section, "Some Blues Songs," contains stanzas from three songs, "found by Mr. A. H. White to be very popular among the negroes working in the oil fields north of Shreveport" (p. 36). She suggests that these might be from phonograph records; however, in this instance, none can be directly tied to a particular 1920s commercial recording.

Two clues locate her efforts near Shreveport: her mention of the oil fields north of Shreveport, mostly found in and around Caddo Lake and Oil City, and her reference to Price's Free-Will Macedonian Baptist Church (p. 4), which is located outside Homer, Louisiana, in Claiborne Parish. As the earliest collection of African American folk songs from northwestern Louisiana, Tinsley's thesis stands as a significant historical document.

Note

1. Page numbers refer to original manuscript; photocopy in authors' files.

Introduction and Acknowledgments.

Almost all that I can say concerning the difficulties of collecting folk songs, has been said already by Miss Scarborough and other collectors. My experiences were similar to theirs. Collecting is a delicate task and requires a great deal of patience and persistence. . . .

I ran as fast as I could toward Aus and the wagon to get there before he finished his song, but I could never catch the words. And when I asked him what he was singing, he said, "Nothin', Miss, jes' holl' in." I slipped along behind the oaks to catch Bob's song while he mowed the grass. But not a word would he say or sing them. And when I asked the old blind negro on the corner to sing me some old reel tunes, he said, "I uster sing dem when I wuz young, Miss , but den I wuz a-servin' another master; now I'z a-servin' de Lord."

So I searched in the fields, kitchens, churches, and in the memories of the old and the young, with the hope of being able to add a few songs to those already collected and published. My findings, made in a short time and from a small district (one or two parishes of north Louisiana) and collected here in this small book, are only a few rays from the million sunbeams of song pouring over those hills and valleys. Almost every kind is represented here—spirituals, "blues," lullabies, reels, and rhymes.

I have made no attempt to classify them, but have put them in with a few words concerning the background, for without the background and the negro, a negro song is less than a quarter of a negro song. This little collection gives to me many times the pleasure it can possibly give to anyone else, for the reason that each song has a story back of it—a story either sad or humorous with a most interesting principal character—and I am on the inside of the story.

I examined many collections of folk songs in order to see if mine were known elsewhere, and I found lines of many of them in various places. I have indicated this along with the songs. Otherwise to the best of my knowledge, these songs have not been published before. I omitted many of mine because I found them given so nearly the same in other places.

Using as a guide *Kenyon's American Pronunciation*, I have attempted to give through phonetic transcription the dialect of the negro as used in these songs. I may be accused of not being consistent in spelling and in phonetic transcription of these words, but that is because the negro's speech varies. . . . In one line he says "de" and in the next "the." For example, the negro would say, "Death is in <u>de</u> lan'," but "<u>The</u>" one she wuz savin'."

I am indebted to Mrs. L. C. Starr (Eloise Melton) for her kind assistance in setting to music those songs of which I had been able to learn the tunes. I wish to thank those friends, the colored and the white, who so kindly assisted me in making this collection. I have mentioned their names along with the respective songs.

My thanks are due also to Dr. W. A. Read for his suggestions, encouragement, and other assistance.

Searching for Spirituals.

In my quest for spirituals I accompanied my colored friends to several churches, of which I remember the names, Pine Hill, Bethel, and Price's Free-Will Macedonian Baptist. I found them all tucked off behind the hills and pine thickets at the ends of rough wagon roads.

On my first visit I was accompanied by Azzie, wearing a large red hat and a sleeveless red silk dress and carrying her shoes in her hand. When we arrived about nine o'clock, a low humming was rising from the rude cabin. There were as many negroes on the outside of the church as inside, and I was impressed by the quietness of them all. They moved about like black spirits, veritable shades in Pluto's dark regions. I have heard them sing at the top of powerful lungs as they worked in the fields; I have heard Teather's mighty booming call three miles away in the middle of the night as he came home from his nocturnal prowls. So I was surprised at their subdued tones here.

I found the singing of two kinds. The first was like the song of soldiers where "each heart spoke a different name but all sang 'Annie Laurie.'" In this case they were attempting to sing unfamiliar songs from "white folks' books"; and although they were all saying the same words, each had a different tune. After they had wailed in this way for a while, they all knelt, bent their backs, and tucked their . . . heads down until they completely disappeared behind the seats. They did not cease to sing, however, but lowered their voices to a hum that rose and fell like a distance-mellowed echo of the song itself. In a short time out of this humming a single voice became audible and grew louder, while the humming became fainter and gradually died away.

"O Lord, dear Father, guide us through the shiftin' scenes of life — — — — — and finally take us somewhere, Lord, where there won't be no sickness an' sorrow, somewhere in the sweet Beuleh Land, jest somewhere, Lord," prayed the sweet voice of a woman, while the whole audience accompanied her with a perfectly rhythmic chorus of "amens" sung out at exactly regular intervals regardless of where she was in a sentence.

At my request the older negroes sang some of those wonderful old spirituals—of which I am including a few in this book—and the young ones joined in with embarrassed grins on their faces. When I asked a young girl if they sang the spirituals at her church, she smiled tolerantly and said, "Yas'm, sometimes de ole foks raise dem ole tunes." She said it in the same way that the modern flapper says, "O, Mother doesn't understand, but she's a dear anyway."

So it is that the younger negroes are trying to get away from the songs that have come to them from the days of slavery, and collectors who would preserve them must work rapidly. With the dying of the old negroes of the present day will die most of the old spirituals.

[From Pine Hill Church]

TEACH ME JESUS.

Teach me, Jesus,
Teach me right,
I'll be yo' servant if you teach me right.

Teach me, Jesus,
Teach me right,
I don't mind dyin' if you teach me right.

Teach me, Jesus,
Teach me right,
If I die on the battlefield, teach me right.

I DONE DONE.

You tol' me to preach,
I done done,
You tol' me to preach,
I done done,
You tol' me to preach,
An' I done done what you tol' me to do.

You tol' me to shout
I done done,
You tol' me to shout,

I done done,
You tol' me to shout,
An' done done what you tol' me to do.

You tol' me to moan,
I done done,
You tol' me to moan,
I done done,
You tol' me to moan,
An' I done done what you tol' me to do.

PREACH THE WORD.

Preach the word,
Preach the word,
Preach the word,
If I never, never see you any more.

Sing the song,
Sing the song,
Sing the song,
I shall meet you on the other shore.

WHAT SHALL I DO?

(This was a favorite of the negroes, and they often sang it in the fields as they picked cotton together.)

If I wuz you, I'd stop right here an' pray;
If I wuz you, I'd stop right here an' pray;
If I wuz you, I'd stop right here an' pray;
O, my Lord, O, my Lord, what shall I do?

O run, sinner, run, an' hunt you a hidin' place;
O run, sinner, run, an' hunt you a hidin' place;
O run, sinner, run, an' hunt you a hidin' place;
O, my Lord, O, my Lord, what shall I do ?

O what you gwineter do when death comes a-creepin' in de room?
O what you gwineter do when death comes a-creepin' in de room?

O what you gwineter do when death comes a-creepin' in de room?
    O, my Lord, O, my Lord, what shall I do ?

Chris' tol' Nicodemus dat he mus' be born agin;
Chris' tol' Nicodemus dat he mus' be born agin;
Chris' tol' Nicodemus dat he mus' be born agin;
    O, my Lord, O, my Lord, what shall I do ?

I NEVER HEARD A MAN.

(This is the most powerful and appealing spiritual I have ever heard sung. The little old negro preacher sang the stanzas, and the congregation joined in the chorus.)

    King Jesus is a preacher;
    He spoke in Palestine,
    Proclaimed to all the nation
    His power to redeem.
All the days of my life, ever since I been born,
I never heard a man speak lak dis man befo'.

    Chorus
I never heard a man speak lak dis man befo'
All de days of my life, ever since I been born,
I never heard a man speak lak dis man befo'.

    He spoke over in Jerusalem;
    His parents they were gone;
    "I want to ask some questions;
    I'm from my father's throne."
All de days of my life, ever since I been born,
I never heard a man speak lak dis man befo".

    He spoke at the grave of Lazarus,
    When a congregation met;
    The Lord God folded up His arms;
    I'm told that Jesus wept.
All de days of my life, ever since I been born,
I never heard a man speak lak dis man befo'.

He spoke to the Jewish nation,
"I am the solid rock;
Behold I am your Savior,
I stand at the do' an' knock."
All de days of my life, ever since I been born,
I never heard a man speak lak dis man befo'.

A GREAT CAMP MEETIN'.

(Led by a very earnest, old negro preacher. They could invent and add stanzas
to this as long as they wished.)

Great camp meetin' over yonder,
Great camp meetin' over yonder,
Great camp meetin' over yonder,
    On the other shore.

Heap of people over yonder,
Heap of people over yonder,
Heap of people over yonder,
    On the other shore.

I have a home over yonder,
I have a home over yonder,
I have a home over yonder,
    On the other shore.

I have a father over yonder,
I have a father over yonder,
I have a father over yonder,
    On the other shore.

I have a mother over yonder,
I have a mother over yonder,
I have a mother over yonder,
    On the other shore.

By an' by we'll go an' see them,
By an' by we'll go an' see them,
By an' by we'll go an' see them,
    On the other shore.

Jes' keep reachin' over yonder,
Jes' keep reachin' over yonder,
Jes' keep reachin' over yonder,
    On the other shore.

(This is given slightly different and with many more stanzas in *The Negro and His Songs*, Odum and Johnson.)

BE READY WHEN HE COMES.

O don't let him fin' you lak he did befo',
Fiddlin' an' dancin' on the ballroom flo',
Raisin' confusion everywhere you go.
        He's comin', yes so soon.

        Chorus.
        Be ready when he comes,
        Be ready when he comes, O Lord,
        Be ready when he comes,
        He's comin', yes, so soon.

O be lak Nora in de days of ole,
Build you a house fo' to shelter yo' soul;
Don't let it be neither silver nor gold.
        He's comin', yes, so soon.

DO LORD.

O when my name is cast abroad,
        Do remember me;
Yes, when my name is cast abroad,
        Do Lord, do remember me

        Chorus.
Do Lord, do Lord, remember me.
When I done all I can do,
        Do remember me.

When my blood run chilly an' cold,
        Do remember me;
When my blood run chilly an' cold,
        Do Lord, do remember me.

(Very similar to the above are the following stanzas, which I find in *The Negro and His Songs*, Odum and Johnson).

Chorus.
Do my Lord, remember me,   (Repeated three times)
    Do, Lord, remember me.
Up on de housetop an' can't come down,
    Do, Lord, remember me.   (Repeat)
When I am hungry do feed me, Lord,
    Do, Lord, remember me.

BLANCHE'S SONG.

Although this is a spiritual that I later heard at the churches, it seems to belong to Blanche, for she taught it to me. Blanche is Bob's wife. She is very ignorant and all drawn with rheumatism. I had no idea that she could sing, . . . So when she came to churn one day and had put the little negro down on the kitchen floor, I asked her to sing and was very much surprised and charmed with her sweet voice. For me it held a most pathetic note.

YES HE'S MINE.

    Yes, he's mine,
    Yes, he's mine,
Ther's joy in my soul,
There is peace in my min'.
    Yes, he's mine,
    Yes, he's mine,
Jesus, I know he's mine.

    He always will be mine,
    He always will be mine,
There's joy in my soul,
There is peace in my min'.
    He always will be mine,
    He always will be mine,
Jesus, I know he's mine.

   I'm singing he's mine,
   I'm singing he's mine,
  There's joy in my soul,
  There's is peace in my min'.
   I'm singing he's mine,
   I'm singing he's mine,
  Jesus, I know he's mine.

Other stanzas: I'm praying he's mine, etc. I'm shouting he's mine, etc.

From My Father's Collection.

Those of the two following groups come to me secondhanded. My father, who is the "Mister Mun" or "Cap" to the negroes, is the real collector of the first group. He learned them from the negroes themselves as he worked with or "worked" them in the fields on "the long summer days"; and at night he propped his tired feet against the columns, and taking his violin under his chin, played their plaintive tunes. I do not know the tunes of some.

   Long summer day,
   Ole massa an' ole missis a-settin' in de shade,
   Drink their coffee and their tea,
   Give po' nigger de black-eyed pea.
   Long summer day,
   Long summer day.

  The same sad complaint with the faintest touch of humor and very much of truth continues in:

   White man go to college,
   Nigger go to the field;
   White man larn to read an' write,
   Nigger larn to steal.

  There came a little yellow negro wandering through the country, and my father hired him. Pretty soon he ran away, leaving this little song for us to remember him by:

   I'm a rovin' little darkie
   All de way f'um Alabam:

> I'm as sweet as anybody,
> An' dey call me Little Sam.
>
>   Chorus.
> I wo'ked in de cotton an' de cane.

...Another "hand" sang these lines over and over:

> Some of dese mo'nings
> An' it won't be long,
> De cap'n gwineter call me,
> An' I'll be gone.

And so it happened. We never saw him again. I find that stanza slightly varied in *Negro Workaday Songs* by Odum and Johnson.

The next little jingle was adopted by our family for practical use. We children often woke each other with it.

> Wake up, Jacob, day's a-breakin';
> Meat's in the pot an' hoe-cake 's a-bakin'.

And he (my father) often told us of the "square" dances for which the black fiddler played "Sally Gooden" and "Sugar in de Gourd."

SALLY GOODEN.

> Had a piece of pie,
> Had a piece of puttin'
> Give it all away to see Sally Gooden.
>
> Looked down the road,
> Saw Sally comin':
> Thought to my soul I'd kill myse'f a-runnin'.
>
>   CHORUS.
> Here dog,
> Here goes a rabbit.
> You don' run,
> You won't ketch it.

SUGAR IN DE GOU'D.

Meat in de smokehouse,
Lard on de boa'd
Coffee in de little sac,
Sugar in de gou'd.

Sugar in de gou'd,
Sugar in de gou'd;
Way to get de sugar out,
Roll de gou'd about.

Sadday night an' Sunday too,
Puty gals on my mind;
Soon's I get up on Sunday mo'nin'
White folks got me gwine.

BETSY MONGER.

Betsy Monger so deceibin'
Tell you a lie an' lieb you a-griebin'.
"Betsy Monger, I want yo' daughter."
Take 'er 'long, son an' treat 'er like you oughter.

SUGAR JOHN.

Sugar John the baby,
Dance a jig for pappy.
Sugar John the baby,
Dance a jig for pappy.

JIMMY HUTTER.

Ole Jimmy Hutter,
You eat de cheap meat, an' I'll eat de butter.
You eat de cheap meat, an' I'll gnaw de bone.
Goodbye, yellow gal, I' goin' home.

Suannie, the wash-woman, remembered this one from her father:

> Step light, ladies,
> De cake's all dough.
> Nebber min' de wedder
> So de win' don't blow.

Talley gives as a part of "Gooseberry Wine" the following stanza, which is similar to the above:

> Oh walk chalk, Ginger Blue!
> Git over double trouble.
> You needn' min' de wedder
> So's de win' don't blow you double.

"IF I CAN"

Dorothy Scarborough, in her book, *On the Trail of Negro Folk Songs*, gives the first stanza of this one as a part of "John Henry's Dead," but it doesn't seem to me to fit there.

All these songs are spontaneous outbursts of real feeling, or as the psychoanalyst would say, the expression of "subconscious desires," only they are not subsconscious. I hear the real cry of hunger in this shameless confession. . . .

> Chorus.
> If I can, If I can,
> I'm gwineter make it to my shanty
>   If I can.
>
> De chicken's on my back,
> De dog's on my track,
> I'm gwineter make it to my shanty
>   If I can.
>
> I'm gwine down de street,
> Steal myself a piece of meat;
> I'm gwineter keep my skillet greasy,
>   If I can.

Steal myself a sack of flour,
Cook an' eat every hour;
I'm gwineter make my livin' easy
       If I can.

(Two lines of this are given in Odum and Johnson's *Negro Workaday Songs*.)

OLE SOW HAD DE MEASLES.

Chorus.
Ole sow had de measles
'fo' she died las' spring.

What will you do with the ole sow's hide?
Make as good saddle as you ever did ride,
Saddle or bridle or any such thing;
Ole sow had de measles 'fo' she died las' spring.

What will you do with the ole sow's nose?
Make as good thimble as ever sewed clothes,
Thimble or needle or any such thing;
Ole sow had de measles 'fo' she died last spring.

What will you do with the ole sow's backbone
Make as good rifle as you ever did own,
Rifle or shot-gun or any such thing;
Ole sow had de measles 'fo' she died las' spring.

What will you do with the ole sow's tail?
Make as good whip as you ever did sail,
Whip or lash or any such thing;
Ole sow had de measles 'fo' she died las' spring.

What will you do with the ole sow's meat?
Make as good sausage as you ever did eat,
Sausage or puddin' or any such thing;
Ole sow had de measles 'fo' she died las' spring.

DE YEAR OF JUBILEE.

A CIVIL WAR SONG.

Darkies, you see dat man dis mo'nin'
Wid de mustache on his face?
He pick up his hat so early in de mo'nin',
He's gwine to leab de place.

Chorus.

Ole massa run away,
De darkies stay at home.
It mus' be de Kingdon Come in de year of Jubilee.

He's five feet one way an' six t' other,
An' he weighs three hundred poun';
Coat so big he can't pay de tailor,
An' it wouldn't go ha'f way round'.

There's wine an' cider in de cellar,
An' de darkies they'll have some,
'Cause it'll all be confiscated
When Lincoln's sergeants come.

DE ODDER SIDE OF JORDON.

Grey goose built in de corner of de fence,
Sparrow built in de gyardin;
If I wuz a goose an' goner build me a nest,
I'd build it on de odder side of Jordon.

Chorus.

Jordon is a hard road to trabble, I do believe.
I looked to de east an' I looked to de west,
I saw a chariot a-comin',
Ole grey hoss an' a bay in de lead,
Gonner lan' me on de odder side of Jordon.

Jacob an' Jack sat down to playing cards,
Jacob meant to beat him;
Jerked up Jack frum de bottom of de pack,
An' landed him on de odder side of Jordon.

(The first part of this is similar to a "Nesting" song in Talley's *Negro Folk Rhymes*.)

HOL' DE WIN'

Satan's mad, an' I am glad.
Hol' de win', don't let it blow.
Lost de soul, he thought he had.
Hol' de win', hol' de win'
Hol' de win', don't let it blow.

Greatest thin I ever done,
Hol' de win', don't let it blow,
Serve de Lord, when I wuz young.
Hol' de win', Hol' de win'
Hol' de win', don't let it blow.

As a part of the song, "What Yo Gwine to Do when de Lamp Burn Down ?" in *Religious Folk Songs of the Negro* , I find this stanza:

Ole Satan's mad an' I am glad;
What you gwine to do when de lamp burn down?
He miss one soul he thought he had,
What you gwine do when de lamp burn down?

MY MOTHER'S CONTRIBUTION.

To my mother I owe the following part of my collection—fragments of spirituals and lullabies gleaned from those sung in the kitchen and at the washplace or handed down from the old negro "mammies" of the past. She in turn sang them to us as we played around her through the long years of our childhood. How my heart grieved in sympathy with "poor little lammie" and Aunt Gracie's "two little goslin's"!

In Miss Scarborough's book I find this stanza in a song with the title of "Ole Cow":

Ole cow, ole cow,
Where is yo' calf?"
"Way down yonder in the meadow,

> De buzzards an' de flies
> A-pickin' out its eyes,
> De poor li'l thing cried 'Mamie'!"

My mother sang it thus:

> "Lammie, Lammie,
> Where's yo' mammie?"
> "Down in de valley;
> Buzzards an' de flies
> A-pickin' out 'er eyes, ah!"
> Poor little lammie cried for mammie.

"GO TELL AUNT GRACIE"

Aunt Gracie is known as "Aunt Tabbie" and " Aunt Patsy" in different places.
I found this song better known and more loved than any of the others. Miss
Scarborough has the first two of mine and three that I do not have.

> Go tell Aunt Gracie,
> Go tell Aunt Gracie,
> Go tell Aunt Gracie,
> The ole grey goose is dead.
>
> The one she was savin'
> The one she was savin'
> The one she was savin'
> To make a feather bed.
>
> She died early this mo'nin'
> She died early this mo'nin'
> She died early this mo'nin'
> Under the ole green apple tree.
>
> She left two little goslin's
> She left two little goslin's
> She left two little goslin's,
> One for you an' one for me.

"EH, MY LITTLE BOY".

"Eh, my little Boy,
Who made your breeches?"
"Mammy cut 'em out,
An' Daddy sewed the stiches."

And, as a friend of mine used to say, the second verse is the same as the first; over and over again they sang it.

"SHOO, MY LOVE."

In a long jingle entitled "Aunt Dinah Drunk" in Talley's *Negro Folk Rhymes*, I found this line:

Oh shoo my Love ! My turkle dove

When I read it, there flew back into my memory like a flock of sparrows to a tree top the following:

Hawk an' turkle dove
Went to the war,
Hawk came back with a broken jaw.

Shoo, my Love,
Shoo, my Love,
Shoo, my pretty little turkle dove.

The following fragment has the tune to which we always sang "Chicken in the Bread Tray," which is given in the Scarborough book. I do not know the title of it unless it is a part of that song.

Chorus.
Granma, 'havie your se'f,
Granma, 'havie your se'f,

You wanter ketch a bell cow,
Ketch her by the tail;
You wanter milk a bell cow,
Milk her in the pail.

And "Chicken in the Bread Tray" as we always sang it goes:

> Chicken in the bread tray,
> Pickin' out dough.
> Grannie, will your dog bite?
> No, chile, no!

The following fragments I do not remember the tunes of. Only their colors cling to my memory, as varied as the bits of silk and cotton in Aunt Lucinda's quilt-scrap box.

> 'Way down yonder in de folks of the branch
> De buzzards had a public dance;
> De ole cow lowed, de ole hoss pranced,
> De ole sow whistled, an' de little pigs danced.

> I'm here today;
> Termorrer I may be a-sleepin' in de grave.
> Zion, Zion, Zion,
> Trabble on, trabble on, trabble on,
> O my Lord.

> In de chariot I'm gwineter ride,
> In de chariot I'm gwineter ride,
> In de chariot I'm gwineter ride,
> Six white hosses side by side.

> Don't you hear dem hosses' feet,
> Don't you hear dem hosses' feet,
> Don't you hear dem hosses' feet,
> Wa'kin down dem golden street?

This is a part of an old Georgia Plantation song. More of it is given with the music in *Religious Folk Songs of the Negro* by The Hampton Normal and Agricultural Institute.

> When de lamp burn down,
> When de lamp burn down,
> What you gwine say to de angels,
> When de lamp burn down?

In Talley's *Negro Folk Rhymes* I find the following stanza, which is the last of three under the title "Susan Jane." It is evidently akin to the rhyme at the top of this page.

> 'Way down yon'er in de middle of de branch;
> Susan Jane ! Susan Jane !
> De ole caw pat and de buzzards dance.
> Susan Jane ! Susan Jane !

AZZIE'S SONG

Assie was . . . very pleasant, and at my request sang in a sweet voice that had the note of [prisoner].

I find a part of her song in one called "Skinner's Song" in Dorothy Scarborough's book. The last stanza of it begins:

> "Looked at the sun and the sun looked red,
> I looked at the Cap'n and he turned his head."

It is there a part of a work-song, but it seems to have a different meaning in Azzie's song. The whole of this seems a jumble, and it probably is made up of lines from several other songs.

> Chorus.
> Let your midnight special
> Shine de light on me;
> Let your midnight special
> Shine de everlovin' light on me.

> Over yonder come Rosie.
> How in the world do you know?
> Well I know her by her apron
> An' the dress she wo'. O,

> Umberella on her shoulder,
> Piece of paper in her hand,
> Gonner tell de captain
> Dat "I won't my man." O,

When you go to Argenna,
Well you better walk right;
Well you better not stumble,
An' you better not fight. O',

A gene'al will fin' you,
Certainly carry you down;
O den we'll fin' you
Passion bound. O,

Well I Looked at de sun, sir,
An' de sun looked red;
Well I looked at my pa'dner,
An' he wuz falling dead. O,

DORTHULA'S SONG

Dorthula was "Mis' Hester's colored girl." When she was a tiny female . . . her mammy had given her to "Mis' Hester." At that time Mrs. Hester had one baby, Tom. Dorthula was then about ten years old, large enough to carry Tom around and amuse him. Afterwards there were two more little Hesters, and Dorthula "tended" to them all. . . . Sometimes they rode on her back; at other times she rocked them and sang:

Cow go, "Moo, moo;"
Calf go, "Baa, baa;"
Guinea go, "Country, country;"
Goose go, "Filly in de field."

When they were asleep, Dorthula dried the dishes and swept the "galleries." That done, she immediately went to sleep on the kitchen floor with her mouth wide open.

Although the following is a favorite in north Louisiana, Miss Mabel Lann recalls it as associated with a little negro boy who sold pralines in Clinton. Pralines are sweetmeats made of sugar and nuts, usually pecans, and poured on corn shucks. They are very popular in south Louisiana, especially among the Creoles.

This particular little negro carried them from house to house in a basket, and many of his sales were due to the popularity of his jig and song. It really should not be called a song, as it had no tune. He set his basket down and said it as he did a double shuffle and clapped his hands. On one occasion the two-year-old, who had more appreciation for sweets than for dancing, bit every praline in the basket while the family enjoyed the performance. It was then necessary that they buy the lot.

> "Mammy, mammy, look at ole Sam,
> Eatin' all de meat an' soppin' out de pan."
> Mammy, mammy, she hit Sam
> Hard as she can lam;
> Jes' kept on eatin' like he didn't give a damn.

THE BOB WHITE'S SONG.

Another and longer version of this is given in Talley's *Negro Folk Rhymes*.

> "Bob, Bob White,
> Your peas ripe?"

> "No, not quite."

> "Bob, Bob White,
> You dog bite?"

> "Yes, if you come in the night."

BOB'S SONG.

Bob was a little half-starved negro who had a young, thin wife and a two-year-old. . . . He worked hard all day and gambled away his earnings in some "crap" game at night. Towards three o' clock in the morning many times I have been pleasantly called out of my delicious slumber by the long sweet notes of Bob's song coming out of the woods and across the hills, as he came home from his gambling parties. It seemed to rise and fall, to become clearer, and then fainter, and gradually die away to be taken up again in startling, clearness much closer home. I am inclined to believe that it is a part of some old phonograph record.

> E-e-e-e-e-eh! Aint got no mamma now.
> E-e-e-e-e-eh! Don't need no mamma nohow.

FANNIE AND ANGELINE'S SONG.

Fannie and Angeline chopped cotton just over the fence on the hillside near where we played in the pasture branch. As they worked, they sang all day long and over and over:

> Jest over in de Glory Lan'
> I'll jine de happy angel's band;
> Jest over in de Glory Land.

SOME "BLUES" SONGS.

Those of the following group were found by Mr. A. H. White to be very popular among the negroes working in the oil fields north of Shreveport. He does not know whether they made them up or got them from some phonograph records. But he finds them singing them while they work.

NO. 1.

> I laid down las' night
> An' was sleepin' sound;
> The blues overtook me,
> An' turned me round an' round.
>
> I'm a-goin' to town,
> To see the chief of police:
> My good gal done quit me,
> An' I couldn't see no peace.
>
> Did you get dat letter
> I dropped in your back yard?
> I would come to see you,
> But your man got me barred.

NO. 2.

> Jest as sho' as de freight train
> Makes up in de yard,
> It's gonner take two fifty
> To sen' me a postal card.

If you should happen to miss me,
Jes' count de days I'm gone.
I'm gonner build me a railroad
All of my own.

I left sweet mamma
Standin' at de station, crying,
Sayin', "You got a home,
As long as I got mine."

"You leave me laughin',
You gonner come back crying,
Singin' all over town,
'Where is dat gal of mine.'"

NO. 3.

Rocks fer my pillow,
Gravel in my bed,
I aint got no where
To lay my worried head.

I wish I wuz a jay bird
Flyin' in the air;
I'd build my nest
In dat brown-skin woman's hair.

Jerry's Saloon Blues

1940 Field Recordings from Louisiana

—Paul Oliver

Oscar "Buddy" Woods figures prominently in this article drawn mostly from the recordings, field notes, and letters of John Lomax and Ruby Terril Lomax in Shreveport in 1940. Author Paul Oliver describes the adept slide guitar playing of Woods, a style of playing with the instrument flat on the lap shared at times by Lead Belly, among other local musicians. "Jerry's Saloon Blues," which initially appeared as the liner notes for Flyright Album 206 (1975), focuses on this 1940 encounter with Woods, two other local black musicians named Kid West and Joe Harris, as well as members of Lead Belly's extended family. As Oliver describes, West and Harris demonstrated their lively and varied repertoire for Lomax, who recorded older ballad and country dance material like "Railroad Rag," "Bully of the Town," and "Old Hen Cackled and Rooster Laid an Egg." Blues material, like that favored by Buddy Woods, is there, too, but drew Lomax's interest less than the older songster repertoire. Oliver himself took a trip to Shreveport two decades after Lomax, in 1960. There he tracked down pianist "Snooks" Jones, who played with the musicians Lomax had recorded. By that year, Buddy Woods, Kid West, and Joe Harris had died or simply faded into obscurity.

Shreveport, Louisiana, lies in the "Tri-state" region where Louisiana, Texas, and Arkansas meet. It's the capitol of Caddo Parish, the most northwesterly parish in the state and one which has along its western border the mounds that marked the boundary between the United States and the Republic of Texas.[1] Like the parish, Shreveport has a large non-white population, a third of its people being black or Indian in origin, and the booming, hustling city has always attracted blacks from the Tri-State region who have sought to get some spinoff from its continually expanding economy.[2]

Growth is a characteristic of Shreveport. It was the clearing of the Red River by Captain Henry Shreve in the mid-1830s that made the town possible, and it was incorporated in 1839 with a name that honored his Shreve Town Company that laid out the site. It flourished with the trade that its situation on the Texas-bound route encouraged and by the cotton produced on the big plantations along the Red River. They depended on slave labor before the War between the States. Not only was the city on the Confederate side; it was the last bastion of the Confederacy even though it was never devastated by the war.

All this has a bearing on its culture and, incidentally, on the music of its black population. For there was money in Shreveport and when the railroad link with Dallas was established, soon after the war, it continued to thrive even as the river traffic died.[3] Relatively speaking, blacks in Shreveport were well off, sharing a little in the general prosperity and circulating their cash in the bars, saloons, and red-light districts of the city. In 1880 there were still only eight thousand people in Shreveport; nevertheless, this number had doubled by the time Huddie Ledbetter, the celebrated Leadbelly, made his first visit to the brothels of Fannin Street at the turn of the century.[4] Still a small town, even if, to the young rebel in knee-pants from Mooringsport and the Caddo Lake region, it had the temptations of a big city.

It was the oil-strike at Caddo Lake in 1906 which made a boom city of Shreveport. Oil, like cotton, required cheap labor, at least in pre-mechanized years. Blacks were seldom employed at the rig, but there was still plenty of heavy work and, with the discovery of oil, the expanding economy of the city brought many opportunities for domestic, menial, and semi-skilled work. When the strike seemed to have burned itself out by the end of the twenties, the opening of the East Texas field in 1930 and the Rodessa Field five years later gave the city the boost it needed.

The Depression years had been tough for Shreveport as for every other urban district but it recovered quickly and avoided the malaise that affected many Southern cities. But then it had none of the aspects of a Southern city; it was pragmatic, hard-nosed, commercial, unromantic, go-getting. When John Avery Lomax and Ruby Terril Lomax came there in 1940 the population had hit the seventy-five thousand mark and blacks had tipped 35 percent.[5] If they'd stayed longer they would doubtless have found many more musicians among the black community that centered on the West Allendale and Cedar Grove sections. But they stayed only two days, the Tuesday and Wednesday the eighth and ninth of October, before going on to Oil City, the site of the 1906 strike. Writing a few days later Ruby Lomax reported: "After jiggling around considerably in East Texas with Sacred Harp Conventions and a Negro Baptist Assn. and guitar-pickers and an ex-slave, we struck out for Shreveport. Except for some pretty newsboys' cries, all our recordings there were made by Negroes—blues singers from "Texas Avenue," French Creole singers, guitar and mandolin pickers."[6]

Though John Lomax's autobiography was published a few years later and therefore could have thrown light on how he found the Shreveport singers, the event was obviously insufficiently memorable for him to include.[7] But it is likely that he merely encountered them on the street and later followed them to a bar. His field notes report that "Oscar (Buddy) Woods, Joe Harris, and Kid West are all professional Negro guitarists and singers of Texas Avenue, Shreveport, Louisiana. The songs I have recorded are among those they use to cajole nickels from the pockets of listeners. One night I sat an hour where the group was playing in a restaurant where drinks were served. I was the only person who dropped a contribution in the can. I doubt if the proprietor paid them anything."[8] This brief note suggests that all three musicians were working together as a group. But if so, it seems not to have occurred to Lomax to record them as a three-piece band. Instead, Oscar Woods was recorded on the Tuesday; Joe Harris and Kid West on the following day.

In a brief interview at the conclusion of the session, when Oscar Woods had sung and played "Look Here Baby, One Thing I Got To Say," John Lomax elicited a little further information.

LOMAX: Buddy, when do you—when do you play this song?
WOODS: Oh, well, down 'n' around these little hop joints and things like
        that—when they having a good time.
LOMAX: That's a—that's a stimulator?
WOODS: Well, they kinda get a li'l stimulated.
LOMAX: How do you make your living regularly, Buddy?
WOODS: Oh, just different—hanging around the corners, lyin' around the
        joints 'n' takin' up where I can. Once in a while-n-y' know, that way.
LOMAX: You pass the hat around? Don't you. . . .
WOODS: Oh yes, sir, passing the hat around, don't forget it.
LOMAX: How long have you been a street singer?
WOODS: Ohh—I guess around fifteen years.

LOMAX: Done nothing but pick since then?

WOODS: That's all—practically all.

LOMAX: That so? Where did you grow up did you tell me?

WOODS: Always in the State of Louisiana.

LOMAX: Whereabouts?

WOODS: Oh, down near Nachitoches.

LOMAX: Worked on a farm?

WOODS: Yes sir.

LOMAX: Where did you get your music?

WOODS: I guess I just settled on it. Just picked it up somewhere, something. I didn't read up on it.

"Thank you," said Lomax in a rather bored voice; he'd heard it all before, the same vagueness, the same lack of detail. As an interview with a blues singer it was perfunctory but in 1940 there was little to relate it to and no picture emerging that would make a more probing interview necessary. Woods was easy, but respectful, and didn't advance any information of his own accord.

The record session itself was slightly more revealing, though it may have given John Lomax a surprise. He had collected a number of versions of the "Ballad of the Boll Weevil,"[9] and probably requested one from Oscar Woods. At any rate Woods obliged with a song of this title, "Boll Weevil Blues." It was, however, a version of Ma Rainey's "Bo-Weavil Blues," recorded in 1923 and her first issued record;[10] Oscar Woods had transposed the tune skillfully to his individual technique of guitar playing, subtly changing the phrasing to suit the steady rhythm of his own accompaniment. By his own account to Lomax, Woods had been working on the streets since 1925 and may therefore have heard the record at his farm home a year or so before.

Buddy Woods, as he was generally called, was no stranger to recording when the Lomaxes found him. His earliest titles were with a second guitarist who sang blues vocals and played kazoo, Eddie Schaffer; their "Fence Breakin' Blues" and "Home Wreckin' Blues" were recorded a decade before in Memphis, Tennessee.[11] This was only four days after James "Kokomo" Arnold made his first recordings, at the same location and with the same recording crew.[12] The fact is a tantalizing one, for as far as can be ascertained, these may have been the first four recordings made of a comparatively rare style of blues guitar playing. It seems unlikely that Woods and Arnold could have learned this technique with such virtuosity in so short a time and direct influence is therefore unlikely. Arnold claimed to have come from Georgia,[13] while Woods came from Louisiana. Only a few days later, Booker Washington White (and companion, Napoleon Hariston) also made his first recordings of slide guitar, again to the same recording team in Memphis.[14]

Unlike Tampa Red, who used a slide on the treble strings only, Arnold, Woods, and White all played in open tuning with the slide laid across the strings. On occasion, Booker White would play with his guitar laid across his lap, but more frequently he played with a slide made from a length of brass tubing, slipped over his finger, with the guitar in the customary position. Arnold usually, and Woods invariably, played the guitar flat across the lap. Black Ace (B. K. Turner), who learned much of his technique from Buddy Woods, employed the same method.[15] This was also the manner of slide guitar playing used by Leadbelly, who may well have learned it in Shreveport. It appears that the flat guitar technique was particularly favored by Shreveport musicians but seems likely that it was derived directly from the Hawaiian style, which had been made popular by Hawaiian musicians appearing at the Chicago World's Fair and the subsequent annexation of the islands.[16]

Arnold, Woods, and White, who were to make their names in later years, had already formulated their personal styles. Arnold's complex picking on "Rainy Night Blues" and almost frantic playing on "Paddlin' Madeline Blues" was undisputably his own; White's train imitations were in a percussive form that he repeated often later. By comparison Wood's playing was more relaxed, seeming to be less interested in impressing the recording executives. Not that any of them was to owe a career to Victor—though Oscar Woods with Eddie Chafer (sic) made a coupling for Victor under the name "Eddie and Oscar" on 8 February 1932. This record (Victor 23324) which backed "Nok-'Em-All-Blues" with "Flying Crow Blues" was the first recording of the latter title, a popular Texas-Louisiana theme. The session was in Dallas and was probably held at the instigation of Jimmie Davis, a white country singer with political ambitions whose songs were clearly influenced by black records. On the same day Davis made four titles with Woods accompanying, on one of which they shared the vocals, "Saturday Night Stroll" (Victor 23688). Indeed, Buddy Woods may have accompanied Davis recordings as early as 1930, in Memphis. Jimmie Davis was later to become governor of Louisiana in 1944 and was to serve a second term in 1960. Woods seems not to have exploited the connection by seeking more recordings on his own initiative. Within the next couple of years Kokomo Arnold had moved to Chicago where, in September 1934, he commenced his four-year long contract with Decca during which he recorded prolifically.[17]

Buddy Woods, however, stayed in Louisiana, unambitious, disinterested in making a career. "Calls himself 'Troubadour,' 'Street Rustler,'" Lomax noted.[18] When Woods had an opportunity to record for a unit of the Decca company it was in New Orleans in 1936 where he cut "Don't Sell It—Don't Give It Away"; one of the tunes he chose to play for John Lomax four years later.[19] He'd recorded it too, in San Antonio with the band fronted by a Shreveport singer, Kitty Gray.[20] It's not surprising, therefore, to hear the ease with which he plays the tune and the almost casual, swinging manner of his singing. "Words and music by Buddy Woods," Lomax added to his hastily penned transcript, adding, "Buddy Woods claims to have composed the words and music."

Though Buddy Woods had recorded several blues at his few sessions, he made only one for John Lomax, "Sometimes I Get To Thinkin." The verses were slight modifications of traditional lyrics, and the whole blues had only three stanzas. But Woods seems to have considered them as a composition; asked to make a second take he introduced only slight variations, opening with different instrumental phrasing and changing a word here and there while the sense remained the same. Buddy's final item, "Look Here Baby, One Thing I Got to Say" was a remodelling of "Hey Lawdy Mama,"[21] (a theme made popular by Bumble Bee Slim a few years before) played with his customary fluency.

John Lomax could have obtained more music from Buddy Woods if he had been familiar with his records. Lomax was motivated to record songsters rather than blues singers and was far more interested in those singers who reflected in their repetoires the vestiges of an older tradition. Buddy Woods, recording with his "Wampus Cats" and playing, at times, with small jazz-inclined groups, must have seemed too urbane to Lomax.[22] Kid West and Joe Harris were more to his taste; at any rate he recorded more items by them. However, they had even less to say about themselves, and Lomax left no further notes to fill in the biographical details of the two street singers.

Their first title was probably rather unexpected. Though it was called "Railroad Rag"(AFS 3990 A3), it was a novelty ragtime number of the kind that years before they had played to white audiences; decades before, even. After a second take of the song, with its pathetic closing line "Here comes that Choo-choo, choo-choo-choo-(poop-poop)—that's the Railroad Rag," Lomax avowed that it was a "pretty thing" and asked Kid West when he first played it.[23] "Thirty-five years ago." Lomax asked him had he heard "anybody else play it?" "Nobody," Kid West assured him. John Lomax turned to Joe Harris, "what do you do Joe?" "Play music" came the brief reply. "In a drinking place?" Lomax asked. "Yes sir," said Joe. "Play and sing?" inquired Lomax. The interview wasn't going well so Joe played the "Baton Rouge Rag" to a banjo-like theme with a "heel-and-toe" dance timing. Lomax asked Joe where he had learned it. "I jus' studied it up myself." "Didn't you tell me that somebody else started you on it?" Lomax asked in a reproving tone. "Yes sir, the boy—he was a trumpet player and he learned it to me." "How long ago?" Lomax asked. "Been around thirty-three years ago," Harris replied, explaining in answer to a further question, that this was in Bunkie, Louisiana. Harris revealed a little more of himself when he recorded a song in Creole patois, "Creole Song"(AFS 3990 B4). This he learned in New Iberia, he explained, some thirty-six years before. At the time he was sixteen years of age.[24]

LOMAX: Did you speak any French, Creole down there?
HARRIS: Yes sir.
LOMAX: What do the words mean?
HARRIS: "I got no razor, and I got no gun,
                I got no money, and I don't want you."

They moved hastily on to the next tune. It was "Nobody's Business" a version of a traditional theme first popularized by Bessie Smith in 1923 by its full title of "'Tain't Nobody's Business If I Do."[25] On this Joe Harris took the vocal, his voice being stronger than Kid West's, who, on the evidence of the recordings, appears to have been the older of the two men. It was one of three older themes which the duo recorded; the other two were "Bully of the Town" and "Old Hen Cackled and Rooster Laid an Egg." Although "I'm Looking for the Bully of the Town" had been recorded by, for example, The Memphis Jug Band in 1927,[26] it seems unlikely that the Harris-West version was derived from such a source. Part of every songster's repertoire early in the century, this song seems to have survived in the duo's memory in a fragmentary form. Kid West's mandolin playing is sufficiently adept to suggest that he may have been a dab hand at playing the tune in earlier years. "Old Hen Cackle" was more popular with white communities, a dance theme which was recorded by a number of old-time white musicians. There is some relation with "Cacklin' Hen and Rooster Too"[27] by The Skillet Lickers, the Atlanta-based white string band which featured Kid West's contemporary, Gid Tanner, on fiddle. It was in fact a fiddle showpiece permitting instrumental imitations of the fowl. One might conclude that Kid West had been a member of a string band playing for white dances at some time in his life, when a fiddle player performed the mimicry.

Though older "musicianers" [28] than Buddy Woods, both Kid West and Joe Harris played and sang blues. "Kid West Blues" has an engaging touch of irony which declares his intention to stay single and not be bothered by "no worryin' kids." Though Joe Harris's "East Texas Blues" is fairly conventional with its verses derived from Blind Lemon Jefferson, his reference to getting to Texas "across the line" emphasizes the persistence in the folk memory of the boundary between the States and the Texas Republic. His "Out East Blues"(AFS 3991 A2), a wistful blues with echoes of earlier recordings, includes the line stating that he had "a woman in Franklin, one in Donaldsonville." These towns in St. Mary's and Ascension Counties, respectively, have even today populations below ten thousand. Bunkie, incidentally, lies southwest of Natchez-on-the-Hill in Avoyolls Parish. The final blues, well played by Kid West, "A-Natural Blues," is otherwise notable for the inclusion of a verse usually associated with Huddie Ledbetter's "Good Morning Blues."[29]

From Shreveport, John and Ruby Lomax went in search of Leadbelly's family, who lived in Mooringsport, near the site of the first big Caddo Lake oil strike. Meeting Uncle Bob Ledbetter must have been a landmark for John Lomax, for the old man was the uncle of Huddie Ledbetter. Lomax wrote in his notes: "Uncle Bob, renowned singer in his younger days when Terrill Ledbetter (now dead) played the guitar, is now an 80-year-old man. Intelligent, possessing natural dignity and poise, he sits on the porch of his home with one of his granddaughters and looks out over fields of cotton and corn, which he is no longer able to cultivate. Children swarm around—nine in the bunch, the oldest sixteen years. He seems as indifferent to the clamor as the flies he brushes away. We were disappointed in Uncle Bob for he has had a "stroke" and his "remembrance" is no longer trustworthy. "He ain't in his mind," his daughter told us." [30]

One of thirteen children, he was born on December 18, in he believed, 1861. They asked him why, after working in a rich country for fifty years, he didn't save up something for his old age. "I drank too much whisky," he replied. "Every Saturday night I spent all I had earned the week before. But I had a good time." Ruby Lomax's letters added further details, quoting Bob Ledbetter as saying that he was born west of Oil City. He didn't go to school. "My father knew book-printin', he had print-learnin', and he learned me how to spell out of an old-fashioned spelling book. He didn't know nothing about writing ... I was never in jail in my life, I didn't go to see my friends there.

I always said, 'Practice makes perfects,' and I stayed away from the jail. My father learned me what was right to do and I tried to do it. My father sang regular church songs. I sang fiddle reels—not a fiddler though. Everywhere you used to hear me I was singing reels ... I joined the church at 19, married at 20, just started in the '20s. I believe in conjure if you let 'em put it in your coffee or food." Noted Ruby Lomax: "It was from Uncle Bob that Leadbelly learned many of the songs that he 'composed' himself!" They asked him where he learned so many songs, "Jes' broadenin' around, jes' broadenin' around" he replied.[31]

By now he was almost unable to sing, but he took them to see his grandson, Noah, a blues singer and guitarist. "Noah resembles Leadbelly physically (he would like to imitate him as a guitar player, but Noah works at his job too closely, he doesn't practice 'pickin'' enough). All of Noah's tunes are 'Blues,' most of which he claims to have put together. As he played for us in Oil City, the adoration of his comely wife who sat by, the grave regard and esteem manifested by Uncle Bob, made the scene memorable."[32]

The "scene" was set with Uncle Bob being interviewed by John Lomax. "Uncle Bob told all about the lakes and ferries in the old days. 'Lots of good fishin',' he said, 'but I don't like to fish. Don't like anything about the water; the biggest motion I can make in the water is to go to the bottom.'" In half apology for Huddie's troublous career he remarked: "Looks like some people's born for trouble; jes' love trouble." Again, "I tell you how it is wid de nigger nation. If a man goes big wid de women, us men hates him!" He followed this with an unaccompanied "Cleveland Campaign Song"(AFS 3992 B 1) potentially of great interest because of its possible early date; the unlovable but ample Grover Cleveland having been elected to office in the year of Leadbelly's birth and entering the White House in 1886. Cleveland's second term, to which this song may have referred, was inaugurated in 1893, supported by the Populist vote. Though it is unlikely that either Uncle Bob Ledbetter or his local black contemporaries had the vote, he did claim he had himself voted for Cleveland. "When the Sun Goes Down" (AFS 3992 B 2,3,4) on a standard blues theme followed, in no less than three takes, suggesting that the stricken Uncle Bob was not up to recording by himself. He was prevailed upon to sing "Irene," with Noah Moore playing the guitar accompaniment.

"Huddie learned 'Pauline' from Uncle Bob and probably many another tune. 'Pauline,' by the way, says Uncle Bob, came to him from his father," John Lomax recorded in his notes, presumably confusing "Irene," with Allen

Prothro's song "Pauline" (AFS 176 B), recorded some seven years before in Nashville Penitentiary. Uncle Bob concluded with "What She Ate" (AFS 3994 A 2), possibly a minstrel-type number, and then Noah Moore took over.

In spite of Lomax's comments, Noah's first items were not blues. "Mr. Crump Don't 'Low It Here"(AFS 3993 A 1) was the spirited barrelhouse piece that was known to all the Memphis singers and which was recorded as "Mr. Crump Don't Like It" by Frank Stokes in 1927.[33] The identity of Mr. Crump was unknown to Noah Moore, and John Lomax's questions and Noah's replies make it clear that he did not associate Memphis with the song. It seems therefore that he probably adapted the Stokes record but introduced the rhythms and licks that he had learned from his elder cousin, Huddie.

"I Done Tol' You" was not strictly a blues either, but an eight-bar dance reel, with refrain of a kind popular in country districts until the thirties. "You call that a two-step?" Lomax asked. "I reckon so," Noah replied, acknowledging that it was the kind that he used to play for dances. In this item, which he recorded twice, the influence of Leadbelly is strong and the powerful rhythms are extremely well handled. But Noah was a younger man and a man of his time. As Lomax had observed, blues were Noah's music and for these he changed his style. "Oil City Blues"(AFS 3993 B 1) and "Low Down Worry Blues" are played in a rolling style, with occasional bass string runs or hammered treble notes in a manner much favored by Texas guitarists of the thirties. Possibly the shadow of Funny Paper Smith (Howling Wolf Smith)[34] falls across these recordings, but they also link with later singers like Lil' Son Jackson.[35] Less likely but subtly evident is the influence of Robert Johnson, especially in the closing verses of "Low Down Worry Blues."[36] Noah uses the humming phrases and once or twice the high notes of the treble E picked at the 12th fret that Johnson favored. This recording lasted nearly twelve minutes, quite exceptional for recordings of the time. "'Bout the longest one I ever heared," remarked Lomax. "It seems like it still got me in a sweat," Noah replied after his marathon performance.

He emerges from the recordings as a good all-rounder, playing dance reels and blues with equal skill. His "Just Pickin'" (AFS 3995 A 1) is a dance tune adapted from the traditional ballad of the region "Ella Speed."[37] He followed it with a slide guitar piece, "Settin' Here Thinkin'," probably played with the guitar flat, and with a vocal that owed even more to Robert Johnson. The final solo item, "Jerry's Saloon Blues," was in the same vein but again with the guitar played in a manner that suggested at least some awareness of the school of Buddy Woods.[38]

At about seven that evening John Lomax went out for a bottle of milk, a piece of cake, and a sandwich for Uncle Bob Ledbetter. Later they drove him home from the Oil City hotel where the recordings had taken place. "They sure showed me a good time; that was the first time I ever ate at a white people's hotel in my life," Bob told his admiring family when he got home.

The Shreveport-Oil City sessions were over, and none of the participating singers ever recorded again. What happened to them?

Almost exactly twenty years later, in the summer of 1960, with my wife Val and Chris Strachwitz I tried to trace Oscar Woods. It wasn't easy to make any kind of research in Shreveport at that time. The city facilities were still segregated and whites weren't welcome in the tougher black districts. Only a few blocks away the white proprietor of a gas station pretended that he'd never heard of Fannin Street. When we got there, finally, it looked oddly pleasant and shaded, the smaller timber framed cabins that clung to the side of the steep hill appearing very domestic with linen on the washing lines. But a couple of black women soon let us know we weren't wanted.

In 1940 Oscar Woods had given his address as 1403 Patzman Street with a mailing address at 1529 Alston, and Harris and West were living at 816 Lawrence. This information was not available to us at the time of our own searches, but in the event it would have been of limited use. From one poor lead to another we eventually met up with Alex "Snooks" Jones, a piano player and one-time musician in a little band which included Woods, Kid West, and Joe Harris. Sadly we learned that Alex Jones had been one of the pallbearers at Buddy Woods's funeral when he died at the age of fifty-three in 1956.[39] Ironically, Kid West, a much older man, survived him by a year, while Joe Harris "just faded" and nothing more was heard of him. We went out to Club 66 on a deserted, chalky hill-site on the edge of town where the band used to play. A clap-boarded, white painted dance-hall, it had lurid murals on the walls and a jukebox in one corner. We tried to imagine it when the Shreveport string musicians provided the music, but in its silent, stuffy, unused space the images were slow in coming.

As for Noah Moore, he had died long before. His brother Tom, a welder at Riley Baird in Shreveport, wrote the brief details of Noah's life in a letter to Bruce Bastin.[40]

"Noah was born in 1907 in the percentage of Mooringsport, La., born to Mr. and Mrs. Tom Moore Sr. He was reared in Mooringsport, La. He learn some of his music from Huddie Ledbetter . . . they played together all through the piney woods. He worked as a sharecropper and he loved to fish." After recalling the Oil City session, Tom added: "Noah loved to play his guitar, sometimes in his younger days, he stayed up late at nights, some friends would usually gather around for a jam session. Unfortunately, he went to war (World War 2) next he was missing in action."[41]

Notes

1. The term "parish" is used only in Louisiana; elsewhere the states are divided into counties. The term was ratified in the State Convention of 1812. Texas became the twenty-eighth state in February, 1846.

2. Due north of Shreveport is Texarkana, on the Arkansas-Texas border and the other principal city in the Tri-State region. They are linked by the "Flying Crow" line.

3. Fuller historical details of the growth of Shreveport may be obtained from editions of the *Louisiana Almanac*, New Orleans, Pelican Publishing House, and from *Louisiana, A Guide to the State* (New York: Hastings House, 1941).

4. Leadbelly's encounters in Fannin Street are described by John A. Lomax in *Negro Folk Songs As Sung by Lead-belly* (New York: Macmillan, 1936) and are the subject of Leadbelly's recording of "Fannin Street," Musicraft 225, made 1 April 1939.

5. Figures simplified from *Louisiana Almanac*, 1968.

6. Excerpt from letter dated 14 October, from Ruby T. Lomax. Archive of Folk Song files.

7. John A. Lomax, *Adventures of a Ballad Hunter* (New York: Macmillan, 1947).

8. John A. Lomax field notes, Archive of Folk Song files.

9. Leadbelly had recorded "Boll Weevil"(AFS 273 A 1) in Shreveport, prob. October 1934; available of Library of Congress L 51. He made other versions for the Archive, and for Musicraft in New York in 1939 (Musicraft 226).

10. "Bo-Weavil Blues" by Ma Rainey, accompanied by Lovie Austin's Blues Serenaders, was recorded in Chicago, December 1923 and issued on Paramount 12080. She made a "New Bo-Weavil Blues"in December 1927, with her Georgia Jazz Band, Paramount 12603.

11. Shreveport Home Wreckers' "Fence Breakin' Blues—Home Wreckin' Blues" was issued on Victor 23275 and Bluebird B5341. Recorded Memphis, 21 May 1930.

12. Gitfiddle Jim (pseudonym for James "Kokomo" Arnold), "Rainy Night Blues—Paddlin' Madeline Blues," Victor 23268. Recorded, Memphis, 17 May 1930.

13. See: Paul Oliver, "Kokomo Arnold," *Jazz Monthly*, Vol. 8 No. 3, May 1962, pp. 10–15; Jaques Demetre and Marcel Chauvard, interview with Kokomo Arnold in "The Land Of The Blues," *Jazz Journal*, Vol. 13, No. 10, October 1960, p. 8.

14. Washington White, "New Frisco Train—The Panama Limited" Victor 23295, and "I Am in the Heavenly Way—Promise True and Grand." Victor 38615. Recorded, Memphis, 26 May 1930. Napoleon Hariston played second guitar. White was later known as "Bukka" or Booker White.

15. See Paul Oliver, notes to Arhoolie (LP) 1003, *Black Ace*, Berkeley, 1961.

16. The World's Columbian Exposition, generally termed the Chicago Fair or Chicago World's Fair was held in 1893. Hawaiian musicians were featured, as were African drummers from Dahomey. The annexation of Hawaii in 1897 resulted in the spread of Hawaiian music and the use of "Hawaiian bars" in guitar playing.

17. Between September 1934 and May 1938, Kokomo Arnold made 76 issued sides and a number of unissued titles for Decca, recorded in Chicago or New York.

18. John A. Lomax, field note, Archive of Folk Song files.

19. Other titles were "Evil Hearted Woman Blues," Decca 7904 (backed by a Peetie Wheatstraw item, "Southern Girl Bl.") and "Lone Wolf Blues"—the reverse of "Don't Sell It-Don't Give It Away"—on Decca 7219.

20. Kitty Gray and her Wampus Cats made ten titles in San Antonio on 30–31 October 1937. One of these was "Baton Rouge Rag," unissued on 78 and only recently released on 50 Years Of Jazz Guitar CBS (LP) 88225, 1976. This is the same tune as Joe Harris's 1940 recording; indeed, composer-publisher credits on the CBS label show—(J. Harris / J. Davis) Jimmie Davis Publishing—and there is therefore a distinct probability that Harris is one of the guitarists— Woods's slide guitar is also present. Buddy Woods preceeded "Baton Rouge Rag" with two items, "Muscat Hill Blues" and "Don't Sell' It (Don't Give It Away)," Vocalion 03906.

21. Bumble Bee Slim, "Hey Lawdy Mama," Decca 7126, recorded 8 July 1935. This, song is also known as "Meet Me in the Bottom."

22. Buddy Woods's 4 December 1938 Dallas session with the Wampus Cats had two guitars, trumpet, piano, string bass, and drums on "Jam Session Blues—Token Blues" (Vocalion 04604) and "Low Life Blues" (Vocation 04745). The fourth title "Come On Over To My House Baby" (Vocalion 04745) has no string bass or trumpet. The latter instrument has been credited to Herb Morand, the New Orleans born trumpet player who led the Harlem Hamfats. This band, in spite of its name, was Chicago-based in the 1930s. It recorded in New York in April 1938 and again in Chicago in March 1939, and it seems unlikely, though not impossible, that Morand was in Dallas for the Woods session.

23. "That Railroad Rag," lyrics by Nat Vincent, music by Ed Bimberg, was published 3 April 1911, by Head Music Company and subsequently recorded by Walter Van Brunt (Victor 16876). The Kid West–Joe Harris version is available on *Railroad Songs and Ballads*, Library of Congress L 61, with inset notes by Archie Green.

24. Many southern Louisiana blacks speak "gumbo French," a patois derived from "Creole" and "Cajun" elements. For a full explanation of these terms see Paul Oliver, "Creoles, Cajuns, and Confusion," *Blues Unlimited*, No. 4 (August 1963) pp. 5–7; reprinted in Simon A. Napier (ed.), *Backwoods Blues* (Bexhill-on-Sea, 1968) pp. 45–47.

25. Bessie Smith's first recorded title for Columbia was "Tain't Nobody's Business If I Do," made on 15 February 1923 but unissued. It was remade on 11 April 1923 (Columbia A3898).

26. The Memphis Jug Band, led by Will Shade, recorded "I'm Looking for the Bully of the Town" at its second session on 9 June 1927. It was the third record of the band to be issued (Victor 20781). See also note 27.

27. The Skillet Lickers with Gid Tanner, fiddle, recorded "Cacklin' Hen and Rooster Too" (Columbia 15682-D) on 4 December 1930. They also recorded "Bully of the Town" on location in Atlanta on 17 April 1926 (Col. 15074-D). It is possible that Harris and West drew these tunes from white sources. Fiddlin' John Carson, for example, recorded "The Old Hen Cackled and the Rooster's Goin' to Crow"on 13 June 1923 (Okeh 4890) and two years later, in June 1925, a version of "Bully of the Town" (Okeh 40444). Similarly, Earl Johnson, who died at the age of seventy-nine in May 1965, recorded with his Dixie Entertainers in Atlanta, Georgia, on 21 February 1927, "Ain't Nobody's Business" (Okeh 45092), "Hen Cackle" (Okeh 45123), and "Bully of the Town" (unissued). These themes were in fact popular among a great many white entertainers.

28. "Musicianer" was a term used by early (pre-blues) entertainers who distinguished the non-singing instrumentalists from the singing guitarists or banjo-players, who were termed "songsters." Editor's note: This differs from Lead Belly's understanding of the term.

29. Leadbelly worked up a spoken introduction to "Good Morning Blues," and always included a "blues all in my bread" stanza, for example, Bluebird B8791, recorded 15 June 1940.

30. Extracted from John A. Lomax field notes, Archive of Folk Song files.

31. Extracted from Ruby T. Lomax letters to her family, Archive of Folk Song files.

32. John A. Lomax, field notes.

33. "Mr. Crump Don't Like It" by the Beale Street Sheiks (Paramount 12552) was recorded in September 1927. The Beale Street Sheiks were Frank Stokes and Dan Sane, and their tune is the one usually associated with this theme. W. C. Handy in his autobiography *Father of the Blues* (London: Sidgwick and Jackson, 1957), reports having heard the song in Memphis in 1909, and the lyrics show a relationship to the Sheiks' song. Handy claimed to have used this as the basis of a tune used as a campaign theme for Edward H. Crump, who was elected mayor of Memphis in 1910. The tune was published as "The Memphis Blues"(1912) but is clearly a different one, (pp. 93–102).

34. J. T. "Funny Paper" Smith, also known as "The Howling Wolf," had some twenty sides issued in 1930 and 1931. He recorded again in 1935 but the items were unissued. After Blind Lemon Jefferson, Smith was probably the most influential of guitarists in the Texas area before World War II.

35. Lil' Son Jackson recorded for Gold Star and Imperial after the war, and made one session for Arhoolie in the summer of 1960, Arhoolie (LP) 1004.

36. Robert Johnson, Mississippi born but recorded in Texas in 1936 and 1937, was an important bridge between the older and the newer Mississippi styles of guitar playing.

37. "Ella Speed" is one of the most popular Texas ballads. Archive of Folk Song recordings of this theme appear on Flyright-Matchbox SDM 264 by Wallace Chains and by Tricky Sam on Flyright-Matchbox 265. It was also recorded several times by Leadbelly.

38. "Jerry's Saloon Blues" includes the unusual verse with reference to "Texas Avenue and that moving picture show," which was recorded by Leadbelly for the Archive of Folk Song in "I Got Up This Morning Had to Get Up So Soon" (AFS 122 A 2), Angola, Louisiana, 1 June 1934.

39. Interview with Alex "Snooks" Jones, Shreveport, 8 August 1960. The problems of tracing Oscar Woods were summarized in my article "Eagles on the Half," *American Folk Music Occasional*, No. 1, Berkeley, 1964, pp. 91–94.

40. Letter from Tom Moore to Bruce Bastin, 9 March 1974.

41. A photograph taken of Noah Moore is dated 1943. As he died in action he must have met his death between 1943 and 1945.

Jesse "Babyface" Thomas

—Eleanor Ellis

After Lead Belly, Jesse Thomas (1911–95) is arguably the best-known and most widely recorded blues man associated with the Ark-La-Tex. He certainly had the longest career, one that was well documented over a period of more than sixty years. It began in August 1929, when the teenaged Thomas stepped into a portable recording studio set up by the RCA Victor company in Dallas, Texas. The four selections recorded under the name Jesse "Babyface" Thomas were released many months after, when the Depression had decimated the industry. Thomas later recorded several dozen selections for a wide variety of labels beginning shortly after the close of World War II.

In this two-part piece, originally appearing in the August and September 1993 editions of the *D.C. Blues Society Newsletter*, Eleanor Ellis focuses on Jesse Thomas's early career and shares his perspective on musical creativity as a process of lifelong learning. Thomas discusses music making in the Thomas family and differences in earlier and later blues storylines. He also recounts life as a musician in search of work, traveling to different cities across the United States. His memories touch on his songwriting, performing, and recording, beginning with "Blue Goose Blues," a 1929 homage to an African American section of Shreveport now all but erased. Rather than setting this piece as an interview, Ellis edited the questions and retained Thomas's answers. The resulting narrative captures the voice of this legendary Shreveport singer/guitarist. Ellis's interview with Jesse Thomas took place in Shreveport in April 1990.

Thomas's music and life have been subject of a number of short pieces appearing in special-interest print sources like *Blues Unlimited*. This magazine, for example, also printed Gayle Dean Wardlow's "A Quick Ramble with Ramblin' Thomas, Jesse Thomas, Will Ezell, Bessie Tucker, Elzadie Robinson, and Texas talent scouts R. T. Ashford and the Kendle Brothers."[1] Wardlow's piece covers the same 1929 Victor session and mentions the presence not only of Ralph Peer but of Jimmie Rodgers as well. He also records Thomas's sketchy memories of other notable but elusive Shreveport musicians who all made a handful of recordings around the same era. These include Thomas's older brother Willard "Ramblin'" Thomas, as well as Elzadie Robinson and Will Ezell, who played mostly juke houses and turpentine camps in Louisiana, near Shreveport, and in southern Mississippi.

Another related source is the short piece by Ray Templeton in *Blues & Rhythm* that conveys the sketchy information we have on Jesse Thomas's brother, Ramblin' Thomas.[2] The elder Thomas remains a biographical cipher largely because he left home at an early age and never kept in touch with his family. He may have been born in Logansport, Louisiana, (at the southern tip of the Ark-La-Tex) sometime in the 1890s, and split his time between Shreveport and Dallas during the teens and 1920s. He lived until at least 1932—the date of his final recording session—but the date (even the decade) of his death is unknown. The only concrete material on Willard Ramblin' Thomas are his phonograph records, which he first made for Paramount in 1928 (probably by way of the Dallas talent scout R. T. Ashford) and completed his recording career with RCA Victor four years later. Depending on the particular song, his guitar style is reminiscent of two pioneer blues artists, Lonnie Johnson and Blind Lemon Jefferson. In other tunes, his playing style calls to mind the Shreveport slide guitarist Oscar "Buddy" Woods.

Notes

1. See Wardlow, "A Quick Ramble . . ." in *Blues Unlimited* 141 (Autumn 1981): 14–15.
2. See Templeton, "Ramblin' Thomas and the 'Texas & Pacific' Country Blues," *Blues & Rhythm* 34 (1988): 12–13.

Part One

Jesse Thomas recorded for Victor in 1929, using the name "Babyface" Thomas. He made many recordings in the years to follow, but they were on small labels and didn't receive wide exposure. In the 1980s some of these recordings, from the late '40s and early '50s, were included on the Nighthawk anthology *Down Behind the Rise*. It was the first time in years that his music had been given national distribution and the impact, at least among certain other musicians, was considerable.

I first heard a cut from this album on Steve Hoffman's show, *The Blues Experience*, on WDCU 90.1 FM, and was immediately intrigued by the music. In asking around—"Have you ever heard of a man called Jesse Thomas?"—I discovered others who'd been just as impressed as I was. Paul Geremia, Roy Bookbinder, and others less well known, all do songs written by Jesse Thomas from that Nighthawk album.

In the spring of 1990, I went to Shreveport to meet Jesse Thomas at his home. We spent the afternoon talking. He spoke of his musical development, of the way that things like phonograph records and electric guitars influenced musical forms and the ways that music is learned and played, and of various incidents in his life. He has never stopped listening and he has never stopped learning. His personal story and the music he has played reflect many of the changes in life and music that have taken place since the early years of this century and, because he has been an analytical observer as well as an active participant, he is able to give a sense of what it was like to be in the middle of musical history as it unfolded.

Jesse Thomas was born seventy-nine years ago in Logansport, Louisiana, near the Texas border. His parents raised nine children and he began to learn guitar around the age of seven by watching and listening to three older brothers (one of whom later recorded as "Ramblin' Thomas") and by practicing on a little guitar they kept around the house. When his father played violin for parties and dances, the whole house became a percussion instrument.

JT: He played something like folk music with a beat. He kept time by patting his foot. We lived in those frame houses with wood floors, and they were built on blocks kind of high up off the ground, and when you pat your foot on those floors you would hear a sound something like drum beats. And he could keep time with his feet. (Demonstrates with feet as he sits at the kitchen table) and people pat their hands (begins to clap at the same time) . . . it had a beat going, that's the way my daddy used to play. He had the beat going with his feet . . . and he'd play in one chord, but he'd be changing the riffs.

[Neither the Thomas family nor the people they knew had radios or record players when Jesse was growing up. The music he heard was the music of the people around him.]

JT: When we'd get together and have company, if someone could play the guitar, he would play it and people passing by with a guitar stop and have the guitar—was mostly acoustic boxes then small guitars, wasn't no large acoustic guitars. You'd just tie a string on each end and put it on your shoulder and just walk on off with it. Sometimes they'd be walking and playing while they were walking, and stop by and get together. Everybody enjoyed playing, they wanted to play and we didn't know it was any such thing as you could make a living playing music. We thought it was just to have fun and enjoy yourself. That's mostly the way we did. And they would sing whatever they knew. And other people would copy that. So we just started out like that.

[The increasing popularity of record players and the corresponding emergence of the recording industry—the "music business" would eventually result in a standardization of musical forms, the targeting of certain music for certain audiences, and full-time work for many musicians. Prior to that time, however, few people thought of music as a way to make a living. The music was a part of life, a natural accompaniment to everyday activities and was more free-form and personalized.]

JT: Before (W. C. Handy) recorded the blues—from what I've heard and what I believe—what I know—the blues was already there, that sound. It didn't have any form or musical composition or arrangements or nothing. The people would mostly make that sound or they would hum that sound or they would sing a few lines. Like (sings): "I'm down now but I won't be down always— and I won't be down always—and I won't be down always." And they would go around singing like that, and the field workers would be working in the fields in the summertime they would moan (demonstrates). You could hear that, you know, all around. When I was a boy, I used to hear that all the time.

I used to have a cousin lived in a little town, we lived out in the country and he would leave late in the evening, just about when the sun was going down, he'd be walking back and he would be singing to himself, he would say (sings): "By-you by-yo, by-yooo." I really didn't know what he meant. That's the way it was with that type of singing. Sometimes people would sing something or say something, we didn't know what they meant, but we would take it for what we believed they meant, you know. We'd have our own opinion of what they were talking about. Seemed like he was telling us goodbye, that he was gone, or saying to himself "I'm gone," and seems like we would understand.

But the difference in blues in those days and what they are now, see a blues song now is a blues style, a type of music, and the song has to be a song like any other song—it has to have a title that appeals to the public and it has to have a story line with the theme. But back then, you would sing one verse after another, and each verse would be a different theme. And we would still understand what they were talking about.

[Every verse began as an insight, an observation, an emotion or a thought in someone's head. The most vivid verses survived, becoming a part of the poetic body of song that grew from common, shared experiences.]

JT: You could tell two or three stories in one song. You could sing a blues like "I woke up this morning and the sun was rising slow." And you'd say that again; then you'd have a third line "She packed her suitcase and slowly closed the door." We would like that because we liked that sound, we liked that music and we liked the blues. That was one verse; the next verse might say "What make a rooster crow every morning 'fore day?" and he would repeat that line. "That's to let the sweet man know that the working man is on his way." We could understand that and it was a totally different theme or subject. The next verse would be something else: "I'm leaving this town if I have to ride the rods." That means if you have to get up UNDER the train and beat your way without buying a ticket, you'd just get up under the train and . . .

EE: Is that what riding the rods means? You mean you get up UNDER the train?

JT: You get up under those coaches. Not under the engine where all that heat and stuff was. You'd get under those coaches, see they had rods under there that connects you, like a foundation under there, and they would get up under there and get one, hang on to those rods, hold on where that train would be passing . . .

EE: That scares me to death (laughs) . . .

JT: Well, it was tough . . .

EE: You mean you'd be holding on, under the train, and it would be ZZZZ going along . . .

JT: You would be laying down under the train, taking a chance on bumping your head on those crossties . . .

EE: If you let go . . .

JT: It would tear you all to pieces. So that means that he wants to leave here so bad, times so tough, and he wanted to leave so bad til even if he had to ride the rods, he's going to leave anyway.

[Carrying on the verse was as important to the life of a song as was its origination. Before recordings made it possible to hear a song over and over at will, music was learned from person to person and might go through several changes each time this happened. In terms of both words and music, this process is one way that transformation and change took place. Each transformation added to the variety and impact of the whole; each had its own emotional reality and each interpretation made its own kind of sense.]

JT: One time I heard about a lady playing piano at a sawmill town, it might have been in . . . Bogalusa, Louisiana. Whatever she said, the people liked it and they would copy it . . . that's the way a lot of those songs spread . . . people would hear it and they'd say the same thing they heard her saying. I think she said "Oakdale is on the mountain, Craven's on the Santa Fe." Well Oakdale was a town, I guess, in Louisiana on the railroad line called The Mountain, I guess. But when I was a boy . . . when I first heard Oakdale's on the mountain," I thought it meant a person named Oakdale was up on a mountain CRAVING for the Santa Fe, wishing they were on the Santa Fe. They were just CRAVING for the Santa Fe (laughter). It's silly, isn't it?

EE: Well in a way it makes more sense than the other way 'cause I don't even know where Craven is.

JT: I don't either. So they would sing a song, even if we didn't know what it meant, we liked it. You would just understand it and go along with it and you'd FEEL it. And some people used to just break down and just cry when they'd hear those songs. That's how the blues affected us in those days. And it would go over so that it would impress the whole public to see how we were falling for the blues, that would make other people understand what we were going though.

[When Jesse Thomas left home, he went to live with relatives in Shreveport. I asked if he'd left because he was tired of living in the country.]

JT: I think music was mostly the cause of me leaving home. 'Cause see I ran away from home when I was fifteen. I wanted to play piano. I started off on guitar but we got so used to guitars, that's all we could hear in the country, then when I'd go to the towns they had electric pianos in drugstores and different stores . . . and you could put a nickel in those player pianos and make them play a tune. It wouldn't be any singing. But that was so much different from what I had been hearing. In the country they were just rapping on the guitar, no melodies, solos, no patterns, you'd just rap on that guitar. That's all we knew. And the piano sounded so good I wanted to forget about the guitar and play piano.

[After Shreveport, he went to Texas to stay with a brother and work on a plantation in a little town near Dallas. The record business was booming by this time. The blues he heard had become more structured, a recognized and popular musical form. Many famous recording stars made appearances in Dallas, and their success showed that it was possible to make a living as a musician. It was in Dallas that he heard Blind Lemon Jefferson, and was inspired to take up guitar again and pursue a musical career when he saw Lonnie Johnson in a vaudeville show at the Ella B. Moore Theater on Central Avenue, near Elm Street.]

JT: I went in there and saw that man playing that guitar like I never saw anybody, I never HEARD a guitar played like that before. He had a big, expensive guitar, something like a Martin or Gibson. Something I'd never seen before. And then he would play on the stage and do a number or two and go back and change clothes. Come back with a different suit of clothes on. I don't think I had ONE suit and he would change suits ever time he came out on the stage. I never seen anything like that ... I got so excited that made me want to go back to guitar, see I had thrown my guitar away and was crazy 'bout piano, but I wanted to go back to guitar then. I could hear about him all over Dallas ... "Lonnie Johnson, Lonnie Johnson, that man got a check, his royalty check came ... $2,000!" We was working for a dollar a day. Never had no money. I said, if I could make $1,000! And I started running around every kind of way with a guitar, thought I was going to get like Lonnie Johnson ... even learned to play like him. But I still didn't have any money, any connection. I wondered why didn't somebody let ME make some money, after I learned to play ... I was sixteen years old.

[At the time there was no way to be sure where the best musical opportunities were and one rumor was as good as another.]

Part Two

JT: Then I left there and went to Oklahoma City ... trying to hitchhike up north into Chicago and Kansas City. People talking all over ... telling what's happening in Chicago, what's going on in Kansas City; people would tell me and swell my head, brainwash me this way and that way; I'd believe everything somebody said: "If you was in Oklahoma with that guitar, boy, the way you play you'd get rich." Yah, I told them, I'm going to get out to

Oklahoma. Got there, and I mean that was TOUGH when I got there, didn't make nothing.

So when I was in Oklahoma City I got a telegram from Dallas, a fella had told the RCA Victor Company about me . . . I came back from Oklahoma City and I made records . . . I was eighteen . . . I made records for the Victor Company called "Blue Goose Blues" . . . . (Blue Goose) was an area where we used to hang around; it had a club there, a beer joint, barber shop, cafe; it was just a part of town.

But the depression was starting then and the record companies wasn't paying much. That big depression came . . . the bottom fell out; there wasn't any money. So I didn't make much money at that. Next time they got ready to record me they couldn't find me; I was somewhere hitchhiking up and down the road. I never did get to record for them again. But the other guys that I know, that I recorded with and worked with, they was making sessions twice a year. And they couldn't find me so they just wiped me off the list, I guess.

[A group he'd been with in Oklahoma City was playing hits like "My Blue Heaven" and "I Never Knew" and the more complex chordal structure of this popular music made it difficult for him to follow. When he returned to Fort Worth, he enrolled in a music school where he learned to read music and studied harmony, theory, and ear training. These lessons, which were offered only on piano, had a marked influence on his guitar style.]

JT: After I took piano lessons I could make (the guitar) sound like a piano, those chords and chord changes, you know, and progressions. You couldn't tell it much from the piano; except you didn't have melody and bass just like the piano but you could play some tunes and get practically the same sound. Wasn't must difference in it. When I played on the radio one time in Santa Barbara . . . a long time later . . . I had forgotten that I'd learned most of my music from the piano 'cause I wanted to play piano first . . . and a lady told me . . . "I heard you playing on the radio and knew that was you before they announced your name." I said, "How did you know?" She said, "Because you make your guitar sound like a piano."

[Encounters with the big bands that toured through Dallas and Fort Worth influenced Jesse Thomas in several ways. He saw that it was possible to live a musical life, to play the circuits and make a good living without recording or being a big star. The sophisticated arrangements he heard were appealing, a new approach to the blues he had associated with simpler, country styles. He particularly liked the horn section and decided he wanted to make his guitar sound like a saxophone. This was before the existence of electric guitars and the people he told were baffled by the idea. He was talking about a sound and a technique that was not possible at the time.]

JT: Those horn players in there, they excited me, they could play that horn type stuff, solos and riffs and things. I couldn't do that on a guitar and that got in my mind. I wanted to solo and pick the guitar and play melodies. Wanted to make my guitar sound like a saxophone.

After I got about twenty-something years old, I was playing, called myself professional, and I wanted to solo. So I told the piano player one time, I say, "I want to make my guitar sound like a saxophone." He said, "What are you talking about?" I said, "I want to solo and just make it sound like a saxophone." He said, "Why don't you go get a couple of saxophones?". . . . He thought I was foolish. I couldn't make nobody understand what I meant. They couldn't teach me; so it was still in me.

So I asked another piano player . . . in Tucson . . . "I've been trying to solo and play like ya'll and play like horns and things—how do you do that?" He said, "Oh—pat your foot, just pat your foot." Well, I couldn't see that either. How's patting my foot going to get me where I want to go? That didn't work. So in a way I just about give up, but it was still there, I still wanted my guitar to play like a saxophone.

EE: What was it about the saxophone that was different from the way you were playing guitar at that time? Were you trying to keep down all parts of the chords as you played the melody?

JT: That's what held me down, see . . . picked with my fingers and my thumb and I could rap with my thumb and compliment myself as I'd go along. But I couldn't carry the solo and strike those chords too. By me playing by myself so much I had to carry chords and try to carry the bass along with it, a lot of guitar players was doing that in those days, they played by themselves and carried a little melody and a little chords all at the same time.

But those saxophone players was in bands and they wasn't doing all that by themselves. They were just doing one thing on the instrument. And that's what held me back so long. I was trying to do what the saxophone player was doing in the band, and carry the background like I had been carrying it for my own self. . . . That was before they made electric guitars.

EE: I was going to ask you if it was not only the WAY it was played, but the tone.

JT: The tone, and the sustain, all that, it wasn't there ... you didn't have volume, you just had to rap those strings, hit those strings on those acoustic boxes, hit them hard to get volume ... the tone wasn't there. It just wasn't there.

So later on, here come the electric guitar. I got me (one) that put me closer to the saxophone sound and that solo I had been wanting. But I was trying to play the melody and the chords and all that stuff at the same time. It would sound terrible on an electric guitar, trying to do all that.

[It was one particular book on jazz instruction that finally brought it all together and led to yet another guitar style.]

JT: I got that book on jazz and they said, "In order to play jazz you have to know how to play the blues." Well, I'd been playing blues all my life, but didn't know how to sit down and just play one blues run after another, making it up as I go along, to a beat. How many riffs or how many notes to put in one measure. I didn't know that. But I studied that jazz book and it showed me what a pattern is, a solo pattern, a two-measure pattern, a four-measure pattern, and a blues riff. Then that connected me back with what I had already learned, plus what I was learning, and it made me know how to compose blues, how to make up my own blues runs. And that's what I needed to know. When I started doing that, well then it all came naturally. I had it all the time in me, but I couldn't execute it because I didn't know how.

[In 1937 Jesse Thomas went to California with the idea of working in a band for one of the movie studios.]

JT: I was with different groups and we were traveling west ... people were talking about "If you go to California that's where they make the money." Maybe you could have gotten some jobs in a studio playing for certain programs but it wasn't like what they said .... go to work in studios just like that .... altogether different. ... We auditioned for two or three movies but we didn't get in the movies. I wanted to play in a studio backing up other people. I know I wouldn't get a job as actor, I didn't have acting experience, or as an entertainer, I was mostly interested in music. And I probably could have, if I'd known how to call up the studio and tell them what I was, but I didn't even know how to go about applying for a job. I didn't even know how to do that.

I would always wait for somebody to come and get me. It's the way I was brought up, you know. People used to come and get us to go pick cotton or go work at the sawmill, and that's all I knew at that time, wait for somebody to come get you. I didn't know how to go contact: "I can do this; if you're interested in that, I know this, I know that." So when you don't know, it makes a lot of difference . . . . I got a late start and didn't have education. I had to study and learn after I left home, you know. So all that made a difference.

[This education—some formal, some in the school of life—has made Jesse Thomas an all-around musician and, during this long career, he has played and recorded all kinds of music—R&B, country, and jazz, as well as blues. Like many working musicians, his repertoire is geared to the occasion. When I was in Shreveport, I went to hear him play for Happy Hour at the Radisson Hotel with piano player Peaches Sterling who had come in on the bus from Baton Rouge for the job. They played everything from blues—including some originals—to standards like "Don't Get Around Much" and "Satin Doll" to classics like "Drinking Wine" and "Caledonia." At the New Orleans Jazz and Heritage Festival, however, Jesse Thomas did an entire solo set of his own recent blues compositions.

He has composed many songs but prefers his latest work; he has written at least fifteen new songs within the past two or three years. During that time he studied songwriting, just as he once studied music. A recent writing course—although geared toward articles and stories—has been very helpful. The techniques for each song vary, but he generally begins with the music. Instead of writing line by line, rhyming, he starts with an overall theme or idea and he writes several drafts.]

JT: They say the mind is something like a computer, that stuff will be in your subconscious mind. If you write songs, you will see that it works. What you're doing is creating and when you write that down, put it aside, go back to it the next day, you'll be surprised at the ideas that's going to come back and give you some more material to work with.

[During a recent television program on Shreveport's Cablevision, Jesse Thomas was asked his advice to young people.]

JT: I told them to be proud of yourself and set your goal and meet that goal, and be proud because you're young and beautiful and healthy and have a future. Know that you're as good as anybody else. You're not any better and you're not any less. Just be proud of yourself. Go on and be happy and make it. Maybe it'll take you a year to get where you're going, that's not long, enjoy yourself while you're waiting. If it takes five years, that's not long, enjoy those five years while you're reaching that goal. Because the longer you wait for what you want, the better it is when you get it.

Look how long it took me to make my guitar sound like a saxophone or even solo like I wanted to solo, with feeling, and could sell it, you know. And put it over. It's taken me, I would say, about forty years.

I had to wait till they made electric guitars. Look like it'd taken them so long. I wonder why it took them so long to put a pick-up and amplifiers for a guitar. Took them people so long. They made jukeboxes, they had electric pianos, no electric guitars. I guess they just forgot about us . . . . bands wouldn't hire us—don't hire acoustic guitars in the band . . . . big bands didn't have a guitar in it. They had banjos playing in a band before they had guitars. They were louder. Guitars weren't even in bands. We had a hard time.

That's the reason I say to a young person, if they really want to make it, all they have to do is just make it and it won't take them too long . . . See, what it took me forty years to do, a young person now can do that in two years.

I'm seventy-nine years old now . . . . started out playing as a kid and left home when I was fifteen. Got on record when I was nineteen and got with groups and listened to those horn players and wanted to do what they were doing and look how long it took me to do that. And I'm just as happy now as I was when I was eighteen. Because I'm doing what I want to do. I work when I want to work. I have a choice to accept certain jobs and I'm married, buying a home. That ought to be something, you know, to look forward to.

The Flying Crow Blues

—Paul Swinton

"The Flying Crow" was a train line connecting Port Arthur, Texas, to Kansas City, with major stops at Shreveport, as well as Texarkana, another significant hub of the Ark-La-Tex. Recorded by Oscar "Buddy" Woods (see "Jerry's Saloon Blues") and Ed Schaffer, playing together as the Shreveport Home Wreckers, their version of "The Flying Crow" is a Shreveport example of a widespread blues tradition of homage to the railroads. Lead Belly sang about them in "Rock Island Line" and in "The Midnight Special," which details the pleasures brought to Sugarland (Texas) prison inmates when the train by that name brought their loved ones to visit. Often the vehicle of choice for African Americans leaving the South in search of a better life during the Great Migration, trains figure in recorded blues by artists throughout the South beginning in the early 1920s.

When I first heard "Shetland Pony Blues" by Son House, the middle passage seemed to contain some loud swishing surface noise. With repeated listening, it became clear that these sounds were that of a passing steam train picked up by the original recording equipment. I cannot describe the pleasure it gave me, not only hearing this classic blues tune but also discovering this more than welcome intruder. The romanticism and pure nostalgia attached to vintage blues recordings and the steam train will always evoke thoughts of a bygone age.

The steam train has always held an honorary position in the story of prewar blues. "The Seminole," "The Sunshine Special," "The Southern Belle," and others have all been immortalized in the lyrics of countless blues recordings and if the history of one train and its relationship to the blues is worth examining, it would be the Kansas City Southern Railroad's "Flying Crow."

The Kansas City Southern railroad was conceived by Arthur Stilwell in 1886 and incorporated the following year as the Kansas City Suburban Belt Line. Stilwell wanted a railroad to run from Kansas City to the Gulf of Mexico. By 1896, he had reached his goal.

He established the present city of Port Arthur, Texas, which he named after himself, and although he had lost control of the company by the twenties, the line had by then become a major contribution to the region's economy, and the numerous towns Stilwell created along the line remain as minor economic and political centers.

On June 15, 1928, the KCS put into service its flagship passenger train to be hauled by heavy "Pacific" steam locomotives, to journey a distance of 788 miles in twenty-five hours and travel "straight as the crow flies . . ."

". . . the 'Flying Crow' was to be the premier varnish on the KCS for twelve years. To be exact, it was the *only* long distance passenger train on the schedule. The 'Crow' never did set land speed records but you never could find a train that was known personally by more people."[1]

A map from a KCS employee timetable book, dated May 3, 1931, shows most places of significance on the railway. From De Queen, Arkansas, southward, is the area of the KCS in which the black population would have been concentrated. The Ouachita (WASH-uh-taw) mountains begin at De Queen. They extend up as far as Poteau, Oklahoma. The KCS is then in the Ozark mountains from Sallisaw, Oklahoma, to Joplin, Missouri. Above Joplin, the railway is in prairie land to Kansas City. These mountain and prairie regions traditionally lack substantial black populations due to their geographical and agricultural characteristics. South of De Queen, however, the racial composition was markedly different. The valley of the Red River (along the KCS from just below De Queen to just below Shreveport, Louisiana) was prime cotton plantation land and hence had a sizeable black element in its population. A major petroleum drilling boom in the same area during the first three decades of the century, undoubtedly had provided much work for common laborers. From Shreveport southward almost to Beaumont, Texas, the KCS courses through a pine forest region. The great timber era passed its peak here in the 1920s, and the great depression would have found many former loggers and mill workers of both races ready to sing the blues. It was almost inevitable that the "Flying Crow" would be celebrated in song.

The first phonograph recording to mention the "Flying Crow" appeared in February 1932 by Eddie and Oscar . . .

The two guitarists were Ed Schaffer and Oscar (Buddy) Woods. They had previously recorded together as the Shreveport Home Wreckers and Schaffer had previously backed white singer Jimmie Davis who possibly organized this session in Dallas, Texas. Only two titles came out of this session, both released on Victor 23324, "Nok-Em-All" and "Flying Crow Blues" . . .

The Flyin' Crow leavin' Port Arthur, leavin' at 2-3:45. (×2)
I'm going to find my baby and bring her back dead or alive.
She takes water at Port Arthur, stops at Texarkana for a slice of cake. (×2)
And when she gets going boys, that Flying Crow just won't wait.

(Spoken): I thought I heard that Flying Crow blow. Woman when you're leavin' you gonna catch that Flying Crow.

I helped you baby when you could not help yourself. (×2)
Now you got your hands on two-three nickels and you want to help
someone else.
Now she's gone, she gone, boys, got that red and blue light behind. (×2)
That red light's for danger, blue light for a worried mind.[2]

The title would seem to have sold poorly, only one single copy is known to have survived to this date. The composer credits on the label state "Oscar Woods." It is doubtful that we will ever know to what extent this is strictly true as Woods himself, when asked where he got his music, replied, "I guess I just settled on it. Just picked it up somewhere—something—I didn't read up on it."[3] Woods's later recordings would show that he could skillfully adapt other people's songs. It has been suggested by researcher Don Kent and others that the "Flying Crow" was primarily a piano piece.[4] It does seem possible that in the four years between the introduction of the "Crow" on the KCS and the Woods and Schaffer recording, Woods could have "picked it up somewhere" but at this late date, we have little chance of adding any further confirmed detail.

There seems little doubt as to Oscar Woods's influence on Carl Davis and his Dallas Jamboree Jug Band. Their session for Vocalion on 25 September 1935 contained two pieces in the Woods vein, one, "Dusting the Frets" is a version of Woods's "Don't Sell It, Don't Give It Away." Although Davis seemed to have beaten Woods to the studio to record his version, Woods would later claim composer credits[5] and would record the piece three times, each version swinging and confident, topped with superior slide guitar patterns. On the other hand, Davis's version is hectic, Woods's deft guitar playing is imitated with kazoo and skat singing, and the lyrics are badly memorized. This goes some way into explaining their treatment of "Flying Crow Blues"[6] as their next number in the session, again adopting typical Woods chord structuring. Davis's Jug band didn't even have a jug player so it is hardly surprising that they only seem to have bothered to remember the title, interjecting the name into various random, traditional verses. It is, nonetheless, an enjoyable piece of hokum, but it was two years before another truly excellent "Crow" recording came along, this time by Black Ivory King (David Alexander). His piano version was recorded for Decca in February 1937. After "toning" the train's bell on his piano, he takes off on a relaxed and assured journey . . . .

Flying Crow leavin' Port Arthur, why, they come to Shreveport to change
their crew (×2)
They'll take water in Texarkana and for Ashdown they'll keep
on through.
Twenty five minutes from Heavener for a cup of coffee and a slice of
cake (×2)
Flying Crow is headed for Kansas City, and boys she just won't wait.
Yes, she's gone, she's gone with a red and green light behind (×2)
Well now the red means trouble and the green means a ramblin' mind
Well, I hate to hear when that old fireman when he tolls his bell.

(Spoken). "Oh, ring em a long time mmmmmmmm."[7]

Could this possibly have been in King's repertoire for some time? He certainly seemed confident and familiar with this piece and if the "Flying Crow" was principally a piano blues, then King must be a main contender. There seems little doubt that Black Ivory King knew the KCS. Of all the "Crow" versions, he uses the most direct references to railway operations and place names, and his piece certainly aroused the most interest in the people I have contacted and interviewed in the course of the research for this article. Wherever possible, I have tried to provide tape recordings of the relevant titles to my informants and at this point their comments should be of interest. Retired KCS engineer, Mr. Howard O. Blackburn, whose experience goes back to the steam era and the Flying Crow, and who still lives by the tracks in Leesville, Louisiana, had this to say about King's version: ". . . passenger train crew changes between Port Arthur and Kansas City took place at Shreveport, Louisiana; Heavener, Oklahoma; and Pittsburgh, Kansas. Water was taken at a number of intermediate points between crew changes, including Texarkana. The Black Ivory King lyrics are indeed accurate in these respects."

Lowell G. McManus, the president of the KCS Historical Society Inc., also has this to say about the King version: "He seems to say 'Ashtown,' rather than Ashdown. The very next line (sung twice) clearly says, '25 minutes for a cup of coffee and a slice of cake.' What is said in the ellipsis is less clear. I believe it is a reference to a crew change at Heavener[8] (HEAVE-ner), perhaps corrupted to 'Heavenen.' That would have been a reasonable time for taking water, changing crew, etc., and would have provided time for passengers to detrain for a quick snack."

Kate Edwards of Shreveport, Louisiana, travelled on the "Crow" in the thirties and remembered on at least one occasion seeing passengers being entertained by colored musicians at one of these refreshment stops (this possibly could have helped in the development of this song). Unfortunately, Kate could not remember any further detail. One would assume that if the musicians were travelling with the train, they were not piano players!

Dusky Dailey was a fair piano player, equally at home playing boogie and jump blues on his own or in a band format. He produced a solo version of "Flying Crow Blues" in late 1937[9] accompanied by his own piano. He plays well, with a pounding left hand, and it was probably the best title he produced from his complete output. However, it offered little insight into the "Crow's" blues history, consisting of unrelated traditional blues verses (failing to even mention the "Crow"), and he chose to only retain the "red and green lights" final verse.[10] This verse itself was not unique to the "Flying Crow" and had been common fare amongst Texas musicians prior to 1932, most likely popularized by Blind Lemon Jefferson.[11]

The last pre-war (1941) "Flying Crow Blues" was by Washboard Sam (Robert Brown), accompanied by Big Bill Broonzy (gtr) and possibly William Mitchell (bass) for the Bluebird label.[12] Sam recorded prolifically and was one of the most popular blues singers of the thirties and forties. The rich vocals and driving rhythm on his version of the "Flying Crow Blues" shows exactly why. The lyrical content of this piece was certainly drawn from at least one of the previously discussed titles. If Sam had firsthand knowledge of the "Flying Crow," it certainly wasn't recent; his opening verse still had the train taking water on at Texarkana while the "Crow" itself had been streamlined and dieselized back in 1937.

The forties saw the end of the steam era and all its romantic connotations. Many would argue that this period also marked the end of the golden age of blues recordings. The "Crow" in its diesel form continued until May 1968 when declining passenger use forced the KCS to finally lay it to rest, but its glory days are still fondly remembered by many along the Texas/Louisiana border and the batch of fine blues recordings that used its name have all, thankfully, survived, establishing the "Flying Crow's" rightful place in the history of the blues.

I would like to thank the following people: Don Kent for the label pic and detail on Victor 23324 [in the original], Lowell G. McManus, W. D. & Tillie Caileff of the KCS Historical Society, Shreveport, Howard O. Blackburn, Kate Edwards, Lyn Burshtin & Mike Griffiths.

Notes

1. "Kansas City Southern" by Terry Lynch & W. D. Caileff Jr., Pruett Publishing Co. 1987.
2. Eddie & Oscar, "Flying Crow Blues," Victor 23324; 8 February 1932.
3. Interview with John Lomax, Library of Congress, Shreveport, 9 October 1940.
4. Don Kent, notes to RCA Victor LPV577, Washboard Sam "Feeling Low Down."
5. As note 3.
6. Dallas Jamboree Jug Band, "Flying Crow Blues," Vocalion 03132, 25 September 1935.
7. Black Ivory King, "The Flying Crow," Decca 7307, 15 February 1937.
8. Previous transcriptions of this number, including my own, heard this as "evening". Mr. McManus's version is, I feel, correct.
9. Dusky Dailey, "Flying Crow Blues," Vocalion 03893, 26 October 1937.
10. Although the symbolism of the "red and green lights behind" is stated, they were simply the marker lights at the end of the train. In those days, passenger trains carried electric marker lights that had evolved from the kerosene lanterns that were formerly hung high on the rear outer corners of the last car. A green light was displayed forward from the end, and a red light rearward. A trackside observer, therefore, would have seen a green light approaching him and a red one receding in the opposite direction.
11. Blind Lemon Jefferson, "Dry Southern Blues," Paramount 12347, c. March 1926.
12. Washboard Sam, "Flying Crow Blues," Bluebird B8844, 26 June 1941.

The Legend of Old Blue Goose

—Dan Garner

First celebrated on Jesse Thomas's 1929 recording "Blue Goose Blues," the area he sings about does not appear on any official maps of Shreveport, nor will many present-day city residents know its location. Blue Goose was an African American part of town in a segregated area, the "wrong side of the tracks" used by the Texas and Pacific Railroad. It was officially known as Wilson Alley, but its local name derived from the Blue Goose Grocery and Market, located at the corner of Snow and Pickett Streets.

Jesse Thomas's song commemorated this important neighborhood for Shreveport blues, one that barely exists today but constituted a thriving part of Shreveport's black life from the 1920s into the 1960s. He was only one of the musicians who hung around there in its early decades. Oscar "Buddy" Woods played in Blue Goose, as did many of his contemporaries, most of them now lost to history. Dan Garner's description of Blue Goose originally accompanied a 1998 compact disc *The Legend of Old Blue Goose* (BGB Records 427642, 1998). [1]

Note

1. According to Garner, Muscat Hill (celebrated in a song by Woods) may have been another smaller black section of Shreveport located within blocks of Old Blue Goose.

Huddie "Leadbelly" Ledbetter is considered to be an icon of early blues, not only in the Shreveport area, but all over the world. However, many years before Leadbelly was recorded, other blues artists from the Shreveport area had already made records, and they all played music on the streets in a small area of town, which today is officially identified as Wilson Alley, but was earlier known as Old Blue Goose. In 1929, a teenager named Jesse Thomas recorded a song called "Blue Goose Blues " in the Deep Ellum section of Dallas, Texas. After many years and many roads traveled, there came a resurgence of interest in this bluesman in the mid-eighties. At that time I had been performing with Jesse for several years and was dumbfounded to learn that this very talented guitarist had been a recording artist for six decades. Some would suggest that he was an early innovator of what is commonly referred to as jazz-fusion.

I had the good fortune to travel with Jesse throughout the country, performing his music at some great blues festivals. It was on the way back from one of these festivals that I asked Jesse about "Blue Goose Blues." He explained that Blue Goose was just a neighborhood with a cafe, a barbershop, and a grocery store where people used to gather and have some fun. He said it wasn't on any map; it was just a name that people called the area because of a picture of a big blue goose on the side of a building.

"And that place," he said, ". . . it's still there."

During a photo shoot for Jesse's last CD, we ended up where it all began: Old Blue Goose. It was a cool, sunny day. I could see the skeletal rooftop of the Calanthean Temple, where, in the twenties, thirties, and forties, the upper echelon of black society danced to the live performances of Louis Armstrong, Cab Calloway, and Duke Ellington. I could almost hear the music and laughter waft along the dusty road, much like it must have been at the time Jesse first visited these mean streets, so long ago. In between shots I couldn't help asking Jesse what he remembered about the area.

Did he ever perform on the streets?

No, it was just an area that he wrote a song about, a place where people congregated and he had been to a couple of times.

A mutual friend, Monty Brown, had interviewed Jesse years earlier and received a slightly different answer about Blue Goose.

"That's where I stayed when I first came here, and I just—made up some words, put it on record. You know, I didn't even know what I was talking about at that time. I think I saw some old man there and he was real good on the guitar, on the chords. He didn't sing good, just play something like that, and I copied some of that and put the words to it."

Located at the corner of Snow and Pickett streets, in Shreveport, Louisiana, this community of Blue Goose certainly dates back at least to the late 1800s, when the original structure of the Blue Goose Grocery and Market was built. When the area actually received its name will be left to the historians. I went down to Old Blue Goose after Jesse passed away in an effort to recapture something of the man I knew. I entered the barber shop of Nathaniel Hogan and sat down in an ancient barber chair for a haircut and some information.

Had Mr. Hogan ever heard of Blue Goose?

Why of course he had, it had been called that long before he came into the area in the early thirties. It was named for a big picture of a blue goose feeding its young, painted on the side of a grocery store. That store was torn down in the early forties.

Had he ever heard of or met Jesse Thomas?

No, Jesse had left Shreveport in the late twenties before Mr. Hogan had arrived and didn't return until the mid-fifties.

Were there ever any musicians who performed in the area?

Yes, The Blue Goose always had musicians who played on the streets for nickels. There were two guys, Ed Schaffer and Woods (Mr. Hogan could not remember his first name), and they played their guitars "real good."

I feared I had come to a dead end, but I was just starting down the road. That afternoon I called my friend Robert Trudeau and mentioned my visit with Mr. Hogan.

Had he ever heard of Ed Schaffer and a guy named Woods?

That would be Ed Schaffer and Oscar "Buddy" Woods, sometimes known as the Shreveport Homewreckers and sometimes calling themselves the Wampus Cats. They recorded in the twenties and thirties, sometimes backing up Jimmie Davis before he became the governor of Louisiana. Some people think that it may have been one of the first times blacks and whites recorded together. They also toured together.

I spoke later with Kip Lornell. He described Oscar "Buddy" Woods as street singer and self-proclaimed street-rustler who was born near Natchitoches, Louisiana, and drifted seventy miles north to Shreveport around 1925. There, as Mr. Hogan had previously stated, Woods played on street corners, passing the hat for nickels, and at an alleged speakeasy, the Blue Goose Grocery and Market where it was said that liquor and dancing abounded.

And there were others who played those lucrative streets.

Babe Kyro Lemon Turner, known as the Black Ace; Kid West and Joe Harris, all performed with Buddy Woods there, and later recorded for John Lomax as a part of a project for the Folksong Archive of the Library of Congress.

There is documentation of Jesse Thomas's older brother, Ramblin' Willard Thomas, wandering through the old Blue Goose, playing street corners. As a matter of fact, it was most certainly his frequent trips between Shreveport and Dallas, Texas (about 290 miles) west by rail and road, that led to his nickname "Ramblin'" Thomas.

Some speculate because of the association with Ramblin' Thomas, as well as specific geographical clues, that many other blues pioneers such as Dennis "Little Hat" Jones, J. T. "Funny Paper" Smith, King Solomon Hill, and Henry Thomas may have passed through Blue Goose on a circuit of train rails and troubadour-friendly venues. The word, it seems, had gotten around about this little corner of Shreveport.

But what brought these blues legends to these dusty back roads in the first place?

According to historian Willie Burton, the area might have been the seat of an original colony of black settlement after the Civil War. Its proximity to Texas Avenue (the Texas Road) and the Union Railway Station accounts heavily for that argument. The boats on the Red River that brought goods from Texas, Oklahoma, and up from Alexandria, Louisiana, and supply stations along the way, eventually made their way to market on Commerce Street and some, eventually, to the train stations. Draymen (ones who drove long carts that carried goods) could be seen transporting goods from the docks down to Union Station.

Blacks moved to the areas allowed for them off Texas Avenue to be near the job market. In the Blue Goose area were found draymen, barbers, brick masons, seamstresses, stablekeepers, woodchoppers, welldiggers, warehousemen, washerwomen, and hustlers.

Another historian, Eric Brock, contends that the original Blue Goose structure was built in the 1890s and during prohibition, became a speakeasy, operating ostensibly as a cafe.

The building was pulled down in the early forties and replaced by a structure similar to a 1939 annex to its immediate west. The only known photograph of the front of the Blue Goose shows stacks of bricks for the new building. In the photo, the Blue Goose was literally in its last days.

The new structure became the Silver Slipper Cafe and in the 1980s the Ebony Club. During WWII the Blue Goose was a popular stop for troops coming into Union Station nearby.

In its speakeasy days and earlier—indeed throughout its life—the Blue Goose saw many noteworthy musicians play there. At the time many were virtually unknown. Like the WWII soldiers, they found the Blue Goose because of its proximity to the railroad tracks and Union Station.

Mr. Hogan's barber shop also had an interesting history. According to Brock, it is the oldest continuously operating shop in Shreveport, originally opened by a black barber named Oscar Vena in 1916. Vena was succeeded by

Walter Van Dyke, who in 1935 hired Nathaniel "Tilo" Hogan, then twenty-five. Mr. Hogan has been there ever since and now owns the shop.

Ironically, there is no mention of Blue Goose on any map, government document, or any other official publication. It is only mentioned in a blues recording from 1929. Other locations throughout the city of Shreveport suffer the same fate. Dirty Thirty is casually mentioned in Ramblin' Willard Thomas's song "Jughead Blues" (some list this song as "Jighead Blues," which may be a racist corruption or refer to various speakeasies, that were also referred to as "jig joints") and is an area commonly called Jones Alley today.

This group of thirty "shotgun" houses lay hidden directly behind the Antioch Baptist Church and has a long history of being known for gambling, prostitution, and illicit acts. It is a stone's throw from Blue Goose and is similarly unrecorded.

Some areas mentioned by name in the songs of Oscar "Buddy" Woods may never be located or perhaps no longer exist due to the construction of an interstate highway, which cut a wide path through most of the surrounding area of Blue Goose. Muscat Hill, a location where wineheads congregated for "one drink of whiskey, two drinks of Muscat wine" during prohibition, could possibly be another name for Bachelor Hill, located about a mile east of Blue Goose, or it may refer to a location closer to the Dirty Thirty.

Perhaps one of the more interesting revelations about Woods's music comes from an obscure song called "Flying Crow Blues." According to a local train expert, the Flying Crow was a predominant railroad line which ran from Kansas City to Port Arthur. In the last line Woods sings "She's gone, she's gone, got that red and blue light on behind, oh the red lights for danger, blue lights for worried mind."

It would be five years later that Robert Johnson would record the song, "Love In Vain," where he sings, "when the train left the station there were two lights on behind, well, the blue light was my blues, and the red light was my mind."

Johnson traveled from Mississippi to San Antonio, Texas, for his first recording session in 1936 and from Mississippi to Dallas, Texas, in 1937 for his second and last recording session. It doesn't take a great imagination to place him on the streets of old Blue Goose as he made his way into legend.

I walk those streets now with no pretense [sic] of how it used to be. The Blue Goose was every bit a rough and tumble area then, as it is today. Nathanial Hogan is open Tuesday through Saturday each week and if you've got $7.50 and a few minutes, you can sit in his chair for a trim. If you know the right questions, maybe he'll tell you a little about the legend of old Blue Goose.

Down-Home Postwar Blues in Shreveport

—John M. Shaw

Shaw's research for this piece began with a paper for a 2000 University of Memphis graduate seminar. He surveys the recordings of local blues musicians in the late 1940s and early 1950s by small labels based in Shreveport and those based elsewhere. The labels were part of the post–World War II wellspring of small record companies across the country that caused a stunning increase in the number of opportunities to record. This burst of new companies resulted in part from the entrepreneurship bottled up by the wartime constraints, in part from the development of magnetic tape recorders that allowed more people to set up studios, and in part by frustration with the limited musical vision of the major companies. In Shreveport, these small labels often existed under the shadow of Mira Smith and Stan Lewis, who owned larger operations. Lewis is particularly important in and around Shreveport because he not only operated Jewel (and its associated labels), but he was also a major record distributor.

The documentation of Shreveport's blues scene began about four years after the close of World War II, with the bulk of the recordings done by independent companies (most notably Imperial Records) based outside of the Ark-La-Tex. Shreveport eventually spawned its own small record industry that looked to local country, pop, religious, and blues talent. Mira Smith's Ram label emerged in the mid-1950s, while Stan Lewis began his Jewel operation a few years later. This brief article surveys the recording of local blues before Smith and Lewis started their own efforts, between the years 1949 and 1952.

All the early recording by blues musicians associated with Shreveport— most notably Lead Belly and Oscar "Buddy" Woods—were undertaken by major companies like RCA Victor or by the Library of Congress. According to Mike Leadbitter and Neil Slaven's blues discographical research, the first two truly local sessions occurred in 1949.[1] The last local sessions of the era occurred in 1952 under the direction of Art Rupe for Specialty Records.

By far the oldest of the Shreveport bluesmen was Nathaniel Hammond, who was born in 1896 in Dallas but moved to the Taylortown area of Bossier Parish in the 1910s. He apparently wore a pegleg, from which he acquired the name "Stick-Horse."[2] The logistics of his recording career are fuzzy at best. An article in *Blues Unlimited* states that Stick-Horse had previously recorded for the J&M Record Shop, and that he died without recording again. He supposedly frequented the 700 block of Texas Street where Stan Lewis had recently acquired the old J&M Record Store, and may have performed on the streets. However, in a 1973 interview, Lewis described an abortive attempt to visit Stick-Horse at a plantation south of Bossier City. As he recalled the anecdote, a white plantation manager allegedly chased Lewis and Leonard Chess off the land with a rifle.[3] Perhaps the "plantation effort" was just the first of several attempts by Lewis to record Hammond, and that ultimately the efforts were successful. Alternatively these selections may have been recorded before 1948 and accrued to Lewis when he purchased the J&M shop in that year.

At any rate, six songs comprise the entire recorded legacy of this remarkably effective blues artist. "Little Girl" and "Too Late Baby" both make use of the same, slow guitar riff, but "Too Late" follows a sixteen-bar form, using a set of chord changes (I-I-IV-I-I-V-I) usually heard in gospel music. "Gamblin' Man" shows how low Stick-Horse's voice could reach, while "Truck 'Em on Down" is an upbeat effort. "Highway 51" must be related to a popular Mississippi blues song, as there is no Highway 51 anywhere in the vicinity of Dallas or Shreveport. With so much of Hammond's life a question mark, there is no way of knowing whether he could have spent time in Mississippi. "Highway 51" could as easily have been based on the well-known Bluebird recording by Tommy McClennan. The upbeat "Alberta" shows a vocal laugh similar to the type used by Bob Dylan in some of his early recordings. All Hammond's recordings appeared on the obscure Louisiana-based JOB label except for the final single "Little Girl" b/w "Truck 'Em on Down," which was released on the Gotham label. The only certain fact of Hammond's life is that he died on May 17, 1964, and was buried in Taylortown in Bossier Parish. His grave is unmarked, as parish historian Clif Coulter has noted all tombstone inscriptions in Bossier Parish, and Hammond is absent from this list.

Pianist Jimmie Bell, a man from Peoria, Illinois, and closely associated with St. Louis and Chicago, recorded in Shreveport in 1949. He had previously recorded for Chess Records, though he doesn't seem to have been under exclusive contract with that company. It appears likely that the songs were recorded at the recording studio at KWKH, almost certainly in the middle of the night since the studio was only open for custom work after the station went off the air.[4] Probably the recordings were made while Bell was in town for a performance or passing through to a show elsewhere in the South. In a 1978 interview, Bell mentioned a 1948 concert in Lafayette, Louisiana, so it is evident that Bell's band toured the South at least occasionally.[5] Alternatively, it is possible that Bell had relatives in the Ark-La-Tex. Regardless of whether the two songs in question, "Boy Day" and "Stranger in Your Town," were recorded for Chess or for someone else, neither song was released until 1979 when they were included on an album of Bell's work on the British label JSP.[6]

James Bledsoe, arguably Shreveport's most prolific bluesman of the 1950s, remains something of a mystery. Neither liner notes nor discographies yield anything of his biography or dates and places of birth and death. His recording career started as "Hot Rod Happy" for Pacemaker in 1949 and ended with his participation in the March 12, 1952, session for Specialty Records, but those three years revealed a bluesman of unique talent and vision. Though Bledsoe must be considered a country blues stylist, his song titles and lyrics reflect a growing urban sensibility. Shreveport-based country bassist Tillman Franks, himself a musician on the *Louisiana Hayride* that broadcast over the high-powered KWKH, produced Bledsoe's earliest session. Franks and Webb Pierce started the tiny Pacemaker label, primarily to record the country music they knew best. But they also recorded two songs by Bledsoe and, for reasons known only to the label's owners, the artist's name was changed to "Hot Rod Happy."[7] The single "Hot Rod Boogie" is a slice of proto-rock-and-roll, a driving ostinato with guitar accompaniment that sounds more "urban" in character than the downhome B-side "Worried Blues" with its slow, almost stomping pattern and lyrics that express a premonition of death. Bledsoe's use of recurring ostinato figures or "riffs" (somewhat reminiscent of John Lee Hooker) is a characteristic of most early postwar blues in Shreveport. Bledsoe was Pacemaker's only foray into the field of blues; it continued to record country artists until it was sold to Philadelphia-based Gotham Records in the summer of 1950.

Meanwhile, Bledsoe went on to record for Imperial and Specialty as "Country Jim," another mysterious moniker. The sessions for Lew Chudd's Imperial label took place in January and April of 1950. The January session produced four songs: "Old River Blues," "I'll Take You Back," "Rainy Morning Blues," and "Avenue Breakdown." Two of these imply a Shreveport locale: "Avenue

Breakdown" because there are no avenues in rural areas and "Old River Blues" in reference to the name of an oxbow lake in southeast Shreveport near the Red River. All four songs are in the same key and make use of a repetitive stomping guitar riff. Despite the fact that all four are roughly the same tune with different sets of lyrics, Imperial released all four. The April session also produced four songs, with two distinct versions of the "Philippine Blues," about going "across the ocean," which may have referred to the draft and the Korean War. The other songs were "Sad and Lonely Blues," "Good Looking Mama," and "Plantation Blues." None of these songs are particularly urban in spirit, but "Plantation Blues" may have referred to the plantations near the Red River south of the city, like the one where "Stick-Horse" Hammond resided. Once again, Imperial released all this material, though none of these 78s sold very well.

Apparently Bledsoe began to record for Art Rupe's Specialty label in 1951. Like the Imperial Sessions, the Specialty cuts were likely recorded at KWKH studios after hours. Many of them underscore Bledsoe's growing concern with Shreveport as a city. For example, "Travis Street Blues" and "Texas Street Blues" are named for streets in downtown Shreveport, while "Hollywood Blues" almost certainly refers to the black neighborhood on Shreveport's west side rather than the showbiz mecca in California. Several titles, including "Jesus Said I'll Go," "Undertaker," and "I'll Be Waiting Up There" seem to be gospel and might have been recorded at a separate session from the secular titles. Other titles among the latter are "Mean Little Girl," "Jimmie's Jump," "Lonesome Today," "Travis Street Blues," "Hollywood Blues," "Texas Street Blues," "Going Away Baby," "Gonna Leave Baby," "Last Winter Blues," "Come Back Baby," "Run Around," and "It's So Lonesome." Exact dates for these recordings are not known. Mike Leadbitter lists a number of titles presumably recorded for Specialty, many of them unreleased, and lumps them together under the dates 1951/1952.

One of these sessions occurred on March 12, 1952, a session for which Specialty has released a CD of almost all the recorded material. By 1952, "Country Jim" was probably the Shreveport area's best-known blues artist. These were apparently Bledsoe's last known recordings. "Dial 110 Blues" refers to the telephone, which was becoming more commonplace in post–World War II Ark-La-Tex. "Hollywood Boogie," again a reference to Shreveport's black Mooretown neighborhood, consists of a guitar riff based on an atypical harmony and a sound reminiscent of blues-influenced rock bands of the 1970s. Bledsoe's increasing urban mentality is expressed in the use of "hip" slang such as the lyrics, "In Hollywood, baby, I believe I can play my hand." "One Thing My

Baby Likes" is Bledsoe's first recording with drums, although only snare brushes can be clearly heard. This song seems to be influenced by the stylings of big-city jazz singers and, perhaps for that reason, was not released by Specialty at the time. Only "Stormin' and Rainin'," accompanied just by Bledsoe's guitar, maintains a traditional rural sound.

Like "Stick-Horse" Hammond, David "Pete" McKinley had two songs released in 1950 on the Gotham label. "Ardelle" uses a set of traditional lyrics often heard in the New Orleans standard "Roberta" (and grafted by Dr. John onto his version of "Tipitina"). "Shreveport Blues" is the earliest postwar blues to mention the city's name. It is a tribute to a foul-mouthed woman apparently onerous enough to force McKinley to leave Mississippi and return to "old Shreveport." McKinley may have been a native of the Shreveport area and may have recorded at the same session with Hammond, likely at the instigation of Stan Lewis; there is no hard evidence on either count. Musically, McKinley makes use of a similar guitar pattern as Jim Bledsoe, but the tempo is more upbeat, and McKinley's style is fuller, with more ornamentation.

With Bledsoe, McKinley participated in the March 12, 1952, sessions for Specialty. According to his publicity information, McKinley was a nephew of Bessie Smith. He was by far the most productive artist at the March 12, 1952, session, though, in the words of musician and writer Billy Vera, "much of his stuff . . . is merely the same song with slightly altered lyrics."[8] Nevertheless, Vera still found seven unique songs by McKinley to place on the Specialty reissue CD, and they reveal McKinley as another artist in transition from rural to urban style. "Black Snake Blues" maintains a traditional rural sound except for the inclusion of the drumset. "Cryin' for My Baby" includes corny crying sound effects. "Look' a Here Boy" is a jaunty, up-tempo effort. "Whistling Blues" is exactly that and demonstrates McKinley's skill as a whistler as well as a guitarist. The tune seems to be a stylized, northern urban blues rather than the country variety. "Don't Want Me Blues" is a duet with Country Jim, who is credited with writing the song, and "David's Boogie" displays a remarkable similarity to the white rockabilly sound to come in a couple of years. The final cut was a cover of an Amos Easton (aka "Bumble Bee Slim") composition, "Sail On, Little Girl." Like Bledsoe, McKinley apparently never recorded again.

Lonnie Williams recorded four songs for the Sittin' In With label in 1951, including "I'm Tired of Running Around" and "Wavin' Sea Blues," similar tunes in the same key. Williams's style is by far the most sophisticated of the Shreveport artists of the 1950s. His vocals are accompanied by guitar, bass, and harmonica, as opposed to previous recordings which were made by artists accompanying themselves. Furthermore, the guitar accompaniment is in a blues/jazz hybrid style reminiscent of the legendary blues guitarist Jesse Thomas, employing many seventh chords and explicitly dominant chords. Bob Shad recalled in a 1968 *Blues Unlimited* interview that Lonnie Williams had recorded in a Shreveport radio station, which was undoubtedly KWKH.[9]

Big Joe Williams, who was born in 1903 in Crawford, Mississippi, had recorded for a number of labels by the time he cut four sides at the 1952 Specialty session. The most well-known among the artists gathered, it is not clear why he would have been in Shreveport on March 12, 1952. Perhaps he was traveling with Art Rupe, working as an A&R man. Regardless of the circumstances, Williams's cuts included a double entendre song "Ride My New Car with Me" and "Rather Be Sloppy Drunk," which describes "staggering down the street."

Art Rupe remembered the elusive "Pine Bluff Pete" as a "very black man" who had been running errands during the session. In Rupe's words, "when it was felt that the other singers couldn't perform effectively any more because of alcohol, fatigue, or both, Pine Bluff Pete asked to record. He looked like he could use the recording fee, and everybody was feeling good, so we recorded him. We never actually intended to release the records, so we paid him outright, not even getting his full name."[10] Billy Vera mentions that the pseudonym "Pine Bluff Pete" was given to him by Barry Hansen, who discovered the tape in the Specialty vault. Pete was a good singer, but it is not clear whether he played an instrument. Two of the three songs he recorded credit James Bledsoe as the writer. "Uncle Sam Blues" is a protest-oriented recording about the Korean War and the draft. The piano accompaniment sounds remarkably like Eddie Williams, who recorded with Oscar "T. V. Slim" Wills later in the 1950s. "A Woman Acts Funny" is accompanied by guitar, played in a style reminiscent of Country Jim; and since Bledsoe is credited with writing the song, the guitarist is likely him.

Clarence London was a Shreveport construction worker who had been hanging around Stan's Record Shop, begging Stan Lewis to record him.[11] When Art Rupe came to Shreveport, Lewis obliged. London's style was strictly rural compared to many of the others present. "Goin' Back to Mama" and "Got a Letter This Morning" are slow blues based on the "stomping" kind of guitar riff preferred by Country Jim. "Want to Boogie-Woogie" is up-tempo but still rural in its avoidance of the dominant chord. Like so many others in the 1951 sessions, London apparently never recorded again. There is some gray area regarding London's recordings: Billy Vera places London in the March 12, 1952, session, but Mike Leadbitter places his recordings at another (and final) Specialty session in Shreveport on April 28, 1952.

Art Rupe of Specialty Records had come to Shreveport from California at the suggestion of Stan Lewis, renting out the studios of KWKH for an all-night session, which began when the station signed off the air at 2 A.M. The March 12 results were something of a transitional session, as some elements of modern urban blues were present alongside more rural sounds. Besides singers and guitarists, there was at least one pianist, and a drummer. If this marathon session can be viewed as the pinnacle of the city's country blues era, it was also its end, for soon afterward, the out-of-town independents left Shreveport, seemingly for good. It is unclear why. KWKH may have quit allowing rentals for custom sessions and the out-of-town independent labels may have lost interest in the area, perhaps because these records had not sold well.

Stan Lewis began to have success with country and rockabilly artists and may have chosen to focus on his white artists. For whatever reason, the city's black music recording scene seemed to vanish until 1955, when new studio facilities opened in Shreveport and a new chapter in the recording of black musicians unfolded that eventually resulted in the documentation of local soul and funk artists some ten to twenty years later.

Notes

1. Mike Leadbitter and Neil Slaven, *Blues Records, 1943–1970: A Selective Discography* (London: Record Information Service, 1987).

2. Chris Smith, liner notes to *Alley Special*, Collectables CD 5320, 1990.

3. Leadbitter, "Serving the South," *Blues Unlimited* 105 (December 1973/January 1974): 6.

4. Leadbitter, "Serving the South," 6.

5. Mike Foster, "Swing, Boogie & Blues: Jimmie Bell," *Living Blues* 41 (November/December 1978): 14.

6. Jimmie Bell, *Stranger in Your Town*, JSP Records 1007, 1979.

7. Billy Vera, liner notes to *Bloodstains on the Wall: Country Blues from Specialty*, Specialty CD 7061-2, 1994.

8. Ibid.

9. "Blues News," *Blues Unlimited* 49 (January 1968): 17

10. Vera, liner notes to *Bloodstains on the Wall*.

11. Ibid.

Radio, Records, and Rhythm

We devote this section of *Shreveport Sounds* to vernacular music that fits neither the broad categories of country or blues, as well as to the people and institutions that made the business of music happen in Shreveport. This latter group includes record company owners like Stan Lewis, Mira Smith, and Dee Marais. It also includes local disc jockeys like Don Logan, whose autobiographical memoirs are excerpted here. Other pieces in this section focus on individual musicians Gene Austin, Dale Hawkins, Eddie Giles, and Reuben Bell. We open with an excerpt from a dissertation that describes how radio station KWKH functioned, thus grounding this section in Shreveport's most prominent media institution. John Andrew Prime's account of Shreveport's colorful rock scene during the 1970s and 1980s emphasizes a little-known chapter in Shreveport's musical life and closes the book, underscoring the fact that work still needs to be done in exploring northwest Louisiana's musical significance.

Shreveport's role in various forms of popular music and its supporting mass media has been overshadowed by two larger cities in relatively near proximity—New Orleans and Memphis. Since the 1940s, in particular, both Memphis and New Orleans have nurtured well-documented and influential popular music traditions; Memphis, first with rockabilly and early rock-and-roll and then soul, and New Orleans for its R&B tradition. Shreveport's story has much to reveal about how America's popular music industry takes local shape and how specific artists reach out to influence music and genres far beyond the Ark-La-Tex. Arguably the most influential guitarist to emerge in the rock-and-roll era (and Elvis Presley's guitarist beginning in the late 1960s), James Burton was raised in Shreveport and lives there today. As one of rock's true enigmas and a group with a loyal cult following, the Residents began as a high school band in Shreveport, though they found fame when they migrated to and eventually recorded in San Francisco during the early 1970s. Blues-rock fans around the world today are familiar with Shreveport-born guitarist Kenny Wayne Shepherd, whose father (Ken Shepherd) was a local disc jockey for many years before managing his son's career.

Despite the fact that Shreveport has produced more than its share of highly regarded musicians, the local mass media have long struggled to sustain commercial success. Even though KWKH quickly became a powerful voice across the mid-South by the late 1920s, no major record companies developed in northwestern Louisiana. Stan Lewis's Jewel/Paula/Ronn Records remains the strongest contender for the most prolific and important among the dozen or so smaller labels based in the city. But no one was able to build a company like Capitol (Hollywood), Chess (Chicago), or Stax (Memphis) that reached a national audience, if only for a finite period of time.

Digital media and the internet have changed everything about the music industry, opening it to creative forces that lack the financial capital of large studios and major distributors. In some ways, this process mirrors the rise of radio so well represented in Shreveport by KWKH. Artists from the nationally successful to the locally important share access to digital media, thereby shaping the documentation and dissemination of popular music in Shreveport. For example, an artist like Kenny Wayne Shepherd, with albums on a multinational label (Reprise/WEA) and contributions to Hollywood film soundtracks like *Batman Returns* and *3000 Miles to Graceland*, also maintains his own website (http://www.kennywayneshepherd.net) with links to videos, tour news, and his fan club. Likewise, Dan Garner for a long time maintained an informal and informative website for his own Blue Goose Blues Records, advertising his catalogue of six releases, all with a distinctive Shreveport focus. (Notes for *The Legend of Old Blue Goose* appear in reprint in this book's "Blues" section.) The German blues enthusiast Stefan Wirz has for years maintained an often-updated site with many links and discographical information related to American vernacular music of all sorts, including Shreveport blues man Jesse Thomas.[1] Another example is the web site (http://www.dandydonlogan.com) operated by veteran Ark-La-Tex disc jockey "Dandy" Don Logan, which includes photos, links, and discographical information, as well as a full version of his autobiography.

In a sense, the internet is only the most recent resurgence of a popular culture cycle in which Shreveport has participated across the twentieth century. Financial capital and creative control tend to get concentrated until something unexpected emerges. In Shreveport during the 1920s it was W. K. Henderson's radio station, over which he broadcast his record collection as well as live local musicians and ranted about politics and commercial culture. In the late 1940s KWKH featured a distinguished regional radio barn dance that would ultimately introduce the era's most notable honky-tonk stars and rockabilly sensations. In the early 1960s, it was small record labels started by local entrepreneurs like Stan Lewis and Mira Smith. In the 1970s and 1980s, it was a local contingent of club owners and musicians who created a lively and distinct cultural climate. Taken as a whole, *Shreveport Sounds* suggests that the picture of popular music in the United States is incomplete until it takes into account the people who create musical meaning in everyday ways and the places that nurture musical sounds far away from business centers like Los Angeles and New York City.

Note

1. See [http://www.wirz.de/music/thojefrm.htm], which includes birth and death dates, photographs, as well as details (when known) of personnel and precise recording dates.

A Historical Study of Programming Techniques and Practices of Radio Station KWKH, Shreveport, LA, 1922–1950

—Lillian Jones Hall

This excerpt is edited from a dissertation chapter titled "The Period of W. K. Henderson, 1925–1933," where Lillian Jones Hall connects Henderson's story with the development of federal-level regulations governing radio. She based her description on newspaper articles, congressional records, and a scrapbook of related documents Henderson published with the title "KWKH Fights for a Square Deal." In addition, Hall conducted interviews with Carter Henderson, son of the radio man; Bill Antony, the engineer who constructed Shreveport's earliest radio transmitters and kept the Henderson equipment in working order; and Stedman Gunning, a long-time Henderson employee and "disc jockey" before the practice was common or even the term invented.

Hall's excerpt begins with descriptions of employee life at Henderson's Kennonwood estate, the innovative broadcasting set-up, and the *modus operandi* for nightly phonograph request shows. She places KWKH's practice of broadcasting records in the context of its time, when today's symbiosis between radio and recorded music was far from apparent. In fact, the Federal Radio Commission frowned upon phonograph records as an undesirable alternative to live programming and feared their broadcast was potentially misleading to the public. Henderson and his KWKH occupied a central position in the era's debates over the right of the government to regulate the airwaves and freedom of on-air content.

In describing the conflicting opinions in this debate, Hall quotes excerpts of written communication between Henderson and key figures in shaping federal radio policies, including FRC Chair W. H. G. Bullard and Louisiana Senator Joseph E. Ransdell. In his responses, Henderson articulates his populist defense of KWKH operations with his usual audacity, characterizing the commission's actions as a threat to independent radio stations and the communities they served, particularly in the South. To use words Henderson himself might have chosen, KWKH programming was none of the FRC's doggone business.

_____

[W. K. Henderson was a prominent local businessman in Shreveport, owner of the Henderson Iron Works and Supply Company, who became infamous as owner of station KWKH. During the early 1920s, he purchased a one-quarter interest in radio station WGAQ from W. G. Patterson, along with three other investors. The station broadcast from the Youree Hotel in downtown Shreveport until 1924, when Henderson bought out his partners, changed the call letters to match his initials (KWKH), and moved the station to the grounds of his country estate, Kennonwood, eighteen miles outside town. Because a fire destroyed the main buildings of Kennonwood on March 26, 1955, Henderson's scrapbooks and files were lost. This loss makes Hall's work a critical piece in understanding early radio in Shreveport and the life of one of radio history's most colorful mavericks. This excerpt draws from interviews conducted not many years after the fire and research into Henderson's communication with government officials.]

When Henderson moved his station to Kennonwood, he hired almost anyone who asked him for a job. However, those employed were expected to perform any task connected with maintaining the station. The owner was a commanding person who demanded that the staff members be proficient in performing the many and varied duties assigned to them. Those persons who attained his high standards were paid well. The main staff of ten persons moved to Kennonwood, where facilities were provided them. The unmarried men and the unmarried women lived in separate "dormitories" in the main residence. Married personnel were assigned separate cottages on the estate.[1]

Following the general policy of demanding every member of the staff to perform any and every task connected with the successful operation of the station, Henderson hired no announcers. Persons who operated the control board also announced. According to Antony, the station personnel and staff were expected to remain on call twenty-four hours a day. Stedman Gunning illustrated this demand by his own experience. On Labor Day, 1926, Gunning began his employment. From that time until Henderson disposed of the station in 1932 he worked without a holiday. However, those staff members who remained with Henderson were intensely loyal to him as was evidenced during the years from 1930 through 1932, when the entire staff served without pay.[2]

Perhaps the foremost staff member of KWKH was William Antony who had served as chief engineer for all radio stations in Shreveport. Antony's full time employment was in the capacity of chief testboard man for the American Telephone and Telegraph Company. It appears that Antony was an employee upon whom Henderson relied heavily. According to Carter Henderson, his father knew enough about engineering to have an idea of what engineering feats could be performed. Whenever the broadcaster wished greater performance or some new improvement for the station, he told Antony who apparently proceeded to work out the details. In addition to his work with the telephone company, with KWKH and other radio stations, Antony continued to experiment with radio on his own free time. In 1928 Antony became a full-time employee and moved his family to Kennonwood where they remained until the station was removed.

Stedman Gunning had been a radio enthusiast in high school. He used empty chalk boxes in which to assemble crystal radio sets and sold them for one dollar. After he was employed at KWKH he went to Kennonwood every afternoon, worked until the station went off the air, and then returned to Shreveport where he worked at the Henderson Iron Works for eight hours. He continued this type of employment until March 1928, when he moved to Kennonwood as a full-time employee of the station. This young man, unmarried at the time, lived in the men's dormitory.[3]

When KWKH went on the air with 1000 watts of power on September 25, 1925, there were no definite program schedules.[4] Broadcasts consisted of phonograph records, talks, and live performances by artists who came to Kennonwood. "Old Man Henderson," as he came to be known, was a major attraction of the station. According to Carter Henderson, listeners especially enjoyed hearing records. Henderson pioneered in the method of broadcasting music directly from the electrical transcriptions. This is the method used today in broadcasting recordings [editor's note: Hall here refers to 1959].

According to a January 1931 article concerning radio transcriptions in *Radio Digest*:

> When the recorded programs are broadcast from a station they are not played on a phonograph placed in front of a microphone, such as was done in the early days of broadcasting. Instead, the output from the pick-up placed on the record is directly fed into the transmitter. The pick-ups used are much more costly than those found in phonograph-radio combinations designed for the home, and are generally operated in pairs so that as one record ends the next one can be cut in without pause.

Radio Station KWKH was using this method in 1925. The music was transmitted clearly, and the announcers never identified the music as phonograph records. Consequently many persons believed that KWKH had performers in their studios.[5] According to Antony, the broadcasts were so nearly perfect that a manufacturer of radio transmission equipment sent twenty-one engineers who posed as visitors to study the method. However, the staff members, unaccustomed to seeing twenty-one men unaccompanied by their families, took special note of the group. When they began asking questions that only a radio engineer would understand, KWKH engineers realized that the men were sent to the station to discover how the music was broadcast.[6]

Henderson stated that his station probably had more money invested in records, in the music library, and in catalogs and the supplements than some other radio stations had cost altogether.[7] In a letter to Judge E. O. Sykes, member of the Federal Radio Commission, dated September 15, 1927, Henderson wrote: "... We have issued beautiful catalogues, of which I gave you one, with supplement, showing the records we play and, since that time, we have issued another, with other supplements, and will continue to do so ..." Copies of the catalogs in the possession of Antony and Gunning are undated, but it is understood that *KWKH Music Catalogs* were available to listeners prior to 1927.

The catalogs were booklets containing the names of all the records in the musical library of KWKH, listed alphabetically. Catalogs were sent to listeners in order that they might request their selections by numbers rather than by the title. One booklet contained forty-three pages of closely typed song titles. Examples of these titles follow: "Abide with Me," "A Kiss in the Dark," "A Cup of Coffee, a Sandwich and You," "Alice Blue Gown," "Bringing Up Father in Prohibition," "Any Ice Today Lady?," "Black Bottom Stomp," "Harmony Blues,"

"Faust," "Frolic of the Coons," "I Know the Lord Laid His Hands on Me," "Hugs and Kisses," "I Keeps My Kitchen Clean," "Say Lister [sic] Have you Met Rosie's Sister," and many others which are similar and dissimilar. Gunning estimated that KWKH always had five to six thousand records in the library, and he recalled that the following five seemed to be favorites with listeners: "My Horses Ain't Hungry," "Missouri Waltz," "Hand Me Down My Walking Cane," "Dead Cat on the Line," and "Golden Slippers."

Broadcasting at KWKH was done at night in order to assure clear reception for listeners. During the time when the station did not share broadcast time with another station, Henderson opened the programs by talking two or three minutes. Then he would say something like "Stedman's going to play your records now. You can call us or send a telegram and he will play your request." Gunning recalled that, from the year 1926 until 1929, programming over the station was almost totally requests. According to station personnel, after Henderson asked listeners to telephone or telegraph, the one telephone line available to the broadcasting studio was used constantly by the long distant operator and the telegraph office. No local callers could contact the station because the two operators kept the line busy.

Gunning was the announcer who handled the request programs. He said that his duties included answering the telephone, writing the name or number of the request and the name of the person making the request. When he received a number of requests for one record, he looked up the record, announced the title and read the long list of persons requesting that selection. Then he played the record on the panatrope. In addition he operated the transmitter. The station remained on the air as long as the requests came, often until eight o'clock the following morning after beginning broadcasts at 7:30 the previous evening. Concerning the requests, Gunning said that there was no program ratio between classical, religious, or hillbilly records played. About 1928 the telephone situation became so congested that the telephone company hired two operators for the station and Western Union Telegraph Company installed a printer at KWKH at their own expense. The telephone operators worked in the broadcast studio and used foot-operated switches to cut off the microphone while they talked over the telephone.[8]

Henderson did not hide the fact that the programs consisted of playing records as evidenced by his issuing the musical catalogs to listeners. However, the Federal Radio Commission was opposed to the playing of records without having each record announced as "recorded." The Commission issued General Order No. 16 which required that all records be announced as such. Henderson would not comply with this order. Admiral W. H. G. Bullard, Chairman of the Federal Radio Commission wrote a letter, dated September 13, 1927:

> Under the date of August 31st, 1927, this Commission has received a report from the Supervisor of Radio in your District, that your station—KWKH—does not comply with the Federal Radio Commission's General Order, which requires that each phonographic record be announced as such before being rendered.
>
> Please read General Order No. 16 again and see if you cannot find it convenient to fully comply with the Order, which requires that "all broadcasts of music performed through the agency of mechanical reproductions shall be clearly announced as such with the announcement of *each and every number thus broadcast.*"[9]

Despite the General Order of the Commission, Henderson continued to broadcast those request programs without credit until he disposed of the station.[10]

By his management of his radio station and his personal use of the microphones, William Kennon Henderson soon established a distinct personality among broadcasters. In the very beginning, his ownership of the radio station was a hobby with him. At the time he entered the field of radio, he had established himself already in Shreveport as a civic-minded man. His interest was in a "Greater Shreveport." In the November 1924 issue of *Shreveport*, the Chamber of Commerce's monthly publication, there was a picture of a sign donated by Henderson. This was a hundred-foot tall sign on the Henderson Iron Works property that read "Prosperity," on one side and "Buy your goods in Shreveport," "for More Factories," "Bigger Payrolls," "Bigger Business," on the opposite side. In May 1925 he was elected president of the Chamber of Commerce. This was the year that plunged him deeply into radio broadcasting.

His business, the Henderson Iron Works and Supply Company, employing seven hundred persons, was the largest business concern of its type in the South. The 1937 book *History of Shreveport and Shreveport Builders* documented his local prominence as follows:

> The name of Henderson suggested machinery, and the railroads, large lumber mills, and major oil companies were his largest customers. His machine plant and foundry was the largest and best equipped in the country. Every class of machine work was handled in his large plant, from the rebuilding of railroad locomotives

to the setting up of sawmill and oil field equipment. His business interests were vast, reaching into seven figures annually for a number of years.[11]

Since the business occupied most of his time, Henderson continued operation of the station in the same manner as the previous owners. However, when he moved the station to Kennonwood, changed the call letters to KWKH, and began broadcasting with 1000 watts of power, the response to the station was overwhelming. Then the new owner realized the power inherent in radio. According to the Shreveport *Times*, June 28, 1935, KWKH received almost one thousand letters within a few days after the station began broadcasts with increased power.

When Henderson first acquired his radio station he did not make lengthy talks over the air, but limited his presentations to two or three minutes before turning the microphone over to the announcers. However, as different situations arose, he took the microphone any time he had an idea he wished to express, stopped the program in progress, and expounded on his idea over the airwaves.[12] Henderson began his talks with a greeting that became very familiar to listeners: "Hello, World, doggone you! This is KWKH at Shreveport, Lou-ee-isiana, and it's W. K. Henderson talkin' to you." This greeting won for him the title of "That doggone man of radio." When he talked over the microphone, this man sounded as if he were seventy or more years of age. Actually, he was nearing fifty.[13] As Henderson became more involved in various campaigns he conducted over KWKH, he increased the length of his talks until, according to Gunning, by about the latter part of 1929 or the early part of 1930, he devoted almost his entire time on the air defending his views.

A friend wrote:

> To see him in action before the microphone is a rare experience. He never plans nor rehearses an address. Whatever he is saying is what he is thinking at that particular minute. Observing him, one can see that he is not conscious of any separation whatsoever between him and his audience. That world—that lil ole [sic] North American continent—which he doggones and to which he calls hello is right across the table from him when he broadcasts. In fact, you might use his own expression and say he's got it right in his pocket.
>
> With his shoulders hunched and lips close to the mouthpiece of his crimson microphone, he (talks).[14]

Henderson spoke on any topic that interested him. He often talked about the national debt on the airways. He would say: "Everything we have is mortgaged, every cow, every blade of grass. We owe more than everything in the whole country is worth. Our mortgage is 100 percent."[15] When telegrams arrived for Henderson personally, he tried to answer them over the air. Since he was famous for "sizzling expletives," he would spare no words in voicing his feelings if the telegram were one objecting to his programs or his manner.[16] Gunning recalled that at such times he would conclude his speech by saying, "If you don't like my station, turn your dials." Henderson prided himself on being right at all times. He would say, "If you can show me where I am wrong, I'll admit it." His son said that he had a "determined will to move all obstacles" and that "he was a one man chairman of all the people."

When the United States Congress introduced bills concerning radio regulation in 1926, Henderson took an active interest in each one.[17] He talked about the various bills over the air and wired the two senators from Louisiana, the Honorable Joseph E. Ransdell and the Honorable Edwin S. Broussard, concerning his views. Henderson felt that the bills before the Second Session of the 69th Congress on January 26, 1927, favored chain stations to the destruction of independent stations such as KWKH. On February 19, 1927, Senator Broussard telegraphed Henderson the news that despite efforts to have the pending bills recommitted, the Radio Bill was approved and sent to the President.[18] ... These communications ... suggest further the scope of the total Henderson personality that had developed in the field of broadcasting. Nevertheless, the bill referred to by Senator Broussard in the telegram to Henderson created the Federal Radio Commission. It was approved by the president on February 23, 1927, and has since been known as the Radio Act of 1927. Among other provisions the act provided for the division of the United States into five geographical zones and for the appointment of five persons to serve as commissioners, one from each zone. The president appointed Judge E. O. Sykes of Jackson, Mississippi, as Commissioner for the South and Admiral W. H. G. Bullard as Chairman of the Commission.

While the Federal Radio Commission was in the formative stage, Henderson increased the power of KWKH from 1000 to 3000 watts without permission. On July 1, 1927, the members of the newly elected Federal Radio Commission began a tour of inspection of radio facilities throughout the United States. Soon after they began the tour, the commissioners discovered that KWKH was using 3000 watts of power. According to Henderson, he did not attempt to conceal the power hike. Instead, he told the inspector of the amount of power KWKH was using and the inspector included this information in his official report. Furthermore, according to Carter Henderson, during broadcasts

W. K. Henderson called the commissioners "the illegitimate children of the Hoover administration" because President Hoover instead of Congress appointed them.

In a letter to Henderson, Senator Ransdell mentioned Henderson's radio criticisms of the commission.

> The Judge (Eugene O. Sykes) said that he had listened in on your station several times and learned therefrom as well as from communications made to him, that you were criticizing the Radio Commission pretty severely—especially Admiral Bullard.[19]

Henderson answered:

> I certainly am and I am going to criticize every move they make that I think should be criticized just so long as I am denied what they are giving to others, or what they have given to others—UNLIMITED POWER to certain sections and VERY LIMITED POWER to other sections.[20]

Henderson wrote:

> There was no intention on our part not to work with the Federal Radio Commission in our using the 3000 watts. It was not thought of in that way. We were rendering the service and not hurting anyone and we had ample time to make any change to hide the wattage we were using when the Radio Inspector called.[21]

Later he discussed this matter further:

> . . . We don't care to just broadcast to Shreveport and Caddo Parish. We want sufficient power to be heard throughout the United States. We want WHAT THEY HAVE BEEN GIVING TO THE OTHER FELLOW. Is it fair to have UNLIMITED WATTAGE given to one locality and VERY LIMITED WATTAGE to another locality? Is it fair for KDKA, Pittsburgh, Pa., to have 30,000 watts—practically as much wattage as the eleven Southern States?—and to be on a wave length by itself?[22]

While Henderson continued his fight for what he claimed was his rightful place on the airwaves, he had to defend his station against the charge of using only phonograph records for broadcasting. The Federal Radio Commission issued the order that was discussed earlier in the chapter. The order read as follows:

> ... [T]he failure clearly to announce the nature of such broadcasting (mechanical reproductions) is in some instances working in effect a fraud upon the listening public. The Commission therefore hereby orders that effective August 21, 1927, all broadcasts of music performed through agency of mechanical reproductions shall be clearly announced as such with the announcement of each and every number thus broadcast. ...[23]

Henderson told the commission that he would never guarantee to make weather reports, broadcast baseball news, advise about high water stages, or make anything a regular part of programming, although he was not adverse to presenting any of those things. He maintained that programming should be at the discretion of the owner of the station and the listeners. Furthermore, he stated that he did not intend to schedule a group of artists for his station merely to receive permission for a power increase grant. His contention was that KWKH should have an increase in power for whatever programs that he might care to use and that he might believe to be in the interest of the listening public. He declared that the radio station was "never intended to please the Commission, but the listeners."[24]

Notes

1. Stedman Gunning, Personal Interview, March 1959.

2. Both Gunning and Antony told the writer in interviews in recent months that they served without pay during those depression years. Henderson provided food and lodging but no pay.

3. The Gunning interview of 1959. All personal statements about Gunning come from this source.

4. The Antony interview of 1957.

5. [This citation was missing in the original.]

6. The Antony Interview of 1959.

7. Cited in W. K. Henderson, ed., *KWKH's Fight for a Square Deal from the Federal Radio Commission* (Shreveport, Louisiana: An unpublished mimeographed collection of letters in Private Library of W. E. Antony, Dixie, Louisiana), p. 6. This is hereafter cited as *KWKH's Fight for a Square Deal.*

8. Carter Henderson, Personal Interview, March 27, 1959.

9. Admiral W. H. G. Bullard letter to W. K. Henderson, dated September 13, 1927; in *KWKH's Fight for a Square Deal.*

10. Gunning interview.

11. Lilla McLure and J. Ed. Howe, *History of Shreveport and Shreveport Builders* (Shreveport, Louisiana: J. Ed Howe, Publisher, 1937), 251.

12. The Antony Interview of 1958.

13. Margery Land May, *Hello World Henderson: The Man Behind the Mike* (Shreveport, Louisiana: Press of the Lindsay Company; 1930), *op. cit.*, p. 21.

14. May, 56.

15. Carter Henderson interview.

16. "Sizzling expletives" from May, 10.

17. These bills were the House of Representatives Bill Number 9971 and the similar Senate Bill Number 1754. Representative White of Maine and Representative Davis of Tennessee are given much credit for the contents of the bills. Points of agreement included provision for the establishment of a Federal Radio Commission. Both placed administrative authority in the hands of the Secretary of Commerce. Licensing authority would include the fixing of wavelengths, power, and time of operation. Administrative authority included inspection of stations, licensing of operators, and the assignment of call letters. Both bills would permit renewal of license privileges. Important points of debate were how much power should be given the Secretary of Commerce and how to deal with violations of the antitrust laws. Discussion of these bills is found in the House of Representatives, *Regulation of Broadcasting*, pp. 7–12.

18. Edwin S. Broussard, Telegram to W. K. Henderson, dated February 19, 1927; in *KWKH's Fight for a Square Deal*, 6.

19. Joseph E. Ransdell letter to W. K. Henderson, dated September 3, 1926; in *KWKH's Fight for a Square Deal*, 18.

20. Henderson, letter to Senator Joseph E. Ransdell, dated September 6, 1927; in *KWKH's Fight for a Square Deal*, 30.

21. Henderson, letter to Senator Joseph E. Ransdell dated September 1, 1927; in *KWKH's Fight for a Square Deal*, 8.

22. Henderson, letter to Senator Joseph E. Ransdell dated September 6, 1927; in *KWKH's Fight for a Square Deal*, 39.

23. Federal Radio Commission, General Order 16, August 9, 1927; cited in *Supplement to the Second Annual Report of the Federal Radio Commission* (Washington, D.C.: United States Government Printing Office, 1928), 41.

24. Henderson, letter to Judge E. O. Sykes, dated September 15, 1927; in *KWKH's Fight for a Square Deal*, 8.

Lead Belly in the early 1940s.
Photo courtesy of LSU
Shreveport Archives—
Noel Memorial Library.

Vallie Tinsley, ca. 1960s. Photo
courtesy of James D. Karl.

Stan Lewis in 1958 with Tommy Sands. Photo courtesy of
LSU Shreveport Archives—Noel Memorial Library.

Jesse Thomas on the Miltone label in 1951.
Photo courtesy of Kip Lornell.

Country Jim on the Imperial label, ca. 1953.
Photo courtesy of Kip Lornell.

Hello World label shot, ca. 1929.
Photo courtesy of Kip Lornell.

W. K. Henderson at the microphone from a Christmas postcard. Photo courtesy of LSU Shreveport Archives—Noel Memorial Library, Paul L. Carriger Collections.

Just a little How-dy-do!
Here's a line to say to you
A Very Merry Christmas

Madam Sturkow-Ryder presented a series of programs over KWEA and KWKH in 1929 Shreveport. Photo courtesy of LSU Shreveport Archives—Noel Memorial Library, Paul L. Carriger Collections.

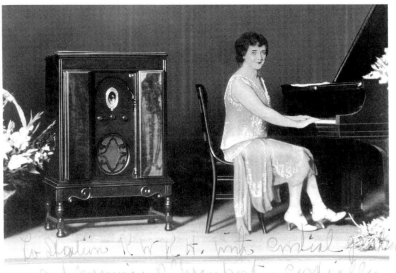

Gene Austin 1934 Perfect Record release announcement.
Photo courtesy of Kip Lornell.

Stan's Record Shop on Texas Avenue in
Shreveport, ca. 1984. Photo courtesy of LSU
Shreveport Archives—Noel Memorial Library.

Pioneering RAM Records owner Mira Smith and
singer Margaret Lewis Warwick. Photo courtesy
of Maggie and Alton Warwick.

Dale Hawkins first promo shot for Chess Records in 1957. Photo courtesy of Dale Hawkins.

CD cover for *The Murco Records Story.*

Eddie Giles promo shot from the early 1970s (spelled "Eddy"). Photo courtesy of John Ridley.

Eddy Giles, courtesy of Bill Millar

MURCO RECORDS
Division of JEWEL RECORDS
728 Texas
Shreveport, La.

EDDY GILES

2

Veterans Park Amphitheater shot, ca. 1978. Photo courtesy of John Andrew Prime.

Allen Ginsberg visiting the grave of Lead Belly in 1991. Photo courtesy of John Andrew Prime.

A Friend in Las Vegas

—H. Allen Smith

The local and national importance of singer, composer, and influential recording artist Gene Austin often goes unremarked. Yet, along with Vernon Dalhart from Jefferson, Texas, within the Ark-La-Tex, Austin emerged as one of media history's earliest stars with strong ties to the Shreveport metropolitan area. His career really took off with his 1927 version of "My Blue Heaven," which sold hundreds of thousands of copies for Victor. During the late 1920s Austin was in great demand across the United States as a live performer. From the mid-1920s into the early 1930s he was a popular recording artist on a par with Paul Whiteman and the young Bing Crosby. His radio appearances began during this same era and continued into the 1940s. Austin debuted in Hollywood movies in 1932 and ultimately appeared in *Sadie McKee*, *Gift of Gab*, and *Melody Cruise*. Nightclub entertainment became his main employment during the 1930s, after recordings slowed down. In many instances, Austin transformed the music that bespoke his southern roots into popular music with wide appeal. Over the course of his lengthy career he composed nearly one hundred songs, most notably "When My Sugar Walks down the Street," "How Come You Do Me Like You Do?" and "Lonesome Road."

Born Eugene Lucas on June 24, 1900, in Gainesville, Texas, (some sixty-five miles north of Fort Worth), he grew up in small northwestern Louisiana towns. His biography includes several fascinating episodes: for example, after joining the United States Army at age fifteen, Austin helped pursue Francisco (Pancho) Villa in 1916 and served in France during World War I. He studied both dentistry and law in Baltimore, but decided on a singing career. Austin was married five times and lived in Las Vegas following the close of World War II. He even mounted an unsuccessful run for governor of Nevada during the 1962 elections.

Sparked by a television dramatization of his biography in 1958, Austin picked up his nightclub appearances and continued to write songs until the last ten months of his life, when his ultimately unsuccessful battle with lung cancer became too onerous. This article was first published in the *Saturday Evening Post* during the late 1950s, coinciding with the resurgence of interest in Austin's career sparked by the TV special. It was later reprinted with slight modification in a collection of essays by its author, H. Allen Smith, brought together as a book with a title from one of its humorous essays, *A Short History of Fingers.*[1] Smith's perspective in itself is of historical interest, speaking for a generation for whom rock-and-roll was an unwelcome musical revolution, and he writes with sympathy, nostalgia, and humor about the singer who, for Smith, represents a gentler musical age.

Note

1. H. Allen Smith, "A Friend in Las Vegas," in *A Short History of Fingers* (Boston: Little, Brown, 1963); this is the version reprinted here.

In the developing folklore of contemporary America there is a story about a newlywed couple holding hands late in the evening on the front stoop of their home. Down the street a cat manages to claw the lid off a large garbage can. The lid hits the pavement with a crash and a clatter, the garbage can falls over, the cat lets out a few frightening shrieks and yowls, and the young woman says softly to the young man, "Oh, darling, our song!"

There must be fogey blood in me because I enjoy that story. I enjoy it because I think that much of the stuff that passes for popular music today is somewhat less melodic than the grunting of hogs in flytime. I happen to hold membership in a generation which grew up on sweet music and a sweet singer named Gene Austin.

Along with almost every other boy and girl of my time I romanced and courted to the music of his records. Those were the days when we cranked up the machine between numbers, and if we ran out of needles we used a straight pin, and if we ran out of anything else to say, we said, "You tell 'em, I stutter."

I've known Gene Austin for thirty-five years. I first met him in Tulsa in the summer of 1927, when he was at the peak of his celebrity. I was a young reporter just barely sapient enough to pour lemonade out of a boot, while he was a national hero of sorts—a young man who was feted and cheered and given the keys to the city wherever he went.

There in Tulsa I talked my city editor into letting me interview him, and then approached the assignment with fear and trembling. "Gene Austin!" I kept saying to myself. "I'm going to interview Gene Austin! In person!" I'm telling you, he was that big in 1927. Yet within two minutes after I had walked into his hotel room he had put me at my ease. He was, if anything, country-er than I was. He not only asked me to hang around with him all afternoon but took me to dinner and then let me go backstage with him at the Orpheum and stand in the wings while he sang his songs.

In subsequent years I knew him in Denver, in New York, in Hollywood and in Las Vegas. He went into a long period of eclipse but then, just a few years ago, the voice of Gene Austin was again being heard in the land. It was a voice out of a seemingly ancient past, vibrant with nostalgia, and all of us who knew it so well in the middle and late twenties somehow achieved a sort of vicarious rejuvenation from listening to it again.

Gene is now in his early sixties. He could easily pass for ten years less than his actual age. I had lost track of him, though I knew he had become a permanent resident of Las Vegas. And then about five years ago things began to happen. Someone in Hollywood started talking about producing a movie to be called *The Gene Austin Story*. Back East the television crowd, remembering, went on the alert. The people at RCA-Victor, remembering, dug into their files and came up with the startling fact that Gene Austin was probably the biggest star that they or any other recording company ever had. What was even more interesting to the Victor people was the report they got from California that Gene Austin was a better singer now than he was when he made "My Blue Heaven" his theme song. They sent out a hurry call for the biggest moneymaker they ever hired.

So Gene headed for New York to fill some new recording dates, to appear on a television show in which a somewhat hopped-up version of his life story was told, and to cut up some touches with his old friends. When I heard he was in New York I went looking for him and found him in an apartment hotel near Central Park. With him were his wife, Lou, and his mynah bird, Jack. As I walked into the apartment the bird said, "My God, why doesn't somebody tell me these things?" A few minutes later he whistled an old familiar refrain and then—I swear it!—he sang the words, "When whippoorwills call, and evening is nigh . . ." After that he asked another question: "Why don't we sell this damn bird?"

There was a portable fold-away electric piano in one corner of the room, gimmicked up with earphones so Gene could write his songs in the middle of the night if he felt the urge. On the piano was a foot-high reproduction of the RCA-Victor dog and beneath it a golden plaque citing Gene's achievements in the recording business. And as for old Gene himself, he was the same easygoing, soft-talking guy I'd known for so many years.

He is a lineal descendant of a woman famous in the history of the American West—Sacajawea, the Shoshone Indian girl who accompanied the Lewis and Clark Expedition from North Dakota to the Pacific Coast and back in 1805–1806. Known as the "Bird Woman" and celebrated for her courage, her resourcefulness and her good humor, she was Gene's great-great-great-grandmother.

He was born Eugene Lucas, in Gainesville, Texas. His parents were divorced when he was three and his mother married an itinerant blacksmith named Jim Austin. "My old man," says Gene, referring to Jim Austin; "was quite a horseshoer in his better days. He worked around the trotting tracks, used to shoe Dan Patch regularly, but he had a hankerin' for that ole whisky bottle, and the good times didn't last, and we found ourselves in Louisiana, roamin' around the lumber country. The old man shoed the mules at the sawmills and I think you might say we could have qualified as poor folks."

Gene was seven or eight when they moved into a house in the little town of Yellow Pine, Louisiana. The previous occupants had left behind an old beat-up piano of Civil War vintage, and Gene began fooling around with it.

"There was a little colored gal," he remembers, "used to come around and do some work for us when we could afford it. I knew she used to sneak into the colored church on weekdays and play the little organ they had out there. So one day I told her I'd give her two bits if she'd show me how to play a song called 'Hard Times.' She did it, and that's the first piece of music I ever learned."

The family settled shortly afterward in the larger town of Minden and the old piano was toted along, despite the protests of Jim Austin. He didn't like it because it produced music, and he had no use for music of any nature or description. "Music," said Jim, "is jest fer ladies."

"What little music I knew," says Gene, "I learned from the colored folks. I used to wander out to the quarters at night and snoop around and listen to them playin' their guitars and their pianos and singin'. Minden was one of those towns where the only music the white folks knew was church music—hymns. Oh, once in a while some white gal would get up at a church supper and sing a soprano solo, somethin' like 'The Little Dickeybird Is Climbin' Up My Garden Wall, Tra-la, Tra-lee.' I didn't go much for that type of jazz; I liked the way the colored folks sang and I liked their songs, especially their blues songs."

When he was fifteen Gene ran away from home, hoboed around the South for a while, joined a circus and learned to play "When You Wore a Tulip" on the steam calliope, and when he was sixteen joined the Army. During the early part of World War I he was assigned to guard duty on the New Orleans docks. "I almost hate to tell you this," he says, "because you hear it from so many singers and musicians, but it's a God's honest fact that when I was off duty I spent many an evenin' playin' piano in New Orleans sportin' houses."

Eventually he found himself in a New Jersey Army camp, where he was put to work in the hayfields. One day he learned that they were rounding up twenty men to fill out a contingent for shipping overseas. So Gene said to himself, "What'm I doin' here? Balin' hay from mornin' to night. Hell, they got hay to bale back home in Looze-ee-anna." He put down his tools and fell in with the group of twenty and soon found himself in France.

One evening an Army dentist heard Gene playing the piano and singing a blues song. "This guy came over and talked to me," Gene relates, "and said he liked music, and he needed an assistant, so I became a dental mechanic. Along came the Armistice and this dentist told me he wanted to stay in Europe and practice dentistry. For some reason he wanted to settle in Lithuania—he said that every tooth in Lithuania had a cavity in it. He wanted me to study dentistry and be his partner, and we'd get dirty rich in Lithuania. I was agreeable, but I had to get an education, so we came back to the States. He opened a dental office in Baltimore and I enrolled in dental school. He had a lot of patients, but they weren't paying their bills, so one day I said as a gag that I'd better switch over and study law so I could collect the bills. Somehow that crack put the notion into my head to become a lawyer, so I entered the University of Maryland Law School."

In the evenings after school Gene began playing and singing occasionally in small clubs in and around Baltimore. Other times he was accompanist for various acts in the local vaudeville houses. He drifted away from dentistry and then he drifted away from the law. Wanderlust, always a strong element in his makeup, led him to sign on as an entertainer aboard a ship headed for the Orient. Within a few days someone decided he wasn't very entertaining and, anyway, they were short a fireman in the black gang. He shoveled coal over and back and when he came home he met a fellow named Roy Bergere.

Bergere liked Gene's singing and talked him into teaming up in a vaudeville act featuring blues numbers. They toured the East and Midwest without setting the country on fire, but they were improving all the time, and finally they wound up in New York. They were still playing club dates and small vaudeville houses when Roy Bergere got married and headed west to try to crash the movies. Out of their association came one song which they wrote together: "How Come You Do Me Like You Do?"

Gene went it alone and got a job singing in the Club Mah-Jongg, which was run by Lou Clayton. Out of that engagement one episode sticks in his mind to this day. Clayton came to Gene one day and told him that the club needed a good trio. "There are three guys over at some little club," said Clayton, "and I hear good reports about them. Drop over there tonight and have a look, and let me know what you think." Gene had the look, came back and told Clayton, "No good. They've got no class." The trio was called Harris, Jackson and Durante and before long Lou Clayton himself had supplanted Harris to begin one of the most memorable associations in all show business.

About this time Gene got married, the Club Mah-Jongg got padlocked by prohibition agents, and Gene turned seriously to the business of writing songs. To sustain life he took a job with a music publisher as a song plugger. He was required to make the rounds of the recording studios, playing and singing the publisher's latest songs, trying to convince people that those songs were worthy of recording.

Nathaniel Shilkret was in charge of music at Victor and one day Gene told him about a new song he had written, called "When My Sugar Walks Down the Street." Shilkret listened to it and decided it was zingy enough for records. He recommended, however, that Gene not try it solo. Gene as a singer was an unknown quantity and the high command wouldn't push his record. Shilkret suggested that they bring in a name singer to do the number with Gene. Aileen Stanley, already a prominent star, was chosen and the record was cut. Gene remembers that he had very little singing to do on that first record. Miss Stanley would sing, "When my sugar walks down the street, all the little birdies go . . ." and Gene would chime in with, "Tweet-tweet-tweet."

Soon thereafter he sang his first recorded number alone—something titled "The Only, Only One"—and Victor gave him a one-year contract under which he would be paid a hundred dollars for each song he did. Next he recorded "Yes Sir, That's My Baby," which made a minor stir, and after that, "Yearning." This was the record that made Gene Austin, and though it sold and sold and kept on selling, his financial take from it remained a flat and feeble one hundred dollars.

Dealers began clamoring for more of this boy's songs, but Victor couldn't find him. He had become unhappy about his contract and had gone off on a vaudeville tour. Victor sent a man to California to beg him to hurry back and make more records. But Gene still didn't like that contract. He wanted the customary royalty arrangements, and he wanted the privilege of choosing his own songs. He got both.

"The most important element in the success of a record," says Gene, "is the song, not the singer. I got an old sayin', 'Hit songs don't care who sings 'em.'"

His first royalty check under his new contract was for ninety-six thousand dollars. He decided it was time to go back and preen himself before the home folks in Louisiana. On his first day at home in Minden, after the big reception at the depot, he was out in the barn with his stepfather.

Old Jim Austin, the music hater, said, "Gene, I hear tell that these here people that sings makes as much jack as a hunnerd, hunnerd 'n' fifty dollars a week. I figger that's all newspaper talk. It is, ain't it?"

"Sometimes it is," said Gene, pulling the ninety-six-thousand-dollar check from his pocket, "and sometimes it ain't. This is what I got for about three months of singin'."

Old Jim Austin's eyes popped when he read the figure on the check. He was about to say something when Gene's mother called him from the kitchen door. Some folks had dropped in and wanted to see him and wanted him to sing a few songs for them. Gene went in and greeted the people and sat down at the old square piano and began singing. Suddenly he sensed an alien presence in the room. Out of the corner of his eye he saw Old Jim Austin, head cocked to one side, forefinger alongside his nose, listening intently.

"I think," says Gene, "that his head was a-bobbin' to the beat; just a trifle, mind you, but a-bobbin' just the same."

Gene bought a comfortable house for his parents and headed back for New York and the making of more records. He resumed his prowling for songs and one day came up with an item called "My Blue Heaven," by George Whiting and Walter Donaldson. This number had been languishing in the files for seven or eight years and hadn't even been copyrighted. Something about it appealed to Gene and he took it along to his next recording session. He knew his own mind about it, but he wasn't sure how the Victor people would react, so he put it last on the day's agenda. By the time they got to "My Blue Heaven" the orchestra leader announced that time had run out and the band was finished for the day.

"I grabbed an old guy with a cello," Gene recalls, "and talked him into standing by. Then I grabbed a song plugger who could play pretty fair piano. And the third fellow I got was an agent who could whistle—bird calls and that sort of thing. I made the record with those three." In the intervening years

Gene has cut fourteen successive versions of "My Blue Heaven" and these records have had an aggregate sale of more than seven million copies.

When I first knew him in Tulsa and Denver, Gene had no inkling of the fact that he and the whole country were riding for a heavy fall. I remember the day in Denver when he was to make a personal appearance in a music store on Champa Street, autographing records for all comers. The entire block was decorated with banners bearing his name in letters four feet high, and traffic had to be blocked off an hour before his arrival.

Several factors combined to thrust Gene into comparative obscurity within the next few years. Radio changed from a hobby to a habit, and then came the depression. People put their phonographs in the attic; they no longer had the seventy-five cents that a record cost and, anyway, they could get their music for nothing on the radio. Another factor, less important, was Gene's affinity for the ole black bottle. He did a lot of drinking in the wild bootleg days and occasionally he got into trouble with the law. It should be remembered, however, that he and the century were in their twenties at the same time, and both he and the century were suffering from severe growing pains. Moreover, it should be kept in mind that Gene was a boy up from the piney woods, a boy who had never had anything; that money was piling in faster than he and all his pals could spend it, and all he had to do to get that money was to appear once each month or so and sing a few songs into a ridiculous recording horn. He played and he played hard in those years. He had half a dozen fancy cars, a mansion on the Jersey shore, a seventy-foot yacht named *My Blue Heaven*, and a host of Good Time Charlies to keep him company. I suspect he was actually a little happy about it when the bottom fell out of things. He disappeared into the West and he remained in obscurity, so far as the national consciousness was concerned, for almost a quarter of a century.

What was he doing in all those years? Surprisingly enough he was making money. And he was still singing. He teamed up with Ken Murray to inaugurate the musical show *Blackouts* which ran for seven solid years in a Hollywood theater. Gene knew a good deal about the economics of nightclub operation, so he spent several years as an entrepreneur. He'd shop around Los Angeles until he found a club that was tottering. He'd buy it for peanuts, move in, change its name to "Gene Austin's Blue Heaven," and build it into a profitable business. For example, he bought one club for thirteen hundred dollars and in six months sold it for thirty-six thousand dollars. He performed this operation with three or four different clubs, and in each case he was the floor show, the attraction that fetched in the customers. A little rinkey-tink piano would be wheeled onto the dance floor. Gene would bounce out, settle himself, and then spend an hour or two singing the old favorites, always finishing with "My Blue Heaven." There were plenty of customers (myself among them) who wanted to hear him sing those old songs again and his clubs were always crowded.

In between times he was involved in other musical shows, in motion pictures, in writing songs, and in nightclub appearances around the country. Once in the 1930s a wealthy auto manufacturer in Ohio heard that Gene Austin was in town. He telephoned Gene, said he had been an Austin fan for years, and then made a proposal. "I'm having a party at my home tonight," he said, "and I'll give you a thousand dollars if you'll come out and sing six songs."

Said Gene, "I'm on my way."

When he arrived at the mansion the auto manufacturer met him at the door and escorted him quickly through a crowd of people and into a library where there was a piano. He closed and locked the door, nodded toward the piano and said, "Okay, start off with 'Melancholy Baby.'"

Gene was perplexed. "But the party's out yonder," he protested.

"The hell with the party," said the host. "I want you to sing just for me."

Gene had many such private engagements, especially back in the twenties when the millionaires of Long Island and Westchester would summon him to their parties and pay him fabulous sums for singing a few numbers.

"Those were usually tough assignments," Gene remembers. "I was the first of the crooners, and some of the men were pretty nasty about it, making loud cracks about me, suggesting that I was sorta ladylike. In those days almost every party I went to ended in a fight, and for the same reason. I'd listen to the cracks and then I'd say, 'Okay, brother, come on outside and we'll see who's ee-femminit.' I'm not much inclined to brag, but the truth is I flattened many a Yale-type cooky pusher in those days."

Gene has been married four times. He has three grandchildren by a daughter who lives in Kansas City. His other daughter, Charlotte Austin, is a stunning brunette beauty who acts in the movies. His present wife, Lou, is a bright and attractive girl out of Springfield, Missouri. She knew Gene Austin's records when she was a teenager, and loved them. About twelve years ago she was living in St. Louis when she read in the newspapers that Gene Austin was singing at the Park Plaza Hotel. That night she was at a ringside table with a friend. When Gene finished his act he wandered down into the audience. He stopped at Lou's table and asked her if there was any special number she would like to hear.

"Oh yes," she said. "I remember a long time ago, the first Gene Austin record I ever heard, and it became my favorite."

"Which one was that?"

"I Wish I Had Died in My Cradle, Before I Grew Up to Love You."

"Great day!" exclaimed Gene. "I forgot that one ninety years ago." But he went back to the piano and noodled around, and it came back to him. When he had finished singing it, he sat for a moment in thought. What kind of a dame would choose a corn-popper like that out of all the songs I've sung? He decided it was a question worth investigating, and returned to her table . . . and so they were wed.

In recent years the Austin home has been a fifty-foot trailer called, naturally, the Blue Heaven. Gene has it based permanently in Las Vegas, with a second trailer serving as studio and office alongside it. He and Lou do a lot of traveling, for he's still in demand in the supper clubs from Key West to Alaska.

Five years ago when Gene was in New York and there was talk of a Big Comeback for him, I decided to try to help matters along by writing a magazine article about him. I turned out a fairly long piece (which was substantially this piece you have been reading) and then sat down and read it through and decided it wouldn't work. There is an axiom in my trade which says that a writer is usually the worst judge of his own product; if he thinks a piece of his work is good it probably smells to middle heaven, whereas, if he judges it to be a malodorous botch, it is very likely a masterpiece. I point to my Gene Austin article to demonstrate the point. I said to myself, after I finished writing it, "Well, I did the best I could. It was a labor of love, an attempt to help an old friend. Nobody will buy it, nobody will publish it. Maybe, because it's show biz, I'll just trim it down and see if Abel Green would like to have it for *Variety*." Still, I felt that I should go through the motions so I handed the manuscript over to my agent. Two days later he notified me that the *Saturday Evening Post* had grabbed it up and was paying me the biggest dough I'd ever had from a magazine for a single piece.

After the article was published in the *Post*, Gene was called upon for various guest appearances on radio and television and one evening he was interviewed on the air by the incomparable Jinx Falkenburg. Miss Falkenburg was famous for her naïveté, her artless simplicity, whenever she was grappling with the seamier side of life, and this night she was stroking par.

"Is it really true," she asked Gene, "that you once were a piano player in the sporting houses of New Orleans?"

"Well . . ." said Gene, a drawling smile in his voice. But Miss Falkenburg, herself once a figure in the sports world, plunged right ahead, and it was obvious that she had no idea of the nature of a sporting house. She suggested that it might have been difficult playing piano in such a place. "All that noise," she said. Gene hemmed and hawed around a bit and finally she asked him if there were lots of sporting houses in New Orleans in those days and Gene brought down the house by answering, "Oh, yes. The Spalding people were opening new ones all over the country."

All of these interviewers asked Gene how it felt to be making a big comeback and he answered each of them the same way: "I'm not makin' any comeback. I ain't been away." This was a normal response for anyone in show business. A performer will withstand thumbscrews and the Chinese water torture before he'll ever admit that he has been in eclipse.

In 1962 Gene came home from a successful singing engagement in Alaska to run for the Democratic nomination for governor of Nevada. The main plank in his platform was that he could do anything his opponent could do and he could also sing. He said, too, that he would be able to give the state one hell of a fine First Lady. It is my impression that he didn't win.

When he was sixty years old he drove down from Vegas to Hollywood and spent a couple of days making a long-playing stereo record which was released under the title, "Gene Austin's Great Hits." On this record he sang "My Blue Heaven," "Lonesome Road," "Melancholy Baby," "Bye Bye Blackbird," "Ramona," "Sleepy Time Gal," "Jeannine," "I Can't Give You Anything But Love," "Someday Sweetheart," "Girl of My Dreams," "Weary River," and "How Am I to Know?" All songs that were closely associated with his name in the days of yore. I speak as a confirmed Gene Austin fan but I also speak with absolute sincerity when I say that he never in all his years sang as well as he does on that record.

And so it was that all of us who belonged to his generation were happy that he was back. Red Barber was happy, and so was John Crosby, and Richard Watts, and Sherman Fairchild, and R. W. Woodruff of Coca-Cola, and Harry S. Truman, and Alfred Vanderbilt. All of these people have remained steadfast Gene Austin fans down through the years—and there was one other.

Jimmy Byrnes, of South Carolina, once told Gene: "I never heard F.D.R. play but one record, and he played that one a lot. It was Gene Austin singing 'Lonesome Road.'"

That, of course, made Gene feel real good, for he not only sang it. He wrote it.

Stan Lewis

—Randy McNutt

This piece is a portion of a chapter from Randy McNutt's *Guitar Towns: A Journey to the Crossroads of Rock and Roll*, titled "Shreveport: Susie-Q," the section focused primarily on Stan Lewis. Lewis's professional career began in 1948 when he opened Stan's Record Shop on Texas Street in Shreveport. He became a "one-stop" operator (other nearby record stores would buy from him to resell on the retail level), distributing independent labels like Atlantic, Chess, Modern, Specialty, and Imperial. In the early 1950s Lewis added a highly successful mail-order operation that lasted for over a decade. This business picked up significantly when Lewis began advertising on R&B disc jockey shows, including KWKH broadcasts by the alter ego of one of the *Hayride* announcers, Frank "Gatemouth" Page. Lewis also advertised on the nightly broadcast of WLAC-AM out of Nashville, famous for its team of disc jockeys, including John R and Hoss Allen. Both KWKH and WLAC operated 50,000-watt clear channels, covering much of the country.

From his beginnings in record sales and distribution, Lewis's business interests expanded in 1963 when he founded the Jewel label, soon followed with the imprints Paula and Ronn. His rosters included a wide range of mostly black artists, among them the Five Blind Boys of Mississippi, Memphis Slim, John Lee Hooker, Reverend Oris Mays, Lowell Fulson, Toussaint McCall, the Violinaires, Lightnin' Hopkins, Reverend Clay Evans, and Bobby Rush. Lewis extended his small empire in 1968 when he purchased the masters of Chicago blues label Cobra Records. Cobra had been particularly active during the middle 1950s and its roster included important Chicago-style blues artists like Buddy Guy, Otis Rush, and Magic Slim.

Lewis still lives in Shreveport and remains active in the music business, though from a semi-retired status. Following a 1993 release on Capricorn of a *Jewel Records* box set, Lewis offered the label for sale, though he wanted to retain control of his publishing companies as well as two small labels, Susie Q and Gospel Jubilee. After protracted negotiations, EMusic.com purchased the master recording rights of the Jewel family of labels during the summer of 1999. Thus, Stan Lewis's work in documenting music during an important era of this (in his words) "regional sound city" continues to circulate musical sounds of Shreveport.

When [James] Burton was appearing on the *Hayride* in the late 1950s, Stan Lewis was selling records across town and starting to build an empire of discs. He turned his record store into one of the South's more prosperous music operations, then turned to releasing R&B, rock, and country hits on his own Jewel, Paula, and Ronn labels. Lewis also built one of the South's larger independent distributors, which helped promote independent labels and regional sounds.

The producer, publisher, label owner, and distributor was born near Shreveport on July 5, 1927, to hard-working Italian parents, Frank and Lucille Lewis. His father worked in a meat-packing house during the Depression, and in 1941 opened a family grocery. Young Stan helped. Even then, he preferred music—big-band jazz by Duke Ellington, Glenn Miller, and others, and the blues and gospel songs that people sang in his racially mixed neighborhood. He also played clarinet in the high school band. In the late 1940s he started buying jukeboxes, pinball machines, and records. The discs came from a little R&B store at 728 Texas Street. In 1948, Lewis bought the store and renamed it Stan's Record Shop. At eight-by-twelve feet, the one-story shop was smaller inside than some people's living rooms, but Lewis crammed it with R&B and a few country records. He continued to work in his father's grocery while his wife, Paula, worked in the shop. They came up with a catchy slogan ("728—Don't Be Late!") and advertised on KWKH, trying to reach a simmering youth market. They even held autograph parties for recording artists, including Elvis Presley. Lewis worked twelve hours a day and became the first local businessman to hire blacks in retail sales.

"I grew up selling newspapers and milk bottles and shining shoes," he said. "I made nickels and dimes. Today, people step over coins and don't bother to pick them up. But they were big money when I grew up. During World War II, I played drums a little to make extra money. The real drummers were off to war. I was too young to go. I saved all my money—$2,500. And that's what I went into the record business with."

His timing was perfect. All across the country, dozens of entrepreneurs were forming independent record companies, including King in Cincinnati,

Specialty and Imperial in Los Angeles, and Chess in Chicago. Their owners sought out Lewis when they came into Shreveport with big dreams and little cash. They stored discs in their trunks next to tape recorders on which they sometimes recorded singers on the road. "I met all these guys when they first put out their records," Lewis said. "As their companies grew into great monsters, my shop grew with them. We did mail-order and retail. I picked up the distribution thing on my own, and grew into it. It wasn't planned. I didn't have board meetings. I just *did* it." By 1954, Lewis did more than sell and distribute records. He produced several Top 10 national country and R&B hits for independent labels. They included blues singer Lowell Fulsom's "Reconsider Baby" for Checker, Jimmy and Johnny's "If You Don't, Somebody Else Will" for Chess, and Jimmy C. Newman's "Cry, Cry Darling" for Dot. By then, Lewis had already forged strong friendships with independents Art Rupe of Specialty and Leonard Chess of Chess Records. When Chess traveled around the South, promoting new releases, he'd always stop in Shreveport to eat dinner with Stan and Paula and give them all of the records he had left in his car—often hundreds of 78s—at no charge.

Lewis stood out among distributors because he was honest and aggressive. He viewed the relationship between record label and distributor as a partnership. Distributors' contributions to popular music are often overlooked, because people prefer the more glamorous work of record labels. But powerful distributors like Lewis—and few were as influential—helped make independent labels a success in the early 1950s. Label owners courted him. Lewis opened new retail stores and provided one-stop and distribution services for far-flung record shops. By the late 1950s, his company ruled western Louisiana and eastern Texas.

I found Lewis, a distinguished-looking man with a soft voice, at his office in a 1950s building at 1700 Centenary Street. Young men and women rushed past me in the halls. Keith Abel, the company's foreign representative, took me into Lewis's small office, where awards and photographs of music stars hung on the walls, and his desk overflowed with papers and audio cassettes. The telephone rang every five minutes—an unusual ring, like the English telephones on a PBS show. Lewis ignored it. He sighed and apologized for delaying me that morning. Problems with distributors, artists—even a missed dental appointment. More succinctly, a problem with time.

For a man of average size, Lewis is distinctive. His wavy gray hair contrasts with olive skin and large, dark eyes that spoke to me. They looked tired at 11 A.M. I thought Lewis was a sincere and friendly man, reserved but forthright and candid. He wore a loud jacket and tie, which gave him the look of a used car salesman. Clearly he understated his company's role in local music history, but he knew that he had achieved something important.

"I was close to our people," he said. "Shreveport was not a distribution center. It was a 'half-percent market,' meaning it wasn't no market, really. So I created a market with mail order, advertising with Wolfman Jack on XERF in Del Rio, Texas; Hoss Allen on WLAC in Nashville; and other early R&B disc jockeys. I sponsored a show called *Stan's Record Review*. We helped the manufacturers break records, and in turn, they stayed with me. Other people like me got out when they were successful and went to New York or Los Angeles. But my roots were here. I had a good thing going. Why should I move? If I went to Chicago or L.A., I couldn't dominate the market the way I did here. I was the big fish in the little pond. Up north, I'd have been a little bitty fish in a great big pond, and I'd have been sliced up ten different ways."

The *Hayride* helped him, too, at least in the early days. It operated in a different world then. "People didn't have a lot of money," Lewis said. "We had no air conditioning, no television yet. Our town had only one radio station company, which picked up three networks to speak of—ABC, CBS, Mutual. Life was simple. What do you do for entertainment? You go to a drive-in movie, get a hamburger, or go window-shopping downtown (this was when there was a downtown). In those times, the *Hayride* was a big, big thing. KWKH owned the local newspaper and other ones. When they used to play country records in the mornin', there was no such thing as ratings. Disc jockeys played whatever they wanted. You had no other station competing in the same market, so you could build a Jim Reeves, Webb Pierce, Nat Stuckey, and others, and play their records. Unfortunately, things didn't work out for the show on television. When television came along, KWKH applied for a license with the intention of televising the *Hayride* on Channel 12, but then one of the owners—they were from an uppercrust family—died, and some interest was lost. That was it.

"If I would have had good sense, I'd have started my own labels back then, in the early '50s. But I was young and lacked the necessary foresight. Shreveport had the potential to become another Nashville. Remember, Nashville didn't have all the studios and labels back then, either. Some people in Shreveport think they can bring it all back here today, but we're living in a computer world with a lot of entertainment options. When I was selling tickets to the *Hayride* in my record shop, people used to come in from New Mexico, all over Texas, Missouri, Arizona, Kansas. They were on vacation, and they came here just like they come to Branson, Missouri, today. I'd like to think it could be that way again, but you can't buy enough advertising to build up an artist today who you built up for nothing in the old days."

Preoccupied by his distribution business, Lewis didn't think seriously about establishing his own labels because he feared he might compete with the labels that he distributed. But he continued to produce records independently for other companies. In 1957 he took Dale Hawkins, a record shop employee, into KWKH to cut "Susie-Q" after the station signed off the air late one night. It was rock-and-roll at its most intimate and primitive: bass, drums, guitar, vocal. They used only three microphones. Although it became a bigger R&B hit than pop, the record showed an early musical fusion that represented Shreveport. The record's opening guitar lick is one of rock's most enduring and identifiable. Hawkins and Lewis talked about writing a song while they worked together in the record shop. Lewis said the title came to him easy enough: he and Leonard Chess both had daughters named Susan. When Lewis mentioned this to Hawkins, they wrote the song. Naturally, Lewis found a sympathetic ear at Chess Records, which released the song on its Checker subsidiary. When "Susie-Q" rose to No. 27 on the *Billboard* charts in June 1957, Hawkins quit the record shop and toured America. The native of Mangham, Louisiana, who also played guitar, shaped the record's mesmerizing R&B beat by listening to Howlin' Wolf records in Stan Lewis's shop. The drummer used a cowbell to give "Susie-Q" its unusual sound. The song—a true rock-and-roll ancestor—remains popular on oldies stations. Creedence Clearwater Revival remade the song—a more driving, eerie version—in the summer of 1968. The band's first hit, it reached No. 11 and created a new audience for the song.

Inspiration struck Lewis again one afternoon in 1963, as he drove around Chicago and noticed a chair store named Jewel. "I told Leonard Chess, 'I think that would be a good name for a label. I think I'll start me one.' He said, 'Why don't you?' I was in business. I named my second label Paula, for my wife, and Ronn after my brother. At first I put my country acts on Paula and R&B on Ronn, but then I gave up on that and just put out what I felt like putting out. To me, a record company should make music that matters—music that tells a story. I like gospel, blues, and country because they tell stories. They're about people. Anyway, the reason that labels resorted to creating other, subsidiary labels was simple: If you got real hot, the disc jockeys would play three or four of your records. Then you'd be accused of giving payola. Atlantic started Atco Records and then Cotillion. I started my other labels because Jewel was my gospel-R&B-type label. I recorded every singer on the Bossier City strip. Of course, most of the time I sold only a thousand copies to jukebox operators.

I got Mickey Gilley started, then he left for Playboy Records. Yeah, I still got tons of Mickey in the can. I bought a Willie Nelson album in a tax-shelter deal. I've got a lot of former Chess artists—Willie Dixon, John Lee Hooker, Elmore James. I've got Ike and Tina, Otis Rush. So many R&B acts."

The company's greatest commercial success came on Paula in 1968, when a Baton Rouge rock show group, John Fred and His Playboy Band, cut "Judy in Disguise (with Glasses)" at Robin Hood Brians's studio in the mini-music center of Tyler, Texas. Fred liked to record for Jewel because Lewis didn't bother him in the studio. Fred's popular band had already scored a few chart records, but the big one still eluded him. Then came "Judy." "We were playing in Florida and the girls at that time had these big, old sunglasses," he told writer Steven Rosen years later. "One of the guys was hustling this chick. She took off these glasses, and she could stop a clock. I said, 'That's it.' That's what gave me the idea. I said, 'She's kind of in disguise.'" With its unusual novelty sounds and solid beat, the record exploded across the country. "It just kept going up until it hit No. 1," Lewis said. "But on the next try, with 'Hey Hey Bunny,' we couldn't break John Fred out of the fifties." Lewis didn't stop. He discovered country singers Randy Travis, Joe Stampley (his rock band, the Uniques, recorded "Not Too Long Ago" on Paula), and Nat Stuckey. But once established, they—and other performers—left Jewel for the larger labels in Nashville.

Somehow, Jewel persisted. I like its slogan: "The World's Most Unique Record Company." At the least it is one of the nation's indigenous labels, for Jewel has thrived primarily on roots music. Most people wouldn't recognize its artists. Lewis has no Madonna clones, no alternative bands, no flavor-of-the-month acts. Jewel's artists include bluesmen Jimmy Reed, Toussaint McCall, and Ted Taylor, as well as the older black gospel singers the Soul Stirrers, the Rev. C. L. Franklin, and the Brooklyn All Stars. Even old Lightnin' Hopkins recorded for Jewel. (Lewis complied with Hopkins's unorthodox demands: payment in cash—no royalties necessary, thank you—for one performance. And no retakes!) Many recordings came from labels that Lewis bought in later years, including Chicago's Cobra Records. Other acts left the major labels like refugees from a storm and sought out Jewel, the unpretentious label that appealed to blues singers like a home-cooked meal. Although Lewis did not sell millions of records, he sold enough to transform Jewel from a commercial label heavily dependent on radio airplay into a successful roots-music independent of the late 1990s.

The transformation did not come without turmoil—and it came at a price. As the record business changed in the early 1980s, developing into a

more corporate environment, Lewis adapted. He sold 300,000 to 400,000 copies of twelve-inch singles by the Conway Brothers, Magnum Force, and Tony
Ballard. But even then, he knew his labels were like small game trying to evade
stealthy hunters. As radio increasingly resisted his more commercial records,
everything began to unravel for Lewis.

"The majors set out to kill the independents, which in the early days
probably comprised 90 percent of the record industry's sales in the roots
field," he said. "By the '70s, my distribution business suffered. The majors
bought Atlantic, so I lost it. Every six months or so we'd lose another label for
our distributorship. Every time this happened, the independent distributors
weakened."

By 1983, his record labels couldn't generate enough income to carry his
entire company. "In this business, we carry on paper," he said. "It's not like a
bank or some store. I had 150 employees, including twelve promotion men
on the road, several salesmen, a sales manager, and many family members in
wholesaling and manufacturing. I got so big that I couldn't watch over it all.
When you get hit with $5 million in receivables, you're hurting. A lot of my
friends in the industry went out of business or hung on by their fingernails.
I had a big team of employees, and all of a sudden I'm in Chapter 11—bankruptcy. I tried to work it out, but there was a lot of backstabbing. I was sold
down the river. Politics as usual. Thank God I emerged from that mess, but
it almost killed me, mentally and physically. It almost destroyed me. You see,
I went from being a poor boy, hustling all my life, to becoming a multimil-
lionaire. And then I lost it, had it taken away. I fell into the bottom of the pit.
That's when you see how many friends you have. There wasn't anybody there
to help me. It wasn't the old days, when I could ask for help. Morris Levy of
Roulette Records helped me at times. He called and said, 'What do you need?'
But I had to struggle."

By the mid-1980s, Lewis emerged with only the record labels and his
music publishing companies. So he concentrated on his strength, roots
music—the music of Shreveport. He had no choice. "We have some of
the greatest musicians in the country in Shreveport and east Texas and
Mississippi," he said. "They play everything from jazz to rock. Imagine what
we could have had here—all the booking agents, managers, studios. But they
never happened. I try to take the music and put it out, but it's a battle. The
majors are just too powerful. Many of the original independents started in
the South, and the others came down here to record our talent. When they
started building more studios on the West Coast, they duplicated our sounds.

Everything changed. Our musicians even went out there. Now not much is left of the regional-sound cities. Chicago is dead, and it used to be a huge R&B market. I used to sell tons of records in Detroit. That's changed."

Lewis handed me a box filled with a dozen compact discs released on Jewel. My favorite title, *Blues Is Killin' Me*, is an anthology from 1951–1953 that features rough-and-tumble singers named Baby Face Leroy ("Pet Rabbit"), Floyd Jones ("Skinny Mama"), and Memphis Minnie ("Kissing in the Dark"). It's the kind of music you won't find too often at the mall's chain stores. Staring at the black and white cover, I realized that Jewel—with its indefatigable owner—was one of the last true American record companies, a feisty operation that would not perish with the twenty-first century.

As I prepared to leave, Stan Lewis walked slowly over to a window for a few minutes and watched the people of his hometown. For a moment he saw a simpler time: his record shop, the autograph parties, the *Hayride*, the hamburger and drive-in days.

"I wish I could transfer everything I have in my head into my employees' heads," he said. "All the history and the knowledge. All the ups and downs. But this is a business that everybody learns on the streets and in the back rooms. You can't learn what I've learned from a book."

"Reconsider Me"

Margaret Lewis Warwick and the *Louisiana Hayride*

—Tracey E. W. Laird

Although this article uses the *Louisiana Hayride* as a point of reference, its focus is not on country music, but on Mira Smith's entrepreneurship as a record company owner, and Maggie Warwick as a songwriter and civic leader in Shreveport's musical life. As the founder and owner of RAM Records, Smith was a pioneer woman in the music industry. Her recording efforts crossed genre boundaries to include country, rockabilly, R&B, and swamp pop. Smith's Lakeshore Drive studio reflected the local DIY (Do-It-Yourself) spirit with its sound baffles built of discarded egg cartons attached to the walls. Dale Hawkins, James Burton, Joe Osborn, and Sonny Boy Williamson (unrelated to either the RCA or Chess blues artists of the same name) were among the musicians who made their way to her studio. RAM recordings of Roy Perkins, TV Slim, and others have been reissued in recent years on the British-based Ace Records—most notably *Red River Blues* (CDCHD 725) and *Shreveport High Steppers* (CDCHD 818).

A songwriter in her own right, Smith moved away from Shreveport in the 1960s as the *Hayride*'s end left little reason for musicians with professional aspirations to stay in town. With Maggie Warwick, then known as Margaret Lewis, she went to Nashville to write songs for producer and music publisher Shelby Singleton. Mira Smith passed away in 1989 after a battle with leukemia. In a recorded telephone interview with Tracey Laird in 2002, Maggie Lewis Warwick recalled Smith's work in the studio on their collaboration "The Cradle to the Blues," and "Just Another Life," recorded by Linda Brannon. As Warwick recalls, Smith was inspired by Les Paul's innovations in multitrack studio recording as well as guitar playing:

> Mira Smith thought Les Paul was the end—she just loved him. And when the Les Paul guitar came out, oh she had to have it. And that's what she used in recording those sounds, that electric guitar, on "The Cradle to the Blues" and Linda's recording of "Just Another Life." Mira was playing the guitar on that and that became a good hit and was actually leased by Chess Records—they wanted to put it on their record label . . . . It was a pioneer time and Mira was very much a pioneer in recording because she just loved it so much and was just fascinated by all of the sounds that you could get by going in and experimenting with these different instruments.

No measure of time
Just the cradle then the blues
Just one second thought
And you win or you lose
Never had to give up so much
Never felt so helpless
Can't stand much more
No wonder it's short
From the cradle to the blues
It's a long lonely road to travel and lose. . . .
              —"From the Cradle to the Blues," Mira Smith and Margaret Lewis, 1959

Hello baby, yes, it's really me.
After all the wrong I've done
I guess you're surprised to see me
Here at your door like a sparrow with a broken wing
Who's come back to beg you, Oh my baby, reconsider me
Oh pleeeeeease reconsider me
I can't make it, not without, oh you can't you see
So if you will let me I will love you eternally
Oh baby, baby, baby,
Reconsider me
              —"Reconsider Me," Mira Lewis and Margaret Smith, 1969

Under the egg crates, two women write. In 1959, Margaret Lewis and Mira Smith composed "From the Cradle to the Blues" in Shreveport, Louisiana.

Ten years later, in Nashville, the two women wrote "Reconsider Me." There are several different ways that these two songs might be used to tell stories about country music. One story might tell of an invisible drain that sucked talent from Shreveport to Nashville throughout the 1950s. Like many musicians and musical entrepreneurs before them, Lewis and Smith honed their skills in Shreveport and then migrated to the citadel of country music, where success was more likely.

Another story might describe the intersecting careers of two women writing songs from the depth of their experiences in a circumstance—both geographic and temporal—where blacks and whites regularly exchanged music and culture in live performance and over the radio. This story begins with an obscure song released only on the regional Ram (Royal Audio Music) label and culminates in the success of "Reconsider Me" on both the R&B and Country charts. ("Reconsider Me" was a hit for soul singer Johnny Adams in 1969 and for Narvel Felts in 1975.)[1]

Then, as with every tale, there is the unabridged version: it unravels both yarns and stretches them further across time in both directions forward and back. It starts when the *Louisiana Hayride* was a radio barn dance, often called the "Cradle of the Stars." The success of the show inspired Mira Smith to build her own recording studio, Ram Records; it also drew Margaret Lewis to Shreveport to join the *Hayride* cast and pursue her aspirations as a performer. This story ends when Margaret Lewis returned to Shreveport after a seventeen-year stint as a Nashville songwriter and became chair of a local non-profit organization she founded with her husband, the Foundation for Arts, Music, and Entertainment (FAME). Two decades later, FAME still works to transform the art-deco Municipal Auditorium (from which the *Hayride* first broadcast) and its blighted environs into a "historic music village" to commemorate and celebrate Shreveport's place in music history.[2]

Lewis grew up with her ear glued to the wireless and her eyes fixed to a Baptist hymnal in the dusty hinterlands of West Texas. From her early childhood, she soaked up radio sounds ranging from Bob Wills on the heels of the sunrise farm report to Peggy Lee in the evenings on stations out of Lubbock.[3] But KWKH was her doorway east to another world. Its AM signal reached from Shreveport to the dry West Texas farm where Lewis lived. She was nearly six years old when the *Louisiana Hayride* first broadcast on April 3, 1948. It soon became a family tradition for the Lewis family to gather around her grandparents' cabinet radio every week, catching the twangy strains of guitars plucked by Johnnie and Jack and the Tennessee Mountain Boys, featuring the sonorous, plaintive tones of Kitty Wells. The quality of reception depended on the weather, as the 50,000-watt AM signal bounced up and down like a strato-sphere yo-yo to the California coast and beyond.

Along with her parents, grandparents, and three siblings, Lewis anticipated and savored the Saturday night mix of country music performers whose pro-cession across the *Hayride* stage and over the airwaves earned the show its nick-name, "Cradle of the Stars": string bands and duets, such as the Bailes Brothers and Johnnie and Jack; honky-tonk innovators like Hank Williams, Webb Pierce, and George Jones; golden-throated crooners like Slim Whitman and Jim Reeves; comic or novelty singers such as Cousin Emmy, Cousin Wilbur, and Bill Carlisle; gospel groups like the Four Deacons, the Plainsmen Quartet and the Deep South Quartet; western swing bands like Paul Howard and His Cotton Pickers; bluegrass talent like Ralph and Carter Stanley, Mac Wiseman, Charlie Waller, Charlie Monroe, and Jimmy Martin;[4] spoken word performers like Red Sovine and T. Texas Tyler; Cajun country musicians like Jimmy C. Newman and Rusty and Doug (Kershaw); and performers who pushed the boundaries of country music like the raucous Maddox Brothers & Rose.[5]

Lewis's musical tastes broadened around the same time her family moved in 1952. Stations like KWKH still broadcast farm news and country music in the early morning hours and around noon. In the late morning and early afternoon, they played soap operas and variety programs that originated from the networks. But in the late 1940s and early 1950s—during the era before for-mat radio—KWKH added afternoon and late-night disc jockey shows of R&B and jive to the daily schedule. *Louisiana Hayride* announcers Ray Bartlett and Frank Page adopted the names "Groovie Boy" and "Gatemouth," respectively, attracting a generation of young listeners, many of whom, like Lewis, were drawn as much to the *Hayride's* country music broadcasts as they were to the rhythm-and-blues shows.

Lewis formed a band, the Thunderbolts, in 1956. They performed coun-try, R&B, and the style of music that came to be called rockabilly. "When we went to Levelland, then the early rhythm-and-blues had come on to the scene. And we had a little radio station there in Levelland that played that in the evening. . . . [The Thunderbolts] were like rockabilly and early rock-and-roll and early [rhythm-and-]blues and country. So we were kind of format-ting just like the radio station. I even liked a lot of the Jo Stafford records . . . and early Peggy Lee, you remember the female singers like that. And especially Ruth Brown and LaVern Baker were real big influences." In Levelland in West Texas, Margaret Lewis and the Thunderbolts were a simulacrum of what was happening all over the South, as the musical and cultural exchange between black and white musicians accelerated, along with the rest of society during the decade after World War II.[6]

The apogee of the cultural dynamic that characterized Lewis's generation was the rock-and-roll moment—that span of five or six years when the long, troubled history of conflict and cultural exchange between whites and blacks in the South culminated in the music of Carl Perkins, Jerry Lee Lewis, Chuck Berry, and Little Richard. The dominant figure in the 1950s rise of youth culture was Elvis Presley, who gained his first widespread national exposure on the *Louisiana Hayride* in 1954. The Elvis juggernaut was, in fact, rock-and-roll inchoate. Furthermore, Presley's promulgation of rockabilly from the *Louisiana Hayride* stage in Shreveport exposed the critical (and sometimes overlooked) country roots of rock-and-roll. As a hybrid of elements from black and white Southern musical traditions, rockabilly had antecedents that extended to the spirituals and gospel songs of the South's more evangelical denominations, as well as to the music of Leadbelly, the Allen Brothers, Bob Wills, and the Maddox Brothers & Rose.

The story of Elvis most famously represents the same compelling cultural force that brought Margaret Lewis to rehearse with the Thunderbolts in West Texas. On the *Hayride,* Elvis Presley performed country songs like "Blue Moon of Kentucky" by Bill Monroe, "Just Because" by the Shelton Brothers (recorded by them as the Lone Star Cowboys in 1933), and "I'll Never Let You Go (Little Darlin')," a 1941 song by Jimmy Wakely. He also performed rhythm-and-blues songs like "That's All Right, Mama" by Arthur "Big Boy" Crudup, "Mystery Train" by Junior Parker, and "Good Rockin' Tonight" by Wynonnie Harris. Presley even performed "I Don't Care If the Sun Don't Shine" (a pop tune omitted from Disney's *Cinderella*), and the famous Rodgers and Hart song, "Blue Moon."[7]

Presley's music, along with that of Carl Perkins, Jerry Lee Lewis, Bill Haley, Chuck Berry, and Little Richard, flew in the face of the record industry's notions of racially segregated musical categories, first established with the "race" and "hillbilly" catalogs of Southern roots music created in the 1920s. Rock-and-roll and its country cousin equally under-mined the industry's understanding of "popular music," as songs by Haley, Berry, Presley, and Fats Domino topped the popular charts in the mid-1950s.[8] Elvis Presley, the Everly Brothers, Jerry Lee Lewis, Johnny Horton—all white performers who originally performed within the context of country music—between 1956 and 1960 recorded songs that simultaneously scaled the country and western, rhythm-and-blues, and popular music charts.⁹ Racial desegregation, which would take painful decades to progress, was significantly occurring with relative speed in the music dubbed rock-and-roll.

For his eclectic repertoire, distinctive rhythmic sensibility, and increasingly brazen but stunning showmanship, Presley found a receptive audience in Shreveport's Municipal Auditorium and on tour with *Hayride* package shows throughout the area. Presley's music made sense in Shreveport, which had long been a crossroads for a variety of musical styles and cultural impulses. Only in such a place could long-held notions of musical categories be slowly—if not quietly—undermined. Presley's music made sense to Lewis when she saw him perform on one of the *Hayride* touring shows, which were always met with enthusiasm in Texas venues.¹⁰

For ambitious young Margaret Lewis, hunkered at the radio to hear every song on the weekly barn dance, the *Hayride* was the doorway of promise to a career as a singer/songwriter of national renown. Hank Williams had set a mythical precedent when he joined the cast three months after it began broadcasting, only to blaze to stardom with vaudevillian Emmett Miller's old tune "Lovesick Blues." The radio barn dance had thus been the natural choice of venue for the nineteen-year-old "Hillbilly Cat" and his Blue Moon Boys, especially after being rejected by the Grand Ole Opry in Nashville. Soon after, Elvis blazed his own trail to fame. He departed the *Hayride,* buying out the remaining months of his *Louisiana Hayride* contract for $10,000 in order to record for RCA Records, at about the time Lewis and the Thunderbolts set their sights there.

In 1957, Margaret Lewis and the Thunderbolts won first runner-up in the Johnny Horton Talent Show sponsored by station KDAV in Lubbock, Texas. Horton, the *Louisiana Hayride's* last big star, sponsored the competitions along with manager Tillman Franks in small cities across Texas. Their prize was a chance to appear on the *Hayride.* Within weeks, Lewis took a Trailways bus with her sister Rose to Shreveport, where she performed Buddy Holly's song "That'll Be the Day" and "some country songs." After returning home, her performance led to several guest appearances whenever the *Hayride* toured nearby. The following year, Lewis moved to Shreveport and joined the *Louisiana Hayride* cast, thereby coming to the attention of Mira Smith, who was bringing the *Hayride's* most promising young musicians into her Ram Records studio on Lakeshore Drive for jam sessions and recordings.

Smith's musical tastes spanned the entire spectrum of regional sounds. She not only recorded younger *Hayride* musicians in Shreveport, she scoured

north and south Louisiana and east Texas for talented black and white players. Since building her own studio with a Crown tape recorder, a Rok-U-Kut
Acetate Disc Cutter in the control room, and sound baffles made from egg
cartons, Smith had recorded players ranging from rockabillies Roy "Boogie
Boy" Perkins and The Lonesome Drifter (Thomas Johnson), rhythm-and-
blues stylist TV Slim (Oscar Wills), and swamp-pop rocker Jimmy Bonin.[11]
Margaret Lewis signed a Ram contract in 1959 at the age of seventeen, releasing her own tune, "Cheaters Never Win," that same year.

    Smith was a songwriter as well as a record producer. Eighteen years her
senior, she became a mentor to Lewis; it evolved into a partnership. The two
women spent hours experimenting with sounds—Smith's guitar and Lewis's
voice, both instruments containing all the impulse and energy wrought by
decades of close and constant contact between white and black culture. Within
a year of their recording "From the Cradle to the Blues" at the Shreveport
studio, the "Cradle of the Stars" broadcast its last show on August 27, 1960.[12]
Hayride management had struggled for several years with dwindling audiences in the wake of cultural phenomena beyond their control: rock-and-roll,
television, and the hive-like centralization of music industry. In the black
hole left after the *Hayride* ended, Shreveport was no longer a viable place for a
professional musician to make a full time living.

    A generation of young musicians left Shreveport for the promise of being
paid to play in Tennessee and California. Their sensibilities had been nurtured
on the ubiquitous country and rhythm-and-blues shows heard on KWKH and
in live local venues. They drew on instincts developed in Shreveport's musical
milieu, and entered the music business in an era when the studio determined
industry success, not the stage. Multi-instrumentalist Jerry Kennedy became
a session musician and record producer in Nashville, producing Roger Miller,
the Statler Brothers, Reba McEntire and others, while also playing bass on
the Roy Orbison standard "Pretty Woman" and dobro on Jeannie C. Riley's
crossover hit "Harper Valley P.T.A."[13] Bassist Joe Osborn became an influential session musician in Los Angeles during the 1960s and early 1970s, later
in Nashville until 1989, when he retired to north Louisiana; over the years,
he recorded with acts as divergent as The Mamas and the Papas, The 5th
Dimension, Barbra Streisand, and Hank Williams Jr.[14] Guitarist James Burton
first performed in Ricky Nelson's band, then became Elvis Presley's guitarist for the last eight years of his career; meanwhile, he recorded in the studio
with Gram Parsons, Joni Mitchell, Emmylou Harris, and John Denver, with
whom he also played for seven years.[15] Kennedy, Osborn, Burton, and others

had grown up in Shreveport, played the *Hayride* stage, and made their earliest recordings in Mira Smith's studio.

Margaret Lewis and Mira Smith wound up in Nashville at the behest of Shelby Singleton, an old contact from Shreveport who had been A&R Director at Mercury Records and was starting his own publishing and record companies, SSS International and Plantation Records. Lewis and Smith joined his small cadre of songwriters, composing more than one hundred recorded songs, including "Country Girl" and "The Girl Most Likely," recorded by Jeannie C. Riley; "Mountain of Love," recorded by David Houston; "Wedding Cake," recorded by Connie Francis; and others.[16] Tunes like "Reconsider Me" and "Soul Shake" cut across soul and country sensibilities.

After seventeen years as a songwriter, Lewis left Nashville in 1981 and returned to Shreveport to marry. Alton Warwick had helped his cousin Mira build her homemade studio back in the mid-1950s, which was where he met Lewis; the two had always remained in contact. Warwick was an executive at the ARKLA Gas Company when he and Lewis decided to marry. Lewis originally planned to move to Shreveport and retire from the music profession, but the city where she began her career seemed to beckon a new vision. In part, this vision was borne of sorrow over the state of dilapidation that had befallen the historic Municipal Auditorium and the area around it, once known as "St. Paul's Bottoms"; the city council renamed the area "Ledbetter Heights" in 1982 in an effort to honor African American folksinger Huddie "Leadbelly" Ledbetter and inspire community revitalization.[17]

In the mid-1980s, Lewis became the North Louisiana representative on the board of the newly formed Louisiana Music Commission, whose state-wide mission was to promote music industry development.[18] From Lewis's perspective, restoration of the Municipal Auditorium was a vital first step: "It was so sad when I came back to Shreveport after all those years and saw the decline in the music industry here and the blighted state of the building where the *Hayride* began, the Municipal Auditorium. The roof was leaking and it was about to fall in and the city [which owns the building] was seriously talking about tearing it down.... When you begin at a place like that, it personally means something to you." The Warwicks had each maintained contacts from their previous occupations that proved helpful, Alton through his political relations work at ARKLA and Margaret through the music industry. At a luncheon with state representatives organized by her husband, Lewis presented her vision of a renovated Municipal as the locus of a Shreveport Historic Music District. They met with city officials, inviting notable figures in the entertainment industry like Joel Katz, the Atlanta-based lawyer and former chairman (currently general counsel) of The Recording Academy (NARAS), to speak about the feasibility of the project. Meanwhile, thanks to the completion of a decades-long lock and dam project by the Army Corps of Engineers, the riverboat gambling industry found a profitable home on Shreveport's Red River, making tourism a feasible industry in the area for the first time. For most of the twentieth century, oil and gas dominated the region's economy. City and state leaders were receptive to the merits of Lewis's vision of a Historic Music District with the Municipal at its center, but neither group was forthcoming with financial support.

Katz, whom Margaret had known from her days as a songwriter, suggested an alternative to the Warwicks. In 1997 they formed a nonprofit organization, FAME, whose goal was to raise funds independently, and then pursue the restoration of the historic district in partnership with the city council. They enlisted the support of local businesspeople, including volunteer assistance from a local architect to draw up preliminary blueprints. They began producing shows to raise funds for the project. "Our first show...was a fundraiser celebrating Governor Jimmie Davis's ninety-eighth birthday.... When we went to visit Governor Davis in Baton Rouge at his home, I wanted to do something real special for him. So I said, 'Governor, who is your favorite singer? Who would you like more than anybody to be on this show with you?' And he said, 'Well I doubt if he would come but I really like Merle Haggard.'" Through Shelby Singleton, Lewis arranged for the appearance of Haggard, who agreed to honor his longtime fan and raise funds for FAME; in exchange, Lewis arranged a paying gig for Merle Haggard at the local Horseshoe Casino.

Since this initial effort, FAME has produced other shows, including *Hayride* reunions and another birthday party for Davis before his death in 2000. With financial momentum behind them, FAME began acquiring state funds for the Municipal renovation. The organization no longer relies on volunteers; they have hired city planning consultant Hunter Morrison, who for over twenty years steered the revitalization efforts in Cleveland, Ohio, to fully flesh out the formal plan for Shreveport. FAME expanded its search for financial support to the federal level, with Washington lobbying efforts that coincided nicely with an invitation from the Smithsonian Folklife Festival for Margaret Lewis Warwick to bring her Louisiana Hayride Band to perform in Washington, D.C. FAME also hosted a Southern American Music Conference in May 2002, which was intended to expand the effort. The next phase of restoration for the Municipal Auditorium includes the construction of a Southern Music Museum inside the building.

Signs of success are already in place. The street in front of the Municipal now bears the name Elvis Presley Boulevard, and FAME is purchasing bronze statues of Hank Williams and Johnny Cash by sculptor Bill Rains, which will be the first in a series of Southern musical figures to line the street on either side. Rains has been commissioned to create others, including George Jones and Kitty Wells. As momentum continues to build, the Warwicks hope eventually to transform the abandoned nearby car lot they bought in 1994 into a Hayride-themed cafe, with live music. Lewis is ready to abdicate her chair of FAME and direct her energies toward more entertainment-oriented development work; to that end, she is searching for a new full-time director of FAME. Her initial moxie redirected, Warwick reflected on what gave her the gumption to pursue her vision: "I guess my tenacity comes from my pioneer heritage because . . . anybody that'll settle West Texas is too stubborn to give up on anything. So I guess that comes from my heritage because to me this is such a natural. It's something that should have been done years and years ago. The value of what Shreveport has is the missing piece of the American music landscape. We're the only city that has this kind of music heritage that has not done something to honor it or re-establish it or in some way do something." The FAME project began with a vision of the Municipal, whose physical structure had fallen into ruin since Hank Williams first yodeled his way through "Lovesick Blues" in the late 1940s, or since a tentative Elvis Presley performed both sides of his new Sun Records release, or even since a hopeful high school-aged Margaret Lewis covered a song by her fellow West Texan rockabilly, Buddy Holly. The catalytic, experimental energy of the *Louisiana Hayride* was suffused in the music performed on its stage, but was also realized in the pursuits of a generation of musicians who cut their teeth there and left to pursue their musical dreams.

In a similar way, FAME's vision has expanded to include the full richness and breadth of Shreveport's music history. The Southern Music Museum plans to honor the exclusively Anglo *Hayride* players alongside the African American musical legends like Leadbelly, blues guitarist Jesse Thomas, and roots recording mavericks Oscar Woods and Ed Shaffer. The formal plans for the Historic Music Village include renovation of structures like the Star Theater, where Bessie Smith played regularly, and the Calanthean Temple, where swing blared from rooftop gardens. If there was promise and beauty in the energy of the rock-and-roll moment, it was the hint, the dream of community—of a space where blacks and whites come together to heal a troubled history and share the intersections of rich traditions of music and culture.

Margaret Lewis Warwick's vision of the Shreveport Historic Music District would be a memorial to the fertile stream of Southern music that flowed from the head of Texas Avenue down to the Red River; at the same time, if fully realized, it would be a space for new creative energies to build. In essence, Lewis has posed a query on behalf of the city of Shreveport: "Oh please, reconsider me . . . ?" She directs this question to the writers of the story of Southern American roots music who have left places like Shreveport largely on the periphery. Only time will provide an answer. Perhaps white and black civic leaders and citizens will begin to imagine new paradigms of community and new dreams of a shared future, as they revitalize the physical spaces where music first made those relationships seem possible. If reconsidering Shreveport's place in music history accomplishes this, then Lewis's question is well worth asking. [Editor's note: Since originally published, the bronze statues mentioned never materialized; however, statues of Presley and Burton stand outside the Municipal. A group called Friends of the Municipal manages the building, including a small museum and gift shop devoted to the Hayride.]

Notes

1. Both versions are available on commercial recordings. See, for example, Johnny Adams, *Reconsider Me: Golden Classics Edition,* Collectables, COL-5741, 1996; and Narvel Felts, *Drift Away: The Very Best of Narvel Felts, 1973–79,* Bear Family Records, BCD 15690, 1996. The original demo of the song, with Margaret Lewis singing lead vocals and Mira Smith on guitar, can be found on a re-release of Ram material. See *Shreveport Stomp,* vol. 1, *Ram Records "Master of the Trail" Series,* Ace, CDCHD 495, 1994. "From the Cradle to the Blues" is included on the follow-up to *Shreveport Stomp:* Margaret Lewis with Grace Tennessee and her Guitar, *Lonesome Bluebird,* vol. 2, *Ram Records "Master of the Trail" Series,* Ace, CDCHD 572, 1994. ("Grace Tennessee" is a pseudonym for Mira Smith.)

2. Margaret Lewis Warwick, telephone interview with the author, 19 September 2002. Tape recording and transcript in author's files. Quotations and biographical information about Lewis are from this interview.

3. KFYO was a 5,000-watt station that broadcast local programming as well as network programming. Under the leadership of "Pappy" Dave Stone, KDAV was an early prototype of format radio, programming exclusively country music from its first broadcast in 1953. Bud Andrews, General Manager of KDAV, telephone conversation, 2 October 2002.

4. Steven R. Tucker, "Louisiana Saturday Night: A History of Louisiana Country Music" (Ph. D. dissertation, Tulane University, 1995), 479. The *Louisiana Hayride* is placed in a social and cultural context that extends back to Shreveport's founding in 1836 as a port and point of division along the Red River in the author's dissertation, "Shreveport's KWKH: A City and Its Radio Station in the Evolution of. Country Music and Rock-and-Roll" (Ph.D. dissertation, University of Michigan, 2000).

5. Tucker, 426, comments on the wide variety of musical styles that appeared on the *Lousisana Hayride:* "*Hayride* crowds came to expect a rich mixture of gospel music, sentimental or 'heart' songs, pop tunes, contemporary country hits, honky-tonk weepers, bluegrass tunes, comedy and novelty numbers, and folk music, a mixture that reflected the image and reality of Louisiana as a musical melting pot."

6. See W.T. Lhamon Jr., *Deliberate Speed: The Origins of a Cultural Style in the American 1950s* (Washington, D.C.: Smithsonian Institution Press, 1990), for an analysis of the "acceleration" of culture in the postwar era.

7. See Peter Guralnick, *Last Train to Memphis: The Rise of Elvis Presley* (Boston and New York: Little, Brown, and Company, 1994), 132. Elvis Presley, *Sunrise Elvis Presley,* CD 67675-2, RCA, 1999, contains five tracks of acetates recorded from *Louisiana Hayride* broadcasts; they are mainly of historic significance because the audio quality is so poor. Some of this material also appeared on a recent release, Elvis Presley, *Good Rockin' Tonight: The Complete Louisiana Hayride Archives,* CD MME-72628-2, Music Mill Entertainment, 2000.

8. See Charles Hamm, *Yesterdays: Popular Song in America* (New York: Norton, 1979), 407.

9. Ibid.

10. Frank Page, interview by the author, 23 February 1996, tape recording in author's files. Page was chief announcer for the *Hayride* throughout most of the 1950s until 1957 when he took over as producer. Page also reflects on the particular fervor of Texas audiences in his spoken narration on Elvis Presley, *Good Rockin' Tonight: The Complete Louisiana Hayride Archives.*

11. Ray Topping, liner notes to *Shreveport Stomp.* These artists can be found on other Ace re-releases produced since the mid-1990s, including Roy Perkins, *Roy "Boogie Boy" Perkins with Bobby Page and the Riff Raffs,* vol. 3; *Ram Records "Master of the Trail" Series,* Ace CDCHD 619, 1995; and *Shreveport High Steppers: Rockabilly and Hillbilly,* Ace CDCHD 818, 2001.

12. Tucker, 516.

13. Jerry Kennedy, interview with the author, 7 March 1996, Nashville, Tenn., tape recording in author's files. For a lively account of Kennedy's early career, including substantial quotations, see John Grissim, *Country Music: White Man's Blues* (New York: Paperback Library, 1970), 27–34.

14. Joe Osbom, interview with the author, 2 August 1999, Shreveport, Louis., tape recording in author's files; also from an advertisement produced by Lakland Basses in Chicago (for the Joe Osborn signature bass) and from the Joe Osborn website.

15. See Steve Fishell, "James Burton: First Call for the Royalty of Rockabilly," *Guitar Player*" 18 (June 1984): 88–101; and Rich Kienzle, "James Burton," in *Great Guitarists: The Most Influential Players in Blues, Country Music, Jazz and Rock* (New York: Facts on File, 1985): 192–97. Colin Escott writes about him in "James Burton: Play It James," in *Tattooed on Their Tongues* (New York: Schirmer, 1996), 163–75.

16. Topping, liner notes, *Lonesome Bluebird.* Ray Topping places Lewis and Smith in Las Vegas when the pair wrote "Mountain of Love" as well as "I Almost Called Your Name," recorded by Margaret Whiting; this would have occurred during a period between Shreveport and Nashville when Lewis sang in Las Vegas clubs and made a handful of recordings.

17. The area was also declared a National Historic District. On 22 October 1994, the Shreveport Regional Arts Council sponsored construction of a $25,000 bronze statue of Leadbelly pointing toward the district. Information about Shreveport's efforts to memorialize the singer can be found in numerous articles in the *Shreveport Times* and in *The Lead Belly Letter,* a quarterly publication devoted to the singer's life and music. See particularly Greg Gornamous and Chester Williams, "Lead Belly Memorialized," *Lead Belly Letter* 3:1/2 (winter/ spring 1992), 1, 5; and Sean Killeen, "Shreveport Lauds Lead Belly," *Lead Belly Letter* 4: 4 (fall 1994), 1.

18. The Louisiana Music Commission was founded and directed by musician/businessman Lynn Orso.

The Making of Dale Hawkins

—David Anderson and Lesley-Anne Reed

The iconic status afforded Dale Hawkins's mid-1950s recording of the rockabilly classic "Susie Q" led numerous writers to include only a vague sketch of his life leading up to the recording and to frame his career after as a variation on the motif of the one-hit-wonder. Anderson and Reed aim to correct Hawkins's dual fate of being glossed over and pigeonholed. Building on numerous interviews with Hawkins, the authors successfully flesh out the years leading up to the momentous recording. They argue against the urge to fit Hawkins into a stereotype of white male youth of his era, emphasizing his unique path to a musical career. The resulting biography is compelling in itself, just as it invites readers to reconsider at-times-romanticized notions of post–World War II southern youth and the birth of rockabilly.

Hawkins's early experiments in the studios of Shreveport's KWKH with Merle Kilgore and Johnny Horton developed both the interest and the skills that led him to later work in studio production. Between the mid-1960s and the early 1970s he produced top-forty hits for a variety of artists, including the Five Americans, Michael Nesmith, and Harry Nilsson. During the late 1960s, Hawkins briefly hosted *The Big Big Beat,* aka *The Dale Hawkins Show* on WCAU-TV, then Philadelphia's CBS-affiliate.

After a nearly twenty-year hiatus from music, Hawkins returned to performing in 1999 with the release of *Wildcat Tamer* on Mystic Records. This was Hawkins's first album of new material in thirty years. The same year he made his first appearance at the New Orleans Jazz and Heritage Festival, followed by a date at the Chicago Blues Festival, where he took part in a historic reunion of Chess recording artists. He also appeared in a film by Robert Mugge, *Rhythm 'n' Bayous: A Road Map to Louisiana Music,* and performed at its 2001 debut at film festivals in Mill Valley, California, Denver, and New Orleans.

I.

Beginning in early 1956, patrons of Stan's Record Shop, a tiny shotgun structure that sat at the head of Texas Street in downtown Shreveport, Louisiana, could make their purchases in quite the unconventional manner, thanks to Stan's singing counter clerk. The clerk, a then-eighteen-year-old Delmar Hawkins—skinny and loud, with a mop of dark hair that never seemed to lie flat—sold the latest releases from independent rhythm-and-blues labels like Chess, Atlantic, and Aladdin, not by their titles, but by a lyric or a guitar lick that a customer recalled. "I could sing it, bam, I knew right what it was," Hawkins—known to most of the shop's regulars as "Del"—remembers, "I knew the songs, I liked the songs."[1] And after his customers headed home with the latest Chicago blues recordings from Howlin' Wolf or Muddy Waters, or uptown R&B by the Clovers or Charles Brown, Del slipped into the building's back room and continued to practice singing the same records he sold. Mastering these R&B records note-for-note, he began to realize, held the key to a completely new life—and a completely different Del Hawkins.

Two blocks west of Stan's Record Shop, where a dull curve in the road turned Texas Street into Texas Avenue, Shreveport's Municipal Auditorium hosted the *Louisiana Hayride*—KWKH's radio barn dance—where the weekly playbill read like a veritable who's who of up-and-coming white country and rockabilly artists. By 1956, Hank Williams was gone, nothing but his ghost remained, and Elvis Presley's appearances were less frequent since he had signed with big-time label RCA in late 1955, but on the same stage one could still see up-and-coming singers like Johnny Horton and David Houston or stellar musicians like pianist Floyd Cramer.[2] But Del Hawkins, a musical dilettante with no performing experience to speak of, rather than immersing himself in the honky-tonk sounds coming from down the street at the *Hayride*, chose to sequester himself inside Lewis's cramped shop, occasionally jamming with an entourage of younger local musicians, some still in high school. Later, he ventured out to play music in the smoky nightclubs an rural high schools throughout north Louisiana, all in order to create the wailing, white rhythm-and-blues—or rock-and-roll—sound that he would become known for.

A little over a year later, in the summer of 1957, a newly-christened "Dale" Hawkins—arguably still a rock-and-roll novice—hit #29 on *Billboard*'s Top 100 chart and #7 on its R&B chart with "Susie-Q," a gritty number that the Rock and Roll Hall of Fame has since named one of its "500 most influential songs" of the rock era.[3] But in late 1955 and early 1956—right around the time he took the part-time job at Lewis's shop —Del Hawkins, a recent graduate of a local business school, was a full-time employee at a nearby creosote mill, and certainly not a "professional musician" by any definition of the term. His musical ascent defies the contemporary image of white rock-and-rollers, and particularly southern ones, as rebellious working-class "teenagers" who fell effortlessly into the music because they possessed some innate sense of country soul or rural rhythm from early childhood.[4] Hawkins's path into the music business—one full of contingencies, chances, and adult choices—was not uncommon among his rockabilly contemporaries, many of whom had reached their late teens or early twenties with little experience on stage or in the studio before they became professional musicians. Before Elvis Presley made his first recordings at Memphis's Sun Studio in July 1954, as his biographer Peter Guralnick has pointed out, nineteen-year-old Presley experienced life as that of an "average" young adult—not of a budding musician. Prior to the summer of 1954, Presley lived with his parents while he drove a supply truck for a local electrical company, dated a girl from a Memphis high school, and perhaps even questioned his dreams—and that's all they were at this point—of being a professional singer. Johnny Cash—twenty-three when he cut his first Sun single—worked at an automobile factory in Detroit for a brief spell and then enlisted in the Air Force, all before he even bought his first guitar. Cash was not the only early rock-and-roller to enter the music business when he was well into his twenties. Chuck Berry had almost reached his thirtieth birthday before he recorded "Maybellene" for Chess Records. And right around the same time Berry cut his first sides in Chicago in the spring of 1955, a twenty-seven-year-old Ellas McDaniel walked into the Chess offices with the lyrics to "I'm a Man" and the song that would become "Bo Diddley."[5]

In fact, for men like Presley, Cash, Berry, and McDaniel, and for Hawkins as well, the decision to make music on a professional basis represented more than a means to simple enjoyment, or even an outlet for artistic expression. For these early rock-and-rollers, becoming a professional musician constituted a conscious, and arguably "adult," decision on their part to live a better life and make a success of themselves. Therefore, the singular revelation that Hawkins never gave music much more than a passing thought until he was on the brink of adulthood does not necessarily make his entrance into the rock-and-roll milieu unique. What makes Hawkins's story intriguing and instructive is the speed and vigor by which he drew on rhythm-and-blues music and other cultural resources available to him in 1950s north Louisiana to forge a new personal identity—one that bore little resemblance to, and drew little inspiration from, his former existence.[6]

II.

Delmar Allen Hawkins was born on August 22, 1936, in Goldmine, Louisiana, a former plantation community, eighty miles southeast of Monroe, twenty miles north from Jerry Lee Lewis's hometown of Ferriday, and near the exact spot on the map where the Franklin and Richland Parish lines meet. As a child, Delmar Hawkins was undoubtedly exposed to a variety of music—hillbilly tunes twanging on the jukeboxes at local honky-tonks, blues moaning in from the Mississippi Delta, and Baptist gospel hymns wafting out through open church windows. But Hawkins himself has never explicitly indicated that any of the music he heard as a child shaped his aspirations for the future.[7] Although images of a small Del joining in on field hollers while he picked cotton with his sharecropper neighbors, both black and white, do contribute a romantic aura to the southern rock-and-roll myth, again, there is no evidence that he put any of these rural experiences to creative use when he began pursuing music in the mid-1950s. Hawkins does admit that he came from a musical, and for that matter, rural family. His father, also named Delmar, arrived in Louisiana via a long line of Hawkinses in northwest Arkansas, and a large part of his extended family still lived in St. Paul, a country crossroads nestled deep within the Ozark Mountains near a series of rushing brooks and rolling green valleys known to local residents as Hawkins Hollow. "All [the family] were musicians," Hawkins explains, "it was in the genes."[8] Several of Hawkins's cousins were in a local string band, and his cousin was none other than Ronnie Hawkins—the rockabilly singer best known for bringing together the Hawks, which included the musicians who would later accompany Bob Dylan as the Band. Despite his impressive musical pedigree, young Del never spent much time with his father's family in Arkansas as a child—only a three-week visit one summer, as he remembers it now.[9] Any insinuation regarding a natural, genetic inclination towards music on Hawkins's part appears like tacked-on afterthoughts to a career spent purposefully debunking precisely that idea.

As a young child, Del started picking cotton and shining shoes as early as he could to contribute to his family's income; if anything, he would have associated music with the broken pieces of his home life and the acute poverty to which his family had succumbed because of it. Del and his brother Jerry, who was seven-teen months younger and would go on to pursue his own brief music career in the 1950s, certainly never witnessed any strong evidence as children that music could provide an adequate livelihood. Their alcoholic father, a stand-up bassist who played in local honky-tonk bands in Arkansas and Louisiana, never made a tolerable living with his music and had located his young family to Goldmine so that he could try his hand at farming. But the elder Hawkins disappeared so early on that neither son can recall more than a faint memory of him from their childhood. Nevertheless, various accounts of Hawkins's early years have cited his father's music as a source for later inspiration, despite Hawkins's claims to the contrary. "My daddy," he insists, "I never saw my daddy [that] I can remember until 'Susie-Q' was a hit [in 1957]."[10] And in 1938, following their parents' divorce, Del and an infant Jerry were moved ten miles north to Mangham to live with their grandparents and various relatives so that their mother could travel unhin-dered to a job at a defense plant in Minden starting around 1942, shortly after the United States' entry into World War II.[11]

In Mangham, music surrounded Hawkins in a ubiquitous drone—in clubs and restaurants, at the local churches, even at neighbors' houses—but he never felt motivated to engage in any of it himself. He does remember music seeping out of the doors of local honky-tonks. "My grandfather was a marshal in the parish," Hawkins explains, "so I got to go with him on Saturday nights [to clubs and shows] and got to hear music on 'both sides of the door.'"[12] In mid-1940s rural north Louisiana, however, live music would have been a regu-lar, possibly even a daily, offering, and Hawkins probably tagged along with his grandfather, more often than not, out of boredom or necessity than pure excitement. Moreover, young Del would not have had to stand outside any door to listen to music—not even black gospel or rhythm-and-blues. By the mid-1940s, radio stations all across the South—especially the powerful 50,000-watt clear channel stations such as Nashville's WLAC, New Orleans's WNOE, and Shreveport's KWKH—had started to play with some regularity the "race" music put out by the growing number of independent record labels intent on exploiting the expanding market for rhythm-and-blues.[13] All Hawkins would have had to do to gain access to gospel or R&B music, therefore, was to stay home and turn on the family's radio. Around this time, though, he and Jerry instead began hitchhiking all over north Louisiana, "because it was the only way to get around," to the popular Flatt and Scruggs bluegrass shows in Monroe and Rayville—anxious, it appears, to leave tiny Mangham behind. The Hawkins boys eventually reunited with their mother in the mid-1940s after she married Luther Diffey, a wounded veteran with two Purple Heart medals to his credit. Diffey drove a dump truck by trade but does not appear to have contributed substantially to the family's income after he returned home from the war. So Estelle worked shifts for a brief spell at "Miss Gertrude's," a tiny cafe in Mangham where Hawkins claims to have huddled around the jukebox for hours at a time in an idle haze—further evidence that he enjoyed listening to music but never quite imagined making a living of it.

Life in Mangham proved far from ideal, even with Estelle's relatives close by, so in 1950 she moved her family to Bossier City, situated directly east across the Red River from Shreveport, and resumed her job at the munitions plant in Minden, which would now be only a thirty-mile bus commute each day. The entire family—Estelle, Luther, brother Jerry, and new half-sister Linda— lived in the Bossier Housing Projects, a place so dismal, in Del's opinion, that it could not have signified the family's frail economic status any more poignantly.[14] Quarters were cramped and noisy—suffocating even—and money remained tight, with Estelle's job appearing to have been the family's primary source of income. Soon, fourteen-year-old Del Hawkins began to look away from home for both personal fulfillment and financial independence, but it was not to music that he would turn just yet.

Although Shreveport beckoned just across the Red River, Hawkins acted more interested in finding a way out of town than picking up a cheap guitar and making his way onto the *Hayride* stage. Del gave his studies at Bossier High School a half-hearted chance, no doubt because one reason his mother chose to settle in Bossier City was so that her children could attend better schools than they could in Mangham or Minden. But he soon began skipping his classes and spent most of his time earning a few bucks delivering newspapers and bagging groceries at the local Pack 'N' Sack store, all the while planning his getaway. "I didn't like school, man," he later confessed, "so after I had got two pay checks" from the Pack 'N' Sack, amounting to "ten, twenty dollars" at most, "I ran away from home."[15]

Thus began an obscure chapter in Hawkins's life characterized by episodes of aimless wandering—a period notably absent in the stories written about him.[16] The first time out, he hitchhiked to Houston and worked "odd jobs, [and] whatever it took" to eat, before he ran out of money and headed back home. On another occasion, he lit out for Dallas, a new Social Security card in hand, and lined up an "actual job" at a department store before the local police picked him up "underage, on the streets, hungry" and packed him back home before he ever worked a day.[17] Despite this brief run-in with the law, young Del was certainly no rebel or budding juvenile delinquent, but he did strain against the barriers of class, reaching out to make his own way in life. More than anything, Hawkins claims, by leaving home he wanted to relieve some of his mother's financial burden. But in his fitful way, he also sensed that there was more to life than staring at the grim, gray walls of the housing projects and passing time mopping floors on the graveyard shift at a grocery store. As with many working-class men of his age in the postwar South, one sure way out of town—and out of the projects—was through military service. At fifteen, Del was a year too young to enlist, but he solved that problem by carefully changing the date on his birth certificate, from 1936 to 1935, with the help of an etching tool and a duplicating machine he had learned to use while working briefly at a local map company. The Del Hawkins who joined the U.S. Navy in February 1953, one could surmise, lacked any sort of real focus, as did the Del Hawkins who returned to north Louisiana a little over a year later, but what he did know was that he wanted a better life than the one he had.

III.

At some point between the fall of 1955 and early 1956, Hawkins underwent a personal transformation that would eventually lead him to pursue a music career. But the transformation actually started in June 1954 when Hawkins returned home from his stint in the Navy. As with the rest of his life up to this point, his career as a Navy seaman ended in disappointment when he was honorably discharged after severely injuring his back in an ammunitions misfire aboard the USS *Maddox* while his unit had been stationed at a port near San Francisco. Even after the Navy transported him back to Bossier City, Hawkins remained incapacitated for most of the summer, propped up in a hospital bed with not much to think about except what sort of future could lay ahead of him. From the window of his hospital room he had a clear view of the Bossier Housing Projects where he had lived with his family just the year before, and where he would return at the end of the summer once his back healed. Desperate for some direction, Hawkins says, he looked to the heavens and pleaded for an answer. "I got on my knees for three, four months" in prayer, he remembers, "begging God for a way out of the projects."[18] Thoughts of music entered his mind at that time, he says, sharp and panging—thoughts that he couldn't suppress, yet remained beyond the realm of his imagination to make happen: "I knew that I could hear things, and I could put things together," Hawkins recalls. "[I] wanted to do it [music]," but, even at this point, "I never saw myself doing it."[19]

Hawkins instead felt pressure from his mother Estelle to complete his education and take a more conventional path to a comfortable middle-class life. So when the military offered to pay his tuition for the Norton Business School, he enrolled in its seven-month program, in part to compensate for the high school diploma he lacked, but mostly because "it was an attempt to do something my mother wanted me to do."[20] "You know," he later reflected on this period, "I was trying to plant a solid foundation in town so I could have an income." Subsequent jobs as a clerk for a creosote mill and later for a local railroad station offered him little personal satisfaction.[21] No doubt, during these half-hearted attempts at what musicians term the "straight life," Hawkins reached out in vain for what other upwardly-mobile young white men of his generation, even those who had come from rural poverty, now perceived as the basic components of the postwar middle-class ideal—an education, a steady and respectable job, and eventually, a nice suburban home. But he would never be content to go about any of it in the conventional manner.

Soon, a curious Delmar Hawkins began to fumble around for a place in the local music scene, something he had not known much about, or cared much about for that matter, while he lived in Bossier City as a young teen—when getting out of town had been foremost on his mind. Of course, the *Louisiana Hayride*, broadcast every Saturday night from the Municipal Auditorium in downtown Shreveport, provided the prime performing opportunity for aspiring musicians in the Ark-La-Tex region. Since its inception in 1948, the *Hayride* hosted a variety of hopeful singers and musicians who used the stage as a springboard to greater fame on Nashville's *Grand Ole Opry*, earning the *Hayride* its "Cradle of the Stars" nickname.[22] By the mid-1950s the *Hayride* also gave a boost to a group of younger singers and musicians, mostly of high school age, who got their professional start as either members of the house band or as back-up singers for headline performers. But Hawkins had never really latched on to country-and-western music.[23] The closest he came to the *Hayride*, Hawkins claims, was through a car-parking scheme that he and his brother Jerry concocted at the Municipal, which actually had a parking lot that was free and open to the public.[24]

What most intrigued Hawkins was dance music pulsing out of the string of nightclubs that straddled Highway 80, known as the "Bossier Strip," where the neon lights, sizeable crowds, and various vices—prostitution, gambling, and burlesque shows, among them—made it, in his words, "one of top ten 'sin cities' in America." The Bossier Strip's various nightclubs, with names like the "Blues Red Devil," "The Boom Boom Room," and the "It'll Do Club," crackled with electric, youthful energy that invited all who dared venture inside to dance and booze the night away. Servicemen from nearby Barksdale Air Force Base greatly boosted the size of the crowds on the Strip, where "unescorted ladies"—many of the clubs' newspaper ads made clear—were "always welcome."[25] In fact, face-to-face with couples who wanted to dance, the musicians who played the Bossier Strip tended to be more solidly rooted in a rhythm-and-blues beat and favored a looser style that swung harder than the honky-tonk boogie played by the country musicians in the *Hayride*'s house band.

Taking his first, halting steps into the music scene on the Bossier Strip, at this point still mostly an observer, Hawkins found a mentor in guitarist John "Sonny" Jones, whose burly brother Al also played guitar and sang, and whose sister Billie Jean, Hank Williams's young widow, was by then married to *Hayride* regular Johnny Horton.[26] "Sonny could play the guitar," Hawkins recalls, "and I used to go out to the clubs and I'd see him." Not only was Jones himself playing in clubs, he also proved adept at organizing young musicians into bands. "Man," Hawkins remembers, "he was finding them and putting them together."[27] Through his friendship with Sonny Jones, Hawkins spotted an opportunity to break into the local music scene. But surrounded by singers and guitarists who had been playing gigs for at least several years, Del Hawkins, already nineteen-years-old and with no real musical experience to speak of, was in over his head.

IV.

Del Hawkins made some big decisions in the early part of 1956, the first of which was to seek out part-time employment at Stan Lewis's record store, which had already garnered a reputation in north Louisiana as the best place to find the latest rhythm-and-blues records. Lewis, a second-generation Italian-American born in Shreveport in 1927, had his first exposure to rhythm-and-blues when he operated a series of jukeboxes in the 1940s, before he opened Stan's Record Shop on Texas Street in 1948. Although the store "carried . . . a little country and gospel," Lewis recalled, it specialized in selling rhythm-and-blues records to a mostly black clientele. By the early 1950s, Lewis not only had expanded his operation to include a thriving mail-order business, he also became the main wholesale distributor (or "one-stop") for

R&B records throughout the Ark-La-Tex region, a position that helped him cement close personal relationships with Leonard Chess and other independent record label owners.[28]

Delmar Hawkins may have first found out about Stan's Record Shop and its music by listening to *Stan's Record Review*, the nightly show Lewis sponsored on KWKH. Like radio stations all across the South, and across the country for that matter, KWKH had hosted nightly music programs since the late 1940s that showcased emerging rhythm-and-blues artists. On Stan's show, local DJ and regular *Hayride* announcer Frank Page—using his on-air blues nickname "Gatemouth"—played a wide selection of rhythm-and-blues releases from independent record labels like Chess, Modern, Specialty, Imperial, and Aladdin—all of which Lewis sold downtown at his shop.[29]

Hawkins was well aware of Stan's Record Shop, but before he could muster up the nerve to ask Lewis for a job, Hawkins "just went in and hung around" the shop. As he recalled, "I just liked to go in and listen to the music."[30] Hawkins's growing fascination with rhythm-and-blues music was shared by other young, white record buyers. By the mid-1950s, white "covers" of black rhythm-and-blues songs were hitting the *Billboard* Top 100 with regularity, but as an increasing number of white teenagers discovered the original records over the airwaves, black R&B vocal groups began "crossing over" and staking their own claim to the popular music charts.[31] Stan's Record Shop carried the cover versions, but also stocked a full selection of straight-up rhythm-and-blues originals, which Hawkins studied with feverish intensity as if prepping for the college exam he never took. "That's why I landed the job at Stan's," Hawkins recalls, "because I knew every one of them."[32] Then he worked in his little performance each time a customer had trouble remembering the title of the song they wanted. And perhaps it was in those moments, singing out on command from behind the counter at Stan's shop, that Hawkins really heard his own voice for the first time—heard that it was capable of evoking both a brazen energy and newfound sense of confidence. At the same time, he studied the reactions his singing elicited in the clientele—both black and white—and began to wonder what it just might feel like to perform some of those same songs onstage. He already had owned a cheap "off-the-wall Stella guitar"—he just needed a band, and a place to play.[33]

After all, north Louisiana was more than just a training ground for *Opry* hopefuls or budding blues cats on the Bossier Strip. The entire Ark-La-Tex region was scattered with venues, large and small, where aspiring musicians could test out both their material and their ability to cut it onstage—which is what Hawkins set out to do in late 1955 and early 1956. Perhaps because he did not feel experienced enough yet to perform in Shreveport or even at the clubs on the Bossier Strip, or perhaps none of them would have him anyway, Hawkins headed thirty miles north through the piney woods to the Horseshoe, a tin-roofed roller rink located in a small rural town near the Arkansas border with the unlikely name of Plain Dealing. Accompanied by Sonny Jones, his mentor from the Bossier Strip, and James Kirkland, a twenty-two-year-old stand-up bassist from Cass County, Texas, Del started out playing rudimentary versions of Chuck Berry's "Maybellene" and a handful of the latest rock-and-roll hits for patrons at the rink—where, on Saturday nights, instead of skates, the teenagers preferred to hop around in their dancing shoes. Hawkins, Jones, and Kirkland formed what was essentially a crude, stripped-down rockabilly trio, right down to their black pants, their blue suede shoes, and the turned-up collars and rolled-up sleeves of their white shirts. "You know [we] went in, we had one amp, had two microphones," Hawkins remembers, and the whole band just "ran those through" and gave it everything they had.[34]

While Hawkins has never pinpointed the exact moment when he decided to pursue a rock-and-roll career, it is easy to imagine that the newfound sense of authority he realized during these first rough performances in Plain Dealing tempted him to do so. The audience responded to him in the most thrilling way that they possibly could—by dancing—and, the teenage girls, Hawkins boasts, "they all crowded around me."[35] Onstage, Del Hawkins was in control—of his voice, of his movements, and, by extension, of his effect on other people—and that sense of control was something he had never quite felt in any of the nearly twenty years of his life. Moreover, no matter when he made the decision to become a professional musician, whether it was during those heady moments onstage at the roller rink or in the back of Lewis's shop one random evening, Hawkins was already living in a rich musical environment—full of ambitious musicians even younger than himself—that would allow him to do so.

I.

Although Hawkins began his own musical education by observing more-seasoned performers like Sonny Jones onstage at the clubs on the Bossier Strip and by playing live with his rockabilly trio at the roller rink in Plain Dealing, his experience working at Stan's selling records made him acutely aware that success in the music industry, and especially the R&B market, would require him to cut a record that could stand out among the ones he sold. So, despite his status as a neophyte, he set out to assemble a group of local musicians who could deliver something resembling an authentic hit sound. First and foremost, Hawkins wanted a guitarist with not only a sharp level of skill but one capable of steeping himself in the blues sound that Hawkins imagined his band would play. Around early 1956 Hawkins found this combination of professionalism and versatility in guitarist James Burton, just sixteen-years-old and still a junior at Shreveport's Fair Park High School.

In the mid-1950s, Burton was part of a perceptible generational shift that took place among the musicians on the north Louisiana music scene. Most of the headliners on the *Hayride*—Presley, Cash, or Horton, for example—were Hawkins's age or older, some even in their thirties, and most of them—again, like Hawkins—had entered the professional music scene as near-adults.[36] Born in the early-to-mid-1930s, this generation of musicians grew up in rural poverty and then migrated to nearby towns and cities during the Great Depression. They were likely to have spent their teenage years in a working-class job or a stint with the military before turning to a career in music. But the musical cohort right at their heels, born in the late 1930s and early 1940s, grew up in relative prosperity, generally lived in stable homes, and were unburdened enough at a young age to take up music as a serious vocation. This more youthful group, which would include guitarists Burton, Jerry Kennedy, Billy Sanford, and singers Margaret Lewis and Linda Brannon, just to name a few, backed headliners at the *Hayride* and played in nearby venues during the mid-1950s—all while still in high school.

But it was not on the *Hayride* stage or local clubs that Burton and the rest of this younger cohort first honed their musical skills. The *Hayride* was a big-time venue, and Burton and those like him—teenagers who had spent the previous couple of years wood-shedding with their guitars in their bedrooms—needed a middle-ground where they could practice with other musicians, even hear themselves on tape, and find out if they had what it took to pursue a music career on a serious, full-time basis.[37] They found such a place in Mira Smith's Ram Recording Studio, located west of the Municipal Auditorium on Lakeshore Drive. Smith built her studio in 1955 because of what she saw as the lack of adequate recording facilities in Shreveport. In addition, Smith operated her own Ram label, which released country, rockabilly, and even blues records from a variety of local—and mostly quite young—singers and musicians. A remarkable woman, Smith, already thirty-years-old when she founded Ram studio, allowed young musicians to practice at her studio, record rehearsal dubs, and perform on recording sessions. It was through Mira Smith that young fifteen-year-old guitar whiz James Burton made his first professional recordings.[38]

Born August 21, 1939, in Dubberly, Louisiana, a small hamlet about thirty minutes east of Shreveport, "so far out in the country we had to drive toward town to go hunting," as he likes to say, Burton grew up in a much more nurturing family environment than Hawkins had ever known. Burton's father held a stable, working-class job and enjoyed playing a little fiddle and guitar, and although he would unwaveringly support James's guitar-playing, he appears never to have pushed his son into a music career. A quiet, observant child, James thus had ample time to soak up the music around him—Top 40 pop songs on the radio, records from guitarists like Chet Atkins, Les Paul, and Merle Travis, and the occasional show in Minden with his father—like the one in which he saw Hank Williams, "sort of like a dream come true," as he remembers it. James's first real exposure to guitar-playing came from Bobby Ray Morehead, a close friend in Minden, where the Burton family made one quick move before settling in Shreveport in 1949. "After school I would go down and hang out with Bobby and he would play guitar," Burton recalls, and "I would try to play his guitar but I couldn't because it was left-handed!" Soon afterward, Burton's parents gave him an inexpensive "Gene Autry-model" guitar as a Christmas gift. He was fascinated with the new instrument and even its cheap "little cowboy" design. "I just played ... that little guitar," Burton later explained, "until I wore the strings [off] of it."[39]

A few years later, right around the time that Del Hawkins began running away from home, James Burton himself took a fateful stroll through downtown Shreveport's business district. "I was walking by the J&S music store," Burton remembers, "and I saw that blonde Fender Telecaster hanging in there." "I just stopped man," he recalls, "and drooled over it." Burton eventually convinced his supportive parents to buy him the expensive guitar and he committed himself to mastering the instrument. At that point, Burton insists, "I wanted to play every chance I got," and spent hours with his ear pressed against speaker of the record player in his bedroom, practicing day and night until he was ready to perform in public. On Labor Day 1954, Burton's father drove him out to the Skyway Club, where local musician Tommy Castle hosted a talent show, and it was there that Burton had his coming out of sorts. "I played behind my back, between my legs and everything, the whole showman thing," Burton recalls, and "won first place" with his own composition called

"Chinese Boogie."[40] By the middle of the next year, Burton was accompanying singers on Mira Smith's Ram records. He became what he termed Smith's
"guest star"—her go-to guitarist who backed everyone from local high-school
rockabillies James Wilson and the Jimmie Cats to fiddle player Larry Bamberg,
teen country-torch singer Linda Brannon, and *Hayride* pianist Leon Post.[41] By
now, Burton admits, he viewed the guitar as a driving force in his life (the only
one, it seems, except for a love of flashy cars) and passed up on the usual teenage pursuits—sports, dating, or even close friendships with non-musicians—
so that he could play wherever and whenever the opportunity arose.

As word of his guitar skills spread around town, Burton began backing
singers on the *Hayride* in late 1955 or early 1956, right about the time he first
met Del Hawkins, who sensed that the young guitarist was a meticulous student who would take easily to mastering an R&B guitar style.[42] To round out
his new line-up, Hawkins drew on a stock of young drummers—all of them
Italian-American. Hawkins had played with Stan Lewis's cousin, D. J. Fontana,
on the Bossier Strip until late 1955, when Fontana accepted a permanent
spot in Elvis Presley's band. After Fontana left town, Hawkins used Anthony
"A. J." Tuminello, Nick Roppolo, and Ronnie Lewis—all three of whom were
Burton's classmates at Fair Park High School—in his live performances and
recording sessions. Hawkins similarly used a shifting roster of bass players,
including Tommy Mandina, Sonny Trammell, and Carroll "Coach" Floyd,
who taught at a local high school. Hawkins would also occasionally pick
up a saxophonist or piano player if one was available and use them on live
dates and on recording dates. But the core of his live sound was always a
basic trio—drum, bass, and guitar—that played black rhythm-and-blues
that he had learned to love from the radio and the records he heard at
Stan's shop.

VI.

Del Hawkins's love of rhythm-and-blues was not unusual among his peers,
but his ability to emulate it made him an anomaly, a fact affirmed by noted
country-and-western songwriter Merle Kilgore, who at that time was working as a disc jockey on Shreveport's KENT radio station. "Rhythm and blues
music was really big down there," Kilgore noted in reference to Hawkins's
appeal, "but nobody had seen a white boy doing it."[43] Hawkins even ventured
the occasional foray into the area's bustling black music scene. Shreveport's

R&B clubs and venues, most of them nestled downtown beneath the Highway 80 Bridge, vibrated with as much rich musical energy as the region's white venues in the 1950s, but, of course, they operated on a strictly-Jim Crow basis. Hawkins remembers sneaking into black-only Club 66 to see B. B. King play several times, which would most likely have been perceived as a bit odd, but Hawkins, unfazed, would go on to use local black vocal groups in his recordings—the only bandleader in the area who did.[44]

Del Hawkins, caught up in a musical whirlwind of his own frenetic design, enjoyed making music too much to care whether or not he was pegged locally as an oddity and outsider. A rare write-up of Hawkins in the Shreveport *Times*, which appeared in September 1956 to plug a Labor Day show he participated in at the Municipal Auditorium, billed him as the "poor man's Elvis Presley."[45] Indeed, Hawkins—less attractive than the erotic Presley, more plainly dressed, and even more awkward in his manner and speech—evoked a much more coarser image than Presley ever did. From this perspective, Hawkins came off as an earnest but second-rate imitator who provided local audiences with an entertaining—yet nonetheless inferior—version of Presley. But Hawkins never aspired to follow in Presley's footsteps. More than anything, he aspired to make a record, one that expressed the spirit of the songs, sounds, and singers locked deep in the grooves of the rhythm-and-blues records he sold off Stan Lewis's shelf. All he needed to do was to come up with the right song. At some point in 1956, he set out to craft the song that would make him somebody, the song that would justify his fitful decision to throw himself into music with such single-minded dedication.

That magical song, Hawkins figured, would synthesize the myriad rhythm-and-blues tunes that had inspired him since the day when he first picked them up over the airwaves, since he first ventured into the dance clubs on the Bossier Strip to hear white musicians actually playing these songs, since he first wandered into Stan's shop to hear them blaring from the speaker system that Stan had rigged up, and since he first began to find his voice singing those songs to customers from behind the counter, some of whom were singers themselves. Hawkins remembers joining in with a "black group that used to hang out at Stan's Record Shop." "When I got off [work]," he recalled, "we'd get out behind the place and sing some of the classy stuff that was out at the time," tunes by uptown R&B chart-toppers Clyde McPhatter and the Drifters and the Clovers, a Washington, D.C. vocal group that recorded for Atlantic Records, the leading independent label in the rhythm-and-blues market.[46] In 1954, the Clovers had scored a #7 R&B hit with "I've Got My Eyes on You."

The Clovers' hit would serve as a blueprint for the song that Hawkins was sure would win him a record deal.[47]

Before he began tinkering with the lyric to "I've Got My Eyes on You," Hawkins remembers that he developed his new song's rhythmic approach. The "beat was there first," he would insist years later, the song "started with that beat." To find this beat, he leaned heavily on his affinity for Chicago urban blues, evoking the drum patterns that kicked off the Chess singles of the first half of the mid-1950s when house drummers Fred Below, Elgin Evans, and Earl Phillips were laying down their strident, syncopated grooves. For this song, he melded their drum sound with the bumpy cadence of the guitar lick in "Baby, Please Don't Go," released by Chess blues singer Muddy Waters in 1953 (as "Turn the Lamp Down Low").[48] Hawkins later explained how he merged brash Chess-style rhythms with the Clovers' slick vocal hit. "[T]he feel of the song was the same as (sings) 'I've got my eyes on you, I've got my eyes on you' and 'Baby, please don't go, down to New Orleans.'" "You know," he adds, the rhythm "was the feel of a guitar—donk, donk, donk-donk."[49]

Hawkins then set out to reinterpret the lyrics of "I've Got My Eyes on You," a process he completed onstage in numerous gigs with whatever local musicians he could pick up at local clubs. When he was finished, Hawkins's revamped lyrics revealed a remarkable contrast between black and white perspectives in the postwar South. In the original "I've Got My Eyes on You," the African American narrator boasts, with some irony, that he is a successful consumer, capable of not only accumulating capital ("some money") but spending it on a good home (on the "avenue"), and expensive merchandise ("a brand new car"). These purchases bring him immense satisfaction; in fact, he's got "everything" except the new object of his desire—a woman. The narrator has a careful "eye on" this new commodity, sizing up her positive attributes the way, one would assume, he would buy a new television set: he notes approvingly the way she can "make a hound dog talk," and the way she dances the "Eagle Rock," a variation on the jitterbug. So intense is his quest for the perfect purchase that he tells her he is watching her "everywhere you go and everything you do." This type of creepy obsession would make the narrator a stalker today, but back then, the song's rollicking backbeat, tinkling piano and swinging stand-up bass, doo-wop chorus, and honking sax solo made it a celebration of the narrator's determination to complete his vision of postwar consumer success by landing the girl of his "dreams."

Hawkins's version of the song would retain some important components of the Clovers' original hit. He would also sing about his desire for a woman and would similarly profess his approval for the way she could "walk" and "talk." Likewise, he would evoke another jitterbug dance step—the "Susie-Q"—to give the object of his desire a name.[50] There, however, the similarities between the two songs' lyrical content end.[51] In Hawkins's case, the narrator is not a successful or discerning postwar consumer reveling in the wonders of the modern marketplace. He is instead a poor man who would be left without anything if not for his darling "Susie-Q," whose fidelity he questions constantly. She is all he has, and without her, he is "nothing but blue." By inverting the Clovers' postwar optimism, Hawkins hit upon the paradox of race and class at the center of the rock-and-roll moment. While the Clovers' uptown R&B vibrantly celebrated black advancement, Hawkins conjured up the sobering reality that for the poor white working-class, the fidelity of a good companion was the only true defense against poverty, which he had known so acutely growing up in rural north Louisiana and living in the Bossier Housing Projects. Yet, despite the song's starkness, Hawkins would not deliver his message in a depressing fashion—and that may be the secret to what made postwar urban blues so compelling to him: even the most dire of sentiments could be packaged in strutting, swaggering arrangement that overwhelmed the song's pessimism. It was as if Del Hawkins put his whole life into this song.

Del Hawkins began assembling his band and putting together a working version of "Susie-Q," less in formal rehearsal sessions and more often in live settings. "We didn't do a lot of practicing," Hawkins recalls, "we just did it."[52] Hawkins's goal was to get a record deal, and he knew enough about the business from working at the record shop that "a lotta deals got made through Stan [Lewis]."[53] For Lewis to set up a record deal, Hawkins would need to produce a rough version or demonstration ("demo") of the song on tape and press it into a cheap acetate record that Lewis could pass on to an independent record label owner. Most likely, Hawkins hoped, Lewis would pitch the demo to his personal friend, Leonard Chess, the head of Chess Records. Lewis had often scouted local talent for Chess and the two had even teamed up to release a brief series of country-and-western records on Chess Records in 1954. While Leonard Chess was willing to experiment by expanding into the country-and-western market, Hawkins, a white singer steeped in urban blues and uptown R&B, was an oddity even for Chess Records. That changed in late 1955 when the label released Bobby Charles's "Later Alligator," an event that would sidetrack for several months Del's determination to turn "Susie-Q" into a hit record.[54]

VII.

In early 1956, Del Hawkins had a budding white rhythm-and-blues sound, he had a band, and his ideal next step would have been to make a demo recording of "Susie-Q." However, a few months earlier, Bobby Charles's "Later Alligator" (Chess 1609) caught his attention with its combination of honking sax, pounding piano, and hipster lingo. In a short time, Charles's record was racking up healthy sales at Stan Lewis's record shop. But the version of the song that Lewis could barely keep in stock was not Charles's original, but a cover version by Bill Haley. Haley had achieved phenomenal success six months earlier with "Rock Around the Clock," the anthem that touched off the rock-and-roll moment when it topped the charts in mid-1955. In December 1956, Haley rushed out his cover of Charles's song as "See You Later, Alligator" (Decca 29791) for major label Decca Records. Haley changed more than the song's title, however. With a quicker beat, a repetitive sax riff, and a short, flashy guitar solo, all topped off by Haley's toastmaster vocals and a peppy cheerleader back-up chorus (not to mention its baby-talk spoken intro), the final product sounded less like Charles's New Orleans R&B bounce, and more like, well, "Rock Around the Clock," more like the teen music that was coming to define popular, mainstream—or white—rock-and-roll. Backed with a major label's clout, Haley's record enjoyed immense crossover appeal, reaching #6 on the pop music charts, while climbing to #7 on the R&B charts.[55]

The success of both versions of "See You Later, Alligator" motivated Hawkins to come up with a similar tune that would attract mainstream listeners. "I was listening to all these people," he later explained, and thought, "I can beat these guys."[56] Putting aside "Susie-Q," Hawkins started working on a new tune, "See You Soon, Baboon," an obvious attempt to mimic the wordplay that had made a hit out of "See You Later, Alligator," which had instantly become a favorite parting phrase for mid-1950s American teens (along with its rejoinder, "After 'While, Crocodile"). Indeed, Hawkins closely copied the plot of "See You Later, Alligator," a simple revenge tale that begins when the narrator sees his girlfriend out with another beau. When the narrator confronts her, she rejects him with the sassy putdown, "See You Later, Alligator." By the end of the song, the narrator's girlfriend realizes her mistake, but when she asks of him forgiveness, he, of course, rejects her with the same line she delivered to him earlier. Both Charles and Haley versions were sophisticated enough to be appreciated by young adults and teens alike—but Hawkins's song appears to be aimed straight for the teen audience.

Hawkins's "See You Soon, Baboon" takes place during the teenagers' favorite time—the weekend—and begins with the narrator "coming from school, Friday afternoon," when he happens upon his girlfriend with "some raccoon"—her new boyfriend. Happy with her current "raccoon," the girlfriend dumps the narrator with the line "see you soon, you big baboon." In the end, Hawkins's "baboon" exacts even greater revenge than Charles or Haley did, not because he is "hurt," as in the original, but because he has found much better "gal," who "can really spoon." From his experience behind the counter at Stan's shop, Del Hawkins surely knew—and if he didn't, Stan Lewis, who encouraged Hawkins to write the tune, did—that derivative or sequel songs were nothing new in the music business. As demonstrated by the Hank Ballard and Etta James popular series of "Annie" and "Henry" songs, along with the multitude of hit "answer" songs in the pop and country markets, record buyers were somehow attracted to songs that contained familiar names or catch phrases. Coming up with derivative songs had been the way most Tin Pan Alley songwriters worked since before the days of Irving Berlin and was still a common practice for the Brill Building songwriters of the mid-1950s, who, by this time, were churning out dozens of songs designed to capitalize on the burgeoning teen market for anything that sounded familiar and resembled rock-and-roll. In adopting this practice, Del Hawkins temporarily abandoned his new persona as an R&B singer moaning for his beloved Susie-Q, and instead adopted the guise of a professional Tin Pan Alley tunesmith who wrote songs for hire—all for the sake of getting a record deal. Hawkins, no doubt, was untroubled by such mercenary motives and figured that a hit record, no matter how derivative or how consciously aimed at the teen market, would be a hit all the same.[57]

Armed with his new song, custom-made for the teen rock-and-roll market, Hawkins gathered together a hand-picked band sometime in the spring of 1956 for a late-night recording session in KWKH's cramped studio. While Hawkins is uncertain of all the musicians on this session, the basic unit was a four-piece band that consisted of pianist Leon Post, a regular on the *Hayride* (where he had once backed Elvis Presley), nineteen-year-old African American tenor saxophonist Elgie Brown, a resident of Shreveport who performed regularly in the area's black nightspots, and a drummer and electric bassist, whose names Hawkins can no longer recall.[58] Hawkins spent some time rehearsing the band, carefully directing them to re-create the sound that only he could hear in his head—and to their credit, each member delivered the goods. With an inventive moving bass line, popping snare drum, Post's tinkling

Fats Domino-like piano, and Brown's sharp riffs and honking solo, the tight ensemble's sound on the final recording of "See You Soon, Baboon" belies its insipid teenage lyric. The song's arrangement effectively captures the rolling New Orleans groove of Charles's original "Later, Alligator"—exactly what Hawkins had intended. "[W]e were really tryin' to get that New Orleans kinda feel," he later admitted, "'cause at that time everything that was comin' out of . . . there was hittin' big."[59] For his part, Del utilized all the vocal tricks he had developed in his few months playing on the stages of the Bossier Strip's nightclubs. At times delivering the words so fast that he reaches the point of breathlessness, he growls, hiccups, drawls, and croons his way through the song, swooping down to the bass register at certain points, elongating words at others, but always pushing forward with every bit of energy he had in him.

After Del put the finishing touches on the record, Stan Lewis took over, and by early June had convinced Leonard Chess to release "See You Soon, Baboon" as a single. Chess made three decisive moves before the disc was sent to the pressing plant. His first move was to add a novelty touch to both the beginning and end of the song in the form a ludicrous "Tarzan" "ape call"— the trademark of Gene Nobles, the influential disc jockey on WLAC, the 50,000-watt clear channel station that blasted R&B records from its Nashville base. Nobles used the "ape call" (supplied by his engineer George Karsch) on his nightly radio show—one of the most important shows in the nation for turning new rhythm-and-blues records into hits.[60] Chess's second move was to secure the publishing copyrights for both songs under the auspices of the Chess publishing arm, Arc Music. When "See You Soon, Baboon" was released, the record's maroon-and-silver label listed as songwriters Stan Lewis and Eleanor Broadwater—who just happened to be Gene Nobles's wife. By the looks of things, Chess was either conspiring with Nobles, or more likely, trying to make it worth his while to play the record by giving his wife a slice of the publishing royalties—a common form of payola at the time.[61] Chess may have had other motives for ensuring that the record received airplay. With control of the song's copyright royalties, he was probably less concerned whether Hawkins's version of "See You Soon, Baboon" sold many copies, and was more intent on using whatever airplay Nobles could give them to entice a major label to put out a cover version, much the same way Charles's "Later Alligator," also published by Chess's Arc Music, had spawned Haley's more commercially successful cover for Decca. In this scenario, the only loser would be Hawkins, who, stripped of the songwriting royalties, would not make a penny off the cover version, which, if it became a hit, would also cut into the sales of his own record. Chess's third and final move would have more profound personal implications for Hawkins. A few days prior to the release "See You Soon, Baboon," a fuzzy long-distance phone call from Leonard Chess in Chicago inadvertently completed Delmar Allen Hawkins's transformation from mere rock-and-roll hopeful to professional recording artist. When Chess asked what his name was, Hawkins replied, "Del." Chess, unfamiliar with Hawkins's southern drawl, instead wrote down "Dale"—and with the stroke of a pen, "Dale Hawkins" was born.[62] Around the same time, Chess also knocked a couple of years off Hawkins's age, turning the nineteen-year-old record store clerk into a seventeen-year-old high school student, because, as Hawkins later explained, "that's what the market was at the time—teenagers."

Chess released newly christened "Dale" Hawkins's first single "See You Soon, Baboon" on its Checker subsidiary in June 1956.[63] Not only did the record fail to attract any major label cover versions; much to Chess's dismay, it also failed to sell many copies, deflating any dreams Hawkins may have harbored of overnight rock-and-roll success.[64] Hawkins may have been temporarily disappointed, but "See You Soon, Baboon," had fulfilled one purpose: "I was trying to get in the door," Hawkins later explained, "and that's the reason I wrote the song."[65] Hawkins was now a professional musician with a new name, a debut record under his belt, and an inside track to Leonard Chess; now, if only Stan Lewis could convince Chess to give the go-ahead for another recording session. Nearly ten months would pass before Hawkins's next release on Chess, and those months would make all the difference both for the development of his own sound and for his desire to become somebody.

VIII.

Hawkins, who now answered to "Dale," teamed up with James Burton and a rotating crew of young band members in the summer and fall of 1956 to fire up dance floors on the Bossier Strip and at local high schools with covers of the latest R&B and rock-and-roll hits. Working his band hard, Hawkins took pride in its live performances. "We'd start out with a set," Hawkins would later boast, "and we'd play until they hit the floor, dancin' all night."[66] "Oh, they were a fabulous band," agreed Merle Kilgore. "Dale was the top draw in Shreveport," he observed. "He would just jam 'em in."[67] Although Hawkins's local reputation rested on his role as a bandleader, his goal went beyond conquering the dance floors of northern Louisiana. He still ached to make a hit record and so returned to working on "Susie-Q," which he was certain would do the job. His confidence in the song itself came from the reaction it received from local dancers. "I mean, all I knew was that 'Susie-Q' was a hit," Hawkins says. "We worked that for at least four months or better on the Strip."[68] On one off-night, he herded Burton and various musicians into radio station KENT to make a demo of "Susie-Q," which survives today on a muffled, scratchy acetate.[69]

Recorded by Merle Kilgore at the rudimentary KENT studio, the demo version of "Susie-Q" provides a fascinating glimpse of Hawkins's band at its rhythm-and-blues peak. Even today, one is struck by the song's faithfulness to the Chicago blues sound of Little Walter, Muddy Waters, and Jimmy Reed. By the time the demo was recorded, Hawkins already had in place one of the song's most important components—the cowbell that kicks it off. Like many creative moments—Elvis Presley spontaneously breaking out into "That's All Right, Mama" as a goof during an otherwise failed recording session at Sun Studios or Leonard Chess naming Chuck Berry's first song "Maybellene" after seeing the name on a stray cosmetics case—the cowbell on "Susie-Q" was also an accident that Hawkins turned into a creative musical idea. One night, as the band was setting up for a show on the Strip, his drummer started warming up by hitting his drums and cowbell simultaneously. Hearing something different, Hawkins said, "Man, hang on to *that*," and had his band kick into "Susie-Q"—instantly, he knew he had his introduction.[70] Otherwise, the demo version of the song has a significantly different feel than the final version—thanks to seventeen-year-old saxophonist Shelton Bissell. Throughout the song, Bissell and Burton share the same jaunty riff, until the bridge, when Bissell steps out with a jazzy solo. Hawkins, for his part, had fully realized his new blues persona, singing in a jive voice full of mumbles and drawls that would verge on minstrelsy if it was not so reverential and so seemingly natural—and by this time it was. As he would later remark, "I just dug the blues," and he owed much to the music, for it had been his faithful companion on his journey out of the projects.[71]

Few white bands would ever get this close to the spirit and sound of Chicago blues again, and it would take until the early 1960s, when the Rolling Stones and the other British blues bands struggled to re-create that sound, to hear something even close to what Hawkins's band played the night that they produced the rough version of "Susie-Q." Merle Kilgore, for one, was already convinced about the song's merits based solely on the sound he heard in the demo version. "I thought it was a damn smash, even at that stage," Kilgore remembered. "I'd never heard that kinda beat," he remarked, "It was so infectious."[72] By late December 1955, Leonard Chess was impressed enough with the demo to give Hawkins the go-ahead for a formal session, with Chess paying the bills.[73]

On February 14, 1957, Hawkins, determined to make a hit record, gathered his band for a late-night session at KWKH studios to record what would become the final version of "Susie-Q." The band recorded two other songs that night, "Don't Treat Me This Way," a blues number based on Little Walter's "My Babe" riff and written by black R&B singer Peppermint Harris from nearby Texarkana, and a Platters-type ballad called "First Love"—both of which featured a local black vocal group that Hawkins had recruited just for the occasion. But Hawkins was there to nail down a final version of "Susie-Q." He wanted a sparse and stark sound, so gone was the saxophone that had riffed and soloed through the demo. Hawkins also told the vocal group to take a break. There would be one voice on this song—his own.

With everything in place, the song kicked off with the familiar cowbell, courtesy of fifteen-year-old Ronnie Lewis, Stan Lewis's kid brother who had gigged frequently with Hawkins on the Bossier Strip. Spooky, yet clanging, with a loose, Latin-ish feel, the cowbell would inspire critics and fans to label Hawkins's sound "swamp rock," as if the mossy landscape of southern Louisiana had somehow seeped northward into the Shreveport recording studio and mysteriously oozed onto the record's grooves—when, of course, the sound was Hawkins's own invention. For a few seconds, cowbell, drums, bass, and handclaps lay down a bed of controlled cacophony that just hints at the menace to come. Out of nowhere, Burton enters with his aggressive finger-picking lick, vaguely similar to the blues on the demo, but something of his own making. Pounding hard on the low-E bass string with mathematical precision, he picks out a syncopated, bluesy melody on the high treble strings, before establishing the repetitive riff that sets up his and Hawkins's classic call-and-response duet. Then it was Hawkins's turn. He begins with a soft, whispery "Oh, Susie-Q"—actually a mistake by engineer Bob Sullivan, who forgot to turn up Hawkins's microphone full throttle, but a mistake that worked. The first sound one hears is the far-off wail of a man desperate for a sign of loyalty from the woman who can save his soul. Hawkins then leans in, and from the start, pours out his feelings, "Oh Susie-Q, how I love you, my Susie-Q," then he tries some sweet talk, "I like the way you walk, I like the way you talk" and, finally he makes his plea, "Well, say that you'll be true, and never leave me blue, my Susie-Q." Gone were the feelings of poverty and humiliation that had haunted the demo version—"Susie-Q" may leave him, but she would not leave him with "nothing." Gone, too, was the Chicago blues mimicry of the demo, for his vocal constitutes nothing less than the full realization of Hawkins's new creative persona, a testimony to the power of rhythm-and-blues to provide him with the transcendence that he needed so desperately just a year earlier. By the time the song was over, "Delmar" was gone, and Dale Hawkins stood alone, a product of his own will and circumstances.

Another rebirth occurs in the song's bridge when Burton unleashes the first of his two solos. Unlike the demo, in which he shared space with a saxophone, Burton would be the only soloist on this cut. Not satisfied with replicating the blues phrases on the demo, yet refusing to copy the country-picking that first drew him to the instrument, he jumps in with a sheet of furious eighth notes that move up and down the fret board; then, he shifts to a series of repetitive two-note phrases, first against the beat and then resolving to reestablish the song's groove, before ending with a flourish, a series of sliding finger-picked notes like no one—not Merle Travis, Scotty Moore, or Hubert Sumlin—had ever played before.[74] By the end of his solo (he would repeat it a verse later), Burton too has realized his goal—to come up with a guitar style that was uniquely his own. As the final version of "Susie-Q" faded out with a series of scattered blues riffs, Hawkins and Burton would never be same. Whether or not the record sold a single copy, they each had completed their apprenticeship and produced their first masterpiece, one that, in its own quirky and primitive way, made a commanding musical statement.

Hawkins could rest assured in the knowledge that "Susie-Q" was no accident. The diligence with which he and Burton collaborated to assemble its unique sound disproves any suggestion that the two merely lucked into a hit record or that it was simply a natural expression of their southern genes or a product of Louisiana's swamps. As Hawkins later noted, the joint creative process in the midnight quest for perfection at KWKH was one of "six or seven cuts of 'Suzie Q' that night."[75] Indeed, the one they chose for the final version was far from perfect in a technical sense. Hawkins, for example, comes in early after the second guitar solo, unintentionally reversing the call-and-response guitar lines of the first two verses. The final version of the song is also punctuated by whoops and yells supplied by the members of the black vocal group and other visitors in the studio, giving it a live feel that conjures up a wild night on the Bossier Strip. While the resulting record appears loose and improvised, it was Hawkins himself who chose which version would make the final cut, and its mixture of musical calculation, chaos, and craft was exactly what he wanted.

With the master tape of "Susie-Q" completed, the only thing for Dale Hawkins to do next was to keeping playing gigs on the Bossier Strip—and wait. Shortly after the session, Stan Lewis delivered the tape to Leonard Chess, who, notorious for his indecisiveness, mulled over what to do with it.[76] After sitting on the tape for three months, still a sore point with Hawkins, Chess finally released "Susie-Q" backed with "Don't Treat Me This Way" in late April.[77] "Susie-Q" was not an "instant hit upon its release" nor was Dale the "archetypal overnight success," as some accounts claim.[78] Although such platitudes bolster Hawkins's claim to the rock-and-roll myth, in fact, he worked hard to make "Susie-Q" a hit. From the outset, the music industry seemed not to know what to make of the record. When "Susie-Q" was first released, the industry's leading trade magazine, *Billboard*, perhaps taking into account that the record came from Chess's Checker imprint, reviewed it in its section for new rhythm-and-blues releases, not in its pop section, reserved for the latest rock-and-roll records. Indeed, consistent with Hawkins's love of rhythm-and-blues, "Susie-Q" first caught on with black radio listeners who pushed the record into *Billboard*'s R&B Top 10 by mid-June. That same day, "Susie-Q" finally entered the magazine's Top 100, a full six weeks after it was first released. By this time, Leonard Chess ordered Hawkins out on the road to promote the record at record hops and local television programs, beginning in May with an appearance in Washington, D.C. on disc jockey Milt Grant's daily teen dance show.[79]

For these events, Hawkins had to undergo yet another transformation. Forced to perform without a live band, he adopted the role of eighteen-year-old teen idol, "Dale Hawkins," lip-synching to the record in front of young teenagers—a far cry from his gigs on the Bossier Strip. Yet, even as a teen idol, Hawkins's promotional efforts on behalf of the record paid off. By July 8, "Susie-Q" peaked at #29 on the pop music charts, a position that gives little indication of the record's actual sales figures or its popularity on the charts. For a record to reach the Top 10, it has to be selling and playing over the airwaves in all the major urban markets at the same time. But "Susie-Q" became popular one market at a time, as Hawkins "had to break it city by city."[80] In July, he traveled to New York to perform at Harlem's Apollo Theater (where he was one of the first white singers to appear at the venue) and on Alan Freed's *Big Beat* television show.[81] On August 7, he lip-synched "Susie-Q" on Dick Clark's *American Bandstand*, the hit-making show broadcast out of Philadelphia that had just started to air nationally the week before. Clark was caught off-guard by the song's popularity, and later recounted that the night before Hawkins appeared on *Bandstand*, Clark hosted a local sock hop in which he was forced to play the song for "21 minutes straight before the kids had enough of it."[82] Judging from these fans' enthusiastic reaction, "Susie-Q" appeared at a time when the rock-and-roll audience was open for Hawkins's type of music, for any little taste of grit, anything that tested musical conventions. Given the song's widespread appeal, it would remain on *Billboard*'s Hot 100 until October before concluding its remarkable nineteen-week run on the charts.

Unfortunately, the musical collaboration between Dale Hawkins and James Burton was already over when "Susie-Q" peaked on the charts in July 1957. By that time, Burton had moved on to Los Angeles to play with *Hayride* regular Bob Luman, a promising rockabilly singer who had signed a deal with Imperial Records.[83] Hawkins, for his part, never missed a beat, and he continued to assemble bands from among the crop of local musicians and to play shows on the Bossier Strip. Now, however, Hawkins was a Chess recording artist and began recording at Chess's brand new Sheldon recording studio in Chicago with some of the same musicians who played on the Chess singles that first inspired him to become a professional singer.[84] And, although the regular interaction between black and white musicians at Chess's studio fostered the kind of collaborative spirit he had created back at Shreveport, neither of the records he recorded in Chicago, "Baby, Baby" and "Little Pig," made so much as a dent on the charts.[85]

But Hawkins would again find success back in the Shreveport music scene, with its rigged-up radio station studios, its feverish Bossier Strip dance floors, and its crop of talented and ambitious youngsters. For his next record, "La-Do-Dada," Hawkins seemed determined to replicate the same conditions that had produced a hit with "Susie-Q." Hawkins not only cut "La-Do-Dada" in the familiar surroundings of KWKH's recording studio, but he also recruited guitarist Joe Osborn and back-up singer Margaret Lewis, two young, ambitious musicians, to play on the session. As with James Burton before them, Osborn and Lewis had first honed their skills at Mira Smith's Ram recording studio, and their unique styles would greatly enhance the final version of the song. Released in July 1958, "La-Do-Dada" gave Hawkins his second Top 40 hit when it peaked at #32 in October.[86]

By this time, the making of "Dale Hawkins" was complete. In fact, Hawkins tucked "Delmar Allen"—the poor young man from the projects who had showed up at Stan's Record Shop just two years earlier, his pockets full of nothing but ambition—so safely away within himself that many who met him afterward would never know "Delmar" at all. By any measure, Hawkins had achieved the goals he set for himself during those late-night prayer sessions in his hospital room after returning from the Navy in 1954. Free, most importantly, from the stifling hopelessness in which he had grown up, and with a couple of hit records to his credit, Dale Hawkins, the musician, had followed his own route to success, one less dependent on his southern rural childhood and more on his experiences in urban Shreveport and Bossier City in the 1950s. One could even argue that his failures to make it in the "straight" life—his dissatisfying jaunt through business school in 1954 and the nondescript jobs that followed—inspired him to pursue a career in music more than anything he ever saw or heard as a child. But more than just a profession or a paycheck, Hawkins made the music, and especially his own interpretation of black rhythm-and-blues, his identity. Still skinny, awkward, and unpolished off-stage, but feverish and in-control onstage, Hawkins headed out on the road in late 1958 in a brand new station wagon, hand-picked backup band in tow, to see if the sound he had constructed within the musical milieu of north Louisiana would garner success outside of it.

Notes

1. Dale Hawkins interview by Dave Anderson, North Little Rock, Arkansas, February 4, 2006; Stuart Coleman, "Repeating Echoes with Dale Hawkins," *Now Dig This*, November 2005, 14.

2. Hank Williams made his debut on the *Louisiana Hayride* in August 1948, the year before the release of "Lovesick Blues" catapulted him to national success as a country artist. Williams's run on the *Hayride* stage, as well as in its regional package tours, helped to cement Shreveport's reputation as a training ground for white country—and later rockabilly—musicians who went to Nashville to join WMS's *Grand Ole Opry*. In fact, the *Hayride*, according to musicologist Tracey E. W. Laird, "nurtured so many successful country music careers that it came to be called the 'Cradle of the Stars.'" Tracey E. W. Laird, "Country Chameleons: Cajuns on the Louisiana Hayride," *Louisiana's Living Traditions*, 1999, http://louisianafolklife.org/LT/Articles_Essays/creole_art_ country_chamele.html. For the best study of the *Hayride*, see Laird, *Louisiana Hayride: Radio and Roots Music Along the Red River* (New York: Oxford University Press, 2005).

3. All chart numbers courtesy of Joel Whitburn, *The Billboard Pop Charts, 1955–1959* (Menomonee Falls, WI: Record Research Inc., 1992); Whitburn, *Top R&B Singles, 1942–1995* (Menomonee Falls, WI: Record Research Inc., 1996); Whitburn, *The Billboard Book of Top 40 Hits* 4th ed. (New York: Billboard Books, 1989). For a complete listing of the Rock and Roll Hall of Fame's Top 500 songs of the rock era, see the Rock and Roll Hall of Fame Web Site, http://www.rockhall.com/exhibitions/permanent.asp?id=677.

4. As historian Glenn Altschuler points out, 1950s social commentators and music critics viewed rock-and-roll as "music for teenagers, about teenagers, [and] performed by teenagers." Glenn C. Altschuler, *All Shook Up: How Rock 'n' Roll Changed America* (New York: Oxford University Press, 2003), 108. The supposed native abilities of white southern rockers was best

expressed by Sun rockabilly singer Charlie Feathers, who claimed, "Rockabilly was natural—it's like when you go get a drink of water, you go get a drink of water." Michael Bane, *White Boy Singin' the Blues: The Black Roots of White Rock* (New York: Penguin Books, 1982), 118–19. Elvis Presley depicted the supposed naturalness of his talent in his second film, the loosely autobiographical *Lovin' You* (1957). At the beginning of the film, his character, truck driver and amateur singer Deke Rivers, jumps onstage to join a professional band and delivers a flawless performance. As numerous historians of Sun Records have shown, the early rockabilly records were hardly natural expressions of the performers' innate talents, but were the result of label-owner and producer Sam Phillips (and later Cowboy Jack Clement) encouraging singers, such as Presley, Johnny Cash, and Jerry Lee Lewis, and the musicians with whom they recorded to experiment with different sounds, genres, and vocal styles.

5. For more on Presley's early years and his Sun sessions, see Peter Guralnick, *Last Train to Memphis: The Rise of Elvis Presley* (New York: Back Bay Books, 1994). For more on Cash, see Colin Escott and Martin Hawkins, *Good Rockin' Tonight: Sun Records and the Birth of Rock 'n' Roll* (St. Martin's Press, 1991). For more on Berry, see Bruce Pegg, *Brown Eyed Handsome Man: The Life and Hard Times of Chuck Berry* (Routledge, 2002). Bo Diddley was born Otha Ellas Bates in Mississippi in 1928, he also took the name of Ellas McDaniel—after his mother's cousin, who legally adopted him as a child—before settling on the musical alias of "Bo Diddley." For more on Diddley, see George White, *Bo Diddley: Living Legend* (Sanctuary, 1998).

6. For the transformative effect of rhythm-and-blues on white southern men during the 1950s, see Michael T. Bertrand, *Race, Rock, and Elvis* (Urbana and Chicago: University of Illinois Press, 2000); Bertrand, "I Don't Think Hank Done It That Way: Elvis, Country Music, and the Reconstruction of Southern Masculinity," in *A Boy Named Sue: Gender and Country Music*, ed. Kristine M. McCusker and Diane Pecknold (Jackson: University Press of Mississippi, 2004), 59–85.

7. Writers who have contributed to the narrative of Hawkins's childhood—in liner notes and scattered articles and interviews—have, for the most part, attributed his success to his exposure to rural music as a child and, notably, to the alleged interaction between a young Hawkins and his fellow African American sharecroppers in his native Goldmine. But Hawkins moved away from Goldmine when he was just two years old and spent the rest of his childhood shuttled among family members in the small towns and, later, cities of north Louisiana. For more on the traditional, and now debatable, narrative of Hawkins's early years, see Colin Escott, "Dale Hawkins: Oh, Suzie Q" in *Tattooed on Their Tongues: A Journey Through the Backrooms of American Music* (New York: Schirmer Books, 1996), 162–75; Bill Millar, liner notes, Dale Hawkins, *Rock 'n' Roll Tornado* (Compact Disc; Ace Records: CDCHD 693: 1998); Bill Millar, "Dale Hawkins," *New Kommotion* 1977, *Rock's Backpages* (subscription only), http://www.rocksbackpages.com/article_with_login.html?ArticleID=5686; Billy Miller, liner notes, Dale Hawkins, *Daredevil* (Compact Disc; Norton Records: 1997); Lauren Wilcox, "Dale Hawkins: *That's Guitar Playing*," *Oxford American* (Summer 2005), 16–20.

8. Dale Hawkins interview by Dave Anderson and Lesley-Anne Reed, North Little Rock, Arkansas, July 20, 2006.

9. Hawkins would later evoke his fond memories of Hawkins Hollow in the 1961 song, "Grandma's House" (Checker 970, 1961).

10. Dale Hawkins interview by Dave Anderson, February 4, 2006. Hawkins felt so distanced from his father that in 1959 he would list the elder Hawkins as deceased when applying for a marriage license, even though his father did not actually die until the mid-1960s. Marriage license 25264, book 52, page 61, Bossier Parish Courthouse, Benton, Louisiana. Hawkins's first marriage to eighteen-year-old Bossier City native Joyce Dixon took place on February 14, 1959 in Benton, Louisiana, the seat of Bossier Parish.

11. Millar, liner notes, *Rock 'n' Roll Tornado*; Millar, "Dale Hawkins"; Dale Hawkins interview by Dave Anderson, North Little Rock, Arkansas, February 4, 2006; Dale Hawkins interview by Dave Anderson and Lesley-Anne Reed, North Little Rock, Arkansas, July 20, 2006.

12. Dale Hawkins interview by Dave Anderson, February 4, 2006.

13. Bertrand, *Race, Rock, and Elvis*; Altschuler, *All Shook Up*; Brian Ward, *Just My Soul Responding: Rhythm and Blues, Black Consciousness, and Race Relations* (Berkeley: University of California Press, 1998); Charlie Gillett, *The Sound of the City: The Rise of Rock and Roll* (New York: Pantheon, 1984).

14. Little is known about the conditions of the Bossier Housing Projects or its requirements for residence. But in the 1950s, housing projects all across the country—despite having earned the reputation as places of only abject poverty and desolation—actually marked a step up for poor rural families with aspirations toward upward mobility. One such family was Elvis Presley's, who moved into the Lauderdale Courts—a housing project in Memphis—in 1949. The Courts, Peter Guralnick explains, seemed more like "a humming, bustling little village, full of kids and ambition" than a poverty-trap; Guralnick, *Last Train to Memphis*, 32–34. Whether or not the Bossier projects ever evoked that same feeling from its residents is unknown, but Hawkins insists that his time there was far from ideal.

15. Dale Hawkins interview by Dave Anderson and Lesley-Anne Reed, North Little Rock, Arkansas, July 20, 2006.

16. Those who have written about Hawkins and his music career have largely neglected the period between 1950 and 1956—the time when he was (barely) attending high school, running away from home repeatedly, and serving in the Navy. Most writers have picked up the narrative conveniently in 1955 or 1956—when Hawkins showed up at Stan's record store and then participated in the north Louisiana music scene. In a 1997, Howard Dewitt does include several paragraphs about Hawkins's high school years and his stint in the Navy, but the accuracy of his account is questionable. For example, Dewitt claims that while attending high school in Bossier City Hawkins "picked cotton alongside black field hands and listened to their guitar and harmonica sounds," while frequenting the local "juke joints." Hawkins has never indicated to the author or any other interviewers that he engaged in either of these activities while he was a Bossier City teenager. Howard A. Dewitt, "Dale Hawkins: Oh Suzie Q and Beyond," *Blue Suede News* #40, Fall 1997, 16–22, quote on pp. 16–17.

17. Dale Hawkins interview by Dave Anderson, February 4, 2006.

18. Dale Hawkins telephone conversation with Dave Anderson, July 26, 2006.

19. Dale Hawkins interview by Dave Anderson and Lesley-Anne Reed, July 20, 2006.

20. Dale Hawkins interview by Dave Anderson, February 4, 2006. According to Hawkins, his mother had been a teacher in north Louisiana rural schools around the time of his birth, which may account for her desire that he complete an education.

21. Dale Hawkins interview by Dave Anderson and Lesley-Anne Reed, July 20, 2006.

22. Beginning with Hank Williams in 1949, the *Hayride* launched the careers of Kitty Wells, Slim Whitman, Webb Pierce, Faron Young, Jim Reeves, Billy Walker, Johnny Cash, Johnny Horton, George Jones, and of course, Elvis Presley. See Laird, *Louisiana Hayride*; Steven R. Tucker, "The Louisiana Hayride, 1948–1954," *North Louisiana Historical Association Journal* (Fall 1977), 187–201. For more on Hank Williams's tenure at the *Hayride*, see Colin Escott, *Hank Williams: The Biography* (Little Brown and Company, 1994). For more on Presley's tenure at the *Hayride*, see Guralnick, *Last Train to Memphis*.

23. In the liner notes to Hawkins's first album, R&B disc jockey "Hoss" Allen writes that Hawkins "never would have been a country singer" because, as Hawkins told Allen, "I've got to have that beat." Bill "Hoss" Allen, liner notes, Dale Hawkins, *Oh! Suzy-Q* (Argo LP 1429, 1958). Journalist-rocker Cub Koda likewise notes that Hawkins "had absolutely no ties to country

music." Cub Koda, liner notes, Dale Hawkins, *Oh! Suzy-Q: The Best of Dale Hawkins* (Compact Disk; MCA CHD-9356; 1995)

24. Dale Hawkins interview by Dave Anderson, February 4, 2006.

25. Shreveport *Times*, October 12, 1955.

26. Bill Millar, liner notes, various artists, *That'll Flat Git It*, Vol. 12 (Compact Disc; Imperial Records/Bear Family Records: BCD 16102: 1998).

27. Dale Hawkins interview by Dave Anderson, February 4, 2006.

28. Wayne Jancik, "Comments from Stan Lewis," in liner notes, Various Artists, *The Jewel/Paula Records Story: The Blues, Rhythm & Blues and Soul Recordings* (Compact Disc; Capricorn Records: 9-42014-2: 1993). See also, Guralnick, *Last Train to Memphis*, 138; Laird, *Louisiana Hayride*, 128; Nadine Cohodas, *Spinning Blues into Gold: The Chess Brothers and the Legendary Chess Records* (New York: St. Martin's Griffin, 2000), 84, 97, 175.

29. Jancik, "Comments from Stan Lewis," liner notes, *The Jewel-Paula Records Story*.

30. Dale Hawkins interview by Dave Anderson and Lesley-Anne Reed, July 20, 2006.

31. The Crows, a black doo-wop group from New York City, scored the first major R&B crossover during the last few months of 1953 with "Gee," which would peak at #14 on *Billboard*'s pop chart and #2 on its R&B chart. The Moonglows' 1954 hit "Sincerely," released by Chess, went all the way to #1 on the R&B chart and, more importantly, "crossed over" to #20 on the pop chart.

32. Dale Hawkins interview by Dave Anderson, February 4, 2006.

33. Dale Hawkins interview by Dave Anderson and Lesley-Anne Reed, July 20, 2006.

34. Dale Hawkins interview by Dave Anderson and Lesley-Anne Reed, July 20, 2006.

35. Dale Hawkins telephone conversation with Lesley-Anne Reed, August 3, 2006.

36. In addition to Hawkins (b. 1936), this group would also include Sonny Jones (b. 1934) and James Kirkland (b. 1934). Many other early rockabilly stars fit much of this older cohort's profile, including Scotty Moore (b. 1931), Tommy Blake (b. 1931), D. J. Fontana (b. 1931), Johnny Cash (b. 1932), Carl Perkins (b. 1932), Elvis Presley (b. 1935), Jerry Lee Lewis (b. 1935), and Gene Vincent (b. 1935).

37. For a more comprehensive analysis of this younger generation, see Laird, *Louisiana Hayride*, 133–47.

38. Ray Topping, liner notes, various artists, *Shreveport High Steppers: Ram Rockabilly and Hillbilly* (Compact Disc; Ace Records: CDCHD 818: 2001). Burton played at Ram with a group of young guitarists that included Joe Osborn (b. 1937), who would go on to play with Hawkins, his brother Jerry Hawkins, Bob Luman, and Ricky Nelson, all before becoming a major L.A. session musician as a bass player; Billy Sanford (b. 1940), who would become a Nashville session stalwart; and Jerry Kennedy (b. 1940), who would achieve success as a Nashville session player and record producer. Female singers who were also part of this cohort were Linda Brannon (b. 1941), who married Jerry Kennedy, and Margaret Lewis (b. 1942), who was also a skilled songwriter whose compositions include the country soul classic, "Reconsider Me."

39. James Burton interview by Dave Anderson, Shreveport, Louisiana, June 16, 2006.

40. James Burton interview by Dave Anderson, Shreveport, Louisiana, June 16, 2006; Shreveport *Times*, September 5, 1954.

41. James Burton interview by Dave Anderson, Shreveport, Louisiana, June 16, 2006; Burton made his recording debut on Carol Williams's "Just for Awhile"/"You Never Mention My Name" (Ram 45MS-101, 1955), recorded in Williams's living room in 1955 while Mira Smith awaited the completion of her Ram recording studio. Escott, "James Burton" in Escott, *Tattooed on Their Tongues*, 166.

42. Oddly enough, Hawkins would later claim to have converted Burton—who was more solidly rooted in honky-tonk country sounds of KWKH and the *Hayride* than Hawkins ever was—"off Merle Travis and [on] to the blues." Dale Hawkins interview with Dave Anderson and

Lesley-Anne Reed, North Little Rock, Arkansas, July 20, 2006. Burton, however, insists that he was already aware that to make it as a professional musician he would have to develop his own unique style rather simply imitating his heroes Merle Travis, Chet Atkins, and Les Paul. With this goal in mind, Burton assimilated the style of blues and R&B guitarists such as Hubert Sumlin, Jimmy Rodgers, Robert Lockwood, Jr., Clarence "Gatemouth" Brown, and Chuck Berry. Burton melded all his influences to develop a signature guitar style—a hybrid of Atkins and Travis's country finger-picking, pop, blues, and rock-and-roll. In addition, Burton learned to imitate steel guitar licks in duets with local steel guitarist and *Hayride* regular James "Sonny" Trammell. Escott, "James Burton"; James Burton interview by Dave Anderson, Shreveport, Louisiana, June 16, 2006. For more on the development of Burton's style, see "James Burton" in John Tobler and Stuart Grundy, *The Guitar Greats* (New York: St. Martin Press, 1984), *Rock's Backpages* (subscription only) available on-line at http://www.rocksbackpages.com/article_with_login. html?ArticleID56079.

43. Billy Miller, liner notes, Dale Hawkins, *Daredevil* (Norton 256), 1997, 11.

44. There is no single study of Shreveport's black music scene in the 1940s and 1950s. For some helpful background, see Laird, *Louisiana Hayride*; Ray Topping, liner notes, various artists, *Red River Blues* (Compact disc; Ace Records: CDCHD 725: 1999). Shreveport also had an active civil rights movement in the 1950s and 1960s. See, for example, Adam Fairclough, *Race and Democracy: The Civil Rights Struggle in Louisiana, 1915–1972* (Athens: University of Georgia Press, 1999).

45. Shreveport *Times*, September 1, 1956.

46. Miller, liner notes, *Daredevil*, 11.

47. Although it reached #7 on the R&B charts, "I've Got My Eyes on You" was actually the b-side of "Your Cash Ain't Nothin' but Trash" (Atlantic 1035), which reached #6 on *Billboard*'s rhythm-and-blues chart. "I've Got My Eyes on You" was written by African American R&B saxophonist and bandleader Charlie Singleton and Paul Winley, whose brother Harold was the Clovers' bass singer. The song was recorded on September 24, 1953 and released in June 1954.

48. Muddy Waters, "Turn the Lamp Down (Baby Please Don't Go)"/"Sweet Man" (Chess 1542, 1953). The guitar lick was supplied by Chess stalwart Jimmy Rodgers. For the definitive Waters discography, see Phil Wright and Fred Rothwell, *The Complete Muddy Waters Discography*, available on-line, http://www.bluesandrhythm.co.uk/documents/200.pdf.

49. Dale Hawkins interview by Dave Anderson, February 4, 2006.

50. The authorship of "Susie-Q" remains a point of contention between Hawkins and Stan Lewis. Hawkins has consistently maintained that he wrote the song while gigging with his band in the months before he recorded the song, and that he was also the one who came up with the song's title. Lewis, however, insists that he helped write the song when he and Hawkins would "kick ideas around together" in the record shop. "Susie-Q," according to Lewis, was the result of "bits of conversation that would trigger ideas" in his young counter clerk's mind. Lewis also asserts that the song's title was inspired by the names of his young daughter, Susan Lewis, and Leonard Chess's daughter, also named Susan. Susan Lewis—only two years old in 1957—recalls that her father was a songwriter who "was always walking around the house rhyming everything." One day, according to Susan Lewis, "he was making up a little song about me, and that became *Susie-Q*." Hawkins categorically denies Lewis's account. See Jancik, "Comments from Stan Lewis," liner notes, *The Jewel Paula Records Story*. For Susan Lewis, see *Houston Chronicle*, "Real Life Suzie-Q Is a Fogerty Fan," July 29, 1998.

51. Another possible model for "Susie-Q" was John Lee Hooker's "Dimples" (Vee-Jay 205, 1956), which opens with the line, "I love the way you walk" and contains an introductory guitar lick similar to the ones found in the recorded versions of "Susie-Q." Hooker recorded "Dimples" in March 1956 and Vee-Jay released it some time that year, so it is plausible that Hawkins heard the record and used it as a model for "Susie-Q." However, Hawkins, who has candidly acknowledged

"Susie-Q"'s blues antecedents, insists that he was not familiar with "Dimples" until after he had written and recorded "Susie-Q" between the Spring of 1956 and early months of 1957. Dale Hawkins telephone conversation with Dave Anderson, February 20, 2007. In any case, both "Susie-Q" and "Dimples" constitute rewrites of the Clovers' "I've Got My Eyes on You"—Hooker even uses the title phrase of the Clovers' hit as the hook line that concludes each verse of "Dimples." For a similar conclusion, see "Love My Susie-Q," *Home of the Groove* website, http:// homeofthegroove.blogspot.com/2006/08/love-my-susie-q.html.

52. Dale Hawkins interview by Dave Anderson and Lesley-Anne Reed, July 20, 2006.

53. Miller, liner notes, *Daredevil*, 4.

54. In June 1954, Leonard Chess expanded his operation into the country-and-western market through a partnership with Lewis. According to two leading historians of the Chess label, Leonard Chess would release records that Lewis either "produced himself or obtained from sources in the" Ark-La-Tex region. Chess put out these records through what became known as its special "4858" series. The Chess-Lewis partnership lasted only for seven releases and ended in March 1955, but it did yield a country hit for *Hayride* regulars Jimmy and Johnny, whose "If You Don't Somebody Else Will" (Chess 4859) peaked at #3 on the country charts in the fall of 1954. George R. White, Robert L. Campbell, and Tom Kelly, *The Chess Label Part II (1953–1955)*, http://hubcap.clemson. edu/~campber/chess2.html.

55. The song, which eventually reached #14 on *Billboard*'s R&B chart in March 1956, was written and recorded by Bobby Charles, a white Cajun from southern Louisiana, whose real name was Robert Charles Guidry. Charles and his band were based in his hometown of Abbeville, but they recorded the song in New Orleans at Cosimo Matassa's famous J&M recording studio, which had produced several R&B and "crossover" pop hits for Fats Domino, Little Richard, and Lloyd Price. Charles's Cajun-inflected vocals led many listeners—and initially, Chess's executives—to mistake him for a black singer. Cohodas, *Spinning Blues into Gold*, 122–26; Colin Escott, "Bobby Charles: See You Later, Alligator," in Escott, *Tatooed on Their Tongues*, 12–19; Scott Jordan, "Searching for Bobby Charles," *bestofneworleans.com* http://www.bestofneworleans. com/dispatch/2004-10-26/cover_story.html. Charles's version was actually titled "See You Later, Alligator" and he later bitterly complained that Leonard Chess had shortened the title of the song "because Leonard thought he was being hip." Subsequent releases of Charles's Chess version were labeled "See You Later, Alligator." Escott, "Bobby Charles," 15. Charles would also become known for the hits he wrote for other musicians, including Fats Domino's "Walking to New Orleans" and Clarence "Frogman" Henry's "(I Don't Know Why) But I Do."

56. Dale Hawkins interview by Dave Anderson and Lesley-Anne Reed, July 20, 2006.

57. Cohodas, *Spinning Blues into Gold*, 126; Hawkins also admitted to journalist-rocker Cub Koda that "See You Soon, Baboon" was an attempt to capitalize on the success of both Charles and Haley's version of "See You Later, Alligator." Koda, liner notes, Dale Hawkins, *Oh! Suzy-Q: The Best of Dale Hawkins* (Compact Disk; MCA CHD-9356: 1995). See also, Coleman, "Repeating Echoes with Dale Hawkins," 14. In a similar vein, Hawkins wrote another song he called "Four Letter Word (Rock)" that resembled Haley's hit "R-O-C-K," released in early April 1956 and featured in the film, *Rock Around the Clock*, a low-budget exploitation film that starred Haley and his band, the Comets, in a heavily fictionalized account of their rise to stardom. Hawkins claims not to have consciously patterned "Four Letter Word" on Haley's "R-O-C-K, but he does remember seeing the film when it was first appeared in theaters sometime around late March or early April 1956.

58. Burton remembers having played guitar on the "See You Soon, Baboon" session, but all accounts of the session list Sonny Jones as guitarist, although his instrument is barely audible on the record. Hawkins had previously identified the drummer on "See You Soon, Baboon" as A. J. Tuminello, as have various liner notes, but has since retracted this statement. The name

of the bassist also remains unclear. In addition, most accounts of the "See You Soon, Baboon" session have listed the horn part as "unknown," but Hawkins has since indicated that Elgie Brown supplied the sax on the session. See Koda, liner notes, *Oh! Suzy-Q*; Millar, liner notes, *Rock 'n' Roll Tornado.*

59. Koda, liner notes, *Oh! Suzy-Q*, 5.

60. Millar, liner notes, Hawkins, *Rock 'n' Roll Tornado*, 5; Tapio Vaisanen, Dale Hawkins Discography, available on-line at http://www.pcuf.fi/~tapiov/discographies/dalehawkins.html.

61. In a recent interview, Stan Lewis claimed to have no knowledge of Chess's machinations. Stan Lewis interview with Dave Anderson and Lesley-Anne Reed, Shreveport, Louisiana, December 21, 2006.

62. Dale Hawkins telephone conversation with Dave Anderson, July 24, 2006. For other examples of Leonard Chess's inability to understand a southern American dialect, see Cohodas, *Spinning Blues into Gold*, 127. Cohodas includes an anecdote in which Chess mistook Louisiana native Little Walter's line "my pains are coming down" in the song "Just a Feeling" for "my pants are coming down."

63. Dale Hawkins, "See You Soon, Baboon"/"Four Letter Word" (Checker 843, 1956). Hawkins's record release dates courtesy of Terry Gordon, "Rockin' Country Style (RCS): A Discography of Country, Rock & Roll, and Related Records, 1951–1964," http://rcs.law.emory.edu/rcs/index.htm.

64. Hawkins has always claimed that the record flopped because Chess failed to market it correctly, although given the fact that Chess owned part of the publishing rights to "See You Soon, Baboon," he did tout the record in the music industry's trade press that summer. For a reproduction of a Chess trade advertisement with "See You Soon, Baboon," see Millar, liner notes, *Rock 'n' Roll Tornado*, 4.

65. Cohodas, *Spinning Blues into Gold*, 126.

66. Dale Hawkins telephone conversation with Lesley-Anne Reed, October 15, 2005.

67. Miller, liner notes, *Daredevil*, 11.

68. Dale Hawkins interview by Dave Anderson, February 4, 2006.

69. The demo is available on Dale Hawkins, *Daredevil* (compact disc; Norton Records, Norton 256; 1998).

70. Billy Miller, liner notes, *Daredevil*, 12. Dale Hawkins telephone conversation with Dave Anderson, August 7, 2006.

71. The band also recorded another song that night, a slow, blues stomp called "If You Please Me," in which Hawkins and his band mates—especially James Burton—made an even more definitive statement for the blues. The young guitarist proved his mastery of blues style, laying down the main riff (based on Jimmy Reed's "You Don't Have to Go"), which he punctuated with snaky, trilling single-string lines before the song collapses into a "shave-and-a-haircut" ending. This song is also available on Hawkins, *Daredevil*. For Reed's song, see Jimmy Reed, "You Don't Have to Go"/"Boogie in the Dark" (Vee-Jay 119, 1954).

72. Miller, liner notes, Hawkins, *Daredevil*, 11.

73. See Escott, "Dale Hawkins," 32–35. Escott includes a copy of the union contract, signed by Phil Chess, which shows February 14 as the date for the final "Susie-Q" session. Chess appears to have committed to financing a session for Hawkins by late 1956. Stan Lewis maintains that he and Hawkins entered into a contract with Chess signed December 16, 1956, for sessions to record "Susie-Q" and "La-Do-Dada." Stan Lewis telephone conversation with Lesley-Anne Reed, August 5, 2006.

74. For an analysis of Burton's guitar technique on the introduction of "Susie-Q," see Askol Buk, "Viva Las Burton," *Country Guitar*, February 1995, 103. For a full transcription of the song, see Fred Sokolow, *Genuine Rockabilly Guitar Hits* (Milwaukee: Hal Leonard Publishing, 1993), 124–27.

75. Dale Hawkins interview by Dave Anderson and Lesley-Anne Reed, July 20, 2006.

76. Cohen, *Record Men*, 103–4. Hawkins and his band recorded the final version of "Susie-Q" on February 14, 1957, and Chess released the record ten weeks later at the end of April. *Billboard*

magazine reviewed the record in its May 6, 1957, issue. However, in various interviews throughout the nearly fifty years since the record's release, Hawkins has insisted that Leonard Chess sat on the record for "six or seven months." Impatient with Chess's indecisiveness, Hawkins sent a copy of "Susie-Q" to Jerry Wexler, head of Atlantic Records, who, Hawkins alleges, showed interest in the song—prompting Chess to release the record. Hawkins's account is plausible, but only if "Susie-Q" was actually recorded in late 1956 and the date printed on the union contract is somehow in error. See Escott, "Dale Hawkins"; Millar, liner notes, *Rock 'n' Roll Tornado*, 6; Ted Drozdowski, "Still Q-ed Up," *Boston Phoenix*, October 22, 1998.

77. Dale Hawkins, "Susie-Q"/"Don't Treat Me This Way," (Checker 863, 1957). Unlike "See You Soon, Baboon," Hawkins received one-third writing credit for "Susie-Q." However, Stan Lewis and Eleanor Broadwater also received one-third each.

78. Marty Jones, "Say That You'll Be True," *Westword*, October 12, 2000. http://www.westword.com/Issues/2000-10-12/music/music2.html.

79. Tapio Vaisanen, Dale Hawkins Discography, available on-line at http://www.pcuf.fi/~tapiov/discographies/dalehawkins.html.

80. Phil Carson, *Roy Buchanan: American Axe* (San Francisco: Backbeat Books, 2001), 42.

81. *New York Times*, July 21, 1957.

82. For Hawkins's appearance on *American Bandstand*, see http://www.tv.com/american bandstand/show/2034/episode_guide.html.

83. Dale Hawkins interview by Dave Anderson, February 4, 2006. Although Hawkins complains that he was left to promote "Susie-Q" on his own, he also admits that he and Burton shared an understanding that Burton could play for anyone he wanted. Burton, says Hawkins, was by no means "exclusively mine." Dale Hawkins, telephone conversation with Lesley-Anne Reed, August 3, 2006. Two weeks after playing on "Susie-Q," Burton was in Dallas for a recording session with Bob Luman, who Burton had been backing regularly on the *Hayride* since the first week of February. Bill Millar, liner notes, various artists, *That'll Flat Git It*, Vol. 12 (Compact Disc; Imperial Records/Bear Family Records: BCD 16102: 1998). For Burton's decision to leave Hawkins and his subsequent moves to Luman's band and then Ricky Nelson's band, see Escott, "James Burton"; Steve Fishell, "James Burton: First Call for the Royalty of Rockabilly," *Guitar Player* (June 1984), 88–101; Joel Selvin, *Ricky Nelson: Idol for a Generation* (Chicago: Contemporary Books, 1990), 76–77.

84. Millar, liner notes, *Rock 'n' Roll Tornado*, 6–7.

85. "Baby, Baby"/"Mrs. Merguitory's Daughter" (Checker 876); "Little Pig"/"Tornado" (Checker 892).

86. Dale Hawkins, "La-Do-Dada"/"Crossties" (Checker 900, 1958); Millar, liner notes, *Rock 'n' Roll Tornado*, 7–8; Carson, *Roy Buchanan*, 42; Koda, liner notes, *Oh! Suzy-Q*; Coleman, "Repeating Echoes with Dale Hawkins," 16; Bill Millar, liner notes, various artists, *That'll Flat Git It*, Vol. 10 (Compact Disc; Chess Records/Bear Family Records: BCD 16123: 1999), 36–38. The brother team of Dean and Marc Mathis, originally from Georgia who were playing clubs on the Bossier Strip at the time, also participated on the "La-Do-Dada" session. The Mathis brothers would have a minor hit record in 1959 with "Tell Him No" as Dean and Marc, and would later have a #2 pop hit in 1964 with "Bread and Butter" as members of the vocal trio, the Newbeats. Millar, liner notes, various artists, *That'll Flat Git It*, Vol. 10, 29–32.

The Life and Times of Dandy Don Logan

—Don Logan

This is an edited version of Logan's experiences with Shreveport radio and record companies, most notably as a popular Top 40 DJ on the 50,000-watt Shreveport station KEEL and as an employee with Stan Lewis's record companies in the 1960s and 1970s. The full version of Logan's life story may be found at his personal website [http://www. dandydonlogan.com], which includes links to local radio stations and entertainment venues, family photos dating back to the late 1930s, and personal recollections of figures as diverse as Frank Sinatra, Jimmie Davis, Tillman Franks, and Cajun humorist and chef Justin Wilson.

This version focuses on the late 1950s into the early 1970s, the era of his greatest involvement, and includes his reflections on the symbiotic relationships between radio, record companies, and live performance. In one longer section, he discusses Paula Records, particularly in relation to its artist John Fred and His Playboy Band, whose "Judy in Disguise [With Glasses]" entered the charts on December 16, 1967; by January 20, it had supplanted the Beatles' "Hello Goodbye" as the number one record on the U.S. charts.

Logan also recounts his experience with radio station XERF, the Mexican/U.S. border station that employed him (via transcribed programs) during the early 1960s. Border radio comprises one of media history's most colorful chapters. In many ways, it has a spiritual father in W. K. Henderson, whose eclectic, eccentric, and illegally powerful KWKH blanketed the middle of the United States during the late 1920s. Border radio plagued U.S. station owners across the country in much the same way Gordon McLendon's "pirate" radio station NORD blasted England and northern Europe in the late 1960s. Logan's reminiscences include interactions with fellow DJ Bob Smith, who later became an icon of the era with his radio and film persona "Wolfman Jack," and he remembers other important Shreveport

DJs like Gay Poppa and B. B. Davis who broadcast over the influential black station KOKA.

Although he was born near Stockton, California, in 1937, Don Logan grew up in mostly small towns in Oklahoma, Georgia, West Virginia, Arkansas, and Minnesota, as his father struggled to support his family during the final years of the Great Depression. Logan played music in the various schools he attended during his peripatetic father's quest for employment. Logan's disc jockey interests grew out of his musical interests and he landed his first radio gig in 1952 on KTCS, a Fort Smith, Arkansas, daytime-only station where he served as a jack-of-all-trades. Following a short stint at Eastern Oklahoma State College as a music major, he dropped out and worked in a succession of increasingly more powerful stations in increasingly larger towns. By 1954 Logan found work in the Dallas/Fort Worth market at a time when rock-and-roll radio and the "Top 40" format was in its infancy. Radio great Gordon McLendon, who formed one of the country's largest stable of stations in the decades following World War II, heard him on the air in Dallas, which resulted in a job offer at his station in Shreveport, KEEL.

When Logan was hired by the McLendon Corporation, their stations included KLIF in Dallas, KILT in Houston, KTSA in San Antonio, WAKY in Louisville, Kentucky, KABL in San Francisco, and KEEL in Shreveport, Louisiana. Logan replaced Ron Baxley in Shreveport and worked under program director Al Hart, who went on to become a radio icon in the San Francisco and Los Angeles markets. In [1956] Logan became the program director at KEEL and was responsible for breaking many top artists and records.

Shreveport Radio

When I came to Shreveport, DJs like Bill Randle, Alan Freed, and Dick Clark had already paved the way for rock-and-roll on radio and TV. Hollywood discovered rock and roll in 1955. *Blackboard Jungle* featured "Rock Around the Clock" and because of the movie, it became the first rock-and-roll tune to reach number one on the charts. Gordon McLendon and Todd Storz had invented Top 40 radio and the jocks who had been at KEEL before me made the station number one in the market. They put a lady named Marie Gifford in as manager and she was top-drawer all the way.

One of the first shows I did in Shreveport was in partnership with Mira Smith and Margaret Lewis Warwick. We did a show at Fort Humbug, the National Guard Armory in Shreveport. I didn't have my radio fan base together yet and the show was a flop. Maggie was a local favorite and was responsible for what crowd we had. I also had Mitch and the Misties on the program. The building had a sheet iron roof and the reverberation was terrible and the sound was inaudible. John Fred and the Playboys also did a guest appearance.

Mira and Maggie were to become very successful songwriters. Later, Maggie was associated with some of the top names in the business, like Connie Francis, among others. Maggie Lewis Warwick is back in Shreveport and is currently active in developing the Shreveport music scene. John Fred [Gourrier] went on to have a number one single with Paula Records. The hit made a lucrative contract with UNI records in Hollywood possible. I, along with "Major" Bill Smith, produced a song called "Hey Baby" by Mitch and the Misties; however, the composer of the song, Bruce Channel, had the big hit with the tune. I never booked another show or group into the armory again, but my luck changed and I did have many successful shows and dances later.

My biggest flop found me in the background. One of my business partners, Jiving Gene, did a two-show deal with James Brown, the Godfather of Soul [1962]. The show was in conjunction with Sonrose Rutledge who was known as "Gay Poppa" on the air. James Brown and the Famous Flames did the show for Gay Poppa and KOKA, but refused to do the show we had booked for KEEL listeners. Gene was stuck with the unpopular task of refunding money to disgruntled fans on the steps of the Municipal Auditorium.

At KEEL radio, we had a deal with A. V. Bamford out of Texas for some Sunday package shows at the Shreveport Municipal Auditorium [1957]. Since Shreveport was midway between Dallas and New Orleans, we got a good deal, price-wise, and the shows were always sold out. Usually, we would have to add a second show. The shows would feature about six or seven good acts and a top-selling star. On one of these shows, we had Little Brenda Lee who was hot as a pistol with such hits as "Sweet Nothings" and others.

I was to introduce Brenda on stage. Jerry Lee Lewis was visiting backstage and was not on the program. But the Bamford rep, a guy named Eddie, wanted me to bring out Jerry Lee Lewis just before Brenda. I knew that I did not want to do this. You don't put a tornado like Jerry Lee out on stage in front of the star. Jerry Lee had been down on his luck. That was back when radio involuntarily boycotted him as he had received so much bad press from his marriage to his teen-aged cousin. That was not the reason our station and others were not playing him; he really did not have any new hits at the time. But he did have that tremendous string of hits before the sky collapsed on him. So Jerry Lee needed some good press and wanted to impress the Bamford people. I told Dub Albritton, Brenda's manager, that I was going to bring out the "Killer" before Brenda. He got angry. Brenda said, "O.K. Let's see what he can do." I introduced Jerry Lee. The audience was not expecting him, so he received a minimal amount of applause as the audience really didn't know who he was. Then, he went into his basket of hits and did five of his hottest numbers. The audience knew the songs, and it had dawned on them that this was Jerry Lee Lewis on stage. Jerry brought the house down and then walked off the stage.

I had the impossible job of trying to calm the audience enough to let Brenda come on stage. I went out but the crowd was not to be calmed. I realized that I had pulled a boo-boo, and for once in my life, I did not know what the hell to do. I tried to calm the audience and get Brenda introduced. Then, out of the corner of my eye, I saw Brenda Lee walking out on stage. She changed the order of tunes with the band and made "Sweet Nothings" her lead number. I quickly introduced her as the "Star of the Show," she grabbed my microphone, and by the time she was four measures into the number, the crowd had forgotten all about Jerry Lee, and they were giving her one of the most tremendous ovations one could receive. She went on to do one of the greatest shows she has ever done. She earned my respect that day, as a true professional entertainer. When she left the stage that Sunday, the crowd was jubilant and they wanted an encore from Brenda Lee. I took the stage and played around with the audience for about five minutes, teasing them that Brenda was too tired for an encore and built them up to a fever pitch before I gave them what they wanted—an encore from the "Star of the Show," Brenda Lee. She received rave reviews in both the Shreveport *Times* and the *Shreveport Journal*. Jerry Lee also received a nice mention, and Bamford did book him several times after he proved that he could still move an audience.

During my greatest success at KEEL radio, the general manager was the late Marie Gifford-Wright. She was also heard on the air with stimulating editorials, and she was very imaginative, coming up with great on and off the air promotions. LIN Broadcasting owned the station at the time and they thought highly of her. Ms. Gifford-Wright was well versed in the theatre, and everything she does, she does with a flair—whether it was selling the image of her radio station to a New York ad firm or a bunch of Chicago media moguls or telling the story at a dinner shortly before her death of how she hired a young

Midwesterner named Larry Ryan. She told the story with such drama, I wrote a song about it. When she died, I put it aside, but may release it at a later date. Also to her credit, she was the first female manager of a 50,000-watt station in the great Southwest. She also ran for mayor of Shreveport, Louisiana.

Incidentally, when WHER, a 1000-watt radio station went on the air in Memphis, Tennessee [started in 1955 by Sun record owner, Sam Phillips], I thought that format would become a national trend, but it never happened. This station featured all female announcers. The station had Dot Abbott and Marion Keisker, the first lady to swoon over Elvis when she worked at Sun Records. Totally female stations never became a trend like black radio did. Instead, we do have a vast array of talented females in the mainstream now.

Border Radio

(KEEL was the solid number one station in the market. However, a guy named Larry Brandon came in with a station and tried to knock off KEEL. The KENT frequency had gone dark and Brandon revived it, calling it KREB.)

Brandon was tenacious and played dirty pool. He put a jock opposite me named Dan DeVille. Thank goodness the listeners loved and stuck with Dandy Don.

(Larry and his crew waged a good battle with some McLendon-type promotions, but failed to topple the giant and their station went off the air with the call letters going to a station in Monroe, Louisiana. Larry just could not get his act together [1960]. Brandon then bought all the nighttime hours available on the legendary 250,000-watt XERF in Mexico, from 6:00 P.M. to 6:00 A.M.)

Brandon was a hard ball business man, but a nice guy and I felt bad about beating him in the ratings races. We had crippled his attack by hiring his best two jocks, Bill Berkey and Johnny Mitchell, away from him. So, I, Buddy Blake, and a guy named Bob Smith, who worked for daytime station KCIJ, started recording radio shows on those big ten-inch, one-hour tapes and Larry mailed them down to Attorney Arturo Gonzalez, who would transport them on down to the station, and they would be on the air within the week. Larry had kicked all the preachers off the air down there, so he needed six fresh hours of entertainment daily for the first month they were on the air and then he would start repeating some of the tapes.

The XERF signal got into Shreveport good on a clear night, and this became a problem for both Buddy and me, as we both worked at KEEL. We were sort of competing with ourselves, so I started doing my taped programs in the voice of E. Peabody Rasmussen, a gravely voiced announcer I created. Buddy and I only had a limited amount of time to cut our tapes as we were a full-time station. Bob, working for a daytime station, had from 6:00 P.M. to 6:00 A.M. to record the tapes. Trying to provide six hours of programming nightly for XERF was stressful and caused Buddy to lose his job at KEEL. He joined Shelby Singleton in the record business.

Bob Smith started doing a gravely voiced character of "Wolfman Jack" and added a HOWL that would catch a dead man's attention. I always called him Bob and I kidded him one time by saying, "That howl of yours would wake a dead man and that dead man might be Hank Williams and he, sure as hell, does not want you 'Howling at the Moon.'" The "Wolfman" voice and persona took off and soon Wolfman had to be the biggest thing to ever happen on border radio. Prior to this time, these stations had been strictly religion and country. Wolfman was neither of these. In my radio career, I always included in my Top 40 programming a sound for my Milam street audience. I may have been young, but I knew, even back then, that all my listeners were not young, white teenagers. I had black listeners and my white audience was usually a little older, as I slipped in some big band, easy listening, and country. I could have never been a shock jock as my upbringing just wouldn't allow it. I think Wolfman was the first of the so-called shock jocks with his phrase, "Let's get NAKED."

I was not doing any more tapes for Larry after they offered an autographed picture of Jesus on the air. When I worked in Fort Worth, Ed Hamilton had told me about the working situation from the studios of XERF and I knew that I would never want to have to go down there to work. I also had a top-paying job at KEEL and I wasn't about to leave, but Bob decided to go, as there was no way to keep up the programming by tapes anymore. Doing the show live really brought the Wolfman to life. His voice and delivery and funny stuff blossomed. However, business-wise, Larry and Wolfman had many problems there. Wolfman's new car had bullet holes in it, according to Tommy Moore, and the station at one time was taken over by Mexican banditos who came riding in on burros and firing rifle shots. Needless to say, Bob and Larry split the Mexican scene. Wolfman went to Minnesota and then California where he became a super jock, TV personality, and movie star, and Larry wound up with a chain of stations with headquarters in Buffalo, New York.

The most successful program I ever had after Wolfman left was a record package program that came on just after "The Rev Ike" on XERF. The listening audience Rev. Ike built up and left for me was astronomical. Border radio had a unique way of collecting the money owed them. At first, in the old days, you had to pay for the time in advance. Later as their popularity declined, they would decrease the wattage during your broadcast time, if you were not current with your payments. In other words, you didn't get the full wattage on your program if you weren't paying the bill. They also used a directional signal, even though they were clear channel. They could pinpoint the eastern states when the local daytime stations would be going off the air. A smart programmer would buy more than one segment of air time, so his program could get maximum exposure. Arturo Gonzales was in Del Rio, Texas, and he was the man I dealt with after Wolfman had long gone. Hoss Allen and Bill Mack also did programs from there. The transmitter was actually in Ciudad Acuña, Coahuila, Mexico.

Wolfman was not the only phenomenal thing I witnessed in my lifetime. I once worked for Gordon McLendon. He had a radio station transmitter on an ocean liner known as the pirate station in international waters off the coast of England. The English have always liked rock-and-roll, and McLendon gave it to them. They began by using tape-recorded shows by some of us DJs here in the U.S. who worked for their various stations, but later went with live DJs. England tried many ways to put a stop to their broadcasting, and I think in the end did, but the signal was there for quite some time and, who knows, probably influenced the Beatles and the Rolling Stones.

Jewel-Paula and the Record Business

Bobby Charles and Dale Hawkins worked for the label for very short periods of time before I came on a part-time basis [in the mid-1960s]. Bobby was a singer and songwriter, having written several songs for Fats Domino. The first record Jewel put out was by Bobby Charles, and the label was then distributed by Chess records. Bobby was more interested in promoting himself, rather than a label, so he soon departed. Dale Hawkins and Stan [Lewis] had produced and written the song "Susie Q" for Chess Records in 1957, on which Dale did the vocal. Dale stayed for a while with the label, but there was no big budget to feed off back then, so he left. He was the one who introduced me to John Fred before John started making records for Jewel.

When we released "Not Too Long Ago" on Paula, the label had no design, just the letters PAULA across the top. The record charted, and the Dick Clark office called wanting the Uniques to do *American Bandstand*. His coordinator called back and asked me how many girls were in the group. I told him the group was a male band; however, there were girl background voices, so we found ourselves in much the same dilemma as Buddy Killen did when he had the group, the Little Dippers, an instrumental studio group who had background singers on their hit record "Forever." The Clark office perceived the group as similar to the Fleetwoods. We thought about adding the girls for the show, as Killen had done with his group, but the Uniques said "no" to that, and they appeared on *Bandstand* without the female background singers.

As we started growing, one of my early tasks was designing the Paula and Jewel labels. My original Paula label had a pinkish background, and the black label copy overprint could print the DJ copies and the stock copies, making it more economical and efficient than most labels. The model for the label silhouette was Pauline Taglavore Lewis, Stan's wife. My favorite was the blue-tinted Jewel label, even though the white DJ copies looked a little one sided. When we started the Ronn label, I may have made a mistake by using the full top half of the label for the sig and logo. Excessive label copy did make the finished label look crowded. But most people liked it, so it was left that way until just recently, when all three labels were redone by the new owners and they now have today's look.

In my DJ capacity, I started doing local dances with John Fred and the Playboys and the Uniques. They were super successful. The first dance that I was involved with in Shreveport was a flop, and the second with Bobby Powell was a near disaster with the musicians local not letting Bobby's band on stage because none of the musicians had valid union cards. Dale Hawkins's brother Jerry and Bob Hogan, the vice-president and president of the Shreveport Musicians local were on my back for every show and dance I booked from that time on. The next, a Bo Diddley dance, was a huge success. Al Hart was at the door taking admission money when a kid showed up in blue jeans, saying I had told him to come by and he could do a couple of songs with Bo's band. Since we were crowded, we had already decided not to let anybody in for half price or leave the door unattended during the last thirty minutes of the dance. The dance was a smash, and we wanted to make every buck we could. We weren't greedy, just trying to make up for past losses. So, Al had decided that this was some guy trying to get in for free and was turning him away from the door when Vern Stierman and I walked by. Vern recognized Roy Orbison and invited him on in, and we let him do several songs for the crowd. He received no pay, as I remember. He was in town and just wanted to play for a crowd.

I have always thought that rock-and-roll began back when the big bands played "In the Mood" and the jitterbug became the exciting dance of the day. When economics caught up with the big bands, they disbanded. They never tried to do it with a smaller unit. Being an old clarinet player, I have always liked horns. When I met John Fred, I thought that his band, being a horn band, had something that would go. Now it's true, everybody was a four-piece group like the Beatles back then, but I really thought John's bigger group had tremendous potential. John never knew it, but many people knew of him outside of the region where he was hot. The group known as the Boogie Kings got most of the credit for what John was doing in the beginning. This happened mainly because, prior to his coming with us at Paula, the Boogie Kings had wider representation, and they were getting credit for things Fred had done. With our national distribution, when people talked about the horn band down in Louisiana, we said, "Sure, that's John Fred and the Playboy Band." The one thing I didn't realize and John didn't realize until the hit "Judy in Disguise" was that it is hard to transport a group the size of his band around the country. They were smaller than the big bands of old, but it was still a major job keeping everyone accounted for on the road.

The one thing I could never understand about the record industry was why there were no limits to the number of records a dealer or distributor could return for full credit. The record company is out the expense of the artists' sessions, which kept getting larger and larger back then and has probably quadrupled by now. The record company is out the expense of production, packaging, and promotion. The dealers, distributors, and wholesalers have no risk, they return all unsold merchandise and laugh all the way to the bank. The returns could bankrupt a small company that was just starting up. Of course, most of this expense is charged back to the artist and recouped. That is not a rule I made up; that is the rule you have to go by if you are going to stay in business because that's what the industry does. We worked long and hard for the big hit "Judy in Disguise." It happened at the end of John Fred's recording contract with us, and I felt John would stay with us because we had really worked on our groups. Instead, UNI records, a division of Universal Films, offered him more money that we did, and Fred went with them. I have not seen John since we spent twelve hours one night in 1968, negotiating a new contract with our attorneys Marvin Katz, Mike Meyer, and C. P. Brocato and John's attorney, Harold Lipsius. I was never more frustrated than I was at the end of that session. I knew John would be leaving us, and I thought it was very unfair. It's like the words to a Peggy Lee record, "Is That All There Is to That"?

The horse that we had ridden to the Carson Show and the top of the charts was going to another stable. That was the first time I thought about leaving the record business. I had heard all of our artists, including John, when he was hungry for that hit, ask us to "please get me a hit" or "put another record out on me quickly while I'm still hot from the last one." We did not force our groups to record songs that I wrote or Stan wrote; we gave them the artistic freedom to come up with their own creative hits. Of course, we had our own publishing company and we did like to publish our releases.

(In 1967, Logan became a vice-president of the Jewel-Paula Record complex. Over the next ten years, he directed, produced, wrote songs, signed artists, you name it . . . he did it.)

Deep in my heart, I would like to discover a bright new young talent and unleash that talent on the music world. It is a great rush, to take a chance on new talent. I know what my talent is and it is limited, but new talent, not yet stereotyped, can run the gamut and full circle of music. When I was vice-president of Paula Records, I enjoyed the release of a new artist's material. The adrenalin would start flowing. I enjoyed signing these new artists and once had a chance to sign a singing pig. No, you read right, a singing pig, complete with an overall-wearing manager. This pig could oink out "Sitting on the Dock of the Bay" perfectly. It was a great live act, but I could never figure out how to make it sell on record. Plus, at that time, it was hard enough to get a DJ to play a record by a human being, much less a pig. Anyway, the pig probably would have claimed I used coercion to sign her up and didn't pay her royalties and would hire a Philadelphia music-attorney to sue us, so I took the easy way out and opted not to sign the pig and never even called it to Stan's attention. Incidentally, "Sitting on the Dock of the Bay" was the only tune she knew.

When I was with Paula Records, we paid our artists the royalties due them, but many felt they got shortchanged. When an artist hears his product on radio, TV, cable, or the movies, he always thinks the sales are bigger than what they are. This is natural and part of an artist's self-esteem. Our Paula distributor in Miami, Tone Records, was owned by a guy named Henry Stone. Stone saw our success with the Playboys when "Judy" became number one across America, and we sold a million 45 RPM records. When disco came in, Stone formed T. K. Records. K. C. and the Sunshine Band had many hit records for his label. The first time I heard one of their records, I thought that K. C. sounded like John Fred Gourrier, who was the vocalist on our Paula hit "Judy." However, I'm told that the lead voice was actually that of Harry Casey. Casey claimed that Stone shortchanged him by ten million dollars. That's one thing

I don't have to contend with and don't want to contend with. I will stay small and do what I want to as long as a few people like it and continue to buy it.

On January 27, 1968, the number one song in the nation was "Judy in Disguise" by John Fred and the Playboy Band, Paula 282. We took the group to New York to appear on the Johnny Carson show which was being telecast from Radio City Music Hall. Though I was not allowed in the NBC control room during the broadcast, they did give the following credit at the end of the program: "Technical assistance for Mr. Fred and the Playboy Band" provided by Paula Records." The elation I felt during this time would never be equaled in my record company career. It was like going to your senior prom dressed up in a tuxedo. Years later, Ronnie Lewis [Stan's brother], who was with me for that trip, agreed that this was a most special time for all of us involved with the record label. Incidentally, the week we were number one in *Billboard*, *Cashbox*, and *Record World* magazines, the Beatles were number six with "Hello Goodbye" and the Monkees were number eight with "Daydream Believer." "Judy in Disguise" was the only million seller on the label.

The record business was a potpourri of individuals, both good and bad. I always tried to be the good guy, but sometimes you had to flex your muscles. Stan Lewis was once threatened by Don Robey of Duke-Peacock over a group called the Carter Brothers and Buddy Ace. He said something about putting Stan in a box. Robey disliked us intensely and badmouthed us every chance he had. "Major" Bill Smith, a former associate and friend of mine, threatened to put a contract out on me when I signed J. Frank Wilson, the guy who did "Last Kiss," to a Paula contract, unaware that J. Frank was still under contract to Bill. In an industry that was slow to pay, it was common to resort to threats of violence. Usually, the threats were just that. Others like Morris Levy (we called him "Moishe") wound up in jail. Levy inspired more fear than any other single record mogul in the industry. Nat Tarnopol of Brunswick Records was acquitted on thirty-eight counts of fraud and the conspiracy count on which he was found guilty was later overturned. Nate McCalla never made it to court. He just died under mysterious circumstances and some writer once called all of us in the record business at the time a bunch of cutthroats who cheated everybody out of everything they could, every time they could, every way they could. That remark never bothered me. I knew the reference was not about us.

In the record business, I did just about everything I wanted to do before I got out of it. I had worked so long in the background that I was hesitant about doing something in the forefront. I did actively operate my record labels for a time, but without the enthusiasm of Stan Lewis, I found no personal satisfaction in it. When I started singing the old songs for the people who enjoy hearing them again, I discovered that old sense of urgency and excitement that radio and the record business used to bring me. With the worldwide web, the Internet can be that answer to finding and discovering fresh new talent and quenching the thirst that the public must once again have, as they did back in the 1950s, for something different. I must confess that all radio stations pretty much sound alike to me and even the music sounds the same. Just like we did at Paula Records, creative talent should be unchained, freeing the creative spirit to be innovative.

The Logan Mansion

(After he departed Jewel-Paula Records [1971], Logan tried a comeback in local radio.)

When I attempted a comeback in radio, I was hired to be the operations manager of KCOZ by Jim Reeder, the owner. The station was a good music station that had fallen on hard times ratings-wise. Their studios were in the Logan Mansion. It was a wonderful place to work and had been somewhat refurbished at 725 Austin Place, a one-block-long street. It was built in 1897 for around $15,000 by Colonel Lafayette Robert Logan for his wife, Lavinia "Libby" Wilson Seay Logan. They were prominent citizens of Shreveport. Prior to my being hired by the radio station housed within its walls, they had always used the tag line, "Music from the Logan Mansion."

When I came back to radio, FM was the thing. And there was an overabundance of youthful talent on radio. You had Jeff Edmond and Melinda Coyer at a new station, started by my fellow co-worker Billy Wilson, who pulled off a ratings coup. That team was probably the most popular radio show ever in the market and Melinda is still doing great things. TV news had Liz Swain and Al Pierce or Carl Pendley and Karen Adams, and they would have been tops in any market. I had aged and no longer had youth to fall back on; however, I did manage to work up to the program manager job at KCOZ, the last remaining good music station in the market. I brought it back to a number 4 overall rating in the market, but it was not good enough. They changed the station format to urban and my radio comeback attempt ended.

(Logan also formed his own production company. He booked bands and emceed shows by such stars as Paul Revere and the Raiders, the Monkees, the Uniques, Swinging Medallions, Willie Mitchell, Dave Clark Five, the Rolling

Stones, Sam the Sham, and other hot groups in the Shreveport area. He also owned Cabriolet Music, Cord Record Corporation, and the Cal and Memorial Records.)

Radio Yesterday and Today

As I listen to radio today, I hear a similarity to what we did in the old days. The talent is youthful and their talent probably exceeds that of ours. The troubling thing is, not all stations feature live DJs. A lot of the programming is via satellite. That is not to say it is not good, because it is, but it is not local programming.

I remain thankful for a guy named Martin Block who, in the 1930s, played records on the airwaves on his *Make Believe Ballroom*. Phonograph records were mostly manufactured for home use on the old Edison and Victrola phonographs of the day. It was not until after World War II that radio stations started playing phonograph records on the air with any consistency, and that gave birth to the personality radio jock. When this happened, recording techniques started to change and quality became more important and the record industry broke wide open.

I was also in radio at a time when "Black Radio" expanded to dominance. Black radio first flexed its muscle when Patti Page released, "How Much Is That Doggie in the Window." The tremendous initial sales came from the black DJ playing this record on his show in Brooklyn. The record was a smash in New York, and the power of the black jock escalated from that time. During my stint in the record world, I remember E. Rodney Jones, Ernie Durham, Hamp Swain, B. B. Davis, and Sonrose Rutledge.

I am happy to have been a part of radio in my youth. I will always cherish having been in the same company as Dick Biondi, Murray "The K" Kauffman, Ron Baxley, George Klein, Bruce Morrow, Jim Lowe, Rusty Reynolds, Art Roberts, Hoss Allen, Bob and Ray, George "Hound Dog" Lorenz, Gene Nobles, Bruce Nelson, Moon Mullins, Dan Ingram, John R. Richbourg, and Wolfman Jack. I am glad that a couple of guys named Todd Storz and Gordon McLendon saved radio with their idea of Top 40 radio. That phrase is no longer used, but I can hear it in just about any radio format I listen to these days.

I knew from playing music in bands that rock-and-roll was a crowd pleaser. If it moved a live dance audience, it could also move a captive radio audience. So, when I was contemplating becoming a rock-and-roll DJ, I was aware of what had happened to personalities like Bob Horn, the predecessor of Dick Clark, and as the big payola scandal broke, I saw DJ giants like Alan Freed tumble and fall. I always played it straight in radio. I attended many music conventions in the record business, but I never went to a DJ convention as a DJ. So you might say I missed out on the booze, broads, and bribes. I just believed in what I was doing, and I really liked most of the music. I still enjoy listening to my collection of old scratchy 45s and the few 78s that I possess. It's true that the quality we have today is not in the grooves of these recordings, but these gems possess the feelings of an era that will never return. If I sing one of the old songs on stage today, it will sound like the music of today, because of the up-to-date equipment and sound we now have. The only way to hear that raw, original sound is in the grooves of the old vinyl recordings. Even when you release those songs on a CD or other sound form, it does not sound the way it sounded on vinyl.

Shreveport Southern Soul

The Murco Story

—John Ridley

Smaller and lesser known than any of Stan Lewis's labels, the short-lived Murco label is important because it documented the Shreveport soul scene. Murco's roots were in the Bayou Records store, a retail outlet purchased by local businessman Dee Marais from Shelby Singleton in 1960. In addition to selling records, Marais occasionally recorded local musicians in the back of his store.

The first few years in the 1960s brought uncertain times to Shreveport's music scene, as the city, like the rest of the United States, struggled through an increasingly confrontational Civil Rights Movement, the assassination of President Kennedy, and the escalation of the Cold War. Following the closing of the RAM studio in 1962, the city lacked a full-service recording studio for several years. Local musicians during this period had little opportunity to record a commercial 45 that might gain them airplay and exposure, or even sales to local audiences during gigs.

Although Shreveport never developed as contentious a Civil Rights environment as that in the Mississippi Delta, racial clashes were not uncommon during the mid-1960s. The year 1963 was particularly difficult in Shreveport because of the "Little Union Incident" that brought racial tensions to the fore. On September 22, riot-geared police arrested several local black clergy who were preparing to lead a protest march from the Little Union Baptist Church. The unnecessarily violent confrontation led to weeks of unrest and walkouts. On October 8, Police Commissioner George D'Artois ordered the arrest of legendary soul singer Sam Cooke and his band when they tried to register at the local Holiday Inn. This public encounter added further fuel to the growing fire of tension.

It was during these uncertain times that Dee Marais began to think about starting a record company. Still a few more years passed before the commercial success of soul music, notably that issued by Stax, convinced Marais that a local label for soul talent might be a business success. Between 1967 and 1973, he released approximately thirty soul or soul-oriented releases, mostly on Murco but with a handful appearing on the allied labels H-Sign and Peermont. His efforts included selections by local legends like Eddie Giles and Dori Grayson. Marais's efforts halted in 1973 due to his frustration with the industry and growing distraction by other business interests. This essay first appeared in 2000 as the notes to *The Murco Story*, Kent CDKEND 178.

The Man and His Labels

Murco and the other labels that form this compilation were the vehicles used by Dee Marais to bring his music to the public. From his base in Shreveport, Louisiana, like so many other southern record men, Marais issued most types of music from gospel through country to rock-and-roll. But between 1967 and 1973 he concentrated largely on soul, and this CD contains the best of his output from those years.

This was essentially a down-home operation in the best sense of the phrase. Marais ran a local outlet for local talent, often using local studios and musicians. There aren't many big stars here but several of the 45s have enjoyed excellent reputations among fans of southern soul for many years. This is the first time the vast majority of these tracks have ever been reissued, and the fact that they have stood the test of time so well is a tribute to the TLC that Marais put into his productions and the quality of the material.

Harding Guyon DesMarais was born in Minnesota of French stock and became Dee Marais at the suggestion of Jimmy C. Newman who felt his real name was rather too much of a mouthful. He started his career in music on the country side writing the smash hit "Poor Man's Riches" for Benny Barnes in 1956. He also did promotional and distribution work all over the South in the '50s for labels like Chess and Old Town and tried his hand at recording both rock-and-roll and R&B at the end of the decade but without real success.

Having introduced Shelby Singleton to the music business, he bought Singleton's Bayou record shop in Shreveport in 1960, and it was from this settled base that his productions really started. Murco was founded in partnership with Dick Martin who worked locally for the U.S. Postal Service. Early releases recorded under his Heads Up production company were country angled mostly, but as the '60s wore on, the neighborhood around East 70th Street where the shop was located changed character as more and more blacks moved in. Marais, who was familiar with and liked black music, reflected this change by recording increasing amounts of gospel-based styles and artists. As time went on, other labels wholly owned by Marais were introduced: Hy-Sign for soul, Hy-Tree for country, Hy-Rock for other white styles, Hy-Sign Gospel for religious music, and Peermont as a general label. As ever, mostly music makers from the Shreveport district were featured, with distribution either by Marais himself or his neighbor Stan Lewis.

With the contraction of the music industry into the hands of larger concerns through the '70s, Marais, like so many of the older style record men, was less active, and he closed the Bayou record shop in 1978. These days Marais has returned to one of his early musical loves—the big-band sound—and is still involved in the recording scene. He is currently trying to discuss new ventures with smooth, cool star Harry Connick Jr.

But his productions from the classic soul period are what concern us here, and the fact that he is remembered so fondly by his artists is a tribute to his straight dealings and honest approach. In an era, for example, when so many soul 45s had dubious writing credits, all Marais's 45s pay proper dues to the actual people who penned the songs. And I think that says as much about Dee Marais the man as his music says about his talents.

The Singers and the Songs

Eddy Giles

By far the most successful of Marais's artists was Elbert W. Giles, who was born in March 1938. A native of Shreveport, he sang in local gospel groups like the Humming Bees in his youth, and he and Marais knew each other from the late '50s. However it wasn't till 1967 that Eddy agreed to make a secular recording, but it was well worth the wait. "Losing Boy" was cut at the Robin Hood Brians studio just across the state line in Tyler, Texas, and its lively rhythm and approach was completely at odds with self pity of the lyric. Helped by a meandering, almost jaunty tenor sax, Eddy's positive vocal also helped dispel any gloom.

It sold very well straight away from release, with the Dallas area alone accounting for 10,000 sales, and Marais turned to his neighbor Stan Lewis for better distribution. "Losing Boy" was a big regional seller and registered for five weeks on the *Cashbox* hot 100 in the spring.

The follow-up "Don't Let Me Suffer" was rather too similar to the hit for inclusion here. But the flip "While I'm Away (Baby Keep the Faith)," another of those Soul-in-Vietnam songs, was a line ballad, given greater weight by the delicious extra vocal by Charles Brown and a sparse horn section. This track was also used as the flip to the disappointing "Eddy's Go Go Train" a few months later. But for deep soul fans Eddy's next release "Happy Man" was his best yet, with a really committed vocal over a classic chord progression and a soulful organ. "Love with a Feeling" carried on the mood, after a splendidly sanctified opening, and had a lovely bluesy feel to the horns. His next 45, "Soulful Feeling", was a rather messy funk item, but in the strutting southern groove of "Ain't Gonna Worry No More" Eddy was right back to peak form.

His final 45 for Dee Marais coupled the O. V. Wright deep soul standard "That's How Strong My Love Is" with the upbeat "So Deep in Love." This was cut at Shreveport's premier studio Sound City but instead of a Murco release, Dee leased the masters to Shelby Singleton, who in turn placed them with Leland Rogers's Silver Fox concern in the summer of 1969. The ballad has one of Eddy's very best vocals on it, and we're delighted to be able to include an extra few seconds of the ad-libbed run-out groove where he really cuts loose. Lovely!

Eddy joined the Bobby Patterson/Jerry Strickland partnership and recorded enough material at Sound City for an LP. One 45, a recut of "Losing Boy" and a typically humorous "It Takes Me All Night" was leased to Stax, and a second came out on Alarm, the label they owned with Stewart Madison. This was the superb ballad "Married Lady" and an excellent Patterson/Strickland cheating number "Are You Living with the One You're Loving With," which also gained a U.K. release on Hit and Run. Although the other cuts from the period were never issued in the U.S., several were featured on a Japanese LP, *I'm a Losing Boy*, at the end of the decade. This quite brilliant album also featured a few cuts Eddy made for Allen Orange's House of Orange concern around '73/'74 but which remained in the can as well. Eddy's final secular recordings were a 45 for another local label, Custom Sound, in 1977. One side, "Sexy Lady," has had plays on the modern scene and is now well sought after.

Since then Eddy has returned to the church as a pastor in Shreveport and also acts as a gospel DJ on the local KOKA station. He remains grateful to Marais for his career as a solo artist, but is adamant that he won't cut any more non-Christian material. Our loss is the church's gain.

Dori Grayson

Dori is another local singer, who came to Marais's attention through the efforts of Willie James, a trained pianist and songwriter, and proved to be his most consistent female singer. His numbers for her first Murco 45 in '68, "Try Love" and "Got Nobody to Love," are worthy vehicles for her strong voice. In particular the toe-tapper "Try Love" swings very well, with an insidious hook that really sticks in the mind. "I Can Fix That for You" is almost as good, and the other side of her second 45, "Never Let Go," is a solid southern groover. The hard-driving "Sweet Lovin' Man" rocks along and the tuneful "Be Mine Sometime" completes a sextet of quality southern soul. These days Dori still lives locally and earns her living as a teacher.

Marcus Brown

James was also involved in Marcus Brown's blues ballad "I'm Coming Home." Although Marais didn't think much of his voice and only recorded and issued the one 45 at Brown's request, it deserves a better press—if only thanks to the fine lead guitarist.

Charles Crawford

Yet again, Willie James was the writer of Charles Crawford's celebrated "A Sad Sad Song." This is, of course, rightly hailed as a deep soul masterpiece, as Crawford takes his time to set the scene for his tale of woe, then in his rather Otis Redding–flavored way delivers an emotion-filled vocal over a sympathetic backdrop provided by the Sound City regulars led by drummer James Stroud—Southern soul in the classic 6/8 tempo, delivered in the grand manner. This cut is an undoubted highlight of this collection and should have been just the first of many such singles—but sadly this was not to be. Crawford, who now lives in Dallas and still does a little nightclub work every once in a while, only has this 45 to his name.

Reuben Bell

Arguably Reuben Bell was the most talented artist to work with Dee Marais. A first-class writer, he collaborated with Geater Davis, Bobby Patterson, Jerry Strickland, and others to leave an enduring canon of southern soul songs, and was also a splendidly gifted singer. His high tenor vocals were at their best, in my view, when extracting every ounce of emotion from those slow, often almost unbearably sad ballads he specialized in. His first 45, "It's Not That Easy," is a marvelous example of this, with its minor-keyed bluesy feel. Marais used his backing group to reinforce the mood on Bell's next release, "You're Gonna Miss Me," to excellent effect. That Bell could also handle more uptempo material well is demonstrated on the lively flip "Another Day Lost."

His final 45 for Marais, "It's Too Late Now" was perhaps the best of them all, an anguished vocal over a typically heartfelt Bell lyric. Like Eddy Giles's "That's How Strong My Love Is," this came out on Silver Fox but not before a brief issue on Murco. A great single ably backed by "Action Speaks Louder Than Words," which has had some plays on the Northern soul scene.

Bell moved on to Allen Orange at the end of the '60s and had a couple of 45s on his House of Orange logo, of which the best was "What's Happening to the World." Orange also leased four sides to Deluxe including the bluesy "All the Time" and "I Hear You Knocking." But Bell's best work in the '70s was for Alarm, who put out four outstanding 45s. "Asking for the Truth" was undoubtedly one of the deep highlights of the decade, and "I Still Have to Say Goodbye," his recut of Danny White's blues ballad "Kiss Tomorrow Goodbye" and "One-Sided Love Affair" weren't far behind it. After a longish gap, Bell resurfaced in 1982 with a first-class LP on the tiny Port City label in Shreveport, from which two 45s were lifted to heavy critical acclaim in Europe.

Bell still lives in the city—is it too much to hope that he might enter a recording studio again? In any event he deserves much wider appreciation for his vinyl efforts than he has received to date.

Ann Alford

Unlike almost everybody else showcased here Ann Alford was just passing through Shreveport with her man Don when she cut the sides for her only single with him. "If It Ain't One Thing (It's Another)" has a terrific funky feel with some tasty JB-style horns, and Ann's rather sassy vocal and "blue" phrasing fits it perfectly. "Got to Get Me a Job" is hardcore street funk, beautifully played by the Sound City boys, over which Ann chants and shrieks. It didn't do much at the time, but the strength of the disc has recently been recognized by the PBS in the locality who are using it as part of their educational program.

It's obvious that Ann was a good enough vocalist to have made a career in the music business, and indeed had already cut for Groove and Vik in the late '50s, but it seems her lifestyle wasn't settled enough for that to happen.

Abe and Marion Ester

Husband and wife team Abe and Marion Ester cut several singles for Marais in a variety of guises. The upbeat "That's Why I'm So Sad" and the charming, naïve "Let Me Be the Fool," both cut in Tyler in '67, are really Marion solos despite both names being on the label. Under her own name Marion cut the excellent "Not Guilty," long a cult deep soul favorite while Abe, as Abraham, had a series of funk singles such as "Hook and Boogie" and "Soul Power." Possibly the strongest of these, "Kangaroo," was leased to Wand who, according to Marais, so messed the tape up as to make the track virtually unlistenable—but still released it! The unissued ballad from him here, "Everyday," is well arranged but perhaps shows that vocally he was more suited to the funk side of things rather than the slowies.

Although they are now divorced, both Abe and Marion still live in the Shreveport locality.

The Final Words

Although the big labels like Stax and Atlantic were the most visible aspect of southern soul in the Golden Age, in my view it was the small labels that were its backbone. Often these were one-man operations, run by all-round music men, who not only wrote and produced music but also pressed, distributed, and promoted the records as well.

The high days of these entrepreneurs are now long gone but in the legacy of people like Dee Marais we have a rich and lasting body of the best music ever recorded. Murco and the other labels weren't huge concerns, but their products still give a great deal of enjoyment to discerning fans.

Eddie Giles and Reuben Bell

Synonymous with Shreveport

—John M. Shaw

John Shaw's piece draws well-deserved recognition to two musicians, Eddie Giles and Reuben Bell. Giles, a fixture on the Shreveport music scene since the mid-1950s, has combined secular and sacred music throughout his career. His musical beginnings in rock-and-roll soon turned to professional pursuits in gospel. He sang with the California-based Pilgrim Jubilee singers during the early 1960s. By mid-decade, he turned to soul and, from 1967 to 1977, made a series of highly sought-after soul records on three local labels (Murco, Alarm, and Custom Sound); he also recorded one release for the Stax label. Today, the Reverend Eddie Giles continues to perform, playing and recording with Shreveport's Ever-Ready Gospel Singers and others. In addition, he continues to broadcast over KOKA, a local black gospel radio station.

Reuben Bell is a more reticent, though significant figure among southern soul singers in Shreveport. His recording career began in the same year and on the same label as Giles, and continued sporadically until 1983, when he seems to have lost patience with the music industry. Along with another soul artist with Ark-La-Tex roots, Geater Davis, Bell appeared on the House of Orange label in 1971. He also recorded an album with local entrepreneur Roy Mahoney eleven or so years later, but his records never sold well. Thereafter, he made only rare public performances. Bell lived in or near Shreveport until his death in 2004, while living in Shreveport's Cedar Grove neighborhood.

Shreveport, Louisiana, a town some 240 miles northwest of the state capital in Baton Rouge, is but a mere twelve-mile hop from the Texas border. Over the years, Shreveport has become famous in soul music circles for Stan Lewis's Jewel-Paula-Ronn group of labels and distribution and a smaller group of labels owned by Dee Marais and Dick Martin, led by Murco. Acknowledging the latter, in 2000, Ace Records in Britain issued a compilation CD titled *Shreveport Southern Soul: The Murco Story* [Kent Soul CDKEND 178]. Of the twenty-six tracks, seven were credited to Eddie Giles [either as Eddy Giles, Eddy "G" Giles, or Eddy "G" Giles and the Jive Five] and five to Reuben Bell [as Reuben Bell, Reuben Bell and the Beltones, or Reuben Bell and the Casanovas]. Both artists went on to record for other labels in the not too distant vicinity, notably Alarm, also based in Shreveport.

These features on Eddie Giles and Reuben Bell have been built around taped interviews with the artists, conducted in February 2000 by John Shaw, a devotee of Shreveport soul, then a student at the University of Memphis and currently employed by Select-O-Hits Distributors out of Memphis, Tennessee. The interviews were originally planned for inclusion in *Voices from the Shadows* magazine, and it is with gratitude to its editor, Rod Dearlove, that the tapes have now been made available for use here.

Eddie Giles

Eddie Giles was born in March 1938, in a little town called Frierson, Louisiana, about thirty miles south of Shreveport itself. His musical activities began when he decided to pick up on playing the guitar, as he told John . . .

"I need to go back to when I first picked up the strings. And when I say 'strings,' this was a two-string guitar. I don't know how many other musicians have played the two-string guitar but this started back in the town of Frierson, in the frame house. We'd buy hay for cows and what not and they had what we called hay wire. And I got two strands of hay wire and I cut it and made up a two-string guitar on the side of my grandmother's house and, oh boy! I was having a good time but when she found out what I had did, she had a good time! And I had to get rid of that. So, from that point on, I was looking in a magazine and I saw something that said 'sell three-hundred garden seeds and you can have a prize of your choice' . . . baseball gloves, bat, radio, guitar, and so forth. My thing was a guitar. I ordered the seeds and I waited the next day for the seeds to come but it was too soon, it took about two weeks. So when the seeds came back, I went to the community and I sold all three-hundred packets of the garden seeds. And then, I sent the money off and my prize was an acoustic guitar. Six strings. There were some instructions in there, how to play the guitar and so forth, and I tried and I tried but my problem was I had to learn how to tune the thing. I wasn't educated, I had no music teaching or anything but just messing around. Eventually I found out it had to be tuned.

Once I found a way to tune the guitar, I just started playing around and playing around. I was never able to accomplish anything much but I could 'rap.'

"There were talent shows at the school I was attending and I would appear at the talent show. I had already tried doing some singing with what we call a quartet. It was kind of like a boys club type thing; in fact we were part of a group in competition with other schools. We had no music, we just sung à capella. We won second place one time. It was secular stuff and by this time and with my guitar, I'm thinking that Chuck Berry was on the rise, maybe Elvis Presley and guys like that. I'm doing 'Blue Suede Shoes,' 'No Particular Place To Go,' just 'rapping,' not really playing the thing but singing the tune. So I appeared on talent shows from time to time and then my senior year . . . I was determined to finish high school, but I lived on a farm and they wanted me to just farm and get my schooling later. But I was determined, so I left Frierson in 1958. I would work as a hotel bellboy from 11 P.M. until 7 A.M. and then I would go home and be to school.

"From that point on, although I still hadn't really learned how to play the guitar properly, I joined a gospel quartet called the Humming Bees. Musicians weren't plentiful then, and they allowed me to play with them and, at the same time, I'm practicing. Finally, I kept on and I got pretty good, good enough to just play behind them. Soon I was about the best thing in Shreveport because, when the Pilgrim Jubilees out of Chicago came to Shreveport, I was introduced to them by the late Willie 'Uncle Bill' Caston. I went for an audition with them, they accepted me, and I left the next day. We went to Mississippi and from Mississippi to Chicago. So now I'm playing . . . well, it should have been bass guitar with the Jubilees but now I had a six-string guitar but I converted it. It wasn't too hard because, when you look at a guitar, the first four strings on top are the same as the bass guitar. So there I was, doing religious music."

Eddie had joined the Pilgrim Jubilees in 1962 and stayed with them for about year. However, as a young married man, being out on the road was not the ideal way to keep a fledgling marriage alive, as he explained: "Since high school, I had got married and, having got married . . . we were together two years, my wife was younger than I was ... while I was on the road with the Jubilees she said, 'It's me or the group.' I finally thought about it, and I gave up the group and came home to her. Back in Shreveport, I continued in the restaurant business because, through working in the hotel, I got familiar with the restaurant business as well. We stayed together for a while, but it didn't work out. She left. So I said, 'Well, I'm going to wait thirty days and if she doesn't show up' ... I waited and she didn't show. I was working at the Fountain at Fairfield here in Shreveport. I would take my guitar to work with me because I was working split shifts and, rather than go home, I would just stay on and lounge around the place.

"Dick Martin [co-founder of Murco] got in touch. He'd read about the band I was with, playing around at different places. There was only three of us then, we hadn't named ourselves. We had guitar, bass, and drums. We started at a little place called Three Corners. My drummer's mother had a place called Three Corners. . . . The first night we played, people were coming in and having a good time. We were charging on the door. The first night I made seventy-five cents! We continued on and people got the word around town and we started playing at a lot of social clubs. Dick said, 'You guys are good. Have you ever thought about recording?' I said, 'No.' Dee Marais [the other Murco co-founder] had a record shop. He had a tune that I listened to but it didn't fit our style so I said, 'I'm going to write a song.' In the meantime, I'm working at the Fountain, and I thought about the situation of me and my wife and that we had separated and I said, 'Well, I'm going to write about it.' So, I wrote 'I'm such a lonely boy,' and then I thought that's not strong enough so 'lonely boy' became 'losing boy.' That's it! Then I knew that song, its verses and chorus. I said, 'I'm going to write two verses and a chorus.' So my first verse I was asking myself why am I a losing boy? Well, I'm a losing boy because my baby is gone. . . . That's verse one, then verse two. . . . I'm giving up romance, I'm through with love. . . . So okay I've got my two verses. So now my chorus. . . . well, you don't know what this woman meant to me, if you did. . . . This was in, let's see, 1966 that I wrote it." As for the tune, in his liner notes to *The Murco Story*, John Ridley describes it aptly with the words ". . . its lively rhythm and approach [is] completely at odds with the self-pity of the lyric. . . . "

"Losing Boy," like much of the Murco label material, was cut under Dee Marais's supervision nearly a hundred miles away from Shreveport, across the Texas border at Robin Hood Brians's studio in Tyler. Eddie remembered it was a drive of some hour and twenty-five minutes. It transpired there were only four musicians in at the session as Eddie confirmed: "Charles Lawrence on bass, Ray 'Cave Man' Harris on drums, James Earl Stewart playing the sax, and yours truly on guitar and singing all at the same time. It was a full sound. I know they say the bigger the band the sweeter the music but, then again, all of us had to play full all the time. It just made it sound like a full band. Actually when you listen to that song and a lot of the groups that came along after us, we were before our time." Asked if the musicians were still around in Shreveport, he replied, "All except Charles Lawrence. He now resides in Atlanta and he has a gospel group called the Saints. Ray Harris is a truck driver here and James Earl Stewart works for the city of Shreveport, driving a bus."

Released in 1967, the song soon began to take off in regional markets and Eddie was in demand. He said: "Once the song hit the market, they wanted me right away. It sold some two thousand copies in Shreveport and then the orders for it got so big. Dee did not have the capability. He had to sub-lease the record for distribution to Stan Lewis. Because Stan at the time had a spot, either thirty minutes or an hour on radio out of Nashville—John Richbourg's station—and that song started playing on radio and it hit the mountains. There was a guy named Doctor Bob in Milwaukee, Wisconsin, and he heard it and boy he got the song. When we went to Milwaukee to play, we hit the ceiling. That was all I could hear on the radio. Dallas was a big market for us too, amazing. There had been times when that song made the Dallas market and went all the way to the top, to number one, and it stayed number one for six weeks before it started coming down. Aretha Franklin had out 'Respect' at that time and the charts would show Aretha Franklin's 'Respect' at number one and Eddie Giles's 'Losing Boy' at number two. Some places, Eddie Giles was number one and 'Respect' was number two. It was just that popular. You know, I never thought first of all that I could write a song. Then there was the thrill of going and performing with people like Bettye Swann [another Shreveport native]. . . . We all gave up our jobs you know and we just hit the road."

The band became the Jive Five with the addition of an organ player, and Eddie continued to record, not just for himself but as a support musician to other artists on Murco, most notably Dori Grayson. Eddie's own recordings were issued variously as by Eddy Giles, Eddy "G" Giles, and Eddy "G" Giles and the Jive Five. "My birth-name is Elbert Wiggins Giles," he said, "but when I was on the road with the Jubilees in '62, they started calling me 'Eddie.' So then when we came back home and I organized the band, I started using 'Eddie'—that's how it started. I'd been using 'Eddie,' 'i-e,' but I know on some of the record pressings it says 'Eddy' with a 'y' and others 'Eddy "G" Giles,' I don't really know why. We had an organ player called Willie James. He wrote the song 'Try Love' [recorded by Dori Grayson], and so now we've got the Jive Five and then of course Dori Grayson. He wrote the song for her. She had a unique voice, she could sound like Aretha Franklin, Gladys Knight—we just had an all-rounder. And I had the privilege to put the guitar on it."

John raised the matter of some of Eddie's follow-up titles, citing both the flip of "Losing Boy," "I Got the Blues," and the later "Love with a Feeling," contrasted with the upbeat sounds of "Eddy's Go Go Train," "Happy Man," "Music," and "Baby Be Mine." Eddie responded: "I really never classified or listed myself as being a blues singer but when I realized a certain tune came I just said, 'Yes, that's in a blues category.' But I guess I'd got over the 'Losing Boy' situation, so now I'm in love, so deep in love, you know. Hence 'Happy Man,' the opposite of 'Losing Boy.' So I guess my writing was autobiographical. With 'Eddy's Go Go Train,' at the time they had groups out with all kinds of trains. So I said now, 'Why not have an Eddie's Go Go Train?'. What I was trying to do was a little selling too. By naming cities, I was calling major markets so we'd get played."

The flip to "Eddy's Go Go Train" was a much more profound number, "While I'm Away (Baby Keep the Faith)," and had, in fact, also been used as the b-side to the previous single ["Don't Let Me Suffer"]. (The second male voice on the track is that of the lead singer of the Violinaires, Charles Brown.) Referring to the Vietnam War but in a rather more positive way than some of the "Vietnam songs"—well-documented in Greg Burgess's article in issue #25 [of In the Basement]—John asked Eddie if he disagreed with the militants and the younger element that felt America never did anything for blacks. He replied: "Not so much, because my thing was about people. I never had any problem with people at that time. I remember I had a brother to go in service, another brother to go in service. I missed service I guess by being the only male left in my grandmother's house, even though I had registered to go but never got called. Freda Payne had out a song called 'Bring the Boys Home' and, on the love side scene of it, I thought I would come up with some lyrics that had to do with going to fight for our country and . . . 'while I'm away you just keep the faith . . . ' because I'll return. It's kind of like I'm going away but I'm coming back. I wanted to do something that, lyric-wise, I would be encouraging to the person who was going into armed service and was leaving his wife or sweetheart back home."

Further controversy centered on Shreveport in 1968 as a [black] movement developed, which began to boycott a lot of the different businesses in the city and staged demonstrations, including against the school system. At one point, a lot of activities were led by a man named Larry "Boogaloo" Cooper and these even included an urged boycott of Stan [Lewis]'s Record Shop. Asked his reaction, Eddie said: "I guess at that time I wasn't doing a lot of listening to radio nor television. Of course, I would hear about these things but our thing was music and we would be always on the go. A lot of time, when these things were going on we were on the road, we were traveling. We were one of the few bands, certainly one of the first black bands in the city of Shreveport, to kind of break the ice. We played on the strip—a number of places—and being associated with the Shreveport Federation of Musicians . . . we were part of the Shreveport Federation of Musicians. So, through the week, we would play through various parts of the city at the recreation parks for the schoolchildren, and they would dance and then go home to bed. At one point I was appointed as the first black to the Shreveport Federation of Musicians board."

Eddie became a well-known face around Shreveport—"Oh yes and actually that hasn't died down"—as other musicians came, passed through . . . Geater Davis ("When he first came to Shreveport, I knew of him but I didn't know him. I knew he sounded just like Bobby Blue Bland.") . . . or stayed . . . Bobby Patterson . . . "I knew Bobby Patterson very well. Actually I met Bobby before he came to Shreveport because, during the touring and playing in Dallas, we met up. Also in Dallas, we played at a club that had a revolving stage, and we went in there for a whole week and like, on Sunday night, one band closed and another came in and they stayed for a whole week.

They said, 'You got to start playing at nine o'clock as the other band finishes.' We had no idea who was on the opposite side [of the revolving stage], so we got set up and all and got dressed in our uniforms. When we started playing, they just hit the button and the stage revolved and the other band were coming off. We found out it was Tina Turner. I think the place I ran across Bobby was called something like 'Chicken in the Basket.' I saw him and he's not much larger than I am. I said, 'Oh boy, you're another small guy who plays the guitar and sings.'"

Although his previous recordings had all been cut in Tyler, Texas, Eddie's last recording with Dee Marais at the helm, coupling his own "So Deep in Love" with a version of "That's How Strong My Love Is," was cut at the recently opened Sound City studio in Shreveport. Issued only momentarily by Murco, it was then leased to the Silver Fox label out of Nashville. Said Eddie, "We would do 'That's How Strong My Love Is' at our gigs and boy . . . it was just like a tribute-type song. It fitted my style. I always tried to pick songs that fit my style, if there was something I liked." Talking gigs, Eddie added, "We, Dori Grayson, Reuben Bell, often combined and did a complete show. We were in Dallas when we opened up for Gladys Knight and the Pips. We had a female group of ladies singing, we had Dori Grayson, we had Reuben Bell and the Beltones, and we had Eddie Giles and the Jive Five. So there was nothing in the music arena that we couldn't do because, if it came to the Temptations, we had Reuben Bell and the Beltones, if it came to the Supremes, we had this female group, if it came to Aretha Franklin we had Dori Grayson."

Nevertheless, Eddie had cut his last record for Dee Marais and Murco. He remembered: "I think, after Dee had tried so hard and I had a two-year contract with him and Murco, the interest was not there. He didn't get treated properly I guess in his record dealing and what not, so he didn't want to go on. By this time I'm known well enough, and I got approached by Alarm." Based at Sound City, owned by Stewart Madison with Bobby Patterson and Jerry Strickland, who had become a prolific songwriting team, Eddie crossed from East 70th Street to 3316 Lime Street. His first recording paired a remake of "Losing Boy" with a Patterson/Strickland song with somewhat tongue-in-cheek lyrics, titled "It Takes Me All Night" (to which can be added " ... to do what I used to do all night."). Not issued on Alarm, however, it was leased to Stax, and Eddie, rather naturally, expected bigger things from the label, despite being less complimentary about the "Losing Boy" remake.... "I don't think it did well at all because, first of all I played no instrument. The track was cut and I sang to the track so the feel lost what the song was all about. I was excited though, because it was on a big label like Stax, but I don't think they tried either. The flip side of that—'It Takes Me All Night'—was strong. African Music Machine were the musicians."

Despite further Alarm recordings, seemingly only one single was released by the label. Other tracks, however, always believed to have been unissued at the time, have subsequently appeared on the Japanese LP release titled *I'm a Losing Boy*. Four such tracks were produced by Allen Orange but, despite the inference that these were intended for Orange's own House of Orange label, both Eddie and John state having been of the impression these were all meant for Alarm release. Indeed, Eddie did seem to recall there having been an *I'm a Losing Boy* album hesitantly released by Alarm.... "It must have been about the mid-seventies—it didn't do very well, there were only about five hundred pressed. I've only been able to get a copy of that Japanese pressing."

Eddie's next—and last—recording appeared in 1977 on another Shreveport label, Custom Sound. Pairing "Sexy Lady" with "Jelly Roll," it was issued, for some reason, as by Eddie Giles and the Numbers although, given Eddie's telling of the tale, the "Numbers" would appear to have been a band called Chocolate Unlimited.... "We had to regroup because Jive Five kind of went their way. At this time, we had stopped traveling so much and we were managing a nightclub called Club Rio. It had a lot of space to it, and we made a bandstand there, so I thought I should organize a band to play there and this became Chocolate Unlimited. But we never gained the recognition or the popularity we had with the Jive Five. I used Dale Douglas from that group. Bill Wheat had the music track to that song and he gave me the music track and I listened and finally I got the title. It's a strange thing because I got to have a title before I can write a song. So, after I got the subject, 'Sexy Lady,' then I started writing the lyrics and listened to the music track and making sure that the words were in meter with the music track. After that, that was it. Even right now, the song 'Sexy Lady' has today's sound and the style is different from the old stuff. It had the 'Tyrone Davis' style to it."

Eddie was about to abandon secular music but, given his grounding with gospel groups, John wondered if he had previously been uncomfortable with his decade of "the devil's music." "At that time, I was just doing my thing," he said, "and I wanted to see how far I could go with it. But then, after being in it for at least ten years, I could see kind of like the failure, because the opportunities that I had, or I realized that I had after I'd gone as far as I could go.... People weren't interested in the artist, they were only interested in the record itself. You know I even understand that a gentleman from Motown came looking for me. Stevie Wonder was one of the staff writers who had prepared for us, and all we had to do was just go into the studio and record and keep on traveling. But that never materialized, so I kind of just stuck out on the road with secular music. I certainly didn't feel like it was anything wrong, because it was happy time music. Music, music, even now I love all music. No one should feel bad for having sung secular songs. Look at Paul, who was Saul before he was converted. He was persecuting the churches but he got changed on his Damascus road. So God can use whomever he wants to but then he takes us through a process to bring us out. Now we know who we are and I know who I am now."

It would be an exaggeration to infer that Eddie had undergone his own Damascene conversion as he had always been conscious of his gospel background, but a major affirmation that he had taken the right path of returning to the church came by way of an incident that occurred while alone at local radio station KOKA, where he had become a gospel music dee-jay and as the consequence of a serious road accident. To précis Eddie's tale.... "I was coming down off being in the lights and so forth. I was grounded in the church from birth so it was kind of like I came back to God. My pastor invited me to come to the Lakeside church and just play the guitar. I said, 'I can't play in church' but I built up enough courage and went and I joined and started playing with the choir. There was some controversy with people, preachers and all, saying 'he's a blues man and shouldn't be playing in church' but before long they were asking me to go and play for them ..."

Eddie joined the Ever Ready Gospel Singers.

"After I had done Lakeside and getting closer and closer to my pastor and his wife—my pastor is from Memphis—he was a radio announcer as well, for KOKA. I started training [there] for two weeks. Then I would play the gospel on the radio whenever he was out of town. From that, eventually, he got completely out, and I ended up being on KOKA in his place. We used to have a show that came on at four o'clock in the morning. A song was playing and I just got caught up in a rage.... There seemed just all kinds of things happening in the building yet there was nobody in there but me and the music playing. And I just went into a crying rage. Then the voice came to me and said, 'Now I need you to carry my word....'

" ... KOKA had moved off my area and moved onto another area because they had changed frequency but this particular morning I had gone to work like five—it's not four any more, we're talking five years later—and I had to go around a place they called 'Dead Man's Curve.' We had moved so we didn't have a production studio. We had to do our stuff at another station and then bring it and play it at KOKA. So I had some cartons on the dashboard, on the top and I went round the 'Dead Man's Curve' and they sort of span off to the side. I was holding the steering wheel and trying to pick them up and, when I did that, I lost control of the vehicle and it just went round and down the embankment into a ravine and hit a tree. There was a sun roof top on the car and my head hit the tree. But I was able to get out of the vehicle. I left it running, I left the lights on and walked back up the embankment and walked a quarter of a mile.... Eventually, I was taken to the hospital and I stayed in the hospital.... After I got out of hospital, I was just so anxious to get back into the groove. I even went back to work at the radio station with my mouth wired up, and I made up in my mind that I was going to carry the word. So, after I got all right I went to my pastor and I said, 'I've been called to preach.' When I made my first sermon, he said, 'Well, God always keeps his promise' and I've been going ever since."

Interview with Eddie Giles (conducted at Salem Baptist Church in Shreveport, Louisiana): 5 February 2000.

Reuben Bell

Despite being highly revered in soul music circles, very little is known about the background and early years of Reuben Bell and, unfortunately, this feature will not necessarily redress that balance, some of Reuben's recollections being a little hazy. Because of the year of his first recordings—1967—and how he has described (below) how it came about, it is probably safe to assume he is junior in age to Eddie Giles, although even their label paths did not diverge greatly between the mid/late-sixties and mid-seventies. However, listening to the interview tape, the impression was that the years had been less kind to Reuben than to Eddie. We can only wish him well—something that could doubtless be assisted by another trip to the recording studios.

Of the early years, Reuben recounted: "I was really born in Jefferson, Texas, but I was raised in Shreveport. Really what got me into thinking about entertaining was the fact that at five-foot three-and-a-half and weighing about 135 pounds, I was out of the basketball team and the football team. I heard some guys sing in high school — I was at the junior high school—they came to campus after school and the girls went crazy. So, being as I was too short to play basketball, too short to play football, I knew what I wanted to do. Because I had never sung before, I didn't expect it to go as far as it did. I was just happy singing in nightclubs and I got involved with some friends in a recording studio and what I thought was a demo wound up being a record out on me."

That "demo" was "It's Not Easy" and, demo or not, it also marked Reuben's songwriting debut. A mournful ballad, Reuben is backed by the Casanovas and the recording was cut at Robin Hood Brians's studios in Tyler, Texas. "I was trying to sing the song but it proved to be a sure good demo." Dee Marais has subsequently suggested the back-up band may not have been the Casanovas as he did not remember this being so, but Reuben assured John that was the case. . . . "Yes, it was. Dee cut records on them too [backing "Abraham"/Abe and Marion Ester]. I got with Dee Marais and Murco because he had recorded a song on a friend of mine, who's a minister now, Eddie Giles. He had a record called 'Losing Boy.' He put us in touch."

Asked the inspiration for his songwriting, Reuben said, "Just by listening to other artists, especially people like Smokey Robinson and Sam Cooke.

It's just like you're telling a story; you have your music, your lyrics, which are nothing but poetry set to music and you tell a story." As for the feeling when "It's Not Easy" started making local noise, Reuben recalled: "Oh man, some things you feel what is happening. It's the spur of the moment thing. You have a record, you're not looking to do anything but you start finding out people are playing your record in different cities, in different states. . . . You're playing local clubs. There were quite a few bands back then and we had the Flamingo Club, Hollywood Palace . . . there was the Three Dimensions, which was more like a concert club. Then there were the disc jockeys of the KOKA radio station. These guys really were the reason we became Reuben Bell and the Beltones. They gave us the chance to be seen by a lot of people that don't go into nightclubs. They were the reason for us being on headline shows, because we were really just opening up. We would perform with Jackie Wilson, the Temptations, Gene Chandler, the Drifters. . . . They used us as the opening act. From then on, most of the big shows that came to Shreveport, they would put us on as opening act. We always had something different when we went on stage. The Beltones were Jimmy Jackson and James Hayes. There was just three of us."

Another sad number, "You're Gonna Miss Me," marked the second Murco A-side, while the more upbeat flip, "Another Day Lost," featuring male support vocals, was billed as by Reuben Bell and the Beltones. Again, both songs were penned by the man himself, demonstrating his songwriting versatility. The third Murco single, an up-tempo "Action Speaks Louder than Words"—which has found favor on Britain's northern soul scene—and the anguished "Too Late" was released shortly before the label closed its doors and was subsequently reissued on Silver Fox—#8 (as Eddie Giles's "So Deep in Love" took #9). Reuben suggested there may have been material for two further singles left behind at Murco but, at the time, he was on his way to Allen Orange's House of Orange label, where he would work extensively with Geater Davis.

"I met Geater Davis when he first came to Shreveport," said Reuben. "He had just got out of the army. He came to Shreveport and every Monday at a club downtown called the Zebra Room, every Monday they would have a blues band. All the musicians, local musicians and anyone from out of town who could play an instrument, they were welcome to come in and just get together . . . blues, jazz, pop, rock-and-roll, it didn't matter. And the first time I met Geater Davis he said to me, 'You're Reuben Bell? You're too small to be sounding like that.' Then he met a lady friend of mine and they started courting and then he moved to about a block-and-a-half from me and we would go back and forth to each other's house when I wasn't on the road, because Geater was still playing locally. He was with Elgie Brown and the Soul Searchers at that time." The two began writing songs together. "It was ... we was close, it was like Isaac Hayes and David Porter. It was just natural that Geater sounded like Bobby Bland. It was just natural. He wasn't going out of his way. He just had that growl in his voice like Bobby. . . .

"I was the first black entertainer they had on the strip in Bossier City [across the Red River from Shreveport]. They didn't mind if you just came in and sat in and did a couple of songs with the band and be on your way. I went with a friend of mine, and I got up and we found a couple of songs the band knew and I knew and, by the time we'd done the two songs, you'd have thought James Brown or someone was in the club. The manager went and told the man that owned the club, and he told me, 'Be back on Monday for rehearsal.' He told me how much he would pay me for five nights, and we were there for about three or four weeks when B. B. Davis, a disc jockey with KOKA, he called Allen Orange to attend to hear me. Geater was working down the street and when they got through playing, they had to go out the back and sit down. He was playing the other end with Eddie Giles and they would always come up to where I was—to Kim's—because you had all the freedom you wanted in Kim's. And Allen Orange was catching the flu, but B. B. Davis brought him by and I asked him to stay and just listen to Geater do one song. We didn't hear anything from him for about a month, then he called me one morning and told me he was sending me and Geater tickets, and he wanted us to come to Nashville. That's how we got in with Allen Orange. Nobody knows where he is now. I've been trying to find him for a lot of material. . . ."

Both Reuben Bell and Geater Davis signed to House of Orange towards the end of 1970. House of Orange issued two singles on Reuben—both the flip of the first and the A-side of the second was a fine ballad called "What's Happening to the World"—before leasing two further outings to Deluxe, the first being the Tarheel Slim song "I Hear You Knockin'," echoing Bell's earlier "Too Late" recording and providing his only chartster [#38 Billboard, #30 Cashbox]. "Right after James Brown left King, Allen Orange got with [King subsidiary] Deluxe, and he produced the song," Reuben said. "It started out in Nashville, WLAC. They had the most powerful radio station in the south. They didn't really have to get out and promote it, the record took off on its own." It also gave momentum to Bell's touring career "I was with Continental Booking Artists, and Eddie Davis at Continental would always get me on the shows with someone, like five or six weeks with Bobby Womack. I did eighteen days with Aretha Franklin. I worked with Al Green before he reached the big time, people like Clarence Carter, Ted Taylor, Joe Simon. . . . "

Despite the success, only one further record was issued by Deluxe—"Leave My Kitten Alone" c/w "All the Time," cut in Nashville—and, by early 1975, Reuben was back with a Shreveport-based label, having signed with Alarm. "It was Dee Marais's idea that I go with them," he explained. They were down at Sound City. Stuart Madison was running the label—and Jerry Strickland. In the liner notes to *The Murco Story* CD, John Ridley states: " . . . Bell's best work in the '70s was for Alarm, who put out four outstanding 45's . . . . " Again, there may well be further material in the vault, enough overall for Alarm to have issued an album but still Bell remained essentially a singles artist. Asked his view on that, he responded: "What happened was the same thing that always happened. I never was with a major label and the ones I got with, they'd record something, put it out, it gets played in Dallas, Forth Worth, Marshall, Tyler, and comes down to Shreveport through to Jackson, Mississippi. So, you pay a hundred thousand dollars to get a complete album ready to be shipped out and of the hundred thousand dollars you sell these albums at ten dollars, fifteen dollars an album. You could put it out in four states and sell three hundred thousand records. You have tripled your money, then the artist has four states he can go and perform in. Without that sort of thing, you cannot go and demand top dollars no matter how good you are. . . . "

There was a four-year hiatus between Alarm and Reuben's resurfacing on Port City, another Shreveport-based indie. This time, Bell did get his one and only U.S. album—titled *Blues Get Off My Shoulder*—and a pair of singles, seemingly more highly acclaimed in Europe and Japan, where affection and admiration for the man has remained constant to this day. For Reuben, however, it was not the best of times as the product's potential was stifled by the label owner. "This was a guy named Roy Mahoney," he said. "The man wanted total control. He was approached by at least three of the top people for distribution but he wanted total control. When he saw it was getting build-up that might slip out of his control, he shut the whole thing down.

"You know I walked away from the music business [then] because of the fact that you can spend all the time recording, recording, and recording and really, if you're a small record company, all you can do is hope and pray for a hit record and that some distributor would pick that record up and then maybe you can get on a major label but the way it is, man. . . . You still had to know somebody to get your foot through that door. What really hurt me, twice, two times in my career, I had a chance to be with major labels but I was with someone who would not release me from a contract. They were asking too much money to release me. The second time that happened, the people wanted distribution on the particular record but they said they wanted more than was being offered."

As the conversation flagged, John suggested to Reuben that, especially given his overseas popularity, the time might be right to return to the recording studios. Reuben, however, did not sound entirely convinced, citing the current "bluesoul" approach to music and the lack of real musicians as things he viewed as downsides. Forthrightly, he stated, "But I don't want to do blues. I want to do what I call the 'mainstay R&B', like 'Asking for the Truth.' I don't mind writing blues for somebody else. . . . 'Sweet Woman's Love,' me and Geater wrote that for my wife. We didn't have anything to go into the studio with. But let's forget that one! We also wrote 'Your Heart Is So Cold.' But what people are calling the blues now, I call it soul. It's a feeling and everyone is leaning so far to the blues in black music, there's a gulf right now from that soul sound, from the days of Otis Redding, William Bell, the earlier days of Johnnie Taylor. . . . If they would let the artists do it like we used to, with studio musicians. . . . And I don't want to do these x-rated songs about low down dirty women and stuff."

Would he perform again? "I'd do a show in an auditorium or somewhere that was big enough but to go back into nightclubs, no man. You don't get a chance to do anything, there's no money." And songwriting? . . . "I keep my ideas up here in my head. I got all these ideas but the thing is getting someone to set them down to music. It's never so fine unless I can find a melody to wrap around my lyrics. Sometimes I hear melodies but, by the time I go to sleep and wake up in the morning, I can still remember what the words were but the melody might have gone. That's where you need someone to sit down with, like I did with Geater. There were times he did not need to even pick a guitar up . . . we wrote a song called 'Sad Shade of Blue'. . . . "

Interview with Reuben Bell: 5 February 2000.

Acknowledgments: John Ridley; Rod Dearlove.

Shreveport's Pop/Rock Music Scene

The 1970s and 1980s

—John Andrew Prime

Shreveport native John Andrew Prime documented music and culture in his role as reporter for the Shreveport *Times* during the late 1970s and 1980s. During that era, he kept tabs on the flourishing of art rock that happened in the city, centered around bands like the Picket Line Coyotes and A Train, and venues like the now-defunct four-thousand-seat amphitheater in Veterans Park. In this piece, drawn from his years as a journalist, Prime ties this musical culture with the city's economic, political, and social history during the same era. He also notes pop musicians from Shreveport—such as Victoria Williams and Joe Osborn—who have influenced music well beyond the boundaries of the Ark-La-Tex. His piece ends the volume on a note that is not only informative, but poetic as well. Clearly, the Ark-La-Tex has more stories to tell than those contained within these pages.

While it managed to escape the worst of the violence and flux of the 1960s, Shreveport and northwest Louisiana had a reputation, deserved or not, with both residents and outsiders as being a conservative, sometimes reactionary enclave that did not welcome or want change. This was as true of the arts as in other areas of life, and so few people in Shreveport at the start of the 1970s would have predicted that decade, and the 1980s after, would leave the city with any measurable music and entertainment equity.

To be sure, the 1970s and 1980s were marked by demographic changes wrought by the rise of the oil industry and the flight of money and jobs from the area. Firms such as United Gas fled the city for major business capitals, notably

Houston, and others closed as wells were shut down or capped and exploration ceased. Also by the end of the 1980s and in the 1990s, manufacturing peaked and began a decline, with AT&T the best example of an operation that once employed thousands seeing its work force thinning and finally disappearing.

A similar music exodus had occurred in the 1960s, exemplified by the demise of the *Louisiana Hayride* radio show that had provided a modest living and some exposure for new artists. There was some unrest in the 1960s—Sam Cooke was detained and humiliated by authorities in Shreveport, and at least one near-riot occurred in the city's Allendale neighborhood on September 22, 1963, when police stormed a black church, dispersed a crowd, and beat a local black leader, the Rev. Harry Blake. And questions lingered about the February 1964 suicide of Ann Brewster, secretary of the local NAACP chapter as well as a participant in sit-ins at the lunch counter at a downtown store the previous year and in the Freedom Riders movement in 1961.

Part of the exodus was due to the siren lure of major population centers on the young talent of the day. Two stellar studio players who would literally shape world rock, pop, and country of the '60s through the end of the century—guitarist James Burton and bassist Joe Osborn—left to work in Los Angeles, New York, and, of course, Nashville and Memphis. Burton's guitar work can be heard on releases by hundreds of artists as can Osborn's bass lines. Burton, now in the Rock-and-Roll Hall of Fame, is mainly associated with Ricky Nelson, Jerry Lee Lewis, John Denver, Emmylou Harris, and, especially, Elvis Presley. Osborn, who doubtless will join Burton in the R. & R. H. O. F. sidemen's gallery some day, has appeared on works by hundreds of artists, notably Johnny Rivers, the Fifth Dimension, and the Carpenters, whom he discovered. Others who left and found fame and fortune, as well as trial and tribulation or early deaths, were players such as Dale Hawkins, Roy Buchanan, and Tommy Blake, the stage name of singer Thomas LeVan "Van" Givens.

But by the 1990s, Shreveport's reputation for music was finally more positive. Burton and Osborn returned to become involved in local clubs or recording, as did Hawkins and, briefly, Givens. Top national and international songwriters and producers—Keith Stegall and Michael Garvin come to mind—made no effort to cloud or obscure their origins. And top national artists with local roots—Eric Leon "Kix" Brooks of Brooks and Dunn and guitarist Danny Johnson, sideman to Rick Derringer and Rod Stewart, to name but two—also make sure their local origins are known.

So what changed the musical environment? As in many other areas in life, a change at the top of civil government and law enforcement played a big part, as did the unique setting of that era. Locally, the government of Mayor Clyde Fant ended in 1970, and more importantly, there was the fall from power and death in the mid-1970s of George d'Artois, Shreveport's authoritarian public safety commissioner.

After Fant came Calhoun Allen. Genial and affable by nature, he was an easygoing, smiling man who had been part of previous administrations as an elected commissioner, but promised change. An able administrator, his term in office (1970 to 1978) marked the community's metamorphosis from reactionary Southern enclave to a more moderate, welcoming city eager to be rid of its past but uncertain of its future. But that was before and after. In the context of this discussion, what he had to offer during his term of office was an attitude and atmosphere receptive to experimentation and, perhaps most important, the creation of a venue that provided a superb, but lamentably short-lived stage for the dreams and aspirations of local artists.

Allen was Shreveport's chief elected official in 1975 and 1976 when it prepared for the celebration of the nation's Bicentennial. Chief among planners and movers with the Bicentennial Planning Commission were Bill Fountain and Steve Primos. The two men were instrumental in helping plan and open what would become a center of Shreveport's music scene of the era, the Veterans Park Bicentennial Amphitheater.

Today, it is a ruin, a hovel, and a dangerous place to hang out unless you are big and bad and mean yourself. But when it opened in 1976, at a cost of $350,000, it was a dream. A large lake formed by the confluence of several historic natural drains surrounded a multilevel, cedar stage surrounded by four large towers for speakers and lights. The natural bowl setting was terraced, and the hills around the natural amphitheater featured trails with wooden picnic pods strategically placed for listening to music or for family picnics. Crowds upward of four thousand people could gather comfortably for daytime or evening shows, though bands would use the stage to practice to the empty hillside as well. The acoustics were as superb as the ambience and invited the creative and the adventurous.

Singer Esther Rolle opened the park with an Independence Day weekend show in 1976, a Bicentennial tribute, but the setting soon drew rock bands. Artists who performed there and delivered memorable shows included Joan Jett and the Blackhearts, Stevie Ray Vaughan, Michael Martin Murphy, and Louisiana's LeRoux. But it was local talent that made best use of this facility, as evidenced by one of the earliest concerts there, in August 1976. It featured Heart's Island, one of the Shreveport's earliest entries into the realm of jazz-inspired, rock fusion jambands.

While the Veterans Park Bicentennial Amphitheater might have been the warmest facility for local bands wishing to present their music to growing audiences of college-aged students from Centenary College and the newly arrived LSU-Shreveport and Southern University campuses, it wasn't the only such setting. Heart's Island had previously staged free concerts at Ford Park on the south shore of Cross Lake, just west of Shreveport. Primos was involved in the staging of those shows, which demonstrated that local bands had original music to offer and that it was worth listening to. The reception shown to the players by the young, energetic crowds, and favorable reviews in local press that had earlier only acknowledged more traditional sounds, encouraged local bands to break out of the cover-music club scene that had dominated the musical landscape for the past decade.

Increased public acceptance, more stages on which to work, and a more receptive, or at least less stodgy civic leadership, encouraged local artists who, like creative peers in other population centers that decade, emerged from the milieu of the times. Heart's Island was one of the more visible local bands of the mid-1970s, but it had strong and vital company. High among the solo artists was Michael Grady, known as "Howdy," a lean, tall, heavily bearded singer-songwriter fond of hand-rolled smokes. He surrounded himself with an often-changing sea of backup players, a fixture among whom was a talented, intense, and often moody guitar player named Randy Arthur, affectionately nicknamed "Goat."

Early entries in the '70s band scene were the Otis Wheat Band, Axis, and Graveyard, the first-named nascent country-rock fusion, the latter two hard rock outfits. Axis was fronted by talented guitarist Danny Johnson and bassist Jay Davis, both of whom would later work with Rod Stewart. Johnson would later head to the West Coast to work with a number of other bands, including Steppenwolf, and to pursue a solo career. The Otis Wheat Band—named after a noted, older fiddle maker and headed by veteran guitarist Don Jobe, keyboards player Hassell Teekell, and banjoist John Peck—and Graveyard, formed by brothers Glen, Gary, and "Tag" Graves, would create memorable music for a few short and glorious years and then see members break away, form other bands, leave Shreveport, and be inevitably drawn back.

Along the way, the evolution and flux would train younger musicians who would people the club and concert scene for the next two decades. With local artists eager to gain exposure and seasoning and attractive venues in place, entrepreneurs, producers, and promoters began to explore the potential of the market in greater numbers in the 1970s and 1980s. Some were regional, such as Beaver Productions, while others, such as Concerts West, were national.

But many others were homegrown. One was Steve Timmons, who opened SOOTO Records in the early 1970s and provided an alternative to the lock Stan Lewis had on music sales at his nationally known Stan's Records. Lewis also operated Paula Records and Jewel Records, which offered an avenue to radio airplay that helped propel some performers to fame, notably John Fred Gourrier and his Playboy band, who had a hit in "Judy in Disguise (With Glasses)" in 1967.

Shreveport was also home to Murco Records, with Harding G. DesMarais at the helm. (Many artists and even some music historians just refer to him as "Dee Marais," due to the pronunciation of his name.) The best-known artist on that label was Eddie "G" Giles, who had a regional hit in "Losin' Boy," but it also fostered such talents as Reuben Bell, Dori Grayson, Ann Alford, Ted Taylor, the Peermonts, and Marcus Brown. In turn these artists drew on the talent of gifted sidemen ranging from bassist Herman Wallace "Buzzard" Lott to guitarist Raymond Blakes.

Timmons brought several acts to Shreveport, notably Neil Young in 1983, and he offered moral support to local acts ranging from A Train to singer-songwriter Kix Brooks, whom you could run into in SOOTO Records during the early 1980s, looking through stacks of records. Another producer was "Shotgun Ken" Shepherd, a popular deejay who worked at a number of local stations but is mainly associated with the FM rock station that once was known as KROK. Shepherd melded two interests—music and fund-raising for charities—by sponsoring concerts using local talent to help the Muscular Dystrophy Association in its local efforts.

One of Shepherd's most successful ventures of the period was a June 12, 1983, benefit concert for the Muscular Dystrophy Association at the Veteran's Park amphitheater, featuring some of Shreveport's top bands of that era: Louisiana Hot Sauce, South Paw, Savage, Danny Johnson and a new band for him, the Bandits, and the inevitable Michael Grady. A few months later, many of these acts and others—the Kidz, Jaxx, Lucky, and Private Life, to name a few—also appeared at Rockfest '83. Shepherd's concert, like the Heart's Island show of seven years earlier, was recorded, capturing those moments in time like ancient bugs in amber. Parallel to those open venues were the smokier, booze-soaked confines of the local club scene that grew more vibrant in the 1970s and into the middle of the 1980s. In the 1960s, the most famous grouping of nightclubs locally was in Bossier City, a two-mile stretch of U. S. Highway 80 north of Barksdale Air Force Base tagged "the Bossier Strip" by novelist Erskine Caldwell. The strip produced many acts whose popularity hardly lasted a year, let alone decades, but a few players stand out for their creativity and longevity.

Perhaps foremost among these was Jerry Beach, a guitarist and bandleader of almost legendary local standing, who penned Albert King's standard "I'll Play the Blues for You." Beach was a survivor in more ways than one, having survived being shot several times with a rifle in the parking lot of a Bossier City club in the 1960s. Like many of the artists named here, he continues to perform into the twenty-first century, now often with his daughter, singer Robin Beach.

Another, of a later vintage, is Dan Garner, who in the early 1970s wore a bowler hat and performed for customers at Shaky's Pizzas, when he wasn't contributing Furry Freak Brothers-style cartoons for *The Third Paper*, one of the few local underground newspapers operating in the region that decade. Garner would later venture into video at the local cable stations, long before that was considered wise or cool. The combination of theater, art, and music led Garner to help start what was arguably one of Shreveport's more gifted, though regrettably short-lived, musical phenomena, the Wedgeheads.

That was a brash, punk/garage band that was more theater than music, though if you listen to its few recorded remnants that have lasted the quarter-century from its demise, the band strangely holds its own against time. Tunes with names like "Puppy Slicer," "Force It," "Eat My Bazooka," "Gimme Gimme Raw Meat," and "Dancing with the Manson Girls" didn't endear the group to authorities or to mainstream music fans, but they drew the curious and the wanna-be hip, and they opened eyes and ears to the notion that you could be bizarre and flow against the stream in Shreveport and survive. Survive Garner did, and he continues to work and support Shreveport music well into the 2000s.

"Survivor" also describes the late Johnny "Slim" Campbell, who lived a life of desperate musical creation and experimentation following a horrific car accident in the 1960s. He developed a powerful, percussive, and captivating blues picking style, honing his art performing with guitarist Buddy Flett and his brother, bassist Bruce Flett, who would go on to form A Train, the band that defined Shreveport's rock sound in the 1980s. Campbell was poised on the edge of stardom in 1993, living in New York City and touring, when he died in his sleep of an apparent heart attack at age forty-one.

Victoria Williams, a Shreveport native, is another survivor born of the local music scene and tested by life. Encouraged in the mid-1980s by producer Tom Ayres, an iconoclastic, moody genius who also helped such bands as A

Train and the Wedgeheads after a career spent with ABC, Dot and Hanna-Barbera Records, Williams moved west, marrying Plimsouls leader Peter Case and developing a whimsical, provocative, and probing musical style that was eclipsed, then amplified, by the crisis she faced and survived: the discovery in 1993 that she had multiple sclerosis.

The artists who stayed, such as Beach and Garner, and those who stayed a while and then left, like Campbell and Kix Brooks and Keith Stegall, polished their sound and stage presence in local clubs. The clubs nurtured a succession of talented, hard-working bands, with names like the Arthur Jones Band, Zip-a-dee-doo-dah, Philadelphia, the Edge of the Wedge, the Caddo Band, the Crawdads, and more. They worked hard, recorded and released albums, gained and lost fans, and helped weave the tapestry of sound that was Shreveport.

One of the best clubs at which to catch Grady and other early '70s performers was the Lakecliff Bar and Road House, a rambling, funky honky-tonk on the southeast shore of Cross Lake. Not far from a city water treatment plant, it was nestled in the Lakeside neighborhood, a middle-class, largely black community that uneasily tolerated the club that drew an odd mix of old-timey white truck driver-country fans and younger, long-haired, pointy-booted proto Prankster types.

The Lakecliff had been around for decades and had its own collection of legends. It had been known as a hangout for *Louisiana Hayride* artists, including Hoot and Curley, talented backup players for Slim Whitman. Cabins behind it had once been let for modest fees to musicians, and it was long said that one in particular had been used many times by a young unknown named Elvis Presley. One of the last operators of the club was Johnny Hall, who would later open his own downtown saloon, Johnny's Cimarron Club. Long-haired—unusual for that time in the Shreveport area—and sporting a desperado mustache and a cowboy hat that Pigpen of Grateful Dead would have envied, he ruled the club with an iron hand.

Over the next twenty years, a variety of clubs would come and go, with two of the best-known anchoring the former Shreve Square. Those were Humpfrees-in-the-Square, later called the Shade Tree, and Steamboat Annie's. Fronting the Shreveport footing of the Texas Street Bridge, they were the place to be Tuesday through Saturday nights. The same '60s club scene that begat Beach and Campbell repelled others, though. The mysterious players who became the San Francisco pop-art band the Residents left Shreveport and Caddo Parish in that era, never to return.

Many also got involved with local studios, where they worked with talented sidemen like guitarist Dino Zimmerman and keyboards player Hassell Teekell, to name but two of the scores who picked and played. Commercial studios had been opened in the early to late 1960s, notably Harding DesMarais's Murco (and affiliated Bayou Records) in Cedar Grove and Sound City on Line Avenue, not far from Byrd High School, under the hand of engineer George Clinton. That morphed into Southern Star Recorders, and later it was joined by Night Wing Studios, with former Stax/Volt engineer Ron Capone at the helm of what was arguably a state-of-the-art facility.

For people who didn't mind the two-hour drive, Robin Hood Brians ran a studio of legend in Tyler, Texas. His genius and ear helped mold the early, raw, nasty sound of ZZ Top, and he helped countless northwest Louisiana artists find their direction. Private studios flourished as well, with Tom Colquitt, keyboards player of the 1960s-vintage Tom and the Cats, long operating a funky, high-tech musical mecca near his South Highlands neighborhood home.

Of course, the local music scene was not a vacuum. In the 1960s, the Rolling Stones, the Byrds, even Jimi Hendrix performed in Shreveport, filling the mellow Municipal Auditorium and the great, concrete, fireproof beast known as Hirsch Coliseum with sound. Cavernous Hirsch Coliseum contributed more to the local scene than just the weekly passing headliner. Its acoustics were, and remain, atrocious. But some bands knew that if you could make a show sound good in Hirsch, it would sound good anywhere, and its construction allowed the preparation of almost any pyrotechnics. So a handful of bands booked the hall for weeks at a time to set up shows for national tours. Van Halen was one. ZZ Top put together its "Eliminator" tour at Hirsch.

The Municipal Auditorium, erected at the close of the Roaring '20s in honor of veterans of the Great War, is best known as the home of the *Louisiana Hayride* from 1948 through the mid-1960s. Today it is home to a museum honoring that epochal period that produced or nurtured country acts ranging from Slim Whitman and Red Sovine to Faron Young and Johnny Horton. It has a legacy no other building in the country can touch: It is where the young Elvis Presley first performed regularly to paying audiences, where he was shaped from raw talent into a star.

But the Muni, which was created in an era when amplification was uncertain and acoustics just had to be good, welcomed other acts that inspired local music. As noted, Jimi Hendrix played there, and in 1983 Neil Young staged a memorable show, backed by local promoter Steve Timmons, that drew heavily on the hall's *Hayride* legacy and included fiddler Rufus Thibodeaux, who had performed at the old *Hayride*.

By the time Young played the Muni, the *Louisiana Hayride* was twenty years in limbo and had been operating in a "lite" form in Bossier Parish for a decade. After the death in the 1960s of the show's main booster, Henry Clay, it had been neglected, and was finally sold to Shreveport businessman David Kent. Kent, who had spent much of his radio career working for *Hayride* rivals, had developed an immense affection and respect for the show, and invested a large percentage of the capital of his Jordan and Booth business toward keeping the *Hayride*'s legacy alive.

While many purists sniff at the *Hayride*'s Bossier City years, it did keep the show's memory and name current and provided the basis for what rebirth the enterprise has enjoyed, aside from its considerable legacy, in the last decade. The show also welcomed exotic talent, whether rockabilly revivalists Levi Dexter and the Rockats in 1979 or the Australian folk band Cobbers in the early 1980s. Actor Stuart Margolin sought the hall out for a performance in the early 1980s, and the show provided a stage and seasoning for such artists as Micki Fuhrman, songwriter Michael Garvin, and Branson mainstay fiddler Shoji Tabuki. A young and inexperienced Randy Travis performed there in the early days of his career, Fuhrman says.

Levi Dexter and the Rockats had been brought to the *Hayride* by Tom Ayres, who'd made a name for himself on the West Coast working for Hanna-Barbera Productions and for RCA Records, where he'd befriended and helped sign an unknown singer who later became David Bowie. Ayres later worked with noted broadcaster and punk rock kingmaker Rodney Bingenheimer, but semi-retired in the late 1970s and returned to Caddo Parish to care for his mother. But he was a magnet and musicians, especially talented ones, were drawn to him like iron filings; in the two decades that remained before he died, he helped meld the Shreveport music scene.

At Ayres's urging, members of the Rockats and the band's mentor, Lee Childers, moved to Shreveport's Highland neighborhood to steep in local culture. Ayres also advised, mentored, cajoled, and hectored local bands, suggesting tours, stunts, causes, and sounds that raised eyebrows and, on the occasions when they worked, put the local bands in the national eye. Aside from bringing the Rockats to Shreveport, Ayres was responsible for exporting local talent. He encouraged Victoria Williams early in her career and coaxed A Train, arguably Shreveport's best-known band of the 1970s and 1980s, to appear at the Los Angeles Street Scene Festival in the early 1980s.

For more than a decade, A Train perched at the apex of the local music triangle. Mostly, it was guitarist Buddy Flett, his brother Bruce Flett on bass, and friend John Howe on saxophone, with a bewildering variety of friends and sidemen on woodwinds, keyboards, and drums. For the most of its latter years, the lineup also included singer Miki Honeycutt, earlier known for her growling, gritty vocals with the Mahala Band. Alternately jazzy, bluesy, rock, and soul, sometimes all in the space of a few minutes, the band released more than a half-dozen albums and set the local standard for performances. A Train also traveled farther from Shreveport than just about any band that didn't break into the big time, with its L.A. gig and appearances at the Festival of Friends in Canada. Ayres was also instrumental in stirring local interest in the legacy of folk singer Huddie "Lead Belly" Ledbetter, and would take people to the legendary songwriter's grave in the nearby Trees community at the drop of a hat.

Strangely, while the equity of Shreveport's music capital grew in the 1980s, one of the things that had most contributed to the energy and the ambience died a horrible death. Veterans Park was brilliantly conceived and poorly executed. Its stage was wooden and its location was wooded and isolated. It had no permanent human presence and access control was next to impossible. Fans would sneak into paid shows, and vandals systematically destroyed concessions buildings, sound towers, and even the stage and dressing rooms. By the 1990s the site was a wilderness again, frequented by hard-core drug users, and at least one headline-grabbing murder occurred there.

But it had produced the stuff of dreams. The Heart's Island and 1983 benefits were just a fraction of the whole. Stevie Ray Vaughan, Joan Jett and the Blackhearts, Louisiana's LeRoux and Michael Martin Murphy performed there, inspiring local talent in the casual, inviting atmosphere. Kenny Wayne Shepherd was seven when he heard Steve Ray Vaughan there in 1984, at a show his dad helped produce. Just one year earlier, he'd been at the amphitheater for the Louisiana Music Festival, the MDA benefit his dad staged and later released as an album. One year after Vaughan's show, rocker Joan Jett packed the site with six thousand fans in another Shepherd MDA benefit. Jett's concert ended with raving fans wading out into the lake and trying to clamber onto the stage. They were mesmerized by the sound in the clear night air, with the lights rippling off the shimmering waters from the stage that appeared to float.

But that proved to be but a short-lived dream, as did the heyday of Shreve Square, the various showcase clubs that sprouted around Shreveport like mushrooms after a spring shower, and the intoxicating cash currents from the oil and gas industry. What remained vibrant and alive, though transformed by shock and the rigors of the times, were the musical legacies Shreveport and northwest Louisiana had put on the table at the start of the 1970s and 1980s.

One stood out above others: Lead Belly. Huddie Ledbetter, the late blues singer and songwriter, died in 1949, and his passing was lamented just about everywhere but in his home parish. There, he was remembered as a talented but violent man, more notorious than legendary, and in the 1960s one would have been hard-pressed to find too many people who sought out his grave west of Mooringsport, near the state line.

But he would have been surprised when in the 1970s people in Harrison County, Texas, agitated to have his remains moved there, and people in Caddo Parish didn't let it happen. Then in the 1970s and 1980s, the trickle of musicians visiting his grave turned into a torrent. A marker was erected in his honor near Caddo Lake, and artists such as Robert Plant, Maria Muldaur, and Country Joe McDonald visited his grave. Poet Allen Ginsberg visited the grave of his old friend in early 1991, and there were reports that at least one former Beatle visited in the 1970s, without fanfare.

The greatest irony was in 1984, when the Red River Revel, a growing music and arts festival one year shy of marking its first decade, decided to pay tribute to the singer. Imagine! The festival was the fruit of labors of the Junior League of Shreveport, which in Lead Belly's day would have been white-haired grandmothers serving tea and biscuits. But by the 1980s the group consisted of hard-nosed, odds-calculating, no-nonsense businesswomen and, more importantly, visionaries who weren't afraid to address, and redress, past wrongs. So it was that the city wags have called the Buckle of the Bible Belt, the last place where the national flag of the Confederate States of America waved, a bastion of conservatism, invited Sonny Terry, Brownie McGhee, Oscar Brand, and Pete Seeger to lead the way. It was a magic night where the legacy of music reigned. Thousands of people joined Seeger and his fellow musical travelers singing "Goodnight Irene," meaning every word when they rang out " . . . I'll see you in my dreams."

It was a dream that survived the waking.

Contributors

David Anderson trained as a historian at the University of North Carolina–Chapel Hill and currently serves as assistant professor of history at Louisiana Tech University in Ruston. His primary interests are United States labor history and working-class culture in the American South. His articles and book reviews have appeared in *Labor: Studies in Working-Class History of the Americas*, *Southern Quarterly*, *Missouri Historical Review*, and elsewhere.

Monty Brown (not the professional football player and wrestler of the same name) has lived in the Ark-La-Tex much of his adult life. In addition to writing about local vernacular music, Brown has broadcast a program about Louisiana music over Shreveport's KDAQ-FM (Red River Public Radio). Brown also writes short fiction and drama, and, with his wife Marsha Brown, writes music and makes documentary travel films.

Eleanor Ellis is a guitar player and vocalist who performs blues, mostly from the Piedmont of Virginia and the Carolinas. In addition to playing music, she also produced *Blues House Party*, a documentary film about Piedmont blues that featured John Jackson, John Cephas, John D. Holeman, and members of their extended families. Ellis currently lives in Takoma Park, Maryland, and often plays at clubs and concerts in and around Washington, D.C.

Kevin Fontenot is finishing his Ph.D. in history from Tulane University, writing about the musical and political life of Jimmie Davis. He teaches at Tulane University and the University of Louisiana–Lafayette. The author of articles and reviews in the *Country Music Annual*, the *Jazz Archivist*, the *Journal of Southern History*, and elsewhere, he was also a consultant and commentator for *Making Waves*, a documentary about the history of radio in Louisiana. He is the co-editor, with Ryan Brasseaux, of *Accordions, Fiddles, Two-Steps, and Swing: A Cajun Music Reader* (2006).

Dan Garner is a Shreveport native, local music researcher, and documenter, best known as a musician who has played at dozens of blues festivals as well as practically every stage in the Shreveport music scene, from clubs to casinos. For thirteen years he apprenticed with the late legendary prewar bluesman, Jesse Thomas, recording and performing with him until Thomas's death in 1995. Through his Blue Goose Blues Records, Dan has produced seven releases, which span the genres of acoustic blues, rockabilly, and gospel. Currently Garner works for the Tipitina's Foundation of New Orleans and performs with Cookie and the Kingcakes.

Lillian Jones Hall chronicled the early history of radio station KWKH in her communications dissertation, which she completed in 1959 at Louisiana State University. She is professor emeritus at Louisiana State University in Shreveport, having taught there from 1967 until her retirement.

Tracey E. W. Laird trained in ethnomusicology and musicology at the University of Michigan. She is currently an associate professor of music at Agnes Scott College in Decatur, Georgia, and the author of *Louisiana Hayride: Radio and Roots Music Along the Red River* (2005). Her current research focuses on the musical and cultural significance of the long-running PBS live music showcase *Austin City Limits*.

Don Logan worked for decades in music as a performer, promoter, disc jockey, and record company executive. He is probably best known in the Ark-La-Tex as "Dandy Don," a well-known DJ on Shreveport station KEEL. Logan now resides in Benton, Louisiana (less than a dozen miles north of downtown Shreveport). He is semi-retired, though still involved in music.

Kip Lornell teaches in the music department at The George Washington University. Trained as an ethnomusicologist at the University of Memphis, he has written nine previous books, including *The Life and Legend of Leadbelly* (1992), co-authored with the late Charles Wolfe and winner of the 1993 ASCAP-Deems Taylor Award. In addition, he has published over a hundred articles and record notes documenting American vernacular music, as well as numerous record projects and documentary films.

J. Michael Luster has been a tireless force in the documentation and celebration of music and culture of the Ark-La-Tex since the early 1990s. Trained as a folklorist at the University of Pennsylvania, he was director of the Louisiana Folklife Festival for ten years (1995–2005), based in Monroe, Louisiana. During that period, he broadcast weekly on two programs over Monroe public radio station KEDM, and taught at the University of New Orleans in 2004. He is a frequent participant in panels, workshops, and festivals throughout the country and has worked with the Smithsonian's Festival of American Folklife, the Olympics, the National Folk Festival, the Great Lakes Folk Festival, the Lowell Folk Festival, and the New Orleans Jazz and Heritage Festival. In 2005 Luster took a position as director of the Arkansas Folklife Program, affiliated with Arkansas State University and serving the Arkansas Department of Heritage.

Randy McNutt works primarily as a feature writer based in Hamilton, Ohio. He has a particular interest in American music and the recording industry; however, his contributions to newspapers and magazines include articles on topics as varied as Ohio's Bentonville Anti-Horse Thief Society, a man with a Statue of Liberty in his front yard, and Ohio ghost towns. McNutt has written several books about music, beginning with *We Wanna Boogie: An Illustrated History of the American Rockabilly Movement* (1989).

Steven Morewood is a longtime contributor to the British magazine *Country Music People*, for which he wrote his first piece on Jim Reeves at age seventeen. He has contributed to *The Rough Guide to Elvis Presley* and *The Rough Guide to Cult Pop*, specifically on country figures including Reeves, and once wrote an article for the magazine *Now Dig This* on Shreveport legend Tillman Franks's role in bringing Elvis to the *Hayride*. In addition, he is a lecturer in international history in the School of Historical Studies at the University of Birmingham, England, where his courses include "Conflict in the Modern Middle East." Morewood's contribution testifies to the longstanding British interest in American vernacular music.

Donald Lee Nelson is a Los Angeles–based country music record collector, researcher, and writer. Many of his writings about pioneering recording artists like McVay and Johnson initially appeared during the 1970s in the *JEMF (John Edwards Memorial Foundation) Quarterly*. His piece on Buddy Jones initially appeared as the liner notes for *Louisiana Honky-Tonk Man*, released on Texas Rose in 1984. This is the second of Nelson's articles to be reissued in a book; Nolan Porterfield included "The Life of Alfred G. Karnes" in *Exploring Roots Music: Twenty Years of the JEMF Quarterly* (2004).

Paul Oliver is widely recognized as an authority on vernacular architecture, and his appointment at Oxford Brookes University is in this field. His dozens of articles, book chapters, and books on architecture include *Dwellings: The House Across the World* (1987). But Oliver is perhaps best known as one of blues scholarship's most insightful and widely published writers, beginning with an article published in *Jazz Journal* in 1951. Since his first major book, *Blues Fell This Morning: The Meaning of the Blues* (1960), Oliver has written or edited twelve books on blues. His most recent work, *Broadcasting the Blues: Black Blues in the Segregation Era* (2005), is based on his own renowned radio broadcasts from the BBC that began during the 1950s.

Earl Porter conducted the interview with Horace Logan found in this volume during the mid-1970s for a course at Louisiana State University–Shreveport while finishing his BA in history. After years of working, first in the building industry and then as a service supervisor on oil and gas rigs, he earned his teaching certification from Mansfield University in Pennsylvania and his MA in educational psychology from SUNY-Albany. He currently teaches in the New York state prison system, helping inmates work toward the GED.

John Andrew Prime has worked as a journalist in Shreveport for more than three decades. He is co-author of *Barksdale Air Force Base* (2002), now in its third printing. Although his current beat is primarily focused on military news, he wrote for years on music and culture, documenting local legends like Michael "Goat" Grady and the darkly sardonic and highly theatrical Wedgeheads, whose ranks included a much younger and less well-mannered Dan Garner.

Lesley-Anne Reed began working with Professor David M. Anderson on the collection and documentation of oral histories related to music in the Ark-La-Tex region while his student at Louisiana Tech University. She is now pursuing a Ph.D. in history from the University of Georgia. Her research interests include labor and environmental history in the twentieth-century U.S. South.

John Ridley is an English collector whose passion for black American music began during the early 1970s. Murco Records is merely one among numerous obsessions that have arisen during a longstanding enthusiasm for R&B and, especially, soul. He and his wife have since built a collection of around 25,000 meticulously indexed sound recordings. Ridley has annotated dozens of these recordings, including the one reprinted in this collection.

Susan Roach trained in anthropology (folklore) at the University of Texas at Austin and in English at the University of Arkansas. She has been active in documenting north Louisiana folk traditions since 1978. Her latest book-length publication is the exhibition catalog for the touring exhibit *On My Way: The Arts of Sarah Albritton*, which won the 1999 Eli Kongas Maranda award from the American Folklore Society Women's Section. Other publications include chapters in *Re-Situating Folklore: Folk Contexts and Twentieth-Century Literature and Art*, *Public Folklore*, and *Women's Folklore, Women's Culture*. Her current research includes the Louisiana Quilt Documentation Project published as a searchable online database by the Louisiana Folklife Program. At Louisiana Tech University, she serves as professor of English and folklorist for the Louisiana Regional Folklife Program, covering the northeast Louisiana area and funded by a grant from the Louisiana Division of the Arts.

John M. Shaw works for the one-stop Selecto-Hits in Memphis and has extensively researched Shreveport's postwar black music scene, most notably blues of the post–World War II era and soul during the late 1960s and 1970s. He focuses on the record labels, the personalities, and the music that never gained the widespread popularity and critical recognition that music in other cities, even Shaw's hometown, has received over the years. He began his research while attending the University of Memphis and hopes the work will bring greater attention to this neglected musical era.

H. Allen Smith was a prolific writer whose pieces appeared in *Playboy*, *Reader's Digest*, and other popular magazines. He began his career as a newspaper writer, most notably for the *New York World-Telegram*. With the 1941 publication of *Low Man on a Totem Pole*, a collection of short pieces that wed his reporter's eye for observation with a rare wit, Smith gained fame as a humorist and turned to writing full time. By his death in 1976, he published more than thirty-nine books.

Paul Swinton lives in Fleet, Hampshire, UK. A longtime blues enthusiast and record collector, Swinton often contributes articles and reviews to magazines such as *Blues & Rhythm*. He also operates Frog Records and Truetone Records, two labels that specialize in reissuing blues, jazz, and gospel recordings from the 1920s through the 1940s. Swinton is currently working on a biography of the well-known, but elusive Texas bluesman, Blind Lemon Jefferson.

Vallie Tinsley was born in Claiborne Parish on November 27, 1897. She graduated from Haynesville, Louisiana, High School and then from Louisiana State University at a time when few women were found in its Baton Rouge classrooms. She taught school many years, including stints in Missouri and Greenville, Mississippi, where she also instructed soldiers at the local air base. Following the completion of her MA thesis reprinted here, Tinsley's interest in folk culture did not diminish. After her retirement from teaching, she spent the summer of 1950 in Bloomington, Indiana, at the International Folklore Convention and the summer of 1959 touring and studying in Europe. Tinsley died on August 26, 1974, and is buried in Claiborne Parish, Louisiana.

Charles Wolfe, born in Missouri in 1943, became one of country music's most important scholars. His interests ranged from bluegrass to African American gospel and blues. Wolfe's contributions began with the first scholarly study of the *Grand Ole Opry* and included the important biographies *DeFord Bailey: A Black Star in Early Country Music* (1993), written with David Morton, and *The Life and Legend of Leadbelly* (1992), co-authored with Kip Lornell, as well as many other works. His book about Bill Monroe (co-authored with Neil Rosenberg) was completed in the year before his death from multiple health issues on February 9, 2006. A thirty-year resident of Murfreesboro, Tennessee, Wolfe taught for many years in the English Department at Middle Tennessee State University until his retirement in 2005.

Credits

"Introduction from *Louisiana Hayride: Radio and Roots Music Along the Red River*" by Tracey E. W. Laird (NY: Oxford University Press, 2005), 3–12. By permission of Oxford University Press, Inc.

"The Grigg Family and the Taylor-Griggs Melody Makers: The History of a North Louisiana String Band" by Monty Brown. *Louisiana Folklife* 12 (September, 1988): 16–24. Used by permission of *Louisiana Folklife*.

"The Cox Family" by Susan Roach. Used by permission of the author.

"Remembering Hiter Colvin, the Fiddle King of Oilfield and Gum Stump" by J. Michael Luster. Used by permission of the author.

"Sing It Good, Sing It Strong, Sing It Loud: The Music of Governor Jimmie Davis" by Kevin Fontenot. Used by permission of the author.

Liner notes essay to *Louisiana's Honky-Tonk Man: Buddy Jones* 1935–1941 by Donald Lee Nelson, Texas Rose Records. TXR-2711, 1984. © 1983 Texas Rose Records; All Rights Controlled by Origin Jazz Library; [http://www.originjazz.com]. All Rights Reserved. Used by Permission.

Interview with Horace Logan, October 13, 1976, by Earl Porter. Excerpts used by permission of Noel Memorial Archives, LSU–Shreveport.

"Getting the Sound Right: Bob "Sully" Sullivan, KWKH, and the *Louisiana Hayride*" by Steven Morewood. Used by permission of the author.

"Beyond Country Music" from *Louisiana Hayride: Radio and Roots Music Along the Red River* by Tracey E. W. Laird (NY: Oxford University Press, 2005), 121–47. By permission of Oxford University Press, Inc.

"Fannin Street" from *The Life and Legend of Leadbelly* by Charles Wolfe and Kip Lornell (DaCapo Press, 1999), 26–36. Used by permission of the authors.

"Some Negro Songs Heard on the Hills of North Louisiana" by Vallie Tinsley. An unpublished MA thesis, Department of Music, Louisiana State University, Baton Rogue, 1928. Used by permission of the family of Vallie Tinsley.

Liner notes to *Jerry's Saloon Blues: 1940 Field Recordings from Louisiana* by Paul Oliver, Flyright-Matchbox, FLY260, 1978. Used by permission of the author.

"Jesse 'Babyface' Thomas" by Eleanor Ellis, *D.C. Blues Society Newsletter* (August 1993): 1, 10; and *D.C. Blues Society Newsletter* (September 1993): 10–11. Used by permission of the author.

"The Flying Crow Blues by Paul Swinton, *Blues and Rhythm* 83 (October 1993): 12–14. Used by permission of the author.

Liner notes to *The Legend of Old Blue Goose* by Dan Garner, BGB Records 427642, 1998. Used by permission of the author.

"Down-Home Postwar Blues in Shreveport" by John M. Shaw. Used by permission of the author.

Excerpt from "A Historical Study of Programming Techniques and Practices of Radio Station KWKH, Shreveport, LA, 1922–1950" by Lillian Jones Hall. An unpublished Ph.D. dissertation, Communications Department, Louisiana State University, Baton Rouge, 1959. Used by permission of the author.

"A Friend in Las Vegas" from *A Short History of Fingers* by H. Allen Smith (Boston: Little, Brown, 1963), 44–57. © 1963 by H. Allen Smith. Renewed 1991. Permission to reprint granted by Harold Matson Co., Inc.

"Stan Lewis," excerpt from "Shreveport: Susie-Q" from *Guitar Towns: A Journey to the Crossroads of Rock 'n' Roll* by Randy McNutt (Bloomington, IN: Indiana University Press, 2002), 65–72. Used by permission of Indiana University Press.

"'Reconsider Me': Margaret Lewis Warwick and the Louisiana Hayride" by Tracey E. W. Laird from *The Women of Country Music: A Reader*, edited by Charles Wolfe and James Akenson (Lexington, KY: University Press of Kentucky, 2003), 75–87. Used by permission of the author.

"The Making of Dale Hawkins" by David Anderson and Lesley-Anne Reed. Used by permission of the authors.

"The Life and Times of Dandy Don Logan" by Don Logan. Used by permission of the author.

"Shreveport Southern Soul: The Murco Story" by John Ridley, liner notes for Kent Records CDKEND 178, 2000. Used by permission of the author.

"Eddie Giles and Reuben Bell: Synonymous with Shreveport" by John M. Shaw, *Down in the Basement*. Used by permission of the author.

"Shreveport's Pop/Rock Music Scene: The 1970s and 1980s" by John Andrew Prime. Used by permission of the author.

Index

Ace Records (England), 256, 324
Antony, Bill, 226, 228
Ark-La-Tex, concept of, xii–xiii, 3
A Train, 338, 345, 347
Austin, Gene, xvii, 50, 223, 237–47
Ayers, Tom, 344, 346

Bartlett, Ray, 12, 14–15, 66, 67, 113
Bell, Rueben, 321, 323–24, 333
Black Ivory King (David Alexander), 207
Bledsoe, James ("Hot Rod Happy"/
    "Country Jim"), 217–20
Burton, James, 15, 105–6, 113, 117–19, 124–27,
    223, 256, 262, 280–1, 288–90, 293, 339

Cajun music, xiv–xv, 184
Clay, Henry, 76, 78, 81, 85, 97–98
Colvin, Hiter, xvii, 43–45
Cox Family, xvii, 4, 5, 30–41

Davis, Jimmie, 4, 29, 31, 40, 46–55, 58, 60, 61,
    131, 182, 302

East Texas Serenaders, 5
Ever Ready Gospel Singers, 138, 323, 332

Fontana, D. J., on growing up and music in
    Shreveport, 119–24
Foundation for Arts, Music, Entertainment
    of Shreveport, Bossier, Inc. (FAME),
    xvi–xvii, 258, 264
Franks, Tillman, 11, 95, 98, 113–15, 123, 129,
    217, 302

Fred, John, and the Playboy Band, relation-
    ship with Stan Lewis, 308–13, 342

Garner, Dan, and the Wedgeheads, 343–44
Giles, Eddie, 138, 223, 317–20, 323–32
Gotham Records, 216–19
Grand Ole Opry, 8–13, 19, 25, 31, 36, 68, 72, 77,
    85, 92, 116–18, 275
Gray, Kitty, 183
Gunning, Stedman, 226, 228, 230

Hammond, Nathaniel "Stickhorse," 216,
    218–19
Harris, Joe, 178, 180, 183–85, 188
Hawkins, Dale, xviii, 4, 98, 124, 126–27, 223,
    252, 256, 268–91, 308, 339
Henderson, W. K., 4, 18, 22, 24–25, 46,
    226–36, 302

Jefferson, Blind Lemon, 140, 154, 185, 193,
    198, 209
Jones, Buddy, 5, 58–62

KEEL (radio station), 302–6
Kennedy, Jerry, 7, 15, 105–6, 113, 117–18,
    121–22, 129–31, 262, 289
KENT (radio station), 281, 288
KOKA (radio station), 323, 331–32, 334–36
Kilgore, Merle, 3, 7, 268, 281, 288–90
King, Claude, 3
KWKH radio, 3, 4, 18, 19, 22, 24, 28–29, 46,
    59, 63–101, 105–7, 111–15, 117–31, 138, 217,

219–21, 224, 248–49, 251–52, 258, 302; early history of, 226–36; and the *Louisiana Hayride*, 8–15

Lead Belly, xvii, xviii, 47, 120, 131, 138, 140–55, 154, 210, 215, 263, 265, 268–69, 272, 277, 286, 290, 347–48
Leadbetter, Uncle Bob, 185–88
Lewis, Stan (Jewel and Paula Record Labels), 89, 113, 215–16, 220–21, 223–25, 248–55, 269, 276–79, 282–84, 287–88, 308–13, 316, 319, 324, 327, 329, 342
Logan, Horace, 4, 5, 7, 63–73, 81, 82–87, 95, 116
Lomax, John, and Alan Lomax, 141, 178–79, 183–88
London, Clarence, 220–21
Louisiana Hayride, xvii, xviii, 3, 18–19, 31, 32, 40, 63–75, 78–101, 105–6, 108–26, 129–31, 217, 249, 251, 256–67, 269, 272, 275, 280, 286, 339, 346; and KWKH, 8–15
Louisiana Music Hall of Fame, 47

Maddox Brothers and Rose, on KWKH, 111–12, 259
McKinley, David "Pete," 219
Moore, Noah, 186–89
Municipal Auditorium, and *Louisiana Hayride*, 8–15, 80–81, 85, 97, 105, 116, 121, 161, 263–66, 275, 279, 304, 345
Murco Records, and Dee Marais, 316–22, 326–27, 329–30, 334

New Orleans, Louisiana, and music, xiv

O Brother, Where Art Thou?, 4, 35, 37–38
Osborn, Joe, 7, 15, 105–6, 117–22, 126–28, 256, 262, 338–39

Peer, Ralph, 25–26
Pelican Wildcats, 5
"Pine Bluff Pete," 220
Plain Dealing, Arkansas, 278
Presley, Elvis, xviii, 3, 7, 10, 14–15, 61, 63, 69, 74–75, 83, 85, 95–97, 105–18, 121–25, 131, 223,

249, 260–62, 265, 269–70, 279, 282, 286, 289, 306, 339, 344

Ram Records, 215, 256, 258, 279–81
Record companies (independent, post–World War II), importance of, 87–99, 214–22, 249–55, 282–85, 311–13, 316–22
Reeves, Jim, early recordings, 90–93
Rodgers, Jimmie, 25, 44, 47, 50, 51, 55, 58, 59, 111

Schaffer, Eddie, 51, 138, 181–82, 204–6, 265
Shreveport, Louisiana, 4, 178–79, 223–24; and Blue Goose, 210–14; defining, xv–xvi; Fannin Street, 146–50; location, xii–xiv; and sense of place in 1900, 146–50
Smith, Mira, 256–57, 261–64, 279–81, 304
Southern Maid Donuts, 65, 70
Sullivan, Bob, 4, 5, 74–101, 124
Susie Q, 287–93

Taylor-Griggs Louisiana Melody Makers, xvii, 4, 5, 24, 29, 30
Thomas, Jesse, xvii, 138, 192–203, 210–12, 224, 265
Thomas, Willard "Ramblin'," 192–94, 212, 214

Veterans Park Bicentennial Amphitheater, in Shreveport, 340–41

Warwick, Maggie, 256–66, 304
West, Kid, 178, 180, 183–85, 188
Williams, Hank, 3, 7, 47, 53, 63, 66, 70, 74–76, 82–87, 100, 106, 131, 259, 265, 269, 276, 280; and *Louisiana Hayride*, 9–15
Williams, Lonnie, 219–20
Woods, Oscar "Buddy," 51, 138, 178–89, 193, 204–6, 210, 212, 214–15, 265

"You Are My Sunshine," 46–49, 52, 53